Writing in Response

SECOND EDITION

Matthew Parfitt

Boston University, College of General Studies

Bedford/St. Martin's
A Macmillan Education Imprint

Boston • New York

For Bedford/St. Martin's

Vice President, Editorial, Macmillan Higher Education, Humanities: Edwin Hill
Editorial Director, English and Music: Karen S. Henry
Publisher for Composition: Leasa Burton
Executive Editor: John E. Sullivan III
Executive Editor for Rhetorics: Molly Parke
Editorial Assistant: Jennifer Prince
Senior Production Editor: Rosemary R. Jaffe
Production Manager: Joe Ford
Marketing Manager: Emily Rowin
Copyeditor: Arthur Johnson
Indexer: Jake Kawatski
Photo Researcher: David Stockdale
Senior Art Director: Anna Palchik
Text Design and Illustration: Castle Design
Cover Design: Marine Miller
Composition: Graphic World, Inc.
Printing and Binding: LSC Communications

Manufactured in the United States of America

0   9   8   7
f   e

For information, write: Bedford/St. Martin's, 75 Arlington Street, Boston, MA 02116   (617-399-4000)

ISBN 978-1-4576-7269-9 (Student Edition)
ISBN 978-1-4576-9955-9 (Instructor's Edition)

Writing in Response

Preface for Instructors

Some years ago, I realized that my students were having a hard time getting a purchase on the smooth surfaces of the academic readings I assigned. Since they didn't have the repertoire of reading skills that this kind of prose demands, the students weren't able to read closely or write thoughtful responses to these texts. To provide them with the analytical tools they needed, I developed materials that have become *Writing in Response*. This book is a short rhetoric designed for first-year composition courses, especially those that include a focus on academic writing. Academic writing typically means writing about texts because the academy functions through dialogue, through conversations that take place mostly in writing — yet many students have never written a serious, thoughtful response to a text, especially a nonfiction text. Frequently, students have very little sense of how scholarship proceeds. They need to learn how they can participate in these conversations by responding to what they read, by approaching their reading as a kind of writing.

In addition to offering concrete strategies for academic reading and writing, *Writing in Response* strives to shed light on the conventions of academic discourse, in particular the relationship between the genres of student writing and the genres of academic writing — between what students are expected to do as writers and what faculty scholars do as writers. The book places a strong emphasis on reading and rereading, not just repetitively but actively, so that note-taking flows smoothly into extended prose writing. An equally important theme is the notion that academic writing addresses a genuine *problem* of some kind, whether it is a practical problem or a "knowledge problem" (a purely intellectual problem). This essential element in student writing frequently takes a backseat to the notion of a thesis, but a thesis has no purpose or motive unless it somehow speaks to a need. Too often, a student essay reads merely like a perfunctory performance of academic prose — or certain qualities of it — because the writer lacks a clear sense of what the problem is and why it matters. This accounts for the book's introduction of the exploratory essay, a less common form of academic writing (not to be confused with personal writing) yet a powerful way to encourage more complex, deeper thinking.

v

Writing in Response presumes a deep connection between reading and writing and so begins with an extensive discussion of active reading. It continues with further strategies for critical reading as well as for reflection and response, aiming to give students the tools they need to work seriously with texts, particularly challenging ones. The book models practices that help students view the composing process as dialogic, nonlinear, and recursive. It presents a method of composition that includes engagement with other texts, has overlapping phases, and embeds revision as an essential component. With a model of reading and writing that is accessible yet grounded in theory, students learn to connect the texts they read to the texts they write in response.

The process of making those connections necessarily involves informal as well as formal writing. Here, "informal writing" is envisioned both as a product, an end in itself, and as a crucial phase in composing a formal essay. The kind of writing encouraged by many composition instructors today reflects the more exploratory, personal, and even experimental style of recent academic prose, and this development represents a return to the possibilities of the essay as it was first conceived. *Writing in Response* carries an emphasis on craftsmanship and creativity through to the task of composing a final paper. Informal writing is presented as much more than just drafting, prewriting, or brainstorming — writing that serves no purpose except as a stage on the way to a finished product; informal writing is the occasion for real thinking and learning. Such writing is vital to this book's purpose: *Writing in Response* aims to restore to college composition the pleasures and rewards of exploring, imagining, questioning, reflecting, and speculating.

Throughout *Writing in Response*, samples of student writing (showing both works in progress and finished products) are included as illustrations, yet the emphasis is on broadly applicable principles, concepts, and strategies rather than on rules and formulas; therefore, these samples are provided to give students ways of imagining what *they* might do as college writers, to show them possibilities for how they might carry out their *own* plans. "Try This" activities appear in each chapter, giving students the opportunity to practice skills and strategies as they learn them. These activities are invitations to exercise the responsiveness, flexibility, and creativity that are central to this book's purpose. Most ask for a fairly substantial piece of work, suitable for an evening's homework. Checklists and guidelines throughout provide practical references. These cover such topics as evaluating evidence and developing an argument. *Writing in Response* also discusses style, emphasizing the principles of plain style best suited for academic writing. The book includes strategies for managing the research process — finding, evaluating, and using varied sources purposefully and documenting them appropriately. Throughout, student and professional readings provide engaging models and topics, with a cluster of eight professional essays in Part 5.

Organization

The organization of *Writing in Response* falls into five parts: (1) responsive reading, (2) composing and revising, (3) issues of style, (4) research, and (5) readings. An appendix provides an overview of documentation.

Writing in Response assumes that the writing process begins in active reading: students should be writing as they read — though this writing may be in the form of only marginalia and journal notes — so that they begin to generate ideas, to formulate a response, well before they sit down to draft a full-length essay. If writing begins with reading notes and then progresses smoothly into low-stakes informal writing and from there into drafting, students should never have the numbing experience of sitting in front of a blank computer screen with nothing to say. In addition, their writing will begin and end as a response, as an original statement that is anchored in a text or in multiple texts, a statement that makes a contribution to a scholarly conversation. The structure of the book thus mirrors the incremental nature of the writing process — reading, informal writing, and formal writing — yet it emphasizes reflection and revision rather than linearity. The discussions in each chapter show how the process is recursive and seamless, an arc of interpretation that begins in attentive listening and ends in thoughtful discourse.

Part 1, "Responsive Reading," offers students three chapters on general concepts and specific strategies for reading actively and initiating a response to a text. These chapters aim to show students how, starting from their own knowledge and experience, they can arrive at insights, formulate arguments, and enter scholarly conversations, thereby making essay writing a more exciting and satisfying undertaking.

Part 2, "Composing the Essay," presents three chapters that offer varied practical strategies for structuring an essay, shaping paragraphs (the building blocks of an argument), and revising for organization and meaning.

Part 3, "Attending to Style," includes two chapters on crafting and revising prose at the sentence level, asking students to consider not only meaning and grammar but also stylistic elegance for vigorous and compelling writing.

Part 4, "Conducting Research," consists of two chapters providing instruction in conducting academic research. The chapters guide students in finding, evaluating, and incorporating sources.

Part 5, "Readings," includes eight professional essays to provide good models of thinking while offering possibilities for student response.

An Appendix, "Documentation," offers an overview of citing sources in MLA, *Chicago*, and APA formats.

New to This Edition

Readings on topics that matter — to students and the public at large. We've added readings to Part 5, which now features eight contemporary selections about issues in the news today. Written by public intellectuals, these essays invite students to join ongoing conversations about topics that matter, such as racial disparities in arrests and sentencing for drug-related offenses (Alexander); the ways in which America has become "the land of less opportunity" (Foroohar); and how American individualism may be sliding toward narcissistic and anxious social isolation (Esfahani Smith).

More help for writing and argument. We've added more on strengthening paragraph cohesion and varying paragraph length, guidance for organizing an expository essay, background information on punctuation for crafting strong sentences, and an overview of Rogerian rhetoric.

More on working with digital tools. We've revised *Writing in Response* throughout to include more on the unique opportunities for researching, writing, and revising in digital environments.

Research coverage now in two chapters. The previous edition's research chapter is now separated into two chapters — Chapter 9, "Getting Started on a Research Project," and Chapter 10, "Working with Sources" — to better reflect the units of work that students are typically asked to do.

Documentation chapter now a streamlined appendix. In response to instructor feedback, we've moved our discussion of documentation to a streamlined appendix that serves as a brief reference for MLA, *Chicago*, and APA styles, presenting only the information students need, without unnecessary details.

Acknowledgments

I am grateful for the suggestions from reviewers who provided feedback at several stages in the development of the first edition. They include Thomas Amorose, Seattle Pacific University; Reine Bouton, Southeastern Louisiana University; Jeffrey Cain, Sacred Heart University; Joan R. Griffin, Metropolitan State College–Denver; Jane Hoogestraat, Missouri State University; Kathleen Lawson, Oakland University; Jennifer Lee, University of Pittsburgh; Karen Bishop Morris, Purdue University Calumet; Cary Moskovitz, Duke University; Rolf Norgaard, University of Colorado, Boulder; Irvin Peckham, Louisiana State University; Nedra Reynolds, University of Rhode Island; Judith Rodby, California State University, Chico; Mary Sauer, Indiana University–Purdue University Indianapolis; Marti Singer, Georgia State University; Donna M. Souder, Colorado State University–Pueblo; Laura H. Thomas, University of Colorado, Boulder; Greg Van Belle, Edmonds Community College; and Michael Wallwork, Oakland University.

We are grateful to the users of the first edition who responded to our questionnaire with valuable feedback: Rhonda Armstrong, Georgia Regents University; Lisa Chinn, Emory University; Christina Durborow, Rutgers University; Laura Hill, Brandeis University; Sonja Jackson, University of Nebraska at Kearney; Sarah Jacobson, Northern Virginia Community College; Patricia Portanova, Bentley University; Robin Smith, Towson University; Martha Webber, University of Puget Sound; and George Weinschenk, Broome Community College.

We thank those instructors who examined the first edition of *Writing in Response* and helped us to consider changes that would improve it: Christine Cucciarre, University of Delaware; Violet Dutcher, Eastern Mennonite University; Sara Eddleman, University at Buffalo; Ellen Feig, Bergen Community College; Devon Fisher, Lenoir-Rhyne University; Seamus A. Gibbons, Bergen Community College; Thomas Richard Johnson, Tulane University; Elizabeth C. Jones, Wor-Wic Community College; Neal Lerner, Northeastern University; Chanomi Maxwell-Parish, Northern Michigan University; Adele Richardson, University of Central Florida; Brent Simoneaux, North Carolina State University; and Stephen Skalicky, Washington State University.

We are also grateful to those reviewers who chose to remain anonymous.

I would also like to thank the people at Bedford/St. Martin's who fostered this project. They include Joan Feinberg, former director of digital composition; Karen Henry, editorial director, English and music; Leasa Burton, publisher for composition; Steve Scipione, senior executive editor; John Sullivan, executive editor; Jennifer Prince, editorial assistant; Molly Parke, executive editor for rhetorics; Emily Rowin, marketing manager; Anna Palchik, senior art director; Castle Design; Billy Boardman, design manager; Marine Miller, cover designer; Rosemary Jaffe, senior production editor; Arthur Johnson, copyeditor; Kalina Ingham, permissions manager; Martha Friedman, photo editor; and David Stockdale, photo researcher.

I am particularly grateful to John Sullivan for his expert guidance, steady support, and infinite patience from the start of this project to its end. His help has been invaluable; had I been in less good-natured and capable hands, the writing of this book would certainly have been far more difficult and less enjoyable.

I am also grateful to my past and present students at Boston University for all that they have taught me. In particular, I would like to thank those students who helped me with this project directly, often by writing extracurricular pieces or patiently conversing with me about some aspect of their experience as writers: Gretchen Baker, Brendan Barrett, Zach Benabid, Amal Benaissa, Ben Dauskewicz, Amy Dipolitto, Joseph Christian Greer, Sergio Herrera, Tiffany Massood, Zach Peikon, Yona Porat, Katelyn Richerts, Adam Romines, Nathan Selsky, Dessa Shuckerow, and Negin Taleb. I owe a great debt to my friend and colleague Professor Dawn Skorczewski, director of University Writing at Brandeis University, for her encouragement, guidance, and inspiration throughout the writing of this book. Professor Stephen Dilks of the University of Missouri, Kansas City, taught me to appreciate the radial diagram as a reading strategy, among other things. Dr. Tom Casserly, associate university librarian at Boston University, generously and expertly answered my questions pertaining to undergraduate research. Professor Tina Loo of the Department of History at the University of British Columbia, Professor David Greven of the English Department at Connecticut College, and Professor Dave Hunt of the Department of Criminology, Social Justice, and Social Work at Augusta State University kindly allowed me to quote assignments of their devising. I am grateful to my dean, Linda Wells, for granting me a leave of absence so that I could complete this book. I would like to thank Deanne Harper for her support. And I owe my partner, Jeff Welch, immeasurable thanks for his support and patience throughout the writing of this project. Finally, I would like to express my deep gratitude to my parents, Mary and Tony Parfitt, for encouraging and supporting me in every endeavor.

Get the Most out of Your Course with *Writing in Response*

Bedford/St. Martin's offers resources and format choices that help you and your students get even more out of your book and course. To learn more about or order any of the following products, contact your Bedford/St. Martin's sales representative, e-mail sales support (sales_support@bfwpub.com), or visit the Web site at macmillanhighered.com/writinginresponse/catalog.

Choose from Alternative Formats of *Writing in Response*

Bedford/St. Martin's offers a range of affordable formats, allowing students to choose the one that works best for them. For details, visit macmillanhighered.com/writinginresponse/catalog.

- Paperback   To order the paperback edition, use **ISBN 978-1-4576-7269-9**.
- Popular e-book formats   For details, visit macmillanhighered.com/ebooks.

Package with Another Bedford/St. Martin's Title and Save

Get the most value for your students by packaging *Writing in Response* with a Bedford/St. Martin's handbook or with any other Bedford/St. Martin's title for a significant discount. To order, please request a package ISBN from your sales representative or e-mail sales support (sales_support@bfwpub.com).

Select Value Packages

Add value to your text by packaging one of the following resources with *Writing in Response.* To learn more about package options for any of the following products, contact your Bedford/St. Martin's sales representative or visit macmillanhighered.com/writinginresponse/catalog.

LearningCurve for Readers and Writers, Bedford/St. Martin's adaptive quizzing program, quickly learns what students already know and helps them practice what they don't yet understand. Game-like quizzing motivates students to engage with their course, and reporting tools help teachers discern their students' needs. *LearningCurve for Readers and Writers* can be packaged with *Writing in Response* at a significant discount. An activation code is required. To order *LearningCurve* packaged with the print book, contact your sales representative for a package ISBN. For details, visit learningcurveworks.com.

i-series This popular series presents multimedia tutorials in a flexible format — because there are things you can't do in a book.

- *ix visualizing composition 2.0* helps students put into practice key rhetorical and visual concepts. To order *ix visualizing composition* packaged with the print book, contact your sales representative for a package ISBN.
- *i-claim: visualizing argument* offers a new way to see argument — with six multimedia tutorials, an illustrated glossary, and a wide array of multimedia arguments. To order *i-claim: visualizing argument* packaged with the print book, contact your sales representative for a package ISBN.

***Portfolio Keeping*, Third Edition, by Nedra Reynolds and Elizabeth Davis,** provides all the information students need to use the portfolio method successfully in a writing course. *Portfolio Teaching*, a companion guide for instructors, provides the practical information instructors and writing program administrators need to use the portfolio method successfully in a writing course. To order *Portfolio Keeping* packaged with the print book, contact your sales representative for a package ISBN.

Make Learning Fun with *Re:Writing 3*

bedfordstmartins.com/rewriting

New and open online resources with videos and interactive elements engage students in new ways of writing. You'll find tutorials on using common digital writing tools, an interactive peer review game, Extreme Paragraph Makeover, and more — all for free and for fun. Visit bedfordstmartins.com/rewriting.

Instructor Resources

macmillanhighered.com/writinginresponse

You have a lot to do in your course. Bedford/St. Martin's wants to make it easy for you to find the support you need — and to get it quickly.

Resources for Teaching Writing in Response is available as a PDF that can be downloaded from the Bedford/St. Martin's online catalog at the URL above. In addition to chapter overviews and additional "Try This" activities, the instructor's manual includes five sample syllabi, suggested additional readings and sequences, correlations to the Council of Writing Program Administrators' Outcomes Statement, and an essay by Matt Parfitt, "Teaching the Exploratory Essay."

Teaching Central offers the entire list of Bedford/St. Martin's print and online professional resources in one place. You'll find landmark reference works, sourcebooks on pedagogical issues, award-winning collections, and practical advice for the classroom — all free for instructors. Visit macmillanhighered .com/teachingcentral.

Bits collects creative ideas for teaching a range of composition topics in an easily searchable blog format. A community of teachers — leading scholars, authors, and editors — discuss revision, research, grammar and style, technology, peer review, and much more. Take, use, adapt, and pass around the ideas. Then come back to the site to comment or share your own suggestions. Visit bedfordbits.com.

About the Author

Matthew Parfitt (PhD, Boston College) is an associate professor of rhetoric at Boston University's College of General Studies. In 2002 he received the Peyton Richter Award for interdisciplinary teaching. He is coeditor of *Pursuing Happiness: A Bedford Spotlight Reader* (2016); *Conflicts and Crises in the Composition Classroom — and What Instructors Can Do About Them* (2003); and *Cultural Conversations: The Presence of the Past* (2001).

Brief Contents

Contents

Introduction: Writing in Response to Reading   1

Part One   Responsive Reading   21

1   Reading with a Purpose   23

2 Active Reading   47

3 Further Strategies for Active Reading   69

Part Two Composing the Essay 89

4 Writing to Discover and Develop Ideas 91

5 Developing an Argument 109

6 Organizing the Essay   147

Part Three Attending to Style 213

7 Crafting Sentences 215

8 Writing with Style 239

Part Four **Conducting Research**

9 **Getting Started on a Research Project**

Part Five Readings   339

"The uncomfortable truth . . . is that crime rates do not explain the sudden and dramatic mass incarceration of African Americans during the past 30 years. Crime rates have fluctuated over the last few decades — they are currently at historical lows — but imprisonment rates have consistently soared. Quintupled, in fact. The main driver has been the War on Drugs."

"Thanks to the ubiquity of text on the Internet, not to mention the popularity of text-messaging on cell phones, we may well be reading more today than we did in the 1970s or 1980s, when television was our medium of choice. But it's a different kind of reading, and behind it lies a different kind of thinking—perhaps even a new sense of the self."

"Each morning people are sprawled in the streets, so deeply comatose that even the indifferent kicks of cops fail to rouse them. Throughout the day the destitute and the addicted, the insane and the desperate, sit in pairs in doorways and on steps, heads bowed, hearing each other out or reaching out an arm while the other groans and shivers."

"Behavioral economics tells us that our sense of well-being is tied not to the past but to how well we are doing compared with our peers. Relative mobility matters. By that standard, we aren't doing very well at all. Having the right parents increases your chances of ending up middle to upper middle class by a factor of three or four."

"Each of these statistics matters, but for very different reasons. As a society, we probably care more about efficacy: America's future depends on colleges that make sure the students they admit leave with an education and a degree. If you are a bright high-school senior and you're thinking about your own future, though, you may well care more about selectivity, because that relates to the prestige of your degree."

"The crowding of our space has been reinforced by a crowding of our time, and the only way to protect ourselves is to build structures of perpetual deferral: I'll see you next week, let's talk soon. We build rhetorical baffles around our lives to keep the crowding out, only to find that we have let nobody we love in."

"In a good game, we feel blissfully productive. We have clear goals and a sense of heroic purpose. More important, we're constantly able to see and feel the impact of our efforts on the virtual world around us. As a result, we have a stronger sense of our own agency — and we are more likely to set ambitious real-life goals. One recent study found, for example, that players of *Guitar Hero* are more likely to pick up a real guitar and learn how to play it."

"At a time when we are more connected digitally than ever before, at a time when we live closer together than ever before, rates of social isolation are rising at alarming rates. In 1985, when the General Social Survey asked Americans about the number of confidants they have in their lives, the most common response was three. The survey was given again in 2004 and the most common response was zero."

Appendix: Documentation 406

Writing in Response

Writing in Response to Reading

"What Does the Professor Want?"

Subject: Hi!
Date: Monday, Oct. 15, 2015 3:40 PM
From: Sam Piotrowski <sammyp@bu.edu>
To: Rachel Piotrowski <rpiotrowski87@hotmail.com>

Hey sis: What's up? College is still great. Classes still pretty interesting. And I'm pressing my nose to the grindstone as Dad would say. The only downer is English — which is weird because in high school that was always a personal best. Got As and Bs without even trying. But my prof gave me a C on my first paper, even though I worked really hard on it, and Julio (remember my roommate Julio, smart kid with green hair?) said it was an A, guaranteed.

Honestly, I can't figure out the problem. The course is Writing about Literature — which is something I've done before. Plenty. And I have to give

> " In many ways writing is the act of saying *I*, of imposing oneself upon other people, of saying *listen to me, see it my way, change your mind.* "
>
> **JOAN DIDION**

1

Prof. Hughes credit: he gives a good lecture. I almost always stay awake. I used the five-paragraph structure that Mrs. Kelly taught back in sophomore year, so I know it was organized. I stayed away from saying anything too controversial because I didn't want to be wrong; just made three really strong points.

I used the thesaurus and found some great words to use, like "stentorian" and "pusillanimous." Impressive, no? I also included a classy quotation about narrative by someone named Robert Coover. I opened the essay with it, along with a dictionary definition of "narrative."

So far, my prof hasn't explained the C. I did make some grammar mistakes. Maybe I'll go see him tomorrow. Anyway, I won't let this thing eat away at me! I'm sure I'll do better on the next paper, which is due at midterms.

See ya! Sam

This book is for Sam. He'll soon learn that some of his notions about what Professor Hughes hoped to find in his essay were misplaced, and those misconceptions are the chief reason he earned a C — not because he was poorly prepared in high school or because he lacks brains or writing talent, but because his expectations for the assignment were different from his professor's. And eventually he'll begin to understand what Professor Hughes and his other instructors do hope to find in his papers, and he may even begin to understand *why* they want these things. Assuming that Sam does speak to Professor Hughes and that Professor Hughes explains to him where he went wrong and how he can do better next time, the C grade might prove to be a blessing. Some students spend months, even years, trying to figure out through trial and error what professors want in a paper. One of the aims of this book is to explain what professors want, and why. The other is to provide strategies and exercises to help you not just meet expectations but surpass them — and get the most you can out of the experience.

So this book is also for students who, unlike Sam, might do fairly well on their papers right from the start but would find the process of writing college essays more rewarding, enjoyable, and worthwhile if they were armed with certain concepts and strategies. After all, the point of writing in college is not ultimately to get good grades but to learn, and essay assignments afford an exceptional opportunity to develop ideas of your own and share them with your instructor and perhaps your classmates. Over the long run, many students find that this kind of learning is the most meaningful and exciting they do. One premise of this book is that it should be — and certainly can be.

When college professors read student essays, their expectations are often quite different from those of high school teachers. This difference, which professors sometimes take for granted and fail to explain, can be one of the great obstacles that students face when they begin writing at the college level. The mere fact that a difference exists may become clear early in the freshman year, as it did for Sam, but *what* the difference is and *why* it exists can remain a mystery for years. Some students complete their entire undergraduate program without being quite sure what professors are looking for in their writing or how to go about actually producing it. For them, writing can feel like a game of chance, with grades awarded randomly and unpredictably, or as if there's a secret to it that no one is willing to share. Some students do seem to catch on at some point and do consistently well — though even they may have trouble saying exactly what it is they've grasped and how it relates to their educational goals.

It would be nice if there were a simple one-sentence answer to the question "What do professors want from student writing?" There isn't. But while there may be no foolproof recipe for success, certain concepts and strategies can help anyone be more successful in pursuit not only of grades but also of the more lasting rewards that grades are meant to stand for: meaningful learning, the satisfaction of expressing ideas effectively, a proud sense of accomplishment and craftsmanship. These concepts and strategies can be learned without great difficulty. Nevertheless, "a smooth sea never made a skilled mariner," as the saying goes. Most of the time, good writing takes hard work, and there's no getting around it. But while misdirected effort leads to frustration and disappointment, even very hard work can be deeply satisfying when the rewards, both short- and long-term, repay the cost.

We mentioned concepts and strategies that can help you be a successful college writer. The chief aim of this introductory chapter is to clarify **concepts**[1] — the ideas that underlie the professors' expectations for college writing. Most of the rest of the book is devoted to **strategies** — tools and techniques to help you meet these expectations. Three of the ten chapters in this book discuss reading and note-taking. This might seem odd in a book about writing, but, for reasons that we will explain shortly, reading and note-taking — of a particularly careful and thoughtful kind — play so essential a role in the process of college writing that it makes sense to devote a good deal of time and attention to them.

---

[1] Terms in **boldface** are explained in the glossary at the back of the book.

⊘ **Try** This　**Exploring the Culture of Education**

Option 1. An "ethnography" is a description of a culture or subculture, with particular emphasis on the rules or norms that define the culture. In two or three pages, describe the culture, social and academic, of your high school. Then, in one or two additional pages, describe as best you can the social and academic culture of college, based on your experience so far. Finally, write two or three paragraphs to compare the two cultures and draw conclusions: How are they similar? How are they different? And how did your expectations of the culture of college compare to your actual experience so far?

Option 2. Visit your college or university Web site and review some of the pages that describe its academic programs. What do these descriptions reveal about the culture of higher education in general and of your college in particular? What goals and expectations does your college have for its students? How might a student's work as a writer contribute to meeting these goals and expectations? In a two- to three-page essay, write up your conclusions.

The Values of the Academy

College is not simply a continuation of high school. As an institution of learning, college is different in kind. The function of a college or university in society is not only to educate but also to create new knowledge: to conduct research that advances our understanding of the world — both the natural world and the human world, both past and present — and to develop new technologies and methods that help to make the world better. Most large universities devote a sizable portion of their resources to research, aided by grants from governments, nonprofit foundations, and businesses. Colleges and universities (collectively known as "the academy") exist both to pass on knowledge and to advance it, and this mission shapes the expectations that professors bring to their students' writing.

The habits of mind and values that are necessary for good **research** and **scholarship** — for making discoveries and producing insights — are ones that professors aim to instill in their students; they include a willingness to question conventional wisdom, a capacity to imagine fresh hypotheses, the patience to gather information and sift it with care, and the ability to reason strictly from data to a conclusion. You may have entered college with the idea that higher education will train you to work in your chosen profession and give you the credentials necessary to land a good job. It probably will, but much of what you'll be taught has little to do with job training. Many colleges require every student to take a certain number of liberal arts courses in order to acquire some familiarity with subjects such as literature, history, and philosophy — knowledge that all educated persons should possess, whatever their profession. But the purpose of a college education extends beyond even this kind of core learning (after all, you could acquire it through correspondence courses); more important, it seeks to impart certain skills and values: the ability to attend, to reason and to judge, to think for oneself and to think with others, to examine the basis of belief, to ask questions, to distinguish sound reasoning from flawed, to draw conclusions and communicate them persuasively. Though you are likely planning a career outside the academy — perhaps in business, communications, law, medicine, engineering, or social work — such skills and habits of mind will help you be a more thoughtful, insightful, and useful member of your profession, serving you well no matter where you work. Moreover, they will help you be a better citizen and a wiser leader.

College, then, does not expect you simply to take in more knowledge of the same kind that you acquired in high school. You will learn new things, of course, but you will be expected to take a different approach to your learning. In high school, knowledge tends to be treated as **fact**, as truth that reasonable people accept because the best authorities on the subject maintain that it is true. But in college, knowledge tends to be treated as **current belief**, as what reasonable people today believe because there are good reasons to believe it — even though new reasons might well come along that would force us to revise our views. As one writer put it, "What is treated in high school as eternal and unchangeable fact that human beings have discovered in their continual and relentless progress toward total knowledge will be treated in college as belief that may perhaps be well supported at the present but that could turn out to be wrong."[2] Why is this? The simple answer goes back to the university's role, which is not only to pass along knowledge but also to create it. Teacher-researchers at the college level are aware that if our knowledge is to

---

[2] Jack W. Meiland, *How to Get the Best Out of College* (New York: Mentor/New American Library, 1981), 14.

advance, we must constantly be willing to question the conventional wisdom. We must be willing to reexamine the evidence behind a claim rather than accepting it blindly. At the same time, knowledge can move forward only by building out from what we already know. So scholars strive to combine a healthy *respect* for existing knowledge with a healthy *skepticism* of it. The history of learning is a history of revision — of mastering knowledge in order to improve on it.

Professors consider their students to be members of the university — researchers and thinkers like themselves, if only at the beginning stage — so they expect students to demonstrate these intellectual skills and values in their writing and speaking. If this may seem a little daunting at first, it can also be tremendously exciting: you are being invited to enter into a genuine conversation about ideas, to reexamine everything you thought you knew, and to share your ideas with teachers who take them seriously enough to scrutinize them in the same way they would scrutinize the ideas of fellow scholars.

Academic Discourse

Unfortunately, professors who have been working in colleges or universities for many years — and since it takes five to ten years to complete a PhD, most have been — sometimes take their values and habits of mind for granted and may not always perceive the need to explain them fully or to describe their expectations for what an essay or a research paper should sound like or look like or do. (And even if they recognize this need, they may not find the space to explain it in an already packed syllabus.) Just as there is a certain **culture** that typically prevails in other American institutions such as churches or the military or high schools — social rituals, ways of speaking, unwritten rules of behavior, and so on — so there is a culture of higher learning. It is far from being uniform; just like other cultures, it varies by region, discipline, age group, and other factors. Nevertheless, its members share a certain common stock of ideas and assumptions, as well as certain ways of speaking and writing. As in any culture, members of the academy often take its ways for granted, forgetting or never realizing their differences from the outside world.

The conventional way of speaking and writing in the academy is often called **academic discourse**. Although each discipline has technical terms and concepts of its own, the term "academic discourse" refers to ways of speaking and writing that are found widely throughout the academy, a set of conventions that have grown up over the years in order to facilitate scholarly work. You already know something about academic discourse because your high school teachers probably expected your writing to reflect at least some of its conventions. For example, academic discourse is typically more formal and precise than ordinary speech. When writing a lab report, you would not write, "I saw this ugly squishy thing through the microscope." More likely, you'd write something like, "The microscope revealed a formless, semiliquid object." Academic discourse is typically more exact and less subjectively impressionistic than casual conversation.

Academic literacy, or a familiarity with academic discourse that enables a person to understand it and speak it, distinguishes insiders from outsiders, members of the academic community from everyone else, just as any type of cultural literacy tends to do. Although you're not expected to become fluent in the discourse of higher education overnight, as a member of the academic community you will need to begin to speak the local language in order to communicate effectively. Some students are understandably reluctant to adopt this language, fearing they may sound stuffy or pretentious. Granted, some academic discourse certainly *is* stuffy and pretentious, but as we will see, it need not be. In essence, it reflects the "ethos" or culture of the academy, and while it is impossible to describe that culture fully in just a few sentences, two practices stand out so prominently that they are nearly definitive. First, academic discourse reflects the speaker's awareness of the work of other specialists who have already contributed to our understanding of the subject under discussion. Second, it reflects the need to proceed cautiously and to follow strict reasoning.

Scholars proceed cautiously because they know that reliable conclusions must be based on evidence and that the evidence is always incomplete. Jumping to unsupportable conclusions would be pointless. But this does not prevent scholars from drawing conclusions at all: over time, they build up reliable, well-tested theories, but such theories are rarely, if ever, the work of just one or two individuals. Thus, scholars avoid making excessively grand claims and tend to **qualify** their statements in words that show their claims are provisional, based on the limited data available so far.

Likewise, scholars carefully try to avoid errors in reasoning that would make their conclusions worthless. Since their arguments must stand up to careful scrutiny, scholars must reason strictly from the evidence, avoiding personal bias, overgeneralization, emotional appeal, careless use of language, self-contradiction, and other fallacies. Typically, articles and books by scholars are reviewed by other scholars in the same field before being published. If reviewers find errors or holes in an argument, the author may need to revise or start over.

Thus, academic discourse reflects a set of assumptions about how scholarly work proceeds, how knowledge gets made. We can readily see how scholarly writing embodies the values of the academy by examining a paragraph from Nicholas Carr's "Is Google Making Us Stupid?" (reprinted on p. 347). Although Carr is not a professional academic, his writing is scholarly in the sense that it embodies the values of the academy. His essay raises questions about our use of the Internet and how our electronic devices may be changing the ways we read and think. At the beginning of the essay he is concerned chiefly with his own experience of life with technology. But at a certain point he begins to consider whether the problem is widespread.

> Anecdotes alone don't prove much. And we still await the long-term neurological and psychological experiments that will provide a definitive picture of how Internet use affects cognition. But a recently published study of online research habits, conducted by scholars from University College London, suggests that we may well be in the midst of a sea change in the way we read and think. As part of the five-year research program, the scholars examined computer logs documenting the behavior of visitors to two popular research sites, one operated by the British Library and one by a UK educational consortium, that provide access to journal articles, e-books, and other sources of written information. They found that people using the sites exhibited "a form of skimming activity," hopping from one source to another and rarely returning to any source they'd already visited. They typically read no more than one or two pages of an article or book before they would "bounce" out to another site. Sometimes they'd save a long article, but there's no evidence that they ever went back and actually read it. The authors of the study report:
>
>> It is clear that users are not reading online in the traditional sense; indeed there are signs that new forms of "reading" are emerging as users "power browse" horizontally through titles, contents pages, and abstracts going for quick wins. It almost seems that they go online to avoid reading in the traditional sense.
>
> Thanks to the ubiquity of text on the Internet, not to mention the popularity of text-messaging on cell phones, we may well be reading more today than we did

in the 1970s or 1980s, when television was our medium of choice. But it's a different kind of reading, and behind it lies a different kind of thinking — perhaps even a new sense of the self. "We are not only *what* we read," says Maryanne Wolf, a developmental psychologist at Tufts University and the author of *Proust and the Squid: The Story and Science of the Reading Brain.* "We are *how* we read."

Carr proceeds with caution, acknowledging right at the beginning that more studies are needed, because only multiple, reliable studies that point to the same conclusions can give real confidence ("we still await the long-term neurological and psychological experiments that will provide a definitive picture"). No single study can "prove" anything, but he cites one recent study — a five-year project, involving two research institutions — whose size and scope give us good reason to take it seriously. In scholarly writing, the report on the study would normally be fully cited, but Carr provides enough information to make it easy to find (and it is hyperlinked in the online version of Carr's essay). (The article is "Information Behaviour of the Researcher of the Future" by Peter Williams and Ian Rowlands.)

Carr summarizes that report carefully, emphasizing key findings and quoting two sentences that pertain most closely to his concerns. He acknowledges an argument that might be raised by a skeptical reader: we may in fact be reading *more* today than in the past. But he remains cautious and tentative: he doesn't want to overstate his views; his purpose is not to win a debate or even to persuade us of some settled position, but rather to raise questions and concerns. He does claim, however, that the reading we're doing on our phones and computers — of texts, e-mails, and Web pages, chiefly — is a "different kind" of reading from reading books, and reading differently means thinking differently; perhaps it even shapes our "sense of self" differently. Carr draws on another scholar for support, the developmental psychologist Maryanne Wolf, and he includes the title of her book, *Proust and the Squid: The Story and Science of the Reading Brain*, so that readers can check it for themselves. So he's bringing together two scholarly sources to raise questions about a trend that cannot definitely be verified at this point but is nevertheless a real concern — not only because other people are very possibly experiencing similar brain changes themselves, but because these changes may be just the start of a larger, deeper shift in our way of being and our capacities, and we might fail even to notice this shift before it becomes irreversible.

→ Try This   Learning the Values of the Academy

Working with the following passage from paragraphs 15–18 of Emily Esfahani Smith's "Life on the Island" (reprinted on p. 399), consider how it embodies the intellectual values of the academy. How does the essay embody the values described in this chapter? What other values, or aspects of these same values, can you infer from it? Write up your conclusions in a short essay of your own. Share it with your classmates and compare your views with theirs.

It would certainly be easy to dismiss narcissists as vain egoists — easy and not incorrect. (Later in the song, Perry sings, "I went from zero, to my own hero.") But the problem with narcissism, as Lasch pointed out in his book, is not just self-obsession. The problem with narcissism lies in the *consequences* of that self-obsession. Narcissists, he writes,

> may have paid more attention to their own needs than to those of others, but self-love and self-aggrandizement did not impress me as their most important characteristics. These qualities implied a strong, stable sense of selfhood, whereas narcissists suffered from a feeling of inauthenticity and inner emptiness. They found it difficult to make connection with the world. At its most extreme, their condition approximated that of Kaspar Hauser, the nineteenth-century German foundling raised in solitary confinement, whose "impoverished relations with his cultural environment," according to the psychoanalyst Alexander Mitscherlich, left him with a feeling of being utterly at life's mercy.

This is precisely what we see happening in the culture at large. At a time when we are more connected digitally than ever before, at a time when we live closer together than ever before, rates of social isolation are rising at alarming rates. In 1985, when the General Social Survey asked Americans about the number of confidants they have in their lives, the most common response was three. The survey was given again in 2004 and the most common response was zero. Our connections to others are slowly dissolving, a trend that Harvard's Robert Putnam discussed in his 2000 book *Bowling Alone*. As community goes, so do the values that accompany social connections — values like duty and restraint.

Left unchecked by the constraints of the community, individualism has a nasty underside, as Durkheim came to see and as we are now seeing. This past spring, the Centers for Disease Control released an alarming study indicating that the suicide rates of middle-aged Americans aged 35–64 rose 30 percent between 1999 and 2010, with men taking their lives at higher rates than women. More generally across the population, rates of depression have increased ten-fold since the 1950s. Young people have been particularly affected. Youth suicide, especially among boys, has risen over the past fifty years in most developed countries.

Why Do College Instructors Assign Writing?

To understand what you need to accomplish in a college essay or paper, it helps to have a clear sense of why professors give writing assignments. If they simply wanted to make sure that you had read the textbook carefully or listened attentively to lectures, they could give a multiple-choice test — which takes much less time and effort to grade than an essay. But most tests only require you to regurgitate content that the course fed to you in some form. They ask you to behave a little like a sponge: you absorb knowledge and, when asked, squeeze it out again, in pretty much the same form that you took it in. This kind of learning certainly has its value: much of what a doctor or an engineer or any expert needs to know has to be learned by rote memorization, and tests are a necessary means of making sure that students have mastered the material. But this kind of learning is not necessarily the deepest or richest kind. It doesn't compel learners to *think* carefully about ideas or *do* anything with them. True expertise requires much more than just an ability to recite memorized facts and definitions: in the real world, we need to *use* knowledge, to apply old ideas in new situations, to solve problems, to analyze data and draw conclusions, to see patterns, to make predictions, to make connections between concepts, to assess the merits of a hypothesis, and in a host of other ways to *think* creatively with what we know. These skills define true expertise just as much as — or even more than — the possession of a body of information. So professors typically ask students to write essays in order to give them the opportunity not only to practice such skills but also to get to know key concepts well enough to be able to use them in the real world.

For this reason, essay assignments typically expect a different kind of work from you than exams and tests do. An essay assignment often poses a problem to which there is no single right answer and no tidy solution. Problems of this kind require us to do the kind of deeper analytic, synthetic, evaluative, and creative thinking just described; they compel us to become actively involved in our learning in a way that exams rarely do. Very often, an essay assignment requires each student to develop an original argument in support of the student's own solution or approach or perspective on a problem.

Let's look at some representative college writing assignments. All of these are taken from actual introductory college courses.

A *"Close Reading" Essay on* Paradise Lost (Humanities): Choose a short passage (10–15 lines) from Book I of *Paradise Lost* that in your view stands as a "microcosm" of the work as a whole. Analyze it in terms of form (imagery, style, figurative language) and content (meaning, literal truth), and discuss the ways in which form and content are related to each other in the passage. Provide a very specific analysis of the passage, but also communicate your sense of the ways in which the passage reflects, contains, and synthesizes issues and qualities of the work as a whole. Length: 5–7 pages. Format: MLA.

Analysis of a News Story (Sociology): Write an essay that uses one or more of the sociological concepts we have learned this semester to analyze an article from a newsmagazine such as *Time, Newsweek,* or *U.S. News and World Report.* Choose your article with care, and decide on one or more appropriate sociological concepts that can help the reader understand the sociological dimension of the story. In your essay, you must explain the sociological concept, explain the article, and apply the sociological concept to the article. Length: 5–6 pages. Format: *Chicago* style.

Inferences about Eighteenth-Century Society (History): Choose one chapter from Christopher Moore's *Louisbourg Portraits: Life in an Eighteenth-Century Garrison Town.* Write an essay that explains what the life of the individual in question tells us about eighteenth-century society (e.g., social relations, class, race, gender). Do not draw on outside sources for this assignment. Instead, use the selected chapter and your knowledge of concepts from lectures and discussions to generalize from the particular. Length: 6–8 pages, double-spaced. Include a title page with your name and the name of your TA on it. Format: *Chicago* style.

All three assignments ask students to work carefully with a text and to use concepts from the course to draw conclusions of their own. The first assignment is from a humanities course: students have been reading and discussing the seventeenth-century English poet John Milton's *Paradise Lost* for several weeks. The instructor wants her students to work closely with just a few lines from the poem, but she wants them to demonstrate that they comprehend the major themes and issues of the poem as a whole, by relating the lines to the rest of the poem. She also wants them to practice for themselves the kind of literary analysis that she has been demonstrating in her lectures and discussions. The most interesting papers, and likely the most successful, will be those that work with a passage that hasn't been discussed in class at any length and thus offer original insights into the poem.

The second assignment also requires students to work with a text, but this is not a literary analysis; here, the instructor wants his students to demonstrate that they not only understand sociological concepts in an abstract way but also can *work* with these concepts and show how they apply to and help us understand real-world situations. A successful essay will demonstrate a strong grasp of the concepts and use them in a precise way, but it will also show some creativity and insight in working with the news story, probing details that a casual reader might overlook and noticing patterns that reveal the sociological background.

The third assignment, for a history course, also asks students to work with a text. In this case, the professor wants students to make generalizations based on a particular example — a single individual described in one of the chapters of *Louisbourg Portraits*. Students will need to apply the knowledge of eighteenth-century society that they have gathered from lectures and other texts as they develop their argument. But their argument will need to be supported by specific details from the text. Like professional historians, students will need to pay careful attention to the clues — the telling details — in the source text in order to make inferences about the society of that time. Because students are working with just one life, this assignment will involve some guesswork, and they might not be quite certain that their inferences are valid. But making this kind of educated guess based on evidence from documents is the only means historians have of drawing conclusions about the past. While the assignment does require students to do the sort of work that professional historians do, it also requires students to develop analytical skills that are widely applicable.

When you write an essay, it is more important to demonstrate your thinking skills than to be precisely "right," in the sense of repeating an answer that has already been defined as correct, as you might do on an exam. And essays give you the opportunity to show your professor what you, as a unique individual, can do with the concepts that he or she has been teaching, to explain the distinct meaning and interest that they have for you. Think of an instructor sitting down to read thirty or more essays on basically the same subject. For both your sake and the instructor's, it's a good idea to make your essay interesting. As a colleague of mine used to say, with only slight exaggeration, "It's more important to be interesting than to be right." While a frivolous argument made just for the sake of being clever wouldn't pass muster in most college courses (and probably wouldn't be very interesting), my colleague wanted to address a different and more common problem with freshman writing: the fact that the arguments are often *too* correct — too familiar, too superficial, too simplistic, too dull. By encouraging students to find something *interesting* to say, she wasn't inviting them to develop arguments that were outlandish or implausible. Instead, she was asking them to be willing to take risks, to think deeply enough about a problem to develop ideas of their own, ones that, if not absolutely new and original, were at least fresh and engaging.

With most assignments, a strong essay makes a clear and convincing argument for an original insight. There are two sides to writing this kind of essay: the thinking side and the communicating side. When professors assign an essay, they typically have both sides in mind: providing the opportunity for you to learn on your own as you figure out what you're going to say, and providing the opportunity to share your thinking with your professor. As a rule, these two sides emerge in the writing process as two different phases: in the early stages, you focus mostly on **writing to learn**, figuring out your ideas and finding something to say; in the later stages, you focus more on **writing to communicate**, finding a way of arranging and expressing your ideas that will make sense to, and persuade, the reader. Writing to learn tends to be inward-looking: it involves your own struggle to figure things out in a way that makes sense to you. Writing to communicate is outward-looking: now that you have some ideas, you're concerned with expressing them effectively to someone who cannot see inside your mind and has no way of understanding your ideas except through the words you put onto the page. These twin goals of the writing process — the writer's need to understand and the reader's need to understand — are equally important and will receive roughly equal emphasis in the chapters that follow. Early chapters emphasize writing to learn, and later chapters emphasize writing to communicate. Both phases are essential to a successful paper.

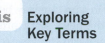

Try This: Exploring Key Terms

Look up the following terms in a good dictionary: *opinion*, *argument*, *hypothesis*, *thesis*, *theory*. Choose two and write a brief essay or journal entry explaining the difference between the two words.

Critical Thinking

Instructors often use the phrase **critical thinking** in connection with writing assignments. This umbrella term refers to the creative ways of using knowledge that we have just described: applying ideas, analyzing ideas (or taking them apart), synthesizing ideas (or putting them together), and evaluating ideas. When used in ordinary speech, the word "critical" often has a negative connotation (for example, "Helen was critical of my taste in clothes"). But it has another meaning that carries none of this negative sense. Deriving from the Greek word for "judgment," it means in this sense "involving careful and exact observation and judgment." College writing instructors often speak of critical reading, critical writing, and critical thinking — all terms that imply attention to detail, careful reasoning, and a mental attitude that seeks out the rational basis for claims rather than accepting them merely on authority. Richard Rodriguez, author of a well-known intellectual autobiography entitled *Hunger of Memory* (1982), recalls his precocious reading habits as a grade school student. By the time he entered high school, he had read hundreds of difficult books that most students would not encounter until college. "But I was not a good reader," he writes. "Merely bookish, I lacked a point of view when I read. Rather, I read in order to acquire a point of view."[3] Now an adult, Rodriguez recognizes that he had formerly been too passive and diffident a reader, too ready to accept what he read at face value, and unable to enter into any sort of dialogue with texts because he lacked ideas of his own. To be able to have a conversation with texts is essential to critical reading and writing. It requires no great fund of learning or special expertise; all it really requires is curiosity, a readiness to pose questions and to wonder, and a degree of confidence in your right to do so. These are precious skills, yet ones that everyone possesses to some degree. They are certainly the keys to critical thinking. Criticism, then, can refer not to the business of finding fault but to the business of analyzing a text closely, entering into a conversation with it, and bringing an independent mind to bear. The result might be a judgment of some kind — positive or negative — but it might equally be a new insight or perspective that emerges from this encounter between a curious mind and a text.

Reading is the principal means by which college writers inform their thinking and develop new ideas. For this reason, three chapters in this book are concerned with reading strategies. The act of reading and the act of scholarly writing are so deeply intertwined as to be almost inseparable. Reading at the college level is never just a passive act of absorbing information; it involves an active dialogue that, like a good conversation, gives birth to new ideas, new ways of seeing, and — as these thoughts find their way into words — new texts. As the nineteenth-century philosopher and essayist Ralph Waldo Emerson wrote in "The American Scholar" (1837), "One must be an inventor to read well. . . . There is then creative reading as well as creative writing."[4] Reading, thinking, crafting an argument, and revising are not

---

[3] Richard Rodriguez, *Hunger of Memory* (New York: Random House/Dial, 2005), 68.

[4] Ralph Waldo Emerson, "The American Scholar," in *Little Masterpieces: Ralph Waldo Emerson*, ed. Bliss Perry (New York: Doubleday, Page, 1901), 160, http://www.archive.org/details/historyselfrelia00emer.

entirely separable activities. To read is to think, to think is to reason and imagine arguments, to make an argument is to revise old ideas, and to revise is to read — creatively.

College professors are interested in your ideas, but students sometimes confuse ideas with **opinions**. By definition, an opinion is a judgment that rests on insufficient grounds, on data and reasoning that are too thin or vague to raise the opinion to the level of a hypothesis or theory. Of course, we all hold opinions about all sorts of things — social, political, religious, philosophical, and so on — that we've never studied in depth but that we know something about from hearsay or personal experience. And opinion is sometimes the best we can hope for: many questions are intrinsically undecidable and necessarily "matters of opinion." (Who's a better artist, Monet or Warhol?) As the cliché reminds us, we're entitled to our opinions. But opinions in the stricter sense do not play a major role in academic writing. Instead, academic writing usually presents an informed argument, working with and against informed arguments made by others on the same or closely related subjects. Such arguments may or may not turn out to be *valid* or *true*, and their claims may or may not be proven. But every such argument aims to stand on sufficient grounds.

But even an uncertain argument is better than no argument at all — a point that Sam seems to have misunderstood. Judging from what he tells his sister in his e-mail, his essay apparently did little more than echo back ideas the professor had already discussed in class. The essay used a rather simplistic structure in a formulaic way; it used words that Sam didn't really understand or need; and it incorporated material, like the quotation and the dictionary definition, designed to produce the *appearance* of scholarship rather than to say anything substantial or interesting or new. These devices did little to support Sam's own argument — if indeed he *had* an argument of his own. But when Sam does start writing the kinds of essays his professors hope to read, he may well find the work much more exciting, creative, and satisfying than it used to be. The process will take more time, and he may still experience the occasional midnight agony when up against a deadline, but he'll be involved in and committed to this work time after time. As another student, Zach Benabid, remarked: "The way I write papers [in college] is completely different from high school. In the past, I'd try to write the final draft right away. Now, when I revise a paper, I *butcher* it; it's a completely different paper. I'm not satisfied or confident in the paper unless I go through seven drafts."

As Zach suggests, there is no simple formula for producing college-level essays. The five-paragraph model that you might have learned in high school will no longer

Try This   Thinking Critically about a Text

Earlier in this chapter, we looked at a paragraph from Nicholas Carr's "Is Google Making Us Stupid?" Now read the rest of Carr's essay (p. 347), and choose one of the following options.

Option 1. Identify at least two other passages that seem to you to embody the values of the academy, as described on pages 4–6. Carr is a journalist, and although he is writing for a general audience here rather than a strictly scholarly community, his writing exhibits some of the characteristics of academic discourse. Identify at least two or three passages or sentences that, in your view, reveal these characteristics. In your notes, explain what qualities each passage exhibits and how it does so. Be prepared to discuss your conclusions in class.

Option 2. Using one of the three sample writing assignments from this introduction (pp. 11–12) as a general guide, write an assignment for Carr's essay that requires students to engage in critical thinking. It might be a formal essay assignment or a short, informal homework or even an in-class activity. But it should ask students to analyze the text, not merely repeat what they learned from it.

suffice, and a rapid, last-minute writing process will no longer work. The remainder of this book offers some strategies for developing ideas about your reading and for expressing these ideas in essay form.

"Live the Questions"

In *Letters to a Young Poet* (1903), the celebrated Austrian poet Rainer Maria Rilke writes to an unnamed younger poet, offering guidance and advice as the youth embarks on a lifelong journey that will demand enormous dedication and hard work. Rilke tells him that he will need patience, that he should not expect to find quick, easy solutions for his doubts and questions. To obtain answers, he will need to "live the questions."

> I would like to beg you, dear Sir, as well as I can, to have patience with everything unresolved in your heart and to try to love *the questions themselves* as if they were

locked rooms or books written in a very foreign language. Don't search for the answers, which could not be given to you now, because you would not be able to live them. And the point is, to live everything. *Live* the questions now. Perhaps then, someday far in the future, you will gradually, without even noticing it, live your way into the answer.[5]

The situation of the young poet might seem very different from that of the average college student. In many respects, it is: student writers are under pressure to meet deadlines, to study for exams, to fulfill the exacting requirements of an instructor's assignments, to earn good grades — and to balance all this with a satisfactory personal life. How different from the poet who can afford the time to "gradually, without even noticing it, live [his or her] way into the answer"!

But looked at from another point of view, Rilke's advice may be pertinent after all. In the end, all those readings, lectures, exams, and assignments must add up to something; they cannot be perfectly disconnected from one another, each an end in itself. In fact, any thoughtful student notices threads that run from one assignment to another, one course to another; together, these threads compose an education. And let's not forget that the point of college studies is to be found not merely in a grade or diploma but in the way it changes us, making us more informed, understanding, and wise. At the center of a liberal education are fundamental questions: Who am I? What is the good life? What kind of world do I live in? How did we get here?

In the thick of reading and writing to complete an assignment, we need to remind ourselves of these questions from time to time. And we need to remember to reflect on the meaning of readings and lectures for our actual lives, our actual selves. To "live the questions" means taking the questions into our lives and making them truly our own — pondering them at any time of day, not only when we're studying but also when we're exercising or commuting or relaxing or talking with friends. It means taking the work seriously and letting it enter the parts of our lives that are not strictly given over to work.

We cannot really respond to a writer unless we are willing to "live the questions," to make connections between what a writer says and all the other things we know or think or wonder about. Responding to a reading means allowing our questions to surface and be taken seriously. It means developing a connection between

---

[5] Rainer Maria Rilke, *Letters to a Young Poet*, trans. Stephen Mitchell (New York: Random House/Vintage, 1986), 34.

schoolwork and the thinking that you do outside of school. Over the long term, this habit will help you make the most of your education. But in the short term, it will also help you write more interesting and satisfying essays.

✔ Checklist for Understanding Academic Discourse

☐ Begin learning the discourse conventions of higher education.

☐ Understand your assignment.
  - Make an appointment with your instructor if aspects of the assignment confuse you.

☐ Understand that writing involves rewriting.
  - Write to discover what you want to say.
  - As you begin to discover what you want to say, focus next on writing to communicate your ideas.
  - All good writers revise. Make revision a step in your process.

☐ Demonstrate critical thinking skills in your writing.
  - Seek to say something interesting and original.
  - Be prepared to take risks.

part 1

Responsive
Reading

chapter 1

Reading with a Purpose

In the academic world, reading is part of the writing process. To respond to a text in a meaningful way, a writer must first listen carefully to what the text is saying. In the case of academic writing, this usually means tracing the main argument — which is something more

> "Read not to contradict and confute, nor to believe and take for granted … but to weigh and consider."
>
> **FRANCIS BACON**

than just the general topic or main themes — and grasping it firmly enough to be able to assess its strengths and weaknesses. Sometimes this poses few difficulties and the argument is sufficiently clear after only one reading, but frequently understanding the main argument requires concentration, effort, and several passes through the text. And even when a text is fairly straightforward, reading it at least twice usually pays dividends if you're planning to write about it.

Academic texts, including the kind that college professors assign to first-year students, are often particularly demanding, so attentive and thoughtful reading is an essential part of college writing. Good academic essays — not just student essays but nearly all academic essays — result from a thinking process that begins in a dialogue with texts, a give-and-take involving listening and responding. Such dialogues require **active reading** and rereading, drawing on just about all of your mental faculties as you question, analyze, reason, weigh, make inferences, and develop ideas of your own. This isn't the kind of reading you do hastily at the start of the writing process and then put behind you. The dialogue continues throughout the writing process: as experienced writers know, reading or rereading is not only the best way to get started but also the best way to get moving again when you're stuck.

Any text you plan to write about should be read more than once, and usually several times. This means that you can hold off making judgments or worrying too much about your own response at first and just concentrate on making good sense of the author's argument. You can develop well-thought-out ideas later: the first thing is to get the most clear and full understanding possible of what the text has to say. Often, this task alone is challenging. The problem many readers have with long or difficult academic texts is not that they fail to understand anything about the texts but that they fail to gather up all the pieces of the jigsaw puzzle, fit them together, and clearly see the big picture, the *main* point. Readers who miss that main point can only produce a response that is to some degree irrelevant and pointless, however inventive and well argued it may be.

Unfortunately, careful reading is an aspect of the writing process that students do frequently neglect. Under pressure to meet a deadline, they are naturally tempted to cut corners, and rereading may seem a time-consuming task that can be hurried a bit. But doing so can thwart all your efforts from the starting gate. In the Introduction, we noted that one cause of disappointing essays is thin, simplistic ideas that are weakly supported by evidence. A clear understanding and full appreciation of another writer's ideas — even if you ultimately disagree with them — is the first step toward developing rich, interesting, strongly supported ideas of your own, whether you are writing a research paper or working on an analytical essay involving just one or two assigned readings.

This chapter concerns some fundamentals of reading with a purpose — that is, reading with the ultimate goal of coming up with something interesting and valid to say. Chapter 2 offers basic strategies for active reading, and Chapter 3 offers several additional strategies for working closely with arguments, strategies that you can use where appropriate but probably will not use routinely.

First, to better understand this concept of "active reading," let's consider what any sort of reading really involves.

Making Sense

Physically, a text is made up of ink marks on a page or dots on a screen: letters, punctuation marks, numerals, spaces. As children, we learn to decipher the code and recognize words that the marks represent. But reading means much more than this: it involves perceiving how a series of isolated letters and words make sense as meaningful phrases and sentences, and tracing a sequence of meanings as they accumulate across a whole page, a chapter, a book. It's what you're doing right now: continually putting together the sentence you are now reading with everything you've read so far in order to make sense of the whole, developing and revising your sense of the whole as you go.

So it is not only the writer's job to "make sense" but also the reader's. When we're reading something that's easy or familiar, we are barely aware of this need to put together the meaning of the text — in a sense, to "compose" it. But when we're faced with difficult or unfamiliar writing, even if written clearly, making sense of the text is a job that calls for great powers of concentration and tenacity.

The ancient Greek philosopher Socrates famously distrusted the written word because he believed it weakened the memory and because the absence of the writer allowed the text to be misunderstood. Indeed, the capacity of most people to remember exactly what they've heard does appear to be much weaker today than it was in Socrates' time, and certainly texts are often misinterpreted. But the modern world relies utterly on writing — from the constitutions that undergird our legal systems to the Twitter feeds that tell us the latest news — so we must deal with the fact that the absence of the writer defines the task that both readers and writers face: both must "make sense" without the benefit of a present speaker who can clarify, correct, or revise. Writing is communication at a distance — but unlike talking on the telephone or through a microphone, it normally takes place across time as well as space. This spatial and temporal distance complicates communication through the written word but also accounts for its tremendous power. "Thanks to writing, man and only man has a world and not just a situation," wrote the French philosopher Paul Ricoeur.[1] Writing makes it possible to know how women lived in

---

[1] Paul Ricoeur, *Interpretation Theory: Discourse and the Surplus of Meaning* (Fort Worth: Texas Christian University Press, 1976), 36.

⊙ Try This   Reading Closely

Read Geoff Dyer's short essay "Blues for Vincent" (p. 358) at least twice. Note that it is divided into four sections that are separated from each other by breaks in the text. What connections and echoes do you see—themes or phrases or feelings that suggest some relation between the sections? What would you identify as the main point or idea that ties the four sections together? How do you interpret the last sentence of the essay?

Compare your reading of the essay with that of other students in your class. Do they differ? How and why? Write one or two pages discussing your answer to these questions.

China a thousand years ago, who won yesterday's hockey game in Philadelphia, how to roast a Thanksgiving turkey, how many moons circle Jupiter, and, of course, what Socrates had to say about writing. (If Socrates' student Plato had not written down his teacher's ideas, we would probably know little about them today.) By reading, we come to know the world and to have a world.

What's the point of all this? It reminds us that reading is never simply the passive act of absorbing information. Making sense of a text does not mean simply figuring out what the author meant; for a text to make real sense, it has to make sense *to you*: you have to recognize the words and phrases, and the text's meanings have to "fit" somehow with other things you know, even if the subject is all quite new to you. Usually we do not know the author personally, but we recognize the world that he or she describes, at least partially. The late English novelist Angela Carter observed, "Reading a book is like rewriting it for yourself. You bring to a novel, anything you read, all your experience of the world. You bring your history and you read it in your own terms."[2] The practical consequence is that reading well means understanding that the reader is an active player in the game of making meaning. Readers can never know *exactly* what the author intended; all they have to go by are the marks on the page. Your reading of a text will differ a little from mine, but this doesn't mean that all interpretations are equally valid. A reader cannot simply invent a text's meaning and make it mean anything at all. Readers have a dual responsibility: they must strive

---

[2] Angela Carter, "The Company of Angela Carter: An Interview," *Marxism Today*, January 1985, 21, http://www.amielandmelburn.org.uk/collections/mt/index_frame.htm.

to work out the author's meaning, and at the same time they must work out its meaning for themselves. This is the basis of the dialogue that generates ideas for writing.

Academic Reading: Reading with a Purpose

We read with many different purposes — to be informed, edified, entertained, stirred, provoked, persuaded. Much of our reading rewards us on several levels at the same time. In college, of course, the principal purpose for reading is to learn, and so the way you read *should* differ from the way you would read a book for entertainment. As you have probably already discovered, reading to learn often requires more effort than reading for pleasure, more focused concentration, and more active involvement. After all, you did not choose these texts for yourself, the subject matter tends to be unfamiliar, and you can't just skim past difficult or tedious passages. Reading in order to complete a writing assignment is even more demanding: not only must you fully grasp the text's meaning, but you must also work out what you have to say about it and perhaps also how it fits into a larger project.

Close reading (reading slowly, with careful attention to the text) is an essential skill for nearly all college students and professors. Good academic writing presents fresh and interesting ideas that are based on solid research and sound reasoning. While research can take many forms (chemists conduct experiments in laboratories, anthropologists observe human culture in locations far and near, archaeologists dig through the remains of lost civilizations, historians study documents in archives, and so on), nearly every kind of research involves reading at some point — and not just casual reading but a careful analysis of arguments made by others concerning the problem under investigation. To produce new and worthwhile ideas, researchers must become familiar with the work that has already been done on the problem; otherwise, they might merely duplicate existing work and pointlessly retrace someone else's steps. Thus, even field and lab researchers must do lots of reading before they get started. Moreover, they need expertise to understand the meaning and importance of whatever they might find in the course of research, and they can develop this expertise only by reading extensively. So the ability to say something fresh and interesting depends to a great extent on careful reading — even in fields that rely heavily on experiment and observation. Reading is the starting point: reading the work of others gives researchers the questions and insights that make it possible to say something new and useful.

Close reading is important beyond the walls of the university too. Nonacademic research projects — such as the kind that journalists do to write magazine or newspaper articles, that lawyers do to build a case, that architects and engineers do to create new structures — also require this kind of responsive and creative reading. Both academic and nonacademic researchers must do more than simply summarize the work of others: their research must be informed by what they read, but it must produce something new as well.

So it's no accident that when reading student essays, professors usually look for signs that students have read the assigned texts attentively and fully grasped the arguments. If you fail to show that you've read the text carefully, your argument will not be based on the kind of evidence your instructor probably expects.

Reading with a purpose, then, means reading with the aim of responding, rather than reading simply to take in a writer's ideas. Like professional researchers, student writers must become familiar with the work of others and then bring something fresh to the conversation. Reading with a purpose is reading as a means to an end, rather than as an end in itself, and it bridges reading and writing — a kind of reading that is itself almost a kind of writing, certainly the first step in the process of academic writing. So academic reading is always a special kind of reading, different from reading a novel for pleasure or reading the newspaper casually over breakfast or surfing randomly across Web pages. Whether you are writing an ambitious research paper or simply a brief response to a single text, reading with a purpose means reading with questions always in mind: "How does this argument work? How strongly supported are the author's claims? What does this argument mean to me? How would I respond? What questions does it raise? What further problems does it imply?" This kind of reading launches a kind of dialogue with the text, as you struggle to figure out where you stand in relation to the writer's argument, or to work out how you might respond to it.

But as we suggested above, the first step is to make sense of that argument fully and precisely. The crucial difference between reading with a purpose well and reading with a purpose poorly is chiefly a matter of recognizing and respecting the author's purpose. In the case of academic writing, this usually means recognizing and respecting the author's argument and the context or situation in which it was made.

Context

Earlier we noted that readers have a dual responsibility: they must try to work out *the author's* meaning and, at the same time, work out what the text means *for them* as individuals. An important aspect of working out the author's meaning involves taking into account the historical or cultural situation in which the author was writing — that is, the *context*. The beliefs and values of one culture can be quite different from another's; this may be true even of assumptions so deeply held that individuals in that culture may be unaware of them. And beliefs, values, and assumptions change through time as well, so that a way of seeing and understanding the world in one century can seem quite foreign to readers in a later century. Arthur Miller's 1953 play *The Crucible* shows how fervently many citizens in seventeenth-century New England feared witchcraft. Indirectly, Miller was condemning the "witch hunts" in his own time (the 1950s) for Communist sympathizers; the mentalities of both periods might seem unintelligible to members of an audience today — unless they strive to see the world through others' eyes and to understand the real fear that gripped people in both those periods as a result of their beliefs. A Japanese writer of two centuries ago might bring to the subject of class relations very different assumptions than those of many readers today. A contemporary Brazilian writer might see issues involved in environmental policy quite differently from the way many Americans see them. Ideally, readers should try to learn as much as they can about the thinking of the writer's time period and culture in order to avoid misapprehensions. When this is impractical, readers should at least make allowances for historical and cultural differences, recognizing that what's strange or puzzling about a text may reflect a different way of thinking and opening their imaginations to a different way of seeing the world. Often, these differences have much to teach us; they help us recognize our own assumptions and put them in perspective. And readers cannot adequately assess an argument without recognizing the cultural or historical differences that might explain the author's point of view.

Books usually contain clues about the time and place in which they were written. Here is some guidance on where to look.

- The copyright page at the front of the book usually includes the date and place of earliest publication.
- A preface or introductory chapter may explain the author's purpose or offer useful information about the circumstances in which the text was written.

- When reprinted in anthologies or textbooks, essays or chapters often include short introductions or "headnotes" that provide background information and a sense of historical and cultural context. The headnotes may also tell you something about the author's career and work. See page 341 for an example.

This kind of information is helpful when available, but readers can gather important clues about context from another source: the body of the text itself. Typically, a writer will reveal a good deal about the context of his or her argument in the first paragraph or two, describing (though sometimes very briefly) an existing controversy or question that he or she intends to address. For example, in "Drug War Nightmare: How We Created a Massive Racial Caste System in America" (p. 341), legal scholar Michelle Alexander outlines the context of her argument in the first two paragraphs, just before she announces her main purpose and thesis, that "racial caste is alive and well in America."

> Ever since Barack Obama lifted his right hand and took his oath of office, pledging to serve the United States as its 44th president, ordinary people and their leaders around the globe have been celebrating our nation's "triumph over race." Obama's election has been touted as the final nail in the coffin of Jim Crow, the bookend placed on the history of racial caste in America.
>
> Obama's mere presence in the Oval Office is offered as proof that "the land of the free" has finally made good on its promise of equality. There's an implicit yet undeniable message embedded in his appearance on the world stage: this is what freedom looks like; this is what democracy can do for you. If you are poor, marginalized, or relegated to an inferior caste, there is hope for you. Trust us. Trust our rules, laws, customs, and wars. You, too, can get to the promised land.
>
> Perhaps greater lies have been told in the past century, but they can be counted on one hand. Racial caste is alive and well in America.

Here Alexander positions her argument as a contribution to a long-standing conversation about race in America, and more exactly about the fate of African Americans since the Civil Rights Act of 1964 put an end to the Jim Crow laws that had enforced segregation. At the same time, she positions her argument in relation to the historical context represented by the election of Barack Obama to the presidency in 2008, an event that for many symbolized the end — or at least the beginning of the end — of African Americans' struggle for equality in the post–Jim Crow era. Most American readers today will be familiar with this social and historical

→ Guidelines **Analyzing Rhetorical Context**

Whenever you read a piece of academic writing, look in the first two or three paragraphs for answers to the following questions. (Occasionally the answers may appear later in the essay.)

- Whom is the writer primarily addressing? Who is the expected audience?
- When was the text written? Where? What do you know about the political and social realities of that time and place?
- How will the argument contribute to an existing conversation? What is that conversation about? Why does this conversation matter?
- What is the author's purpose?

context, so the significance of Alexander's argument is not hard for them to see. But in the case of more specialized academic writing, the first two or three paragraphs of an article may contain clues about a debate or a question that can help us understand the importance of the author's argument.

Scholarly essays invariably make an argument that relates to a *problem* — often a controversial, unresolved, or problematic aspect of a larger project (in the case of Alexander's article, the problem is the persistent social and economic inequality of African Americans). The writer usually aims to contribute something to a conversation that is already in progress. (Occasionally, a writer attempts to launch a completely new conversation, but even then, the writer will often refer to a recognized problem or context that helps explain why this new conversation is needed.) Recognizing this context — the problem that warrants the argument — helps us understand the author's purpose, but we may have to read carefully to find it, and we may need to make a few inferences or even do some quick research to understand it fully when we do.

Your Own Contexts

When assigned as a reading in a college course, an article like Alexander's has another context — the goals of the *course* — and while this context does not normally conflict with the author's purpose, it is not quite identical with it either. If you were reading Alexander's article in a sociology course, it might be paired with one or two other readings that present very different perspectives on the question of race in America. The instructor might expect you to see it as one position statement in a larger debate. In a writing course, the purpose for reading it might be quite different: to illustrate certain features of critical thinking, perhaps, or to show how an academic argument can be structured. You thus need to recognize not only the author's purpose but also the instructor's purpose in assigning it.

Finally, working out a text's meaning involves a third context: the reader's. Not only do writers produce texts in a particular historical and cultural situation, but readers read them in some situation that influences the way the text gets used and even understood. If you read Charles Dickens's *Oliver Twist* (1838) on your own over a vacation, you would likely read it differently than if you were to read it for a nineteenth-century British literature course. There, you might be asked to compare it to other novels by Dickens and to novels by other authors; you might be encouraged to think about its relation to British social problems and political struggles of the nineteenth century; you might read critical essays on the novel by scholars who read it from a Marxist perspective, or a feminist perspective, or a biographical perspective, and these articles might influence your own thinking about the novel. And of course, you would probably be concerned with the exam or paper that you'd have to write. But if you read *Oliver Twist* on your own, over summer vacation, you might be more likely simply to enjoy the plot and the characters and to think about the novel in relation to your own

---

⊖ Guidelines   ## Analyzing the Purpose of Reading

As you read a text, consider these questions:

- What was the instructor's purpose in assigning this text?
- How does this argument relate to the topic or questions currently being considered in the course?
- How does the text's particular topic or question relate to the overall goals and themes of the course?
- How does the reading relate to others that have been assigned?
- What is the importance of the text in the course? (Is it required reading? Are you spending a lot of class time on it? Does your instructor refer to it frequently? Will it play a major role in assignments or in exams?)

life. This is not a bad thing—indeed, it is essential—but the course might lead you to think about the book differently. For example, you might pay closer attention to the possible interpretations of other readers and find yourself justifying your own reading in preparation for any questions that might be raised about it. Reading with these considerations in mind—reading with a purpose—can give you a deeper appreciation and understanding of the book than you would likely get from reading it on your own on vacation.

Identifying the Genre of a Text

In addition to context, readers must recognize and respect a text's **genre** in order to understand it well. The word "genre" (from the French word for "kind" or "sort") refers to the literary category to which a text belongs. The novel—a lengthy fictional narrative or story in prose—is one genre. The essay—generally a brief, nonfiction composition that discusses a limited subject—is another genre. There are countless genres and subgenres—tragic plays, romance novels, Facebook updates, comic books, scholarly articles, blogs, Web sites, tweets, textbooks—and their existence allows readers to know roughly what to expect from a text before they begin reading. College courses assign texts from a wide variety of genres; understanding something about the differences among them can help you adopt an appropriate reading strategy.

Table 1.1 provides a simplified overview of genres. Probably not all the texts you read will fit into these few categories, but the table shows that genre greatly influences how you read. For example, you read textbooks for college courses differently

---

⊙ Guidelines   **Analyzing Your Motives for Reading**

The following questions can help you focus on your motives for reading a particular text.

- What do you personally hope to learn?
- What particular interests and ideas do you bring to the reading?
- How does the reading relate to your goals for your education? To your particular interests and concerns? To your own experience, academic or general?
- How will the reading help you in your coursework?

Table 1.1 Types of Sources and Their Characteristics

Genre	Typical Focus	Typical Author	Typical Audience	Reading Strategy
Textbook (such as this one)	Widely accepted facts and theories	A scholar in the discipline	Undergraduate students	Read chiefly for information
Article from a scholarly journal (such as the *New England Journal of Medicine*)	Specific problem or question in the discipline	Specialist in a particular discipline	Other specialists in that discipline	Read for thesis; weigh the argument
Classic text or "great book" (such as *Moby Dick*)	Human experience	Major author or thinker from the past	Educated general reader	Read for themes and perspectives
Contemporary nonfiction essay (from a periodical such as the *New Yorker*)	Human experience; social, political, and cultural issues	Professional writer, scholar, or journalist	General reader	Read for insight into the subject
Contemporary poetry and fiction (such as *The Girl with the Dragon Tattoo*)	Human experience	Professional writer	General reader	Read for themes and perspectives
Journalistic essay (from a periodical such as *Time* magazine)	Topical issues; social and political problems	Professional journalist	General reader	Read for argument and information
Blog (on a Web site)	Individual opinion or experience	Professional or amateur writer	General reader	Read to understand point of view

from the way you read novels for pleasure, and you read news articles to understand world events differently from the way you read blogs to learn about an individual's experience or opinion. Some texts you read quickly, some slowly. Some you must read with great attention, taking notes and marking up the text; others you can read more casually, sometimes just skimming. Ultimately, your purpose — your needs — determines the way you read.

Genres are really sets of assumptions that writers and readers share concerning the nature and purpose of a text. Having an awareness of genre will prevent you from reading a scholarly article as though it were simply a source of information, or an essay as though it were simply a newspaper report.

Clearing Space to Concentrate

In today's "wired" world, we need to be more deliberate about clearing a space for attentive reading than we did just a few years ago. It takes a positive effort now to set aside thirty minutes or an hour to concentrate on a task without the distraction or temptation of text messages, phone calls, e-mail, TV, chat roulette, and who-knows-what's-next. But it's worth the effort because we read so much better and, in fact, more *efficiently* when we fully immerse ourselves in it — not for just a minute or two at a time, but for an extended period (thirty minutes or an hour at a time). We'd all like to believe that we're capable multitaskers, but research suggests that, like driving, reading requires the mind's full attention. (A recent study found that heavy multitaskers actually perform worse than the average person, even though they feel more confident of their ability.[3])

If you find it difficult to stay focused for thirty minutes at a time, try just ten minutes or even five. With practice, you will gradually be able to increase the length of your sessions. (Use a timer. If your phone has a timer, for now use it *only* as a timer!) Even if you find that ten minutes or so is your limit, you can schedule several sessions an hour with short breaks in between and get the work done more efficiently than if you allow distractions and interruptions.

The right space for reading is also important — with good lighting and a good chair that encourages an upright posture. Not surprisingly, many students discover (sooner or later) that the library affords a better space than home or a dorm room and that in the library they can do better work and do it more quickly, thanks to the freedom from distractions.

---

[3] Eyal Ophir et al., "Cognitive Control in Media Multitaskers," *Proceedings of the National Academy of Sciences* 106 (2009): 37.

Some Sources of Difficulty

Unfortunately, you will occasionally come across an academic text that is hard to understand simply because it is badly written. But more often, academic texts are difficult because they discuss difficult ideas — those that are subtle, complex, and finely nuanced. Such texts unavoidably make demands on the reader's attention and patience. For students, the difficulty can be even greater because many course readings were originally intended not for general readers or even undergraduates but for other specialists in the author's field, who speak the language of the discipline and are familiar with all its terms, concepts, assumptions, and problems. When writing for fellow specialists, scholars do not have to explain the whole context and background of their research, as they might for the general reader; instead, they explore problems and explain their insights in all their complexity and richness, without compromise. Although such texts can be bewildering and frustrating at first, it would be a mistake to conclude that such writing is simply "too difficult." Even if some passages remain a little puzzling, you can still learn a tremendous amount from them, especially with a little persistence and a good reading strategy.

A few other sources of difficulty are worth noting, having to do with **diction**, **sentence structure**, and **tone**. Academic writers sometimes use familiar words in unfamiliar ways, and words that have one meaning in ordinary speech may have another meaning in a scholarly context. (For example, a scholar of eighteenth-century British literature might use the word "sublime" in a technical sense. In ordinary speech, it usually means "very beautiful," but a literary critic might use it, as did Edmund Burke and some other eighteenth- and nineteenth-century theorists, to refer specifically to the aspect of things that provokes an *irrational* response in the beholder; by contrast, the critic might use the word "beautiful" to refer to the aspect that provokes a *rational* response.) Stay alert for familiar words that are being used in specialized senses. In many cases, a good college-level or unabridged dictionary will explain these alternative meanings; occasionally, you might need to refer to a specialized dictionary (see p. 305).

Complicated ideas often require complicated and lengthy sentence structures. This type of writing is necessary when a good deal of qualification is needed to convey ideas precisely, but it requires readers to hold one idea in their heads while other ideas gather round to modify, expand, limit, and revise it. Paraphrasing or mapping long sentences in a notebook or word processing document may help to clarify or untangle them. (Mind-mapping software, such as XMind, FreeMind, or SimpleMind, can be useful for mapping sentences.)

Finally, look for shifts in tone that may affect the text's meaning. Academic writers, no less than other writers, employ humor, annoyance, skepticism, gravity, sarcasm — the whole spectrum of intonations — to express ideas and persuade readers. But because difficult texts demand so much of us, especially the first time we read them, we may miss subtle shifts in tone. Since we cannot literally hear the writer's voice, we must detect such shifts purely from written clues. For example, in "Is Google Making Us Stupid?," Nicholas Carr describes the ideal search engine imagined by the creators of Google, Sergey Brin and Larry Page, by referencing HAL, the mutinous humanoid computer portrayed in the film *2001: A Space Odyssey* (and in the Arthur C. Clarke novels on which the film is based): Carr calls it a "HAL-like machine that might be connected directly to our brains," and he quotes Brin and Page speculating about artificial brains that would give us constant access to "all the world's information." In the following paragraph, Carr remarks,

> Such an ambition is a natural one, even an admirable one, for a pair of math whizzes with vast quantities of cash at their disposal and a small army of computer scientists in their employ. A fundamentally scientific enterprise, Google is motivated by a desire to use technology, in Eric Schmidt's words, "to solve problems that have never been solved before," and artificial intelligence is the hardest problem out there. Why wouldn't Brin and Page want to be the ones to crack it?

Although Carr uses terms that, on the surface, might seem to express nothing but esteem for Google's founders, he subtly undercuts the praise by hinting that Brin and Page might be dangerous, ambition-crazed crackpots, like Dr. Evil in *Austin Powers*: "a pair of math whizzes with vast quantities of cash at their disposal and a small army of computer scientists in their employ." By exploiting the widespread suspicion that "math whizzes" may not be entirely well adjusted, Carr injects a tone of irony or humorous, gentle sarcasm into the paragraph, in keeping with his larger argument that Google and the browsing mentality that the Web engenders may be harming us and our society in ways that tend to escape our notice. In the closing paragraph, Carr returns to HAL and its humanlike intelligence, but now his tone is earnest: "as we come to rely on computers to mediate our understanding of the world, it is our own intelligence that flattens into artificial intelligence." Seen in this light, we realize that (in Carr's view) Brin and Page's ambitions for Google may threaten to deprive us of an essential aspect of our humanity. Unless we are reading carefully and picking up on Carr's tone, we might fail to recognize the connection between these two paragraphs and the way both belong to a single, consistent argument.

Identifying Arguments

Throughout this book, we use the word **argument** in a particular sense, referring not to a debate that ends with a winner and a loser but to a kind of logical structure. The *Oxford English Dictionary* defines "argument" in this sense as "a connected series of statements or reasons intended to establish a position." The way that statements and reasons are connected, the way that evidence supports claims and one claim supports another, makes it possible to speak of the *structure* of an argument, even the "architecture" of an argument.

In any free society, and especially in a liberal democracy such as the United States, *argument* in this sense plays an essential and conspicuous role. Barring physical force, the only way to get citizens to do something or believe something is through persuasion. Candidates for political office must persuade voters to support their platforms. Once elected, politicians must persuade one another to support legislation. In the judicial system, lawyers must persuade judges and juries to convict or release the accused, or to rule in favor of a client. The health of the political and judicial systems depends greatly on citizens' ability to distinguish between a strong argument and a weak one.

Moreover, arguments in the form of advertisements drive the economy. Many corporations live or die by their ability to persuade consumers to buy their products. Every advertisement presents an argument of some kind, whether bold or subtle, aimed at convincing members of the audience to spend money on the company's product — or at least to give the company a few seconds of their attention. Americans are bombarded with advertisements, thousands a day according to some estimates.[4] A century ago, advertisers would pitch their products with slogans that now seem obvious and crude ("Dooley's Yeast Powder. The Best. Try It"). Today, most advertisers use more subtle and indirect approaches, hoping to create positive associations with the product in the viewer's mind or to sell an idea that will ultimately lead to some sort of behavior.

Let's take a look at an advertisement and examine its argument. Figure 1.1 shows a billboard image that was used in an Ad Council campaign for the National

---

[4] "The Harder Hard Sell," *The Economist*, June 24, 2004, http://www.economist.com/node/2787854?Story_ID=2787854. Also, Louise Story, "Anywhere the Eye Can See, It's Likely to See an Ad," *New York Times*, January 15, 2007, http://www.nytimes.com/2007/01/15/business/media/15everywhere.html.

Figure 1.1   This straightforward ad contains a complex argument.

Highway Traffic Safety Administration. This apparently simple ad is not selling a product, but it *is* selling something: the idea that driving while "buzzed" — that is, with a blood alcohol concentration high enough to impair but not enough to make a driver feel positively drunk — is extremely costly. Since drivers on the highway can only glance quickly at billboards, it must be possible to take in the image and text in a second or two. Yet an effective ad will somehow stick with the viewer and have a lasting impact; in this case, the goal is to change the viewer's behavior.

All we see here is an image of a man in his twenties or thirties blowing into a Breathalyzer, and beside it the brief white-on-black phrase, "You just blew $10,000." The man is well groomed and clean shaven, but unremarkable — an everyman that many viewers, particularly young men, could probably identify with. He looks worried, perhaps even bewildered, his eyes not focused on the police officer or the Breathalyzer or anything in particular, as if he's thinking only about the mess he's in. It's clearly nighttime, but he is brightly lit: a harsh yellowish light shines from the right, as if he is in the glare of a spotlight. Unfocused colored lights twinkle in the distance. The police officer is out of focus too, and almost out of the picture, but the figure ".08" on the Breathalyzer is crisply legible.

The words "You just blew $10,000," in all caps, shout directly at us, because we read "you," not "he." Beneath this we read another phrase in smaller, lowercase type: "Buzzed driving is drunk driving." Perhaps the first thing to register is the obvious pun on the word "blew": blowing .08 into a Breathalyzer can mean blowing a large sum of money. But what does this figure of $10,000 refer to? The second sentence doesn't explain. Most drivers know that the actual fine for a DUI (driving under the influence) offense is likely to be much less, at least for a first offense. So it presents a puzzle: How does that number make sense? Many viewers will probably soon guess that it must be a rough estimate of all the costs resulting from a DUI conviction: fines, towing, bail, legal fees, increased insurance rates. (Those who visit the Web site cited at the bottom of the billboard will find videos that explain the amount as the total of the "fines, legal fees, and increased insurance costs" resulting from a DUI conviction.) Importantly, however, the ad has forced the viewer to think, if only for a few moments longer than it takes to read the billboard, about the high monetary cost of a DUI — even if there's no collision, and no one is injured. In a sense, the sign is interactive, and therefore memorable.

The number displayed on the Breathalyzer and the phrase "Buzzed driving is drunk driving" suggest that you don't have to feel positively *drunk* to have broken the law and get arrested: with a .08 blood alcohol concentration you might feel merely "buzzed." The assumption behind the ad seems to be that the potential hit to the wallet will have a greater impact on the target audience than would other deterrents, such as bodily harm suffered in an accident. That may seem cynical, but many drivers believe that they can drive pretty safely after a couple of drinks and won't cause a collision. The ad argues — with great economy but considerable force — that even if that's true, getting arrested can still cause a lot of pain.

Political speeches, legal speeches, and commercials exist in order to persuade, but other kinds of texts also make arguments, though argument may not be their only purpose. Films and novels often make arguments. For example, the film *Avatar* might be said to argue that our modern, industrial civilization's objectification and exploitation of the natural world cannot be reconciled with the longer-term need to live harmoniously with it. Sculptures and paintings make arguments — for example, about what we should consider good or noble or beautiful. In arguments like these, the claim being made is implied rather than stated. But the argument exists nevertheless, and it may be powerful.

For instance, in Figure 1.2, a photograph of the Freedmen's Memorial in Washington, D.C., a nameless slave stoops at the feet of Abraham Lincoln, apparently paying tribute to him. Lincoln is emancipating him, signing a proclamation with his right hand and sweeping his left hand over the slave's head. The figures are slightly larger than life and stand on a column about seven feet high. The sculpture makes an argument about the historical significance of the Emancipation Proclamation, certainly, but in doing so, it makes other claims as well. For example, Lincoln stands upright, as though solely responsible for the emancipation of slaves. The slave, though finally free, still kneels at the feet of a powerful white man. Of course, viewers can draw their own conclusions, but the sculpture — created by Thomas Ball only a decade after the end of the Civil War — does appear to invite the viewer to remember the emancipation of slaves in ways that today would make many of us uneasy.

Figure 1.2 The Freedmen's Memorial
(1876), by Thomas Ball, in Lincoln Park,
Washington, D.C. (Source: Library of Congress)

We can even speak of the argument of a piece of music, such as a movement in a symphony, even if the piece has no words. Here the term would refer to the way that a composer varies and develops musical ideas — themes and phrases — such that the piece has a structure something like that of a written text. And just as music listeners or viewers of visual works of art must often look for an implied argument, so readers of texts sometimes encounter arguments that remain unstated. At times, a text that seems to be simply telling a story, or a series of stories, is actually making an argument. Consider Geoff Dyer's "Blues for Vincent" (p. 358), an unusual essay in four scenes, or perhaps "panels," that clearly relate to one another but in no simple way. At the end of the essay, we become aware that it has been making an argument, and that the last two or three sentences perhaps express that argument in the manner of a thesis statement. Or perhaps not quite: maybe the argument cannot be contained in that way, being so thoroughly entangled in the feelings of sorrow and consolation that emerge only from the stories themselves. The argument may be hard to pin down (Is it about the blues? Love? Pain? Cubism?), but that does not mean that no argument is there.

➔ **Try This**   **Analyzing an Advertisement**

Find an ad, either in a magazine or from television. Study it closely (no detail is insignificant). What claim does the advertisement make? What evidence (implied or stated) does the ad offer for this claim? In your notebook, write out the argument of the ad as fully and accurately as you can. Now, assess this argument. In your view, is the argument rational or irrational? Logical or emotional? Some combination? Neither?

Reading Critically

We said earlier that readers must first listen carefully to what the text is saying, but we have also spoken of the importance of entering into a dialogue with the text: at some point, readers must go beyond just listening if they want to develop a response. Even if readers primarily listen first and figure out their ideas about the text later, both of these activities are part of what we mean by "reading critically." The difference is really a matter of emphasis, since it's impossible to separate them *completely*: it is impossible *not* to reflect, weigh, and even react as you read, even for the first time. (The eighteenth-century Irish statesman Edmund Burke once observed, "To read without reflecting is like eating without digesting.") "Listening" carefully to what the author has to say produces an understanding of the text that inevitably reflects something of your own priorities, interests, and even personality. As such, it becomes the basis of your response.

So good readers take into account the context in which the piece was written and its genre. They attempt to look at the question through the writer's eyes, and they strive to give some thought to what the argument means to them personally. But good reading does not end there. A reader's responsibility is not only to *understand* a writer's point of view but also to *test* it, to see whether the argument holds up under close scrutiny. Put another way, a reader's responsibility is not only to the writer but also to the truth: if every reader simply accepted every writer's claims without question, as if they were the last word on the subject, humankind's quest for understanding would come to an abrupt halt. Only by noticing errors, weaknesses, and limitations in arguments that have already been made by others do we become able to improve on those arguments and get a little closer to the truth. Most writers actually value this kind of critical reading because they see their work not as an end in itself but as a contribution to a larger project, a project of figuring out the answer to a question or the solution to a problem, and this greater goal is one that they share with their readers. In this sense, a critical reader who can see the shortcomings in an argument and correct them is the best reader a writer can hope for. (Note how different this is from merely passing judgment — saying "I liked it" or "I didn't like it." Such blanket judgments don't get us very far.)

But can you, as a first-year college student, raise valid questions against an argument made by an expert? Most of the time, yes. In some situations, you might simply have to take an expert's word for it. But for the most part, if you can make sense of the argument, you can also analyze and assess it. Your knowledge of the subject may be more limited, but you do bring learning and valuable experience to your reading. Your unique perspective may enable you to see something an expert has overlooked. Moreover, you are a reasonable creature, and you can be observant and sensitive, so you are capable of recognizing when something doesn't make sense, when some aspect of the question has been carelessly or superficially argued, or when an important point has been neglected. Questioning whether an argument makes sense is a necessary part of figuring out *how* it makes sense: when an argument doesn't make good sense to you, even after you've considered it carefully, you have as much right as anyone to say so and to explain your misgivings.

The Principle of Charity

But don't be *too* hasty to criticize! Good readers also observe the **principle of charity**. This principle simply states that, as readers, we ought to give the author a chance before we leap in with criticisms and questions. If we find ourselves struggling with a text, we should assume, at least provisionally, that such difficulties stem chiefly from the nature of the ideas being explored, not from the failings of the writer. And we should bring reasonable expectations to the text: a few writers are able to cast their every thought in crystal-clear prose, but we should not expect everyone with good ideas to achieve perfection all the time. So the principle of charity dictates that readers should, within reason, allow for human frailty and accept that even if the writing might be clearer, the text may still be worth reading. (Of course, at the end of the day, you may be forced to conclude that the text was not, in fact, worth the time and effort — but if you make such a judgment before you're sure it's fair, you may be cheating both the writer and yourself.)

The principle of charity has another, more positive aspect. It implies that, to be really good readers, we must temporarily surrender ourselves to the text and let it do its work on us. That is, we must give the writer a chance and, for a time, imagine how the question looks from the writer's point of view. The English romantic poet Samuel Taylor Coleridge wrote in 1817 that poetry requires the "willing suspension of disbelief"; just as poetry and fiction demand that we allow our imaginations to carry us away from our own worlds and into a world created by another, so nonfiction also demands a certain willingness to entertain another person's ideas, and even to immerse ourselves in them. (In "Blues for Vincent" [p. 358], Geoff Dyer writes, "The blues is . . . not something you *play* but a way of calling out to the dead, to all the dead slaves of America." On its own, the claim might seem outlandish, but he has given us, in a few short scenes, a way of understanding his point of view, of hearing in the blues what he hears.) Eventually, of course, we will need to consider the text in a more detached and critical way, but on a first reading the suspension of disbelief is a useful strategy: the deeper our understanding of the author's position, the more well-founded and persuasive our response will be — even if our position differs.

Is it possible to be a sympathetic reader and a critical reader at the same time? Absolutely. Experienced critical readers tend to seesaw as they read, shifting their perspective back and forth, first asking themselves "What does the writer mean?" and then "Does this really make good sense?" The modernist poet and critic T. S. Eliot used the terms "surrender" and "recovery" for this kind of mental circling: readers must first surrender to the text, accepting its way of looking at things, but in good time they must recover their own mind and judge whether this way of looking is acceptable or valid. In this phase, the reader asks questions such as "What is the author failing to see? How else might the question be considered? What are the unstated implications of this argument?"

Clearly, readers who write have many things to do: listen carefully to what the author is saying, taking into account the historical and cultural context; trace the argument and its logical structure; reflect on the argument and start weighing it; begin to think about what they might have to say in response. Readers do not need to do all these things at once, however: that's what rereading is for. And in the next two chapters, we'll offer several strategies for getting all these reading tasks done, effectively and efficiently.

Most students are, in effect, professional readers, and reading plays a central role in the vast majority of college courses. A 2012 national survey of first-year college students showed that 73 percent are assigned at least five books or book-length packs of course readings. Thirty-three percent are assigned eleven or more books, and 11 percent are assigned more than twenty.[5] Your success as a student depends to a great extent on how efficient and capable you are as a reader. And if you think of "success" in education as the attainment of greater wisdom, discernment, and maturity rather than just a matter of grades and credentials, then the way in which you read becomes an even more critical matter. The kind of education you receive — or perhaps "achieve" is the better word — depends not only on what you read but also on how you read. To read attentively, thoughtfully, critically remains an essential skill. In this age of the Internet, information is readily available in vast quantities, but its sheer abundance has made the ability to discriminate between the useful and the not so useful, between the reliable and the dubious, more valuable than ever. "Active reading" means bringing your whole mind to bear on a text, in order to comprehend the text's meaning, to place that meaning in relation to the rest of what you know, and to step back from it to assess its strengths and weaknesses. In the following chapter, we will look at the fundamental strategies for putting this lofty ideal into practice.

✅ Checklist for Reading with a Purpose

Keep the following in mind as you read:

- ☐ If the reading has been assigned, note its purpose in the context of the course.
  - Ask your instructor for guidance if you are confused.
- ☐ Clear a space for reading, free from distractions.
  - Find a quiet setting, such as the library.
  - Turn off your cell phone and other devices, close your laptop, and sit upright.
- ☐ Identify the author and his or her work.

---

[5] National Survey of Student Engagement, Annual Results 2012, 34, http://nsse.iub.edu/NSSE_2012_Results/pdf/NSSE_2012_Annual_Results.pdf.

☐ Identify the text's historical and cultural context.
  - If necessary and appropriate, research the historical and cultural context.
☐ Identify the text's genre.
☐ Identify the main argument.
  - Understand the author's point of view; observe the principle of charity.
  - Hold off any criticism until you have a good grasp of what's being said.
☐ Trace the logical structure of the main argument.
  - Identify key claims.
  - Identify key terms and concepts.
☐ Finally, weigh the argument; note possible weaknesses.

chapter 2

Active Reading

When you have to write about a difficult text, you face a special challenge. Your task is not just to get through the reading, or even to come up with ideas about it, but to meet the author's ideas and develop a response that is *adequate* to them — "adequate" in its root sense: equal, commensurate, or fitting,

> 66 Curiously enough, one cannot *read* a book: one can only reread it. A good reader, a major reader, an active and creative reader is a rereader. 99
>
> **VLADIMIR NABOKOV**

having been brought up to the same level. A careless reading cannot lead to a response that is equal to the text, one that recognizes and respects the text's meaning. At the same time, the reader who is concerned *only* with the text's meaning and does no more than repeat or summarize the main point will not truly be responding to the text at all and will have nothing to say that another reader might find interesting or useful. The real challenge, then, of **response** is twofold: to comprehend the text's meaning and to respond with fresh and interesting ideas. Active reading strategies help you accomplish both of these tasks. This chapter offers some basic strategies — strategies you should consider using whenever you read a text you will have to write about. The next chapter offers some additional strategies for active reading, ones you can draw on more selectively and which will help you dig deeper into an argument; these are useful when you have to work with an especially difficult or complicated text or when an assignment requires you to explore a text's argument very closely.

As we noted in the last chapter, in practice understanding a text and responding to it cannot be separated into completely distinct activities — they inevitably overlap — yet first readings tend to focus more on comprehending, and later readings more on responding. You may need to read a difficult text three times or more before you feel comfortable writing about it. This is not unusual, and in fact many students find that this kind of close, deep work with a writer's ideas — pondering them, questioning them, wrestling with them — is among the most rewarding kinds of academic experience.

So plan to read a text several times if you will be writing in response to it. Though more than three readings may be needed, the process typically has three phases.

- The first reading allows you to get your bearings — to get a general sense of the sort of text you are dealing with and the work that lies ahead.

- The second reading usually provides a better sense of how the pieces fit together into a whole, and now you can begin to map the text's argument or structure so that you arrive at a strong sense of "the lay of the land."

- On the third and subsequent readings, you define, clarify, and strengthen a position of your own.

Although at first the text may feel like a wilderness, if you take the time to explore, survey, and map it, you can soon feel at home in it. With the help of a few strategies, you can approach this kind of work with confidence and even a sense of adventure.

Reading through the Text for the First Time

Read from Beginning to End

The principal aim of a first reading is to develop a general sense of the text as a whole, to "get your bearings," so that when you begin to concentrate on discrete passages, you will be able to use your understanding of the whole to make sense of them. In this first reading, try to push on from the beginning to the end of the essay or chapter with minimal interruptions and without worrying too much about passages whose meaning is not immediately clear. Focus on the main argument, and try to follow the thread that runs through the whole text, connecting paragraph to paragraph and section to section. Glance at footnotes or endnotes, but don't let them distract you from this thread. If for a moment you lose your sense of how the pieces are fitting together, don't get discouraged. Keep reading. Later passages may help to clarify earlier passages, and examples and anecdotes may help to make sense of abstract generalizations. But for now, you need only get a sense of the "shape" of the text, the principal features of the landscape. As you read, keep an eye out for the author's main purpose and argument so that later you can confidently identify it.

Keep a Notebook and Pen Nearby

It's always a good policy to keep a notebook and pen nearby so that you can mark up the reading or write notes if the need arises or inspiration strikes — and if it does, go ahead and write, even if it means interrupting your reading for a few minutes. (Of course, you can also use a computer for your writing.) Capture your thoughts and put them into words while they are fresh. The value of this kind of informal and unstructured writing is immeasurable, and, we contend, "freewriting" at various stages of the reading and drafting process is essential to a good final product. Its purpose is not only to record your thoughts; the very act of writing helps to clarify and develop them and to begin a conversation with the text. Your thoughts may be tentative, random, and sketchy at first, but that should not discourage you. The process of thinking things through on paper is valuable even when the writing itself turns out to be no more than a stepping-stone to more usable writing later on.

Mark Up the Text

A brand-new book, with its crisp pages and clean margins, is an object you may want to keep in mint condition. But textbooks are not coffee-table books. They are the tools of your education, and writing in them does not desecrate them. For centuries, readers have **annotated** — or marked up — books with notes and made their copies into unique records of a thoughtful engagement with the author's ideas. (Notes in the margins of a book are known as **marginalia**.) "Annotation," writes H. J. Jackson in *Marginalia: Readers Writing in Books*, "used to be taught as part of the routine of learning. Marking, copying out, inserting glosses, selecting heads, adding bits from other books, and writing one's own observations are all traditional devices, on a rising scale of readerly activity, for remembering and assimilating text."[1] Owning a book allows you to record your conversation with the author; that conversation begins with your choice of what to underline and what to jot down in the margins. (See Figure 2.1.) Some readers develop their own private codes for

---

[1] H. J. Jackson, *Marginalia: Readers Writing in Books* (New Haven: Yale University Press, 2001), 87.

Figure 2.1 A page from
Ralph Waldo Emerson's
"The American Scholar"
(1837), annotated by
student Katelyn Richerts.

54   NATURE; ADDRESSES, AND LECTURES

tially, or through one faculty; and that you must take the
whole society to find the whole man. Man is not a farmer, or
a professor, or an engineer, but he is all. Man is priest, and
scholar, and statesman, and producer, and soldier. In the *divided* or social state, these functions are parcelled out to individuals, each of whom aims to do his stint of the joint work,
whilst each other performs his. The fable implies, that the
individual, to possess himself, must sometimes return from
his own labor to embrace all the other laborers. But unfortunately, this original unit, this fountain of power, has been so
distributed to multitudes, has been so minutely subdivided
and peddled out, that it is spilled into drops, and cannot be
gathered. The state of society is one in which the members
have suffered amputation from the trunk, and strut about so
many walking monsters,—a good finger, a neck, a stomach,
an elbow, but never a man.

Man is thus metamorphosed into a thing, into many
things. The planter, who is Man sent out into the field to
gather food, is seldom cheered by any idea of the true dignity
of his ministry. He sees his bushel and his cart, and nothing beyond, and sinks into the farmer, instead of Man on the farm.
The tradesman scarcely ever gives an ideal worth to his work,
but is ridden by the routine of his craft, and the soul is subject
to dollars. The priest becomes a form; the attorney, a statute-
book; the mechanic, a machine; the sailor, a rope of a ship.

In this distribution of functions, the scholar is the dele-
gated intellect. In the right state, he is, *Man Thinking*. In the
degenerate state, when the victim of society, he tends to become a mere thinker, or, still worse, the parrot of other men's
thinking.

In this view of him, as Man Thinking, the theory of his
office is contained. Him nature solicits with all her placid, all
her monitory pictures; him the past instructs; him the future
invites. Is not, indeed, every man a student, and do not all
things exist for the student's behoof? And, finally, is not the
true scholar the only true master? But the old oracle said, 'All
things have two handles: beware of the wrong one.' In life,
too often, the scholar errs with mankind and forfeits his priv-
ilege. Let us see him in his school, and consider him in reference to the main influences he receives.

farmer instead of man on farm

*In society he is one finger. In
solitude he is Man (Thinking) or
a whole hand.*

warning

function/duty

benefit

Reality is intelligible

Nature   THE AMERICAN SCHOLAR   *& mind*   55

I. The first in time and the first in importance of the influ- *1st influence should be nature,*
ences upon the mind is that of nature. Every day, the sun; *with time comes intelligence*
and, after sunset, night and her stars. Ever the winds blow; *& science*
ever the grass grows. Every day, men and women, conversing, beholding and beholden. The scholar is he of all men
whom this spectacle most engages. He must settle its value in
his mind. What is nature to him? There is never a beginning,
there is never an end, to the inexplicable continuity of this
web of God, but always circular power returning into itself. *ideas try to explain the world*
Therein it resembles his own spirit, whose beginning, whose *example = circle*
ending, he never can find,—so entire, so boundless. Far, too,
as her splendors shine, system on system shooting like rays,
upward, downward, without centre, without circumfer-
ence,—in the mass and in the particle, nature hastens to ren-
der account of herself to the mind. Classification begins. To
the young mind, every thing is individual, stands by itself. By
and by, it finds how to join two things, and see in them one
nature; then three, then three thousand; and so, tyrannized
over by its own unifying instinct, it goes on tying things together, diminishing anomalies, discovering roots running under ground, whereby contrary and remote things cohere, and
flower out from one stem. It presently learns, that, since the
dawn of history, there has been a constant accumulation and
classifying of facts. But what is classification but the perceiving that these objects are not chaotic, and are not foreign, but
have a law which is also a law of the human mind? The as-
tronomer discovers that geometry, a pure abstraction of the
human mind, is the measure of planetary motion. The chem-
ist finds proportions and intelligible method throughout matter; and science is nothing but the finding of analogy,
identity, in the most remote parts. The ambitious soul sits
down before each refractory fact; one after another, reduces
all strange constitutions, all new powers, to their class and
their law, and goes on for ever to animate the last fibre of
organization, the outskirts of nature, by insight.

ABSTRACTIONS in the world

Thus to him, to this school-boy under the bending dome
of day, is suggested, that he and it proceed from one root; *Root = the soul of his soul*
one is leaf and one is flower; relation, sympathy, stirring in
every vein. And what is that Root? Is not that the soul of his
soul?—A thought too bold,—a dream too wild. Yet when

marginal notes, using math symbols, abbreviations, and pictographs. Your notes in the margins make a book more completely your own.

But on reading a text for the first time, avoid marking it up too heavily. Instead read through the text completely at a steady pace, knowing that later on you'll come back to it and mark it up thoughtfully.

Underline sparingly — just key phrases or sentences that you know you will want to come back to; and in the margins, jot down a question mark next to puzzling passages, or a brief keyword as a heading, and so on. When you reread and have a stronger sense of the shape of the argument as a whole, you will mark up the text more heavily (see p. 59). For this kind of work, a thick highlighter marker may be better than nothing, but in the long run it reveals its shortcomings. After several rereadings, devotees of the highlighter often end up with a text so heavily highlighted that nothing stands out any longer in the great sea of yellow or pink — and so it defeats its purpose. A pencil or a fine-point pen, on the other hand, offers plenty of flexibility — underlining; circling words or phrases; writing words, symbols, and simple diagrams in the margins; and so on — and allows you to mark up pages and write notes in a notebook without constantly switching between tools.

Here is an example of annotations a student made during a first reading. This is the first paragraph of Adam Gopnik's essay "Bumping into Mr. Ravioli." (The full piece is reprinted on p. 386.)

7½ years old

My daughter, Olivia, who just turned three, has an imaginary friend whose name is Charlie Ravioli. Olivia is growing up in Manhattan, and so Charlie Ravioli has a lot of local traits: he lives in an apartment "on Madison and Lexington," he dines on grilled chicken, fruit, and water, and, having reached the age of seven and a half, he feels, or is thought, "old." But the most peculiarly local thing about Olivia's imaginary playmate is this: he is always too busy to play with her. She holds her toy cell phone up to her ear, and we hear her talk into it: "Ravioli? It's Olivia . . . It's Olivia. Come and play? OK. Call me. Bye." Then she snaps it shut and shakes her head. "I always get his machine," she says. Or she will say, "I spoke to Ravioli today." "Did you have fun?" my wife and I ask. "No. He was busy working. On a television" (leaving it up in the air if he repairs electronic devices or has his own talk show).

Here are the annotations of the same paragraph that the student made during a second reading. Note that he has expanded his use of marginalia.

"imaginary friend" *why weird name?*	My daughter, Olivia, who just turned three, has an imaginary friend whose name is Charlie Ravioli. Olivia is growing up in Manhattan,
New York *Charlie - 7½ years old*	and so Charlie Ravioli has a lot of local traits: he lives in an apartment "on Madison and Lexington," he dines on grilled chicken, fruit, and water, and, having reached the age of seven and a half, he feels, or is thought, "old." But the most peculiarly local thing about Olivia's imag-
imitates adults with *toy cell phone*	inary playmate is this: he is always too busy to play with her. She holds her toy cell phone up to her ear, and we hear her talk into it: "Ravioli? It's Olivia . . . It's Olivia. Come and play? OK. Call me. Bye."
pretend frustration?	Then she snaps it shut and shakes her head. "I always get his machine," she says. Or she will say, "I spoke to Ravioli today." "Did you
examples of *conversation*	have fun?" my wife and I ask. "No. He was busy working. On a televi- sion" (leaving it up in the air if he repairs electronic devices or has his own talk show).

Note the Knowledge Problem, Thesis Statement, and Key Claims

As you read, look for an explanation — even a very compressed one — of the **knowledge problem** that the author is addressing — the question that remains unanswered, the mystery that remains unsolved, or the need that remains unfilled. As we noted in Chapter 1, scholars typically identify the important unknowns in their field and attempt to contribute something large or small toward answering these knowledge problems. Usually, scholars tell the reader quite early in the article the nature of the problem, question, or need they are addressing. However, since they are often writing for other specialists in their field, they may refer to this problem in shorthand, with a brief allusion rather than a full explanation. Still, if you look carefully in the first few paragraphs, you can usually find at least a hint of it. And recognizing the knowledge problem will help you understand the author's main purpose and the general direction of the argument.

Closely linked to the problem is the **thesis statement**: a proposition, in one or two sentences, that stands for the argument of the text as a whole. You might think of the thesis as the author's answer to the knowledge problem — perhaps just a small part of the answer, but something worth contributing to the conversation about this problem. Writers do not always position the thesis statement at the end of the first paragraph, as you may have learned to do, but it usually does appear somewhere near the beginning of the essay or somewhere near the end. Writers will sometimes restate a thesis in different forms as their argument evolves; for example, a short version might appear at the beginning of the essay, and a more detailed one at the end. Many accomplished writers resist following predictable formulas, so they might decide to hold the reader in suspense and disclose the argument a little later than expected, or they may want to begin with a lengthier introduction that makes it necessary to place the thesis statement in the fourth or fifth paragraph rather than in the first or second. A complex argument may even require breaking the thesis statement into several parts that appear throughout the essay. So be on the lookout not only for the thesis statement but for all statements that disclose the author's sense of the purpose and direction of the argument.

As you work your way through an argument, you may notice that it contains interlocking parts: one argument has to be made to support another argument, and each argument or supporting argument works together with others to make the author's overall case for the thesis. Each argument contains one or more **claims** (assertions) and support for those claims (see pp. 110–14.). As you read, identify the major arguments and their claims — you will often find them at or near the beginning of paragraphs. Notice also *how* the author supports such claims — perhaps through stories, or with data, or by referring to the work of other researchers. Not all essays make straightforward arguments in support of a thesis, however; some are much more exploratory and questioning (see Adam Gopnik's "Bumping into Mr. Ravioli," p. 386, and Geoff Dyer's "Blues for Vincent," p. 358, for example).

Note Divisions, Turning Points, and Signposts

Whether you're reading an exploratory essay or a thesis-driven argument, note and mark the major divisions in the text; where the author shifts from one topic or theme to another; and how each topic or theme relates to the thesis of the essay as a whole. If necessary, write headings in the margins.

Many writers leave signposts for the reader at key turning points in the text. These signposts may be a single word such as "however" or "nevertheless" that reveals a shift in the direction of the argument, perhaps to introduce some exception or qualification. But sometimes an author very explicitly states where we will be heading or where we have come from, perhaps using a phrase like "I will argue that . . ." or "Having demonstrated that . . ." This kind of writing (sometimes called **metadiscourse**) often helps the reader take a step back from the details of an argument to get a stronger sense of its general direction, or it reminds the reader of the global argument after a long detour. Statements like these often appear at **turning points** in the text. Consider an example from an influential essay by the historian Frederick Jackson Turner, "The Significance of the Frontier in American History" (1893). Because his essay is necessarily full of facts and references that support his argument, he wants the reader to be able to navigate through the wealth of detail and still keep sight of the destination, so he offers an entire paragraph at about the midpoint that functions as a large signpost.

> Having now roughly outlined the various kinds of frontier, and their modes of advance, chiefly from the point of view of the frontier itself, we may next inquire what were the influences on the East and on the Old World. A rapid enumeration of some of the more noteworthy effects is all that I have time for.[2]

This kind of metadiscourse is "programmatic" — it reveals the author's project — and reassures the reader that the vessel is still on course and that the destination is just over the horizon. In any complicated or difficult reading, these signposts are worth looking out for and worth marking or underlining so that you can come back to them whenever you need a reminder.

Note Things That Puzzle You

At this stage, your first reading, don't spend a lot of time trying to figure out everything in the text you find confusing. Simply make a note in the margin of things that you'll want to come back to later on, or copy out a brief phrase from the text and a page number, so that you can identify the passage easily. In one or two sentences, write down your question, as clearly as you can at this stage, or simply put a question mark next to the passages you don't understand.

---

[2] Frederick Jackson Turner, *The Significance of the Frontier in American History* (New York: Ungar, 1985), 44.

→ Try This Mark Up the Text

Read Rana Foroohar's essay "What Ever Happened to Upward Mobility?" (p. 362) steadily from beginning to end, marking up the text as you go. Follow the guidelines offered on pages 48–56 as best you can. Mark or underline Foroohar's statement of the problem, her thesis statement, and some of her key claims. (If on a first reading you cannot identify all those elements, simply make a note of those you need to keep looking for as you reread.) Identify divisions, turning points, and signposts in the essay. And note anything that puzzles or surprises you—as well as anything you find especially interesting or thought provoking. Finally, in the margins or on a separate page, gloss unfamiliar terms and references.

Gloss Unfamiliar References

As noted earlier, one of the most effective and efficient ways of making better sense of a text is to look up unfamiliar words (and familiar words that seem to be used in unfamiliar ways) in a college-level dictionary. Many e-book devices allow a highlighted word to be looked up in a built-in or online dictionary. It is also useful to look up unfamiliar allusions and references, either in a traditional encyclopedia or on the Internet. A quick Web search can provide context.

A *gloss* is an explanatory note that a reader records in the margins of a text or in a separate notebook. Instead of interrupting your reading every few minutes, however, consider using a code to mark unfamiliar terms, and look up several at once when you reach a convenient break in the text. For example, you might underline and put a "d" in the margins next to words you need to look up in the dictionary, and underline and put an "a" in the margin next to unfamiliar allusions or references.

Every reader encounters the problem of changing cultural knowledge. Culture changes constantly, and readers today tend to be much less familiar with, say, the Bible or Greek myths or even Shakespeare's plays than were readers of just a few decades ago. Writers once took for granted that readers would understand allusions to "Niobe's tears," for example, or "the patience of Job." Today, readers may not recognize the source or immediately catch the meaning, but they can easily look such things up on the Internet. Try Encyclopedia.com or one of the reference works at Bartleby.com (bartleby.com/reference).

Reading Journal: Thoughts, Claims, and Questions

Keep a reading journal, either in a notebook reserved for this purpose or in a special folder on your computer. You'll want to be able to review your entries easily, so it's important to keep them together in one place. In your first entry, include three parts: your first thoughts, a list of two or three important claims that you noticed in the text, and a list of two or three good questions about the text.

Don't be too concerned about the quality of your work at this point; you need only lay the groundwork for more productive writing you'll do later on. But this groundwork *is* valuable, as a word or phrase that might seem insignificant now can inspire an important insight later.

Record Your First Thoughts

After reading the whole text once, put it aside and spend at least ten minutes writing freely and unreservedly about what you've just read. First, note the date and time at the top of the page or document. Then write continuously; don't stop to worry about grammar, spelling, word choice, or even whether your thoughts are any good. This freewriting is for your eyes only — a chance simply to record your initial response to the text, however basic or incoherent. Here are some questions you might ask yourself if you're stuck — remember, though, that there are no firm rules for this, and you certainly don't have to cover all (or any) of these questions.

- What is the text about? How would you describe the author's *main* purpose, as you understand it at this point?
- Of everything you just read, what most stands out in your memory?
- What do you think of the author's ideas at this point?
- What was it like to read this text? Hard work? Easy going? Stimulating? Arduous? Describe the experience.
- How do you feel you performed as a reader? (Note your strengths as well as your weaknesses.)

➔ Try This   Record Your Initial Response in a Journal Entry

If you have not already done so, read Rana Foroohar's "What Ever Happened to Upward Mobility?" (p. 362) once from beginning to end. Then put it aside and spend ten to fifteen minutes writing in a journal, either on paper or on a computer. First record the date and time at the top of the page, and then write freely and continuously. If you get stuck or feel unsure of your direction, turn to the questions listed in the "Record Your First Thoughts" section (p. 57). At some point in your writing, attempt to express in your own words the essence of the problem that Foroohar is addressing. In addition, try to record from memory two or three of the claims that she makes. And note two or three questions about the text that occurred to you as you were reading or that occur to you now. (You need not do all these steps in any particular order. The main thing is simply to record your initial responses to the text.)

Here's an example of one student's initial response after reading Rana Foroohar's "What Ever Happened to Upward Mobility?" (p. 362).

Student Sample Reading Journal, First Entry

March 31, 2015, 8:20 p.m.

I was pretty surprised by the things I learned from this essay, as I'd always thought of the USA as "the land of opportunity." But I guess things have been changing in the last few decades, and even if "our national mythology," as Foroohar calls it, was more than just myth 40 years ago, it seems to be less so today. The big question for me, though, is whether the trends that Foroohar discusses can be reversed. I suppose that's what she's getting at by "inflection point": we might still be able to change direction before it's too late. Some of the things Foroohar mentions seem like they may be temporary effects of the financial crisis, but other things, such as tax policies and social safety nets, seem like they're not going to change without a lot of effort. I don't have a problem with social safety nets or fairer tax policies, but I do suspect that super-high taxes would make it harder to start a small business or save for college. I think Americans like the idea of risk more than people in other countries, too. I think they like the idea that they're taking care of themselves, not just letting the government take care of them. Of course, they also like the idea of climbing the economic ladder, so if Foroohar's right, we have some work to do. I'm just not sure we need to become exactly like the European countries. I think I understood this essay pretty well, though there are lots of facts to absorb and lots of issues to think about, so it wouldn't hurt to read it again.

Identify the Problem (If Possible)

If you can, explain in your own words the nature of the problem that the author is concerned with, or as much about it as you can grasp at this point. In some instances, this may be difficult after only one reading; if so, simply write a word or two reminding you to come back to this step after a rereading or two.

Restate Two or Three Claims

Next, identify from memory two or three of the author's claims. If you can confidently identify one of these claims as the author's thesis, then do so. (Perhaps mark a capital "T" next to it in the margin.) But if you're not sure of the thesis yet, don't worry: the claims you identify at this point need not be the most important ones, just ones that you recall. But try to be sure that they are indeed *claims* — arguable propositions — and not simple statements of fact.

Ask Two or Three Questions

Finally, write down two or three good questions about the text. A "good" question is simply a genuine question about some aspect of the text that interests or puzzles you — the sort of question you'd like to raise in a discussion and that might lead to a deeper understanding of the text, or some aspect of it, rather than a merely factual question with a yes/no answer or a "quiz" question that would only be asked to make sure the class had done its homework.

Rereading

Read Slowly

To some, this may not sound like a productive reading strategy; we tend to assume that, as the ads for speed-reading courses tell us, better readers are faster readers. But in fact, good readers vary their pace to suit their purpose and the nature of the material. They might skim quickly through a newspaper article or a Web page, but they will take the time to absorb, weigh, and ponder a densely argued text, especially if they expect to be writing or talking about it. Read at a pace that's comfortable, but don't hurry. Especially for your second and subsequent readings, you'll get much more out of a text if you give it the time it requires.

Develop Your Marginalia

Your most important task is to identify the author's argument and follow it throughout the text. To do so, you will need to mark up the text more heavily. If you don't have a lot of margin space (or are unwilling to mark up your book even with a pencil), consider making a photocopy of the essay so that you can use the larger margins as well as the white space on the reverse. Or you might attach Post-it notes to the book; one advantage of this approach is that, by aligning the edge of each note with the edge of the page, you can easily locate your notes later, and of course you can detach them if needed. If you're working with an electronic text, consider printing it out so that you can annotate it by hand. Or you can use an app such as iAnnotate or a Web-based tool such as Crocodoc to mark up and add marginalia to any electronic text.

A Basic Dialectical Notebook

The **dialectical notebook** is a simple and powerful method of taking notes developed by Ann E. Berthoff.[3] Here's how it works. Draw a line down the center of a page in your notebook. You can also use a computer. At the top of the left-hand column, write "What It Says." Here, you'll take notes about *what the author is saying*. These might be quotations of key phrases, whole sentences, or even whole paragraphs. They might be paraphrases or summaries of parts of the text. Or they might outline a section of the text. The form they take is up to you — but the left side of the page belongs to the author's words and ideas. (Be sure to record the page number that corresponds to each quotation or paraphrase so that you can find it and cite it later.) At the top of the right-hand column, write "What I Think." Here, you'll take

---

[3] Ann E. Berthoff, with James Stephens, *Forming/Thinking/Writing*, 2nd ed. (Portsmouth, NH: Heinemann–Boynton/Cook, 1988).

notes about *what you think* about what the author is saying. These notes might consist of comments, questions, reactions, reflections, or even symbols and punctuation marks (!, ?, *, huh?). They can be as long or as short as you like. At first, your notes on the right side may be quite brief compared to those on the left, but it's important to write something on the "What I Think" side. In particular, write down your questions. The act of formulating your questions in words will help make them clearer and more definite. You can come back to them and rephrase them more precisely later on. You'll be able to try out possible answers to these questions and find patterns that will help you see things that were hidden before.

The word "dialectic" refers to a method of arriving at insights through debate, discussion, or an exchange of ideas. The double-entry format of the dialectical notebook lets you keep one foot in the text, so to speak, and one foot in your own reactions to it. This close and continuous interaction with the text produces a dialectic that, like good talk, leads somewhere. But you've got to keep up your end of the conversation. The notes you take on the right, notes that record and develop what is going on in your head as you reread, may be different from the sort of notes you usually take. Berthoff described this record-keeping as an **audit of meaning**. An audit is a methodical review or examination. Recording your responses, and then reviewing them and recording your responses to your responses, is the key to establishing a real dialogue with the text. This dialogue, as Berthoff argues, is the essence of critical reading and writing: "The reason for the double-entry notebook will become apparent to you as you begin to see that you are conducting the continuing audit of meaning that is at the heart of learning to write critically."[4] This method of note-taking may seem time-consuming, but it helps to generate critical reading and ideas for writing so effectively that it is worth giving it a try.

If initially you have very little on the right side of the page, reread with the sole aim of recording your responses, however vague or inarticulate they might be at this early stage. Then work through your notes and write brief responses to the quotations and paraphrases that you noted on the left — as many of them as you can. If you're at a loss, use these questions as prompts.

- Why did this passage seem noteworthy or puzzling to you?
- What can you say about its meaning?
- What questions can you ask about the passage?

---

[4] Berthoff, *Forming/Thinking/Writing*, 27.

- If the passage is confusing, can you identify where the difficulty lies? For example, is there a particular word, phrase, or sentence structure that is unclear?
- How might you connect this passage to something else in the text, or to other texts in the course, or to your own knowledge or experience?

Don't worry at this point about whether your thoughts are impressive or essay-worthy or "right." You can edit later, and you can use as much or as little of these dialectical notes in your final product as you like. For now, they need only be a record of your own thoughts as you read.

Layers: The Dialectical Notebook as Palimpsest

The real power of the dialectical notebook becomes clear when you start working over the notes that you took on a first and second reading. With each subsequent reading, you can build up the notes on each side, and as they become denser and more fully developed, you can begin working solely with your notebook, amplifying and elaborating your thoughts until you have whole sentences and paragraphs, referenced to relevant passages in the text. For example, on a first reading, you might copy out on the left side a passage you found especially puzzling, and on the right write down nothing more than two question marks next to it. But on a second reading, some ideas about the meaning of the passage may occur to you, and so you jot them down. Returning to this page later, you might realize that your ideas were basically right but that you can now explicate the text with more confidence and more precision, so you edit your notes and add to them. (You might want to write or type each layer of notes in a different color, so that you can later distinguish first-impression notes from subsequent notes.)

In this way, your notes develop layers, and your pages become a kind of "palimpsest." This word derives from a Greek root that literally means "scraped again." Before the invention of paper, writing surfaces were expensive and were often reused rather than thrown out. A palimpsest is a manuscript of papyrus or parchment from which the text has been scraped away, but not completely erased, to make room for a new layer, so that the first layer is still legible beneath. By extension, the word is often used to refer to a text that bears more than one layer of writing, one superimposed on another. In our case, the first layer of writing will not be erased to make room for a new layer, but rather serves as a foundation for subsequent layers that fill in the white space around it.

The three examples that follow provide a glimpse of a student actively using this method of note-taking. These cumulative entries on Rana Foroohar's "What Ever Happened to Upward Mobility?" (p. 362) show the student's newest notes in blue.

Double-Entry Notebook with a First Layer of Notes

WHAT IT SAYS	WHAT I THINK
"easier to climb the socioeconomic ladder in many parts of Europe than it is in the U.S." (p. 363)	
"sclerotic"? (p. 363)	
ABSOLUTE mobility	
↘how much growth has occurred	
RELATIVE mobility	
↘how you're doing compared to other people (climbing ladder)	
"Nordic nations"	= what countries exactly?
In Europe: more equality, more homogeneous populations	
"When the rungs on the ladder are further apart, it's harder to climb up them." (Sawhill)	
"Gilded Age"	?
Role of banking and finance industry	

Double-Entry Notebook with a Second Layer of Notes

WHAT IT SAYS	WHAT I THINK
"easier to climb the socioeconomic ladder in many parts of Europe than it is in the U.S." (p. 363)	Is this just a temporary thing? Or likely to be permanent?
"sclerotic"? (p. 363)	= "becoming rigid and unresponsive"
ABSOLUTE mobility ↳ how much growth has occurred	But doesn't this suggest we're all getting richer together?
RELATIVE mobility ↳ how you're doing compared to other people (climbing ladder)	Complicated
"Nordic nations"	= what countries exactly?
In Europe: more equality, more homogeneous populations	More socialist or welfare state systems in Europe. But still, U.S. should give more mobility.
"When the rungs on the ladder are further apart, it's harder to climb up them." (Sawhill) (Isabel Sawhill, Brookings Institution's Center on Children & Families)	Meaning that the spread between wealth and poverty is greater in the U.S.
"Gilded Age"	? = 1870–1900, roughly, when some Americans got very rich (Wikipedia)
Role of banking and finance industry	

Double-Entry Notebook with a Third Layer of Notes

WHAT IT SAYS	WHAT I THINK
"easier to climb the socioeconomic ladder in many parts of Europe than it is in the U.S." (p. 363)	Is this just a temporary thing? Or likely to be permanent? Impossible to know? How can it be reversed? Become more like Europe?
"sclerotic"? (p. 363)	= "becoming rigid and unresponsive"
ABSOLUTE mobility ↘ how much growth has occurred	But doesn't this suggest we're all getting richer together?
RELATIVE mobility ↘ how you're doing compared to other people (climbing ladder)	Complicated Why is relative mobility a good thing? Isn't absolute really better?
"Nordic nations"	= what countries exactly?
In Europe: more equality, more homogeneous populations	More socialist or welfare state systems in Europe. But still, U.S. should give more mobility.
"When the rungs on the ladder are further apart, it's harder to climb up them." (Sawhill) (Isabel Sawhill, Brookings Institution's Center on Children & Families)	Meaning that the spread between wealth and poverty is greater in the U.S.
"Gilded Age" Role of banking and finance industry	? = 1870–1900, roughly, when some Americans got very rich (Wikipedia) Inequality is a problem, I guess, but if everyone's wealth could increase, not such a big problem, maybe?

➔ **Try** **This**   ## Creating a Dialectical Notebook

You can set up a dialectical notebook on paper or on your computer. Divide the page down the middle and give each column the appropriate headings: "What It Says" on the left and "What I Think" on the right. (If you're using a computer, you can insert two text boxes side by side to create two columns. This takes a few minutes, but you can save the blank dialectical notebook template for future use.) Read or reread your assigned essay with your dialectical notebook open, and take notes in the "What It Says" column as you go. Respond to these notes in the "What I Think" column. Leave some space so that you can develop these notes later. (For further detail, see "A Basic Dialectical Notebook," p. 60.)

After reading and making notes once, read through the text a second time and develop your notes with a second layer. Record new insights and observations, and pay special attention to any notes on the right-hand side that suggest an idea, a question, or a puzzlement that needs to be worked out. Respond to your earlier responses, so that your notebook begins to become an audit of meaning.

Reading Journal: Further Thoughts

After you've finished rereading, spend twenty to thirty minutes with your reading journal. The purpose is to give you an opportunity to collect your thoughts while the reading is still fresh in your mind, to develop these thoughts by the act of writing (remember: writing tends to *generate* ideas, not just record them), and to capture some words or phrases that might be useful later. You've already laid the groundwork with your entries in your dialectical notebook: this is an opportunity to begin building on it — in a very rudimentary way, perhaps, but you never know what might happen. The point is to give your mind the opportunity to create thoughts.

Here is what one student, Stephanie Skinner, wrote in her journal after reading Foroohar's essay and working with her dialectical notebook. Note how she has begun to shape and structure her observations.

Student Sample Reading Journal, Second Entry

After reading Foroohar again, I think I'm persuaded that America has a problem, and we need to make sure that more people have real opportunity in their lives and that the gap between the haves and the have-less isn't quite as crazy wide as it is right now. But maybe this means getting back to where we were a few decades ago rather than imitating European countries. Foroohar admits that those societies are different from ours, smaller and less diverse (for a start). I think I would argue that our model ought to be the America of 1960 or 1970 rather than the Sweden of today. I realize that we can't simply turn back the clock: values have changed and technology has changed and the rest of the world has changed. (For example, women aren't going to quit their jobs in droves and become homemakers; the Internet isn't going to go away.) But we could try to manufacture more products in America, and we could do more to make homes affordable, I think. I'll need to make a list of the things that were different 40 or 50 years ago in America and see which things might be restored and which things can't or probably shouldn't.

Timed Freewriting

First, spend another ten minutes writing continuously in your reading journal. Again, don't be too concerned with the quality of your writing. But focus this time on what you are now able to say about the text, beyond what you could say after the first reading. How has your understanding of the text changed? Did you notice anything different or new this time through? What are your thoughts now about the author's argument?

Two or Three More Claims

Write down from memory two or three more of the author's claims, ones that you overlooked the first time. This will give you a more complete sense of the author's argument.

Respond to Your First Questions

Take a look at the questions you wrote down after your first reading. Can you respond to any of them now? If so, write a paragraph or two.

Write Down Two More Questions

Add two more questions to your entry. Perhaps you'll find this time that your questions are even more penetrating and interesting—that they go deeper into the main concerns of the text.

Of course, you can read the text a third time, or as many times as you wish, and repeat the same process of freewriting, identifying claims, responding to questions, and posing new ones. Beyond providing material you can bring to class discussion, your notebook may well contain good material for your writing too.

✅ Checklist for Active Reading

Here are some guidelines to help you get the most out of reading a text. Remember: difficult texts are difficult for most readers, and good readers expect to reread.

☐ The first time you read a text, read it through from beginning to end.

☐ Mark up the text.
- Underline and make marginal notes — but sparingly.
- Keep a notebook and pen nearby.
- Note key claims, turning points, and signposts.
- Note things that puzzle you.
- Gloss unfamiliar references.

☐ Keep a reading journal.
- Record your first thoughts and questions.
- Identify three or four important claims.
- Write down at least two good questions about the text.

☐ Reread the text.

☐ Read slowly.

☐ Develop your marginalia.

☐ Keep a dialectical notebook.

☐ Add further thoughts to your reading journal.
- Write down two or three more claims.
- Respond to your first questions.
- Write down two more questions.

chapter 3

Further Strategies for Active Reading

The techniques we described in the previous chapter — marking up the text, taking dialectical notes, and keeping a reading journal — are basic tools for active reading, and you'll probably use at least one of them whenever you read for your courses. But other strategies can be useful in special situations, such as when you need to work with a very difficult text, and these will be the focus of this chapter. Reading about these alternative strategies might inspire you to come up with new ones of your own, ones uniquely suited to your own particular needs and habits as a reader.

> "To read well, that is, to read true books in a true spirit, is a noble exercise, and one that will task the reader more than any exercise which the customs of the day esteem. It requires a training such as the athletes underwent, the steady intention almost of the whole life to this object. Books must be read as deliberately and reservedly as they were written."
>
> **HENRY DAVID THOREAU**

In the epigraph on the right, Henry David Thoreau issues a kind of challenge to his reader: to approach reading with real seriousness and dedication — like professional athletes, who push their limits and constantly strive to improve. Perhaps he makes reading sound rather grueling, but another way to look at it is to consider that, like athletes in training, readers do improve with practice and find that the work gets easier over time. At the same time, Thoreau reminds us that the art of reading is one that nobody ever *perfects*, that every text is in some way unique and poses fresh challenges.

Certainly as a college student, you'll find that attentive critical reading is something you'll practice regularly, and you'll find that your skills as a reader will be stretched and strengthened as you tackle more difficult texts. You'll learn to adapt your strategies for different purposes, needs, and time frames; you'll learn what works best for you and for the kinds of courses you're taking.

You may want to experiment immediately with the strategies described in this chapter, or you may choose to store them away for later. But it's important to have such tools available when you need to dig into an argument and probe it deeply, questioning it not in a hostile way but to find out whether it stands up to scrutiny. Just as you might have come to know pieces of music intimately by repeated listening, so too can you become as familiar with a text as its author is (as Thoreau suggests readers should do) through a combination of rereading and close critical analysis. The strategies that follow may seem time-consuming, but that's not a bad thing: spending time with a text and becoming absorbed in it is the surest way to develop your own ideas about it. The common denominator among all these strategies is that they keep the reader focused on the text for the time it takes for those ideas to emerge.

Variations on the Dialectical Notebook

A Question-Centered Triple-Entry Notebook

This is another kind of dialectical notebook, one suggested by David Jolliffe in his book *Inquiry and Genre: Writing to Learn in College*.[1] This method works especially well with texts that take a stand on a debatable issue. As in a double-entry

---

[1] David A. Jolliffe, *Inquiry and Genre: Writing to Learn in College* (Boston: Allyn & Bacon, 1999).

> **→ Guidelines** **Taking Double- or Triple-Entry Notes on a Computer**
>
> If you prefer to work on your laptop rather than with paper and pen, you can still take notes in parallel columns. If you are working in Microsoft Word or Apple's Pages, use the "Text Box" tool (in the "Insert" menu) to draw the columns on a blank page. After filling in a heading at the top of each column, save the page as a blank template that you can use repeatedly. (Avoid using the "Columns" command in the "Format" menu, which is designed to make text flow from one column to the next; it does not let you move back and forth between the columns.)

notebook, you audit meanings in the text in one column and your responses to the text in another, but in a third column you also keep an audit of *the question or problem that the text addresses.* This "question column" helps you focus your responses on the fundamental questions that underlie the argument.

To begin a question-centered triple-entry notebook, divide the page into three columns, and give each a heading: "Question" for the left column, "Text's Answer" for the middle column, and "My Response" for the right column (or your own variation on each heading).

- For the left column, figure out what question each paragraph or section of the text is answering. Usually, the question is only implied, so you'll need to deduce it. (This can be the most difficult part of the task, but it will give you a strong understanding of how the argument works and of the purpose of each section in relation to the whole.) Expect to write roughly two or three questions per page of text, but you might write more or fewer; there are no strict rules.

- The middle column will note how the text answers the question being addressed.

- The right column will record your *own* answer to the question being addressed and your thoughts about how the text's answer squares with your experience and views.

Here is an example of one student's question-centered triple-entry notes applied to Adam Gopnik's essay "Bumping into Mr. Ravioli" (p. 386).

Question-Centered Triple-Entry Notebook

THE QUESTION BEING ANSWERED BY THE TEXT	HOW GOPNIK ANSWERS THE QUESTION	MY OBSERVATIONS AND RESPONSE
How did we in the 21st century get to be so busy?	Trains and telegrams (p. 389). Trains ended isolation, crowding our streets. The telegram crowded our minds (p. 390).	It's hard to imagine telegrams crowding a person's mind, but e-mail and texts certainly do. I'd never thought of it as an issue that dates back to the 19th century.
How is life in New York particularly affected by these developments?	Elsewhere, cars and televisions "pulled people apart"—back into a sort of isolation. But in New York, cars and TV watching never caught on to the same extent (p. 390).	Yes, okay, but cars and televisions certainly don't make us feel less busy. Maybe more isolated. So maybe there is more "bumping into" people in New York. (Which actually sounds like fun.)
Should it worry them if Mr. Ravioli has an assistant?	Gopnik's wife thinks so. But Gopnik? Maybe.	It's just funny and cute.
Is the "bump and run" lifestyle that Olivia seems to be imitating so bad after all? Or can it be lived with?	In the end, Gopnik seems to be answering "yes, we can live with it"—even though Laurie "threw us badly" (p. 391).	Gopnik seems sort of resigned to the inevitable here, and sort of eager to celebrate New York's lifestyle. I don't know whether I'm fully convinced, but I agree that busyness has an upside as well as a downside.

A Quotation-Centered Triple-Entry Notebook

This note-taking strategy is a simple but effective method of producing a close reading of key passages in a text, with your own observations and ideas about these passages attached. The simple act of copying out the words forces your attention to stay on the passage and helps to clarify its meaning. This strategy is especially useful when you are working with very difficult texts.

To create a quotation-centered triple-entry notebook, divide your page into three columns, and give each column a heading: "Quotation," "Exegesis," and "Commentary" (or, again, variations of your own). An **exegesis** is an explanation, interpretation, or paraphrase of a passage of text.

- In the left column, copy out a text passage — no more than a few sentences — that seems to you interesting, significant, or puzzling. Take care to copy it exactly. Note the page number so that you can locate the passage in the original text later on.

- In the middle column, write your best explanation of what the passage means. Use only your own words. You may not be confident that you've got the meaning quite right, and that's okay: just get as close as you can.

- In the right column, write down your own observations, ideas, or questions, or any other kind of response. Here you can write freely, comparing the passage with your own experiences and beliefs, or arguing back against the author — whatever you like.

Your exegesis explores *inside* the text, while your commentary often works from the text to something *outside* it. Exegesis combined with commentary is a good way to work with dense or difficult texts because it lets you work out the meaning of complicated passages but also requires you to think about their meaning *for you.* It allows you to move back and forth between the text's meaning and your meaning. Feel free to write a lot about even a short passage, exploring not only what the passage says but also how the passage says it and what thoughts and feelings the passage suggests. You may be surprised at how much you get out of a passage that might not seem promising at first.

Here is an example of this technique applied to Ralph Waldo Emerson's essay "The American Scholar."

QUOTATION	EXEGESIS	COMMENTARY
"Man is not a farmer, or a professor, or an engineer, but he is all. Man is priest, and scholar, and statesman, and producer, and soldier" (p. 54).	Man cannot only be one thing. If he focuses only on one aspect of life, he is not a full man and is not a fully functioning member of society.	To be taken seriously, I must show that I am knowledgeable of many aspects of life. I must be well rounded and educated.
"Man is thus metamorphosed into a thing, into many things. . . . The priest becomes a form; the attorney, a statute-book; the mechanic, a machine; the sailor, a rope of a ship" (p. 54).	When you are only focused on one field of work, you gradually become morphed into that field and are classified by what you do.	As college students, we are classified by the college we are in and the major we want to pursue.
"So much of nature as he is ignorant of, so much of his own mind does he not yet possess" (p. 56).	Emerson relates the unknowns of nature to the unknowns of human life and experience. Just as we are ignorant of all the nature surrounding us that we must explore, there is still a lot we must explore in our minds as well.	As a college student, I am eager to learn as much as I can while I'm in school. I cannot reject opportunities to learn, and I cannot remain ignorant of all the things going on in the world.

Adapting the Dialectical Notebook Method

Once you've tried some of the dialectical note-taking methods described above, you might begin experimenting with your own versions. For example, some writers like to work with smaller notebooks that are half the size of the standard

8.5-by-11-inch type. In this kind of notebook, you might write your initial notes only on a left-hand page while reading. These notes might be quotations, paraphrases, or reflections. Later, when you review these notes, you can write on the facing page, tying themes together, developing thoughts, sketching out new ideas, and so on. For some writers, a notebook becomes a kind of scrapbook, a repository for all sorts of ideas. They add sticky notes when they run out of space; they incorporate doodles and diagrams; they tape in short articles or images; they use different colored inks to highlight ideas that seem important.

Word processors such as Evernote or Journler and apps such as Noteshelf and Notability work well for keeping this kind of notebook on a laptop or tablet. The medium and even the details of the method are less important than the key principle, however, which is to create an archive of your dialogue with the text, and thus to begin the writing process *during* the reading process. As Ann E. Berthoff notes,

> In all its phases, composing is conversation you're having with yourself — or *selves*, since, when you're writing, you consciously play the roles of speaker, audience, and critic all at once. You do the talking; then you do the answering; and you listen in to the dialogue between the speaker and the respondent. When you're making meaning in sentences, gathering sentences to compose paragraphs and paragraphs to construct arguments, you're doing the same kind of thing you do when you carry on a conversation.[2]

Ideas can come to us at the strangest moments. Keeping a small notebook with you at all times (or having a suitable app on your phone) will let you work on your ideas when they occur to you — on the subway, in the waiting room of the dentist's office, or wherever they happen to find you.

Analyzing the Argument

A good reader will not only follow a text's argument but also evaluate it and notice its weaknesses and strengths. But arguments can be complicated, and readers sometimes need strategies to help them evaluate an argument fairly and avoid mistakes.

As we have already said, an argument is a kind of logical structure, combining **claims** and **evidence**. We produce arguments all the time. "In the long run, my car

---

[2] Ann E. Berthoff, with James Stephens, *Forming/Thinking/Writing*, 2nd ed. (Portsmouth, NH: Heinemann–Boynton/Cook, 1988), 23.

costs less to drive because it gets twice as many miles per gallon as yours." The claim: "In the long run, my car costs less to drive." The evidence: "It gets twice as many miles per gallon as yours." In this case, the argument is only one sentence long, and the evidence is a single piece of data. The logical structure of this argument is as simple as could be, made up of a premise and a conclusion, a simple "if . . . then" relation. If my car gets twice as many miles per gallon as yours (the premise), then in the long run it would cost less to drive (the conclusion). Of course, a full calculation would have to take in many factors, such as the price of each car and the price of gas; but leaving all that aside for the moment, we have a simple argument.

A more complicated argument — and most arguments are a good deal more complicated — will have a more complicated logical structure, combining multiple premises and multiple conclusions. Evidence is rarely a simple statement of fact; often it is itself another claim, and arguments are often complicated structures of claims built on claims. Sometimes claims and evidence can be easily verified with some quick Internet research. But an argument may also be based on some sort of "near fact" that a skeptical reader might question but that is difficult to verify. So arguments can be slippery, and tracing them often demands considerable powers of attention.

Note that this kind of analysis involves thinking about the argument in a different way than we would when reading it simply to understand what it is saying or whether we agree with it. Instead of thinking about *what* the argument is saying, we're looking at *how* the argument is made, how it is constructed. That means putting aside the content of the argument and focusing on its **rhetorical structure** rather than its subject matter.

Let's look at Jane McGonigal's "Be a Gamer, Save the World" (p. 394), a brief opinion column adapted from her book *Reality Is Broken*. Her thesis is not difficult to grasp, but it's the kind of argument that's likely to arouse skepticism in some readers. Analyzing her argument closely will allow us to see more clearly where its strengths and weaknesses lie and may also teach us how to construct stronger arguments of our own.

- Note that in the first paragraph, McGonigal immediately contrasts her own position with conventional wisdom: "We often think . . . ," she begins, suggesting right away that she will offer a different opinion. She describes the common perception of video games as being harmful to kids or society: video games are seen as a "retreat from reality" and "mind-numbing." Her own position starkly contradicts this view; she believes that "the truth about games is very nearly the opposite": they "fulfill genuine human needs" and are "a key resource for solving . . . real-world problems."

- The second paragraph offers statistics about the prevalence of video games and the size of the industry. Why? McGonigal wants to suggest that video gaming is worthy of our attention, for one thing, but she is also suggesting that such a popular pastime must have some value. She uses the term "alternate reality" for the virtual worlds found in video games, rather than "non-reality" or "false reality." This will allow her to shift the reader's perspective on the issue: instead of comparing "virtual reality" to "true reality," she can compare one kind of world to another and find some positive and negative elements in each.

- The third paragraph spells out the first argument that this shift of perspective makes possible. She upends the conventional wisdom about the "real world" by suggesting that, for these gamers, it's not the gaming world that's "missing something" but the ordinary world of physical reality.

- Paragraph four elaborates and supports this idea, making a series of claims (either directly or indirectly through a rhetorical question) about the advantages of experience in the gaming over the ordinary world.

- Paragraph five introduces a new argument, that gamers have an advantage over non-gamers and are starting to use their special skills for "real good." To support this idea, she cites her own research, which shows that games provide four ingredients for a happy and meaningful life. Subsequent paragraphs will detail the importance of these four ingredients and explain how gaming supplies them.

You can continue this analysis yourself by looking carefully at what McGonigal says in each paragraph and asking questions like: How does the paragraph contribute to the argument? What does it *do* (as distinct from what it says)? Figuring out the answer is not always easy and can take a bit of time, but it's an excellent way of learning how arguments work — not in theory but in actual practice.

What It Says/What It Does

The "What It Says/What It Does" technique is an adaptation of the double-entry notebook that facilitates the kind of rhetorical analysis described above. It helps you separate observations about what each paragraph *says* (the content) from observations about what it *does* (how it contributes to the argument's structure) so that you can then go on to construct an outline of the text's rhetorical structure. This method may take a little time, but it produces a clear picture of the argument's main claims and the support for those claims. You will need to approach this kind of analysis in two steps.

- First, analyze each paragraph, and take informal notes on "what it says" and "what it does." For example, does the paragraph set the stage for the thesis by explaining the context or the problem being addressed? Does it introduce a new argument in support of the thesis? Does it further explain or support an argument that has already been introduced? Or does it do something else?

- Second, use this analysis to construct an outline that illustrates the argument's structure. (If the text is lengthy, this may be a good group activity: divide the text into sections, and give each section to a different individual or small group.)

This kind of rhetorical analysis can be tricky, so here are more detailed, step-by-step instructions for creating "What It Says/What It Does" notes.

Step 1 Draw a line down the middle of a page in your notebook, creating two columns. Or set up two columns in a word processing document. (See the Guidelines box on p. 71 for instructions on how to do this.) At the top of the left column, write "What It Says," and at the top of the right column, write "What It Does." For each paragraph in the essay, write one or two sentences in the left column that summarize what the paragraph says, and one or two in the right column that state the *function* of this paragraph within the argument. Figuring out the function of each paragraph can be tricky, but it is the key to any analysis of rhetorical structure. Avoid summary here, and avoid repeating what you've already written in the left column. Instead, work out how the paragraph contributes to the writer's argument, how it moves the argument forward. If the paragraph were absent, what would the argument be missing? What kind of "move" is the writer making? What is the writer doing that serves the larger purpose of the essay?

It's okay if these "What It Does" notes are a little messy—you'll be revising anyway. If a paragraph's function is not immediately clear, leave the right column blank and come back to the paragraph later. But complete the right-hand column before moving on to Step 2.

Although this work may take some time and some trial and error, you'll learn a great deal from it about how experienced writers develop an effective argument. In the following example based on Jane McGonigal's "Be a Gamer, Save the World," the entries on the left briefly summarize the key points in the first six paragraphs, while the entries on the right explain what these paragraphs *do* for the argument. You may want to complete the analysis for paragraphs 7–16 on your own.

WHAT IT SAYS	WHAT IT DOES
¶1. Many think of video games (VGs) as a "retreat from reality" & a waste of time, but they fill needs that the real world doesn't and may be a "resource" for solving real problems.	Introduces thesis. Contrasts this view with conventional opinion. Answers the question, "Are video games a waste of time?"
¶2. A great many people play VGs! A lot. Time spent on WoW alone = 5.63 million years!	Establishes the importance of her argument by giving data about how much time people spend playing VGs.
¶3. Gamers "often feel that the real world is missing something."	Flips the conventional view that the virtual world of VGs is the one that's lacking.
¶4. Reality isn't as engaging, thrilling, or motivating as gaming worlds and isn't "engineered . . . to make us happy."	Presents a major claim to support the main argument.
¶5. Gamers have advantages: VGs provide 4 ingredients of happy & meaningful life. Support: her own research.	Introduces research that supports her views—gives her credibility (U Cal Berkeley, Institute for the Future).
¶6. Games offer "intrinsic rewards," and research shows that these "provide the foundation for optimal human experience."	Implies that something that seems a limitation of VGs is actually a strength (the rewards are all inside the game experience itself).

Step 2 Now construct an outline of the argument's structure, based on the right-hand column of your "What It Says/What It Does" notes. Begin by identifying how paragraphs with a similar function can be grouped together. For example, several paragraphs might all be telling one story, or explaining one example, and these might provide support for a claim; this claim might in turn support one aspect of the author's main thesis.

Once you have completed your "What It Says/What It Does" double-entry notes, you can move on to create an outline of the rhetorical structure, which might look something like this:

Partial Analytical Outline of "Be a Gamer, Save the World"

Paragraphs 1–4 introduce the main argument.

¶1. Establishes her position that video games fulfill genuine needs and help players learn to solve real-world problems, in contrast to conventional opinion that video games offer only a "passive retreat from reality."

¶2. Establishes the importance of the issue by providing data about the popularity of gaming. Shifts the terms of debate by substituting the phrase "alternate reality" for the more common "virtual reality."

¶3. Claims that many gamers feel that it's the *real* world that's missing something. Turns the tables on the conventional view.

¶4. Elaborates by claiming that the real world does not offer the same pleasures, challenges, and opportunities for social bonding as the gaming world. Supports this claim by reasoning that the real world isn't "engineered" to maximize our potential as the gaming world is. This is a major claim in support of her thesis.

Paragraphs 5–10 detail the psychological benefits of gaming for real-world activities.

¶5. Claims that gamers have an advantage over non-gamers and are using their skills to do good. Supports this by citing her own research that shows video games supply four ingredients of a happy life.

¶6. Further claims that these benefits are "intrinsic rewards," and cites studies that show that such rewards form the basis of "optimal human experience."

Try This   Rhetorical Analysis

Complete the "What It Says/What It Does" notebook for paragraphs 7–16, and then complete the outline, devoting a line or two to each paragraph.

(Note the shift in direction that the argument takes in paragraph 11.) The real point is that even a brief argument like this contains a logical structure of claims and support. Analyzing the structure of the argument, whether formally as above, in the margins of the text, or even mentally, reveals the argument's structure and helps us see its strengths and weaknesses. (For example, to support her claim in paragraph 10 that the sense of awe produced by an epic video game makes gamers act more selflessly, McGonigal cites "researchers on positive emotion." But did they study awe and wonder in virtual worlds or in real worlds? Then again, does it make any difference?)

Constructing a Radial Map of the Text

A radial map is a diagram of a text, using boxes, circles, and lines to arrange elements on a single page so that the text's structure becomes visible at a glance. Subheadings radiate out from the main theme at the center or down from the top. (See Figure 3.1 for an example.) Such a map is a useful tool to have on hand as you begin writing about a text, but its benefits lie just as much in the process of working out how to put all the pieces together. The construction of a radial map requires that you collect all the important elements of an argument or exploration, consider how these elements relate to one another, and arrange them all under headings that connect to the central theme so that the entire essay can be visualized at once. This process entails a good deal of analysis and results in a strong grasp of the text's structure. Radial maps are especially useful when working with a text that is full of detail; they are perhaps most helpful for readers who are visually inclined.

If you have access to a drawing program or mind-mapping application on your computer, you can block out themes and main points first and then move them around, experimenting with different arrangements.

Whether working on a computer or on paper, you'll begin by jotting down main headings and themes on a blank sheet of paper, arranging them more or less randomly at first. Once you begin to see patterns and relationships among the

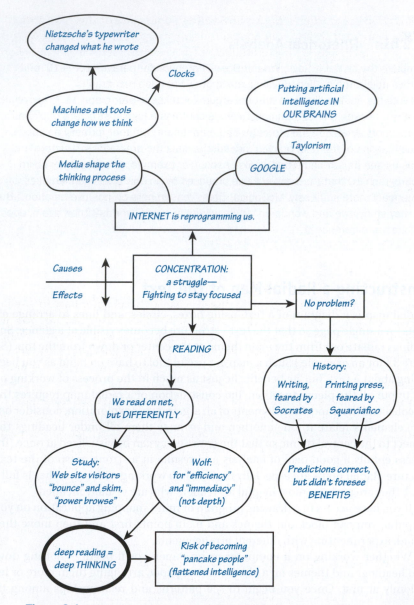

Figure 3.1 Radial Map of Nicholas Carr's "Is Google Making Us Stupid?"

headings, you can start creating a map on a fresh document or sheet. Note that the central theme may shift as you read: for example, the central theme of Nicholas Carr's essay "Is Google Making Us Stupid?" might seem at first to be "Google" (based on the title). But after reading the entire essay carefully, a term such as "concentration" or "attention" might seem to be more truly at the center.

Write down the theme of the essay in a box at the center or top of the page, and then begin arranging main headings around or below this box. Elaborate the map by arranging subheadings and subtopics in relation to each of the main headings. You will see patterns emerge that you might not have noticed otherwise. You will almost certainly find that you need to revise as you proceed: rearranging and even starting over always seems to be necessary as the map becomes more complicated and more complete — and as the structure of the argument becomes more clear.

Evaluating the Argument

Reading with and against the Grain

The note-taking methods we have discussed so far in this chapter have focused on understanding a text more deeply through analysis and exegesis. But you will sometimes need to go further and evaluate the argument as well. Too often, readers pass judgment on a text without really taking the time to consider it carefully. So hold off evaluating a text until after you've spent sufficient time with it to understand it fully.

Your first reading of a text (and perhaps your second and third readings, if the text is a difficult one) should focus on what the author is saying: you look at the question from the author's point of view, and in so doing, you "try on" his or her ideas. The "principle of charity," discussed in Chapter 2, states an essential precept for this kind of thinking: we need to be a "friend" to an argument and give it a fair chance before we can justifiably be its critic. When we read in this way, attempting to look at the world through the writer's eyes, we are reading "with the grain" of the essay: we are turned in the direction that the essay points. But there is also value in reading "against the grain" and bringing a more skeptical mind to bear on the text. (When working with wood, it is easiest to cut with the grain, in the direction of the tree's growth; cutting against the grain is harder due to the wood's resistance.) The point is not to demolish the argument — and certainly not to dismiss it unfairly, forgetting everything we learned from reading with the grain — but to test the argument, to find out its weaknesses, and to imagine alternatives to it.

This exercise might produce any number of outcomes. You might find fatal flaws in the argument and decide that an opposing argument, or counterargument, has greater merit. You might discover that, although other points of view and other arguments are possible, the author's argument is a very strong one, and you are more convinced by it than ever. Often, though, you'll find some weaknesses and some strengths, and you'll have to weigh the former against the latter to see where you stand. This is a necessary part of critical reading and formulating a response.

Believing and Doubting

The "believing and doubting game" is a strategy developed by the scholar and teacher Peter Elbow. The word "game" is used because this strategy requires you to play roles — to step away from what you really do believe for a moment and to pretend you are someone different. Once you've become well-acquainted with an argument, write out all the reasons that someone might have for believing it, and then see if you can imagine other arguments for believing it, in addition to those the writer has given. In other words, be the writer's strongest advocate and ally. Give this the time it needs: twenty to thirty minutes at least.

Now play the "doubting" game. Put yourself in the shoes of a person who is deeply skeptical of the writer's views. First, you'll need to work out what the opposing view — the counterargument — would look like. Write it out as a thesis statement. Then imagine the details of the counterargument. Ask yourself, "What possible reasons could such a person have for taking a contrary position?" Make a list of as many reasons as you can think of, including weak ones: writing out weak reasons may help you think of other, stronger reasons. (And sometimes, on reflection, weak reasons turn out to be not so weak after all!) Then select the most persuasive of the arguments you've listed and write them out as an argument.

An important aspect of the doubting game, indeed of any critical reading, is to identify weaknesses, if any, in the writer's rhetoric. Some kinds of argument are inherently flawed because they involve mistakes of reasoning:

> All Americans love their country. Paul McCartney loves his country. Therefore, Paul McCartney is an American.

Of course, the error in this example lies in the fact that while it might be true that "all Americans love their country," it is not true that *only* Americans love their country. Paul McCartney is English, so it's quite possible for him to love his country and not be an American. The mistake here is obvious, once you give it a moment's thought, but this kind of logical error, or **fallacy**, can be subtle and easy to miss in the context of a larger argument. Other kinds of fallacies are not logical errors but ethically questionable strategies: for example, an argument might appeal to the baser instincts of the reader — the tendency to go with the crowd, perhaps, rather than examine an argument on its merits, however unpopular.

Representing Another's Ideas Fairly and Accurately

A final observation concerns both reading attentively and reading critically. Any writer who works with another writer's ideas may be tempted to shape those ideas to suit his or her own purposes, and thereby risks misrepresenting or distorting them. To do so deliberately would be a serious breach of ethics. But we should also bear in mind that a writer can misrepresent another's ideas through mere carelessness or neglect, without intending to be dishonest. For example, you might need to summarize a writer's argument to give support to an argument of your own. But in doing so, you might accidentally omit certain details and qualifications that make a considerable difference to the writer's point. The result may be that you not only misrepresent the other writer's point but also create an argument of your own that cannot stand up to scrutiny. There's a difference between *using* another person's ideas and *abusing* those ideas — and sometimes the difference is subtle.

Imagine, for example, a student writing a sociology paper about the ways the Internet is changing society and how people relate to one another. Suppose the student wants to argue that behaviors and relationships are now being shaped by large companies such as Facebook, Apple, and Google in ways that were unimaginable thirty years ago. Having read Nicholas Carr's "Is Google Making Us Stupid?," he might want to enlist Carr in support of his argument, and he writes something like this: "Carr argues that Google uses Frederick Winslow Taylor's principles of scientific management to turn Internet users into cogs in a machine or system that works entirely for its own benefit." But Carr doesn't go quite this far, and the difference, though subtle, is important. Carr doesn't say that Google *uses* Taylor's principles; he only suggests that the way it functions is similar to the way Taylor's system functions. Nor does he quite say that Google turns people into cogs in a system that benefits only Google itself; he does suggest, though, that Google, as well as other companies that dominate the way we use the Internet, seems to be pushing in that

➔ Try This   Paraphrasing a Passage

Select a brief passage (10–15 lines) from one of the essays that have been reprinted in Part 5 of this book. Draft a paraphrase of the passage by expressing the writer's ideas in your own words. Now reread the original passage a couple of times (you might also need to reread the paragraphs that precede and follow it, in order to get a clearer sense of the context). Revise your paraphrase so that it represents the writer's thought more accurately, but take care not to use the writer's own words. If you must use one or two phrases from the original, put them in quotation marks to avoid plagiarizing.

direction, and that Google's aims reveal a tendency to want to subordinate individual human beings to a vast artificial intelligence. But directions and tendencies aren't quite the same thing as an actual deed. As Carr goes on to say a few paragraphs later, he is worried — but perhaps needlessly. A careful and responsible summary of Carr's argument would reflect this distinction.

The temptation to misrepresent or oversimplify (even unconsciously) is sometimes great because academic writers (whether freshmen or professionals) face deadlines and high expectations. We are often looking for something when we read, perhaps something specific or perhaps just anything we can use, and it's easy to be a little too eager to find it — and to pretend we've found it even if it's not quite there. We must frequently paraphrase and summarize other writers' ideas, and we must do so in such a way that we show the relevance and meaning of those ideas to our own argument. It's much more difficult to represent the ideas of others accurately than it is to oversimplify or reconstruct or slant or slightly exaggerate those ideas. We shall look further at particular strategies for paraphrasing and summarizing in Chapter 9.

Writing a Letter to the Author

Another way to work out your response to a reading is to write a letter to the author. This technique helps you focus your thoughts, formulate your questions and ideas, and "speak back" to the text. For many writers, the personal letter is a familiar mode of writing, one that allows them to write honestly and openly, whereas note-taking can lead them to write in more formal, detached, and inhibited ways. Writing a letter to the author provides an "enabling fiction": imagining a real person as the audience of your remarks is an effective way to enter into a conversation with a text and to sidestep anxieties about formal, graded academic writing that can restrain your creativity.

Talking Out Your Ideas

Use Class Discussion

In class, your dialectical notebook can do double duty. On one hand, it contains questions and observations that you can put to your classmates, and you can develop your notes on the basis of their comments. On the other hand, discussion can spark ideas to record in your notebook and work out more fully later on. In many college courses, discussion plays a crucial role. Its purpose is to give students the opportunity to think ideas through and to arrive at their own understanding of a text, rather than simply relying on the professor's interpretation and taking it at face value. Students are expected to come to class with comments and questions prepared and to express their views clearly and reasonably for the class to consider. Instructors hope you will work out your own views and come to your own insights; they do not want to see their own views echoed back in a dozen or more identical papers. Class discussion affords an opportunity to figure out where you stand and how your views compare to others so that you can make a strong and interesting argument in your writing. A dialectical notebook can be an essential tool in making such discussions work for you.

Discuss with a Friend, Classmate, Tutor, or Professor

If you read actively, and especially if you use some of the strategies you have learned in Part 1, you will soon reach a point where you have some ideas about the texts you are reading, but these ideas may be vague or confused at first. It might help to get some feedback at this point. Just listening to yourself talk out your ideas can help to clarify them and give you a sense of their strengths and weaknesses. But feedback from a colleague, a friend, or an instructor can be just as helpful. There's nothing wrong with seeking feedback of this sort, and it doesn't make your ideas any less your own.

☑ Checklist of Further Strategies for Active Reading

Although you are unlikely to use all of these methods for one piece of writing, add them to your toolbox of reading strategies, and use the ones that best suit your purpose.

☐ Use a question-centered triple-entry notebook.

☐ Use a quotation-centered triple-entry notebook.

☐ Construct an analytical outline of the text.

☐ Map the text.
- Construct a "What It Says/What It Does" analysis.
- Construct a radial map.

☐ Read with and against the grain.
- Play the "believing and doubting game."

☐ Write a letter to the author.

☐ Talk out your ideas.
- Use class discussion.
- Discuss with a friend, a classmate, a tutor, or an instructor.

part 2

Composing the Essay

chapter 4

Writing to Discover and Develop Ideas

The Value of Exploratory Writing

Writing is in some ways a mysterious business. Some days, we sit down at our desks, and the words just tumble out; ideas delight and surprise us as they parade across the page. It all seems fun and stress-free, hardly like work at all. Yet the next day, for some reason, words refuse to cooperate, and nothing we write seems the least bit interesting or worthwhile. We get distracted, take a coffee break, watch YouTube, return to our work. But it's as if the words we need are bottled up in some hidden recess of the brain, and we just can't seem to get them out. At those times, writing can be brutally hard work, like carving granite with a teaspoon.

It's just as hard to account for the enormous differences in how writers experience the creative process. Some write slowly and with difficulty, others quickly and

> " The formulation of a problem is often more essential than its solution, which may be merely a matter of mathematical or experimental skill. To raise new questions, new possibilities, to regard old problems from a new angle, requires creative imagination and marks real advance in science. "
>
> **ALBERT EINSTEIN**

easily; some keep to a strict routine, others change their methods frequently — yet many different working styles can be equally productive in the end. Each writer must learn through experience how to get his or her best work done, and many aspects of the whole complicated business — how the mind finds words, how words give form to ideas, how one idea leads to another — may never be fully understood.

But even though these mysteries lie at the heart of the writing process, most experienced writers agree on certain productivity strategies. First, the writing process is typically **recursive**: it loops back through the phases of the process as many times as necessary. So reading leads to note-taking, note-taking leads back to reading, further note-taking leads to drafting, then some difficulty arises that leads back to additional reading, and so on. (We'll return to this theme in Chapter 5.) Second, experienced writers tend to agree on the importance of separating out two distinct phases of the writing process: **informal writing** to discover and develop ideas, and **revising** and **editing** this writing to make those ideas clear to the reader.

We're all tempted to believe that we can hammer out good writing in one sitting, simply pouring out our brilliance onto a computer screen. Oh, a bit of editing and polishing might be necessary afterward, but (we tell ourselves) it ought to be possible to express ideas directly and clearly (shouldn't it?), as we do routinely when we speak.

In reality, however, that's not how writing works.

Here's the problem: if we approach the first draft as if it were the final version, we require ourselves *to do two conflicting things at the same time*: we must figure out our ideas for ourselves and at the same time we must make sense of these ideas for the reader. To do both at the same time is not exactly *impossible* — we manage it with simple pieces of writing like text messages and short e-mails, and some of us could even cobble together something resembling an essay this way — but it is certainly inadvisable. It's inadvisable because college-level writing must possess qualities that few of us can achieve all at once on the first pass: preciseness, nuance, clarity, complexity, and logical rigor. We will write a better essay, and the work will go more smoothly, if we separate out the informal exploratory writing from the formal essay writing. When the writing process does clog up and break down, it's usually because we are trying to do both the writerly and the readerly at the same time.

The Writerly versus the Readerly

When writing informally to discover and develop ideas, you are working toward meeting *your own need* to develop and clarify your thoughts. When rewriting, revising, and editing, you are working toward meeting *your reader's need* to understand and appreciate your ideas. Writers sometimes refer to the first kind of writing as **writerly** and the second as **readerly**,[1] terms that express the different audiences and, so to speak, the different beneficiaries of each. In the writerly, exploratory phase, you focus your attention on developing and sorting out your ideas; you allow your ideas to change as they take shape, even if they contradict what you said two sentences before. You never know quite where this kind of writing will lead: you are pursuing an insight — on a voyage of discovery, an expedition into the unknown — and the more surprising and new the revelations, the better.

In the readerly phase, you focus attention on your reader. You try to see your writing through the reader's eyes, to imagine what those eyes will see as they work their way through your text and how the mind behind those eyes will respond. You arrange your arguments in the most effective order; you delete sentences, paragraphs, even whole pages that do not belong; you add new material where something is missing; you iron out wrinkled sentences and find apt words to replace awkward ones. You carefully craft a text designed to persuade readers to believe, think, feel, or do something.

Even if lots of good ideas have already occurred to you as a result of rereading and taking notes, it would be unwise to skip the exploratory, writerly phase. It truly is the energy center of the writing process, the most creative and, for many, the most enjoyable of writing activities. As novelist and screenwriter Evan Hunter said, "The only true creative aspect of writing is the first draft. That's when it comes straight from your head and your heart. . . . The rest is donkey work. It is, however, donkey work that has to be done."[2] Devoting adequate time to working out and developing your ideas — thinking and rethinking them — will result in a final product that is clearer, richer, and more interesting. Informal writing enables you to correct weaknesses that were previously invisible and to become aware of possibilities that at first you could not have imagined. Moreover, low-stakes experimentation with words and strategies smoothes out the whole writing process, reducing the anxiety that can otherwise be overwhelming. It supplies the raw material, the ingredients, that you need for the readerly phase that comes later.

---

[1] These terms were coined by the twentieth-century French critic Roland Barthes; see Barthes, *S/Z: An Essay*, trans. Richard Miller (New York: Hill and Wang, 1974).

[2] Quoted in Jon Winokur, *Advice to Writers* (New York: Random House/Vintage, 2000), 104.

Exploratory Writing

There are, of course, many kinds of writerly, informal writing — journaling, note-taking, planning, and so on. This chapter focuses on exploratory writing for the purpose of developing ideas, a pleasurable and unpressured kind of writing in which there are few rules and no wrong moves. Exploratory writing can feel more like play than work. It gives you the opportunity to puzzle things out, to delve deeper, in a writing space where no one will judge or criticize you. You can freely exercise your creativity and ingenuity, because at this stage even apparently outlandish ideas are just fine. You can safely write about your personal thoughts and experiences too. You can worry later about whether to keep such material in your final paper; for now, just explore. This is writing for no one's eyes but your own.

The twentieth-century English novelist E. M. Forster famously posed the question, "How can I tell what I think until I see what I say?"[3] At first, this may seem counterintuitive: Doesn't thinking come before writing? But what Forster describes is a familiar experience to writers: somehow the act of putting ideas into a sequence of words and arranging words in a sequence of sentences clarifies and *shows* us what we think. We can begin writing with very little sense of what we might have to say about a subject and can use the writing process as a tool for discovery, figuring things out as we go.

Most of us talk to ourselves — if not out loud, then silently. We speak thoughts in our heads in order to consider and test them; we might even improvise a little debate to weigh the pros and cons of an idea. But usually we don't sustain these interior conversations for very long, and we end up with no record of the conversation except unreliable memory. Recording thoughts in writing makes it possible to *see* these thoughts — quite literally — and to work with them. As the teacher and scholar Peter Elbow writes, "A principal value of language . . . is that it permits you to *distance* yourself from your own perceptions, feelings, and thoughts. Try, then, to write words on paper so as to permit an interaction between you and not-you. You are building someone to talk to."[4] Seeing our words makes it possible not only to

---

[3] E. M. Forster, *Aspects of the Novel* (Harmondsworth, UK: Penguin/Pelican, 1962), 108. It must be said that Forster does not quite endorse this view, which occurs in a chapter on plot. There he posits it as the words of "an old lady" who refuses to believe in logic and would agree with the French novelist André Gide, whose book *Les Faux Monnayeurs* (1925) tries to do away with plot and replace it with "real life." Forster is doubtful about the wisdom of this approach. Nevertheless, the old lady's question has justifiably been adopted by writing teachers as a succinct expression of the aims of exploratory writing.

[4] Peter Elbow, *Writing without Teachers*, 2nd ed. (New York: Oxford University Press, 1998), 55.

weigh them but also to respond to them — to improve and extend them — so that writing leads to more writing. Thus writing does not merely express thinking; it *produces* thinking (from the Latin *producere*, "to lead forward").

Many writers enjoy exploratory writing enormously. Their thoughts about scholarly matters and private matters get mixed up together — and this has the effect of enriching and deepening both. Some writers prefer to write longhand, in small notebooks or on blank pages of copier paper; others prefer to type their thoughts on a computer. Many prefer to work somewhere quiet, where there's nothing to distract them — no phone or TV or e-mail. Other writers work best in crowded, noisy environments like cafés or fast-food restaurants, where the music and chatter become a kind of white noise that actually helps them think. Some people need the comfort and privacy of a special writing place — a bedroom or an office. Personalities differ; the important thing is to figure out by experimentation where you do your best work, and then make a habit of going there regularly.

Knots and Questions

With time, writers tend to develop individual methods of exploratory writing to suit their own personalities and situation (such as the particular requirements of an assignment or a project), but the variations typically follow a basic pattern. In all exploratory writing, two types of activity are of particular value: posing questions and playing with "knots." A knot is anything that's puzzling or unclear or even mysterious about the text (or whatever is on your mind) — some difficulty, something that bothers you about it. We're all familiar with crime dramas in which the detective fastens onto some detail that doesn't quite make sense — the butler's shoes weren't muddy — and of course it leads to the solution of the whole mystery: the butler was innocent of murder, after all; it was the baron's estranged half-sister who did it! That little detail is the knot that the detective plays with until it unravels and reveals the truth. A knot might at first look like an awkward inconvenience: a fact that doesn't quite fit with the theory. But knots are frequently doorways to fresh, surprising ways of looking at something. Once you've identified a knot, either from memory or from your notes, toy with it, untangle it, see where it leads you. Be patient: if you just pull randomly on the end of a string, you might only make the knot tighter. Exploratory writing offers the opportunity to approach it with a light touch, to get the knot to yield by taking time to analyze it, prod it, gently interrogate it. It's possible the knot leads nowhere — but it might lead to a whole new way of seeing things.

Questions are the best tool we have not only for undoing knots but also for finding them. Knots can be hard to identify at first, but questions are easy to come by. We can always pose some kind of question to get things started, even if it seems obvious or pointless. The writing process gives us an opportunity to rephrase, correct, or sharpen the question, and a well-crafted question clears a pathway to a good idea. One question leads to another, and a good idea leads to further questions.

We sometimes speak of "entertaining" a question, a turn of phrase that suggests precisely what is needed: invite the question in, offer it a cup of tea, urge it to sit down and chat. Worthwhile questions can't be turned away immediately with a simple yes or no answer. They demand our hospitality before they divulge everything they know. To use a different metaphor, questions function as the engine of the whole process: they keep the exploration moving forward into new territory. If you get to the point where your exploratory writing hits a dead end or seems to peter out, try simply listing questions for a while. Compile a dozen questions and then choose one to work with until it opens up further questions.

Sample Exploratory Writing

First-year student Lea Bright is working on an essay assignment with an open topic. In these exploratory writing sessions, she thinks through the meaning and possible implications of some themes from Emily Esfahani Smith's "Life on the Island" (p. 399), focusing on some of the more promising knots and questions in the essay as she looks for a topic and some ideas to write about.

Session 1, October 12, 2014

I think the main point here is that people don't do so well in places like America where individualism is so strongly emphasized. Strong communities are needed for good psychological health, and they're becoming weaker, even though most people today live in cities surrounded by other people. People can be very lonely and unhappy in cities. American culture is becoming "hyper-individualistic" and narcissistic, she says, and that's dangerous because it leads to higher suicide rates and presumably a lot of unhappiness.

I guess the main question I have right now is whether it's really true that America has become hyper-individualistic and narcissistic. I agree that narcissism is bad, but is social isolation really on the rise? "Our connections to others are slowly dissolving," she says. That doesn't feel quite true to me personally, but I suppose as a college student, my case might be pretty different from the norm. She says that middle-aged suicide has been rising. Levels of anxiety are rising.

The strange thing is that we're so much more connected now than just a few years ago. Esfahani Smith was writing in 2013—only a year ago—so people had exactly the same phones and technology then, and they could text and call each other all the time, the same as today. I suppose the point, though, is that texting and calling someone doesn't necessarily make them a confidant, and she seems to be saying that the number of confidants is falling. In 1985, the most common response was three; in 2004, the most common response was zero. It's possible, then, that some people have a lot of confidants, but a lot of people have none—more people than in 1985? (Not quite sure how this works.)

I wonder if it's true that song lyrics today are more narcissistic than they used to be. I could check it out by comparing the lyrics of the top hits right now to the lyrics of top hits ten, twenty, thirty, even forty years ago. I think that would be possible.

Session 2, October 13, 2014

On second reading, I think I have a better sense of the argument that she's making about individualism. Conservatives, she says, tend to think that individualism is a great thing and one of the things that makes America a great country. I think Esfahani Smith is saying to them: "Yes, individualism is okay, but hyper-individualism can be really bad: people need friends and communities too." So conservatives should be careful about emphasizing individualism at the expense of community, or maybe about supposing that community is always a nonconservative value, a liberal value, and something they would naturally oppose.

I can't get super interested in the conservative-liberal thing, though. And I'm not sure I believe song lyrics are going to make a strong case one way or the other. What I couldn't stop thinking about as I reread the essay was the role that smart phones and social media play in all this. Maybe smart phones make us more disconnected from each other, in a way, rather than more connected? I was thinking about all those times when good conversations have gotten interrupted by calls or texts. Even on the phone: "There's someone on the other line." It's perfectly possible to have a deep conversation, of course, but it just seems like phones make it harder, and they're always with us. Theoretically, they make connections with others easier—and they actually do in many ways—but the connections they make never seem to be very deep. You need to be face to face, or if on the phone, then uninterrupted, to have a deep connection with someone, and phones maybe make that harder, actually. I could write about this from personal experience—and probably the experience of my friends. Will that be enough? It would be great to come up with some neat way of getting evidence like the Google Ngram Viewer. I'll have to think about that.

Maybe we just need to learn how to use our devices better. They're not necessarily good or bad in themselves: as users we do have control. We have to turn off our phones in class. Why can't we learn to turn them off in social situations? Maybe we need a movement! Anyway, I'm not sure why Esfahani Smith doesn't talk about technology in the essay, but I think it could be a good topic. I think my starting point could be the General Social Survey that Esfahani Smith cites, and the decline in the number of confidants that people have. And so that raises the whole question of whether or not phones and social media actually make it less likely that friends will become confidants, or more so. And if they do make it less likely, can we turn it around somehow so that they make it *more* likely? It's probably complicated, but it's interesting.

✅ Checklist for Exploratory Writing

Just as computers and pens are the physical tools for exploratory writing, so knots and questions are the mental tools. But we still need some practical guidelines for this kind of writing. Here, then, is a list. Keep in mind, however, that these are only guidelines. Eventually, you'll develop an exploratory writing practice of your own that might work differently.

☐ Remember that this writing is for your eyes only.
- No one will read it except you, unless you choose to show it to someone.

☐ Plan to write steadily for a set period.
- Try twenty minutes at first. But fifteen minutes or thirty minutes will work too. In any case, decide on your time frame in advance.

☐   To start with, put your notes aside and work from memory.
   - What you remember is probably what interests you most: for some reason, it got lodged in your mind.

☐ If nothing occurs to you from memory, begin anywhere.
   - You may have nothing to say at first. You may have nothing to say for the full writing period. That's okay. Just write "I can't think of anything to say. I still can't think of anything to say" until something occurs to you, however trivial or superficial it might seem. Thoughts are stirring in the back of your mind. When something about the reading or the problem does strike you, write about it.

☐ Keep moving forward.
   - Don't edit. Don't worry about grammar, spelling, punctuation, or formatting. Don't go back and erase or cross out anything you've written, no matter how pointless or silly it seems.

☐ Entertain questions and knots.
   - However silly or inappropriate they may seem, use them as the engines of exploration. Dwell on knots. Stay for as long as possible with the knots that you come across — anything that's puzzling or interesting. Do what you can with them. One may lead to another or begin to change its appearance as you dwell on it.

☐ Open a space for reflection.
   - Talk things out. Speculate freely. Ponder. Give yourself time to focus at length.

☐ Put away your dictionary and thesaurus for now.
   - Use your own words, even if they may not be exactly right. Save perfectionism for the readerly phase.

☐ Expect a lot of garbage in this writing.
   - That's exactly as it should be. You need to generate a lot of material in order to produce a few good ideas.

The Benefits of Writing Daily

This book or any book can teach you only so much about writing. Writing is a craft, and crafts are learned by doing. Like learning to play the piano or paint or jump hurdles, learning to write means doing it regularly, and writers benefit from

→ **Try** This   Practicing Exploratory Writing

Option 1. Try your hand at exploratory writing. Go to your college library or another quiet spot where you can work without interruption. Briefly review the notes that you have made on one of the readings included in this book. Then open your notebook to a new page and write for twenty minutes. Search for a good theme for an essay, on any topic related to the reading. If you find one before twenty minutes are up, don't stop: continue to explore the theme, testing its strengths and weaknesses and developing its implications.

Option 2. As a subject for exploratory writing, consider this painting by René Magritte, entitled *The Liberator* (1947). Try to work out an interpretation: What, in your view, is the painting saying? What does it mean? Devote thirty to forty-five minutes of exploratory writing to this activity.

The Liberator (1947), by René Magritte.
(Source: Gianni Dagli Orti/The Art Archive at Art Resource/
© 2014 C. Herscovici/Artists Rights Society [ARS], New York)

Option 3. Choose an intriguing poem, photograph, painting, or piece of music as a subject for exploratory writing. (Choose one to which you have access so that you do not have to rely on memory and can examine it repeatedly.) It should be a work that is unfamiliar to you so that your exploration of it has a chance to yield fresh and unexpected insights.

> **→ Guidelines** **Keeping the Censor at Bay**
>
> To avoid the negative thinking that blocks writing, keep the following guidelines in mind:
>
> • Recognize that the negative, critical voice in your head is the enemy of creativity and insight.
>
> • Write daily in a journal for no one's eyes but your own. Write whatever you want.
>
> • Permit yourself to write badly in your journal.
>
> • Relax. Go where your mind takes you and enjoy the ride.

practice more than anything else. Instruction is helpful, but we learn far more from sitting down regularly to put words on paper, discovering over time our themes and our voices, steadily gaining confidence and fluency, recognizing our strengths and limitations, developing an ear for what works and what's labored or florid or wordy, getting a sense of how to begin, how to keep going, how to finish.

Although this book deals with writing in academic settings, we strongly encourage you to write a daily journal about whatever you like. Use a notebook or, if you prefer, a computer, and save your entries in a special folder. Write two or three pages a day — and write every day, preferably at a regular time. (The best time is probably soon after you get up, before your busy life eats up the rest of the day.) This journal will be for your eyes only, with no restrictions on what you write about. Though journals are often used for recording experiences, feelings, and speculations, they don't have to be. You can write stories or dreams or fantasies, describe what's around you wherever you happen to be, or just write aimlessly about nothing in particular. It's all perfectly fine. Any kind of daily writing will help you become a more proficient writer. (In fact, the word "journal" comes from an Old French word meaning "daily.")

Writer and teacher Julia Cameron notes that creative people (and that might be virtually everyone) tend to be highly self-critical.

> We are victims of our own internalized perfectionist, a nasty internal and eternal critic, the Censor, who resides in our (left) brain and keeps up a constant stream of subversive remarks that are often disguised as the truth. The Censor says wonderful things like: "You call that writing? What a joke. You can't even punctuate. If you

haven't done it by now you never will. You can't even spell. What makes you think you can be creative?" And on and on.[5]

Daily journal writing helps us learn to ignore the Censor's negative and disabling voice. We can let that voice carp away, while we just keep on writing whatever we feel like writing. In time, we learn that the Censor is merely a "blocking device"[6] that serves no useful function, and it slowly loses its power over us.

Making Meanings

As a college student, you are likely to find journaling particularly valuable because you are bombarded throughout the day with so many new ideas, experiences, and people. You need not only a place to record your impressions but also a way to sort it all out. Ideas and questions occur to you constantly, but you need to take the time to reflect, develop these thoughts, and dwell with them.

Ideas become meaningful to us when we find a way to integrate them into our entire body of knowledge. As long as they float around in a space where they are cut off from the rest of our concerns and experiences, they will never be very meaningful. Notebooks, journals, "morning pages," freewriting—all these are forms of "heuristic" writing, or writing to discover. Done in a sincere and committed way, they become the means of discovering not just ideas but meanings, not just thesis statements and arguments but connections between the readings and your own interests. Too often, schoolwork assigned by instructors in different courses that have little in common exists in isolation, detached from students' actual experiences and questions. One of the most effective ways of making readings and assignments meaningful is to begin by writing for yourself, rather than writing for a grade. Ultimately, the two things can merge so that the writing you do for yourself evolves into the writing you submit for a grade. Exploratory writing can function as the bridge between the two, the means by which schoolwork can become personally meaningful and satisfying.

Exploratory writing is recursive, meaning that the results of one session become the starting point for the next. This writing strategy is sometimes called

---

[5] Julia Cameron, *The Artist's Way* (New York: G. P. Putnam's Sons, 1992), 11.
[6] Ibid., 12.

looping, a rhythm of writing and resting, of tension and relaxation, that helps ideas to form. Here's how it works:

- Write for ten, twenty, or thirty minutes. Take a break, roughly equal to the amount of time you've spent writing. Pick up a promising thread from the writing you just completed, and write for another ten, twenty, or thirty minutes. Then take another break. Keep this going for several loops.

- Enjoy yourself. Don't hesitate to explore thoughts that you don't expect to include in the finished version of your paper. You never know what may spark an idea, so trust your thoughts and let them lead you forward.

The results of exploratory writing are frequently surprising. You might start out in one direction and find yourself suddenly veering off in a different one altogether, and this new direction takes you places you never imagined going. You might write something on Monday that seems unremarkable and insignificant, but when it comes to mind on Wednesday, it opens up all kinds of unforeseen possibilities, becoming the beginning of a whole new line of inquiry. In her essay "On Keeping a Notebook," essayist and novelist Joan Didion explores the purpose of the notes that she has been taking — regularly but unsystematically — for many years. Their value, it turns out, is less in what she actually records on paper than in the memories that these notes can conjure up.

> At no point have I ever been able successfully to keep a diary; . . . and on those few occasions when I have tried dutifully to record a day's events, boredom has so overcome me that the results are mysterious at best. What is this business about "shopping, typing piece, dinner with E, depressed"? . . .
>
> In fact I have abandoned altogether that kind of pointless entry; instead I tell what some would call lies. "That's simply not true," the members of my family frequently tell me when they come up against my memory of a shared event. "The party was not for you, the spider was not a black widow, it wasn't that way at all." Very likely they are right, for not only have I always had trouble distinguishing between what happened and what merely might have happened, but I remain unconvinced that the distinction, for my purposes, matters. . . .
>
> How it felt to me: that is getting closer to the truth about a notebook. I sometimes delude myself about why I keep a notebook, imagine that some thrifty virtue

derives from preserving everything observed. . . . Remember what it was to be me: that is always the point.[7]

Likewise, the point of exploratory writing is always to find out what something means to you. Don't expect any sort of heuristic writing to pay off quickly: most of the time, you won't arrive at the insight or thesis statement that you need for your essay with your very first writing session — or even your second. The process is meant to be recursive. The result of the first session becomes the starting point for the next one. You may be surprised how many sessions you have time for. If you have five days between reading/note-taking and revising/polishing, and if you devote just ninety minutes a day to exploratory writing, broken into three sessions, you will complete fifteen half-hour sessions. At three pages per session, that's forty-five pages of exploratory writing. More to the point, it's a journey that may lead you far from your point of departure and, in all likelihood, toward ideas of real value.

You Can Always Write More

One of the most valuable outcomes of exploratory writing is the effect it will have on your attitude toward revision. When writing feels difficult and demands enormous effort, writers tend to become too attached to their words. They become reluctant to cut or revise passages that, no matter how much perspiration they cost or how delightful they may be in themselves, really must go, for the greater good of the whole. By contrast, writers who know from experience that they can readily generate more writing whenever it's needed can revise with confidence and can revise more effectively, because they are willing to abandon material. To revise well, we need to know that our words are not so very precious: we can always write more. As the late British comic Spike Milligan used to say: "Ingle jingle jangle jom / There's more, my friend, where that came from."[8] And as, more soberly, Annie Dillard writes: "the path is not the work."[9] The writing that we abandon was useful for getting us

---

[7] Joan Didion, "On Keeping a Notebook," in *Slouching Towards Bethlehem* (New York: Farrar, Straus and Giroux, 1968), 133–36.
[8] Spike Milligan, *Muses with Milligan*, recorded 1965, Decca LK 4701, vinyl LP.
[9] Annie Dillard, *The Writing Life* (New York: Harper and Row, 1989), 4.

where we need to be, but once it has served its purpose, we must be willing to part with it. Perhaps every writer finds this process of deleting words and ideas a little difficult to do, but the habit of exploratory writing and unpressured drafting does make it easier. We no longer feel that words are precious, hard-to-find things but instead feel that they are plentiful and easy to come by. We can afford to be generous with them.

Focused Exploratory Writing

As we've seen, exploratory writing can serve many purposes and be about anything at all. But there will be times when you'll want to use exploratory writing to make progress toward completing an academic essay. For the purpose of academic writing, first focus on figuring out exactly what the question or problem or issue is. Once you've got a clear sense of that, you can begin to work on finding a solution to it.

Focused exploratory writing is useful whether you are writing in response to a specific assignment — perhaps one that presents you with a specific question or problem to address — or writing on a topic of your own. Even if the assignment is phrased as a question or problem rather than a topic or a directive, first you'll need to understand the question *for yourself*, in your own terms and in relation to your own thinking. Patiently thinking the question through — figuring out what it's *really* asking, what it's getting at — is the first and most necessary step toward arriving at an answer.

If the assignment asks you to respond to a particular reading, begin by focusing on the problem that the author is addressing. The author may explicitly mention the problem (usually in the opening paragraphs), or you may have to infer it from the text by asking, "What sort of question, problem, or issue does the author's argument shed light on or take a stand on?"

Then, work out your take on the problem. Explain, in as much detail as possible, where you stand and where the author stands. Do you agree or disagree with the author? Your sense of this may be vague at first, and it may shift or even reverse itself as you write, but that's fine: you're just exploring, not laying out a consistent argument.

Pose questions whenever they occur to you. Questions help you see more clearly where you need to direct attention; they will move you forward.

→ Try This   Practicing Exploratory Freewriting

The following activities will give you the opportunity to try your hand at exploratory freewriting, to get the feel of it, and to experience how it works. For now, follow the guidelines that have been offered in this chapter. To get more practice with exploratory freewriting, choose one or more of these activities. Before you begin, decide how much time you will devote to the activity you've chosen, and divide it into segments of ten, fifteen, or twenty minutes so that you can practice looping.

Option 1: Focused Exploratory Writing for an Essay Assignment. If you have been assigned a topic for a paper, use it as a springboard. Read over the assignment instructions carefully. Consider the following questions as you write.

- What is the assignment asking you to do? What central problem does it set for you? Paraphrase the problem as you see it (put it into your own words).
- What can you say in response to this problem as a result of your reading, note-taking, and thinking so far? Work first from memory, but if you get stuck, turn to your notes.
- What passage in the text speaks most directly to the problem given in the assignment? What does this passage say (paraphrase it)? Explain the connection to the problem, as you see it. What conclusions can you draw from this passage? What ideas does it suggest to you?
- What other passages relate to the problem? What do they say? Repeat the step above for each relevant passage: paraphrase it, explain how it relates to the problem, develop the ideas it suggests to you.
- What seems to be the purpose of the assignment? Why might this problem be important? How does it relate to the course and its objectives?
- Does the assignment offer any clues as to the direction your essay should take? Many assignments include both a directive—a statement of what you must do—and suggestions or hints for things you might do, or might want to think about, as you develop your ideas.

Option 2: Exegesis and Commentary. As we said earlier, exegesis is an explanation or interpretation of a text. For this activity, choose a short passage from the text—between two sentences and one paragraph in length. (You might work with one of the essays included in this book or use a text that you've been assigned in your coursework.) It should be a passage that seems important to the meaning of the text as a whole but also contains difficulties or puzzles of some kind—in other words, a passage that seems likely to reward close attention, one that's worth dwelling on for a while.

Begin by stating in your own words what you think the passage means. Try to clarify any parts that seem obscure. (You may need a dictionary; if so, quote useful definitions in your writing.) Work over the passage in detail, so that your writing unfolds its meaning as exhaustively as possible. Consider how its parts work together, how words, phrases, and sentences relate to one another to form a meaningful whole. Stay alert for meanings that might not have been obvious at first, especially ones that differ from—or even contradict—your first impression.

Once you have done all you can with the passage itself and have completed your exegesis, shift your focus to making connections between the passage and something else—other texts, ideas, experiences, and facts. (In the exegesis phase of this activity, you work inside the passage; in the commentary phase, you work between the passage and something else.) Almost any kind of connection could produce a useful insight. How does your chosen passage relate to the major themes of the text as a whole? How does it relate to particular passages in the text that seem memorable or important? What connections do you find between this passage and other things in the world, such as your experiences or other texts you've read or social issues or political events?

After writing about one or two connections of this kind, go back to the text and consider it in isolation once more. What more do you see in it now?

Option 3: Exploratory Writing on a Knot of Your Own Choosing. Use some problem or puzzle in your own work or life as a subject for exploratory writing. You may or may not solve the problem, but write continuously and explore different ways of looking at it. Try to bring greater clarity to the problem, and perhaps some kind of solution will emerge—if not immediately, then later on.

Option 4: Freewriting. Try freewriting without any subject or starting point at all. See what emerges as you follow where the writing takes you. As you proceed, try to identify a topic, a question, or a problem. Articulate and refine it to the best of your ability, and try to develop some kind of insight into it. Use the looping technique to get some distance and perspective on your topic between bouts of writing.

Next, begin working out your reasons for your position. If you get stuck, work on key passages (a few sentences) in the text. Perhaps copy out the most relevant ones, or ones that feel like knots, and focus on answering these questions:

- What is the author saying in this passage?
- What might it have to do with the problem?
- How does it relate to my position?

Keep it loose: you are not yet writing for anyone's eyes but your own. The trick to exploratory writing is to keep moving toward your objective even though you don't know what it looks like. Move toward the articulation of an idea, or the framing of a question, or the formulation of an argument. Eventually, perhaps repeatedly, you will find that the elements of your puzzle resolve themselves in a little "aha" experience as something obscure emerges into clarity. Then you've got something. This something may not be the final thing — ideas can always be polished, developed, elaborated, refined — but it's a beginning.

✅ Checklist for Focused Exploratory Writing

Keep the following points in mind as you write to discover and develop ideas.

- ☐ Identify the problem, issue, or question that the assignment or text addresses.
- ☐ Establish your own position and seek a solution or an answer. Make a contribution to the conversation.
- ☐ List your reasons or justification for this stand.
- ☐ Pose questions.
- ☐ Seek knots.

chapter 5

Developing an Argument

Argument as Structure

If you were to build a house, a barn, or a cathedral — any structure meant to last — you would need not only good materials but also an understanding of structural and architectural principles. You would need to know how to arrange spaces that serve people's needs, how to place doors and windows, how to make the walls and roof strong enough to withstand ice and rain and wind. Developing an argument is similar. Of course, you need materials, like ideas and quotations and notes, but you also need an understanding of the principles that make it possible to bring the various parts together to form a structure that holds up, that invites readers in and leads them through its points, and that can withstand careful scrutiny. Like the best buildings, the best arguments are sturdy, well proportioned, and pleasing. Achieving these goals requires an understanding of some basic principles of logic and rhetoric.

To this point our focus has been chiefly on reading, note-taking, and informal writing — work that generates the sort of ideas you can use for an essay or other piece of writing. By now you should have some sense of what you want to say, so this chapter focuses on planning, designing, and assembling an argument. To construct a strong argument, writers must understand argument's component parts and how these parts relate to one another. In the fourth century BCE, the Greek philosopher Aristotle distinguished between two aspects of argumentation: **logic** (systematic reasoning) and **rhetoric** (the art of persuasion). You might think of logic as the invisible interior principles that hold an argument together — like the structural principles that keep a building standing — and rhetoric as the external features that make it attractive. This chapter is concerned primarily with logic — with making the argument fundamentally sound. (Rhetoric, the art of making an argument appealing, is discussed in the next chapter.)

The Components of Argument: Motive, Claim, and Support

As you will recall from Chapter 1 (p. 38), we use the word "argument" here not in the sense of a two-sided dispute in which one opponent tries to defeat the other, but in the sense of a single logical structure in which one individual *makes* an argument. Like any structure, arguments have several component parts — namely, motive, claim, and support.

Motive

We noted in the Introduction that academic essays usually offer a solution or partial solution to a problem, a question, or an issue of some kind. Very often, this problem (or question or issue) also interests other scholars in the field; the writer will usually mention or explain it in the first paragraph or two. This reference to a problem reveals the writer's purpose and suggests why readers might want to pay attention to the essay. In other words, it explains the argument's "motive": its basic purpose or reason for existing. (As we noted in Chapter 4, sometimes the problem, question, or issue is *implied* rather than stated outright. But if so, the reader can usually figure it out.)

Academic writing is often concerned with problems of an intellectual nature — we might call them "knowledge problems" — rather than practical problems. In many academic disciplines, the job of researchers is to expand our understanding of the world, so their work seeks to answer questions and solve problems at the cutting edge of knowledge. Some practical usefulness might appear somewhere down the road, but often the main reason for solving the problem is simply to satisfy human curiosity. In the academic world, this is motive enough. Arguments published in magazines and newspapers, typically intended for general readers rather than professional researchers, are more usually concerned with practical problems.

While a concern with knowledge problems is a distinctive feature of academic work, academic writing can also focus on practical problems. College writing assignments in particular often ask students to address practical problems: for example, political problems ("Should the electoral college be abolished?"), social problems ("How can American cities best deal with homelessness?"), or technological and engineering problems ("How can a smarter robot be built?"). Whether you are dealing with an intellectual problem or a practical one, you will need to provide a strong sense of the problem, question, or issue you are addressing so that the reader can understand why your argument matters and is worth reading.

Claim

Every argument, including academic arguments, proposes some idea to readers — the solution to a problem, the answer to a question, the correct approach to an issue. In other words, it makes a claim — an assertion that something is true or valid.

A claim differs from a fact in that a claim *awaits* proof or strong evidence, while a fact has already been well established. For example, the following is a claim:

> Information comes to seem like an environment.
>
> (Sven Birkerts, "Reading in a Digital Age")

This is a novel idea, one that readers might not accept without some sort of supporting evidence. However, the sentence that comes next in Birkerts's article can be called a fact because it describes a familiar experience that readers are likely to accept without further argument or support: "If anything 'important' happens anywhere, we will be informed."

On its own, a claim leaves the reader wondering, "Why should I believe that?" or "Why is that true?" A claim is yet to be proven, just as a claim that you stake on something, such as a piece of land, has not yet been fulfilled: it is a demand that you're *expecting* to be fulfilled at some later time. A claim hangs in the balance, waiting to be proven or disproven.

A claim is also different from an opinion, though the difference can be subtle. When you express an opinion — for example, "I think it is wrong to conduct experiments on animals," or "In my opinion, it was a terrible performance," or "I believe that most people are basically good" — you just state a belief, and it may or may not be possible or necessary to make a rational argument for it. It could be an expression of taste, bias, or faith, perhaps a feeling or a hunch — that brussels sprouts are delicious, that Cameron Diaz is the greatest actor ever, that capital punishment is murder — and you are not asserting that your belief is objectively "true." But when you make a claim, you do state it *as true*. You're prepared, at least in theory, to back it up. Here are several actual claims.

> ➔ **Try This**   **Working with Claims**
>
> 1. Make up supporting statements for each of the claims listed on this page. Use your imagination, or search for facts that provide strong support.
> 2. Make up three or four claims of your own. Discuss them in class: What sort of support does each require? (Some possible topics: the effect on children of two working parents; the right to text while driving; the dangers of mixed martial arts or "ultimate fighting"; the need for print journalism in the Internet age.)

> There is no fundamental difference between man and the higher animals in their mental faculties.   (Charles Darwin, *The Descent of Man*)

> To the frontier the American intellect owes its striking characteristics.
>   (Frederick Jackson Turner, "The Significance
>   of the Frontier in American History")

> The current design revolution recognizes that sensory experience is as valid a part of our nature as our capacity to speak or to reason.
>   (Virginia Postrel, "The Design of Your Life")

> It's an overwrought Gothic melodrama that has a nice first act before it descends into shameless absurdity.   (Roger Ebert, review of the film *Asylum*)

These claims come from very different sources, but each one *requires* a supporting argument to persuade the reader that it is valid or true. On their own, they aren't either valid or invalid, true or false. (You can probably imagine directly contrary claims that might be made.)

Support

Without **support** (evidence and reasoning), claims are no more than a series of assertions, backed by nothing (such claims are called "empty claims"). If readers have no reason to believe them, claims lack all force and impact. So support is essential. But what counts as support? Support includes both evidence, such as data and facts, and **reasoning**, a sequence of logically connected statements. There are only two requirements for support: first, it must be *valid* in itself; second, it must be *relevant* to the claim. Consider the following one-sentence arguments:

> Animals should be treated humanely because they are just like you and me.

> Animals should be treated humanely because at least 60 percent of American households include a pet.

In the first example, the claim that "animals should be treated humanely" is supported by a statement that is not necessarily valid in itself. (*Are* all animals "just like" you and me? Are any?) In the second example, the claim is supported by a statistic that may well be accurate but is irrelevant: Why should this fact mean that all animals should be treated humanely?

A stronger argument might go something like this:

> Animals should be treated humanely because they feel pain as acutely as humans do; moreover, scientists have shown that animals also experience similar emotional distress, including feelings of shame, loss, and depression.

(Of course, this argument holds up only if scientists have in fact shown all this. The relevant studies would need to be cited.)

Support gives us a reason (or reasons) for believing a claim to be true, but it is not the same thing as absolute **proof**. (In fact, proofs are rarely, if ever, 100 percent airtight, except perhaps in mathematics.) We can rarely *prove* arguments; all we can do is support them as strongly as possible. There will always be *some* room for doubt.

Still, in the strongest arguments, the relation between claims and their support is a tight fit, so tight as to be virtually irrefutable. In a weak argument, there are holes in the reasoning, gaps between the claims and the support and between different claims. Objections can easily be raised. The whole structure comes tumbling down under the least pressure.

A Typical Workflow

Writing an essay isn't like following a recipe: it's a creative enterprise, and individual writers eventually develop their own processes that work for them. But it is possible to describe a typical writing process, and Figure 5.1 below shows a standard workflow for academic writing. As we've already seen, the writing process begins with active reading and note-taking, and that is usually followed by informal writing to develop ideas. Now we've come to the next stage, which is normally to draft a working thesis statement and then begin developing an argument, perhaps with an outline. Later in this chapter, we'll discuss some strategies for drafting paragraphs, and in Chapter 6 we'll discuss strategies for refining the organization and clarifying the argument.

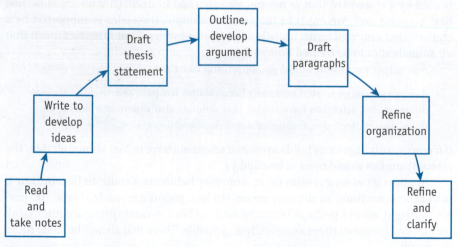

Figure 5.1 A Typical Workflow

Drafting a Thesis Statement

Arguments can be short and simple — a single claim and some support for the claim.

> Come with me to the hockey game. Our star defenseman has finally recovered from his injuries and will be in the starting lineup.

> **THE CLAIM:** You should come with me to the hockey game.
> **THE SUPPORT:** Our star defenseman will be in the starting lineup.

But academic arguments are more lengthy and complicated than this example, so they need a "master claim" to keep them focused and organized. We call this master claim the **thesis statement**. The body of the essay typically provides support for this master claim, support that will include many other claims — supporting claims — along the way. The thesis statement is often presented in one or two sentences somewhere near the beginning, usually toward the end of the first or second paragraph. It represents the argument boiled down to its essence — a single claim that shows what the essay contributes toward the solution of a problem or that reveals the author's stand on an issue.

The purpose of all the thinking you do while rereading, taking notes, and doing exploratory writing is to produce an idea that you'd like to present in an essay — a thesis. If you feel that you still don't have anything to say, return to the strategies discussed in Chapters 2, 3, and 4. (Sometimes the creative process can be a struggle. There's no fail-safe formula for generating ideas, but the strategies and activities that we've discussed in these chapters should move the process forward.)

If you do have a sense of what you want to say, even a vague one, it's time to draft a working thesis statement. Think of your working thesis statement as a building tool: it will help you develop your argument even if it has to be substantially revised several times during the writing process. You need not feel committed to your words at this point, but your working thesis statement will give you a sense of direction as you begin developing an argument.

The Role of the Thesis Statement

As you begin thinking about a working thesis statement, it will be helpful to remember what a thesis statement is and isn't.

The word "thesis" is an ancient Greek term that originally referred to the stressed syllables in a line of poetry or stressed notes in a musical phrase, and to the beating of a hand or foot in time to a rhythm. Eventually, it came to be used for statements that were "put forth" or "put down" in a related way, often in a debate or conversation. This sense is still implied in its modern usage. Just as we sometimes use the expressions "Let me float this idea" or "Let me put this thought out there," the word "thesis" suggests an idea that a writer wants to test or try out. (Similarly, the word "essay" comes from the French verb *essayer*, meaning "to try or test.")

This nuanced meaning of "thesis" is useful to keep in mind as you sketch out a working thesis. Student writers are sometimes tempted to play it safe, feeling that they ought to have the "right answer" to a problem, even if their idea is self-evident or one that anyone else in the class might have come up with. But to construct a lengthy argument to support an obvious point is a waste of your time as well as your reader's. And an essay assignment is not like an exam: instructors rarely expect a "right answer." When they read exams, instructors usually expect to find a certain sameness; but when they read essays, instructors look forward to reading as many different arguments as there are students in the class.

A thesis statement is much more than a **topic** or general subject. It suggests what the essay seeks to accomplish rather than merely what it talks about. A topic is static and lifeless — it makes no particular assertion and needs no proof. But a thesis statement — as a type of claim — requires a supporting argument. And it relates to a recognized problem, question, or issue — it has a motive. Thus a thesis has an energy and a direction that will keep the essay moving forward.

For example, "the problem of greenhouse gas emissions" is a possible topic. Here's a thesis statement from a student essay:

> Congress can take several effective measures to diminish the emission of dangerous greenhouse gases, without limiting either the freedom or the prosperity of American citizens.   (Student writer Amy Britten)

In her opening paragraph, this writer had explained the problem: greenhouse gases contribute to global warming, which scientists agree is changing the climate more quickly than living things can adapt to such changes. She then proposed that part of the solution may be action on the part of the federal government, as action can be taken without great cost to America's freedom or prosperity. So the essay's motive is clear. But the thesis calls out for a supporting argument: the reader needs to know not only what specific measures the writer is proposing but also how these measures can be implemented without diminishing the freedom or prosperity of American citizens.

Here are some further examples of thesis statements from actual academic essays and articles, some by students and some by professional scholars. Note how each of these makes an original claim, related to a problem, a question, or an issue. Each leaves support for later, provoking the reader to ask, "Really? Now, why should you think that, and why should I agree with you?"

> Racial caste is alive and well in America.
>
> > (Michelle Alexander, "Drug War Nightmare:
> > How We Created a Massive Racial Caste System in America")

> In today's society, [video games] consistently fulfill genuine human needs that the real world fails to satisfy. More than that, they may prove to be a key resource for solving some of our most pressing real-world problems.
>
> > (Jane McGonigal, "Be a Gamer, Save the World")

> Why is it that so many of us are obese? . . . Although answers are beginning to emerge, there can be no meaningful discussion of the subject until we resist the impulse to assign blame. Nor can we hold to the simple belief that with willpower alone, one can consciously resist the allure of food and precisely control one's weight. Instead, we must look at the facts dispassionately and uninfluenced by the numerous competing interests that drive debate on this subject.
>
> > (Jeffrey M. Friedman, "A War on Obesity, Not the Obese")

> The athletics scholarship must be abandoned in favor of institutional need-based aid. The athletics scholarship at its foundation is the biggest barrier to athletes' getting a genuine educational opportunity. When you are paid to play, regardless of the form of "payment," everything takes a back seat to athletic performance.
>
> > (John R. Gerdy, "For True Reform, Athletics Scholarships Must Go")

> Although a supporter of states' rights and the Missouri Compromise, President Franklin Pierce signed the Kansas-Nebraska bill into law because he believed that the advantages of a transcontinental railroad were worth the political price: the potential benefits to the country outweighed the anger that the repeal of the Compromise would surely provoke.   (Student writer Zach Peikon)

> Jane Tompkins's main argument is that reflecting seriously about history is a personal moral responsibility. But instead of just stating this argument, Tompkins *shows* the reader what this means and demonstrates how to do it. In the end, the

essay's meaning is to be found more in what Tompkins *does* than in what she says. It presents its "moral" more in the indirect way that films or plays or even paintings do than in the direct way that most scholarly essays do.

(Student writer Diana Taylor)

We wish to put forward a radically different structure for the salt of deoxyribose nucleic acid. This structure has two helical chains each coiled round the same axis.

(James Watson and Francis Crick,
"A Structure for Deoxyribose Nucleic Acid")

Credentialing, not educating, has become the primary business of North American universities. (Jane Jacobs, "Credentialing versus Educating")

To sum up, a thesis statement helps readers recognize an essay's purpose and point, but it also serves the needs of writers during the writing process, in that it gives them a clear sense of their argument's direction and helps them stay in control of their purpose. As you draft your working thesis for the first time, bear in mind that a good thesis has two qualities, which work in tandem:

1. It is fresh, insightful, and interesting.
2. It can be supported with evidence and strong reasoning.

These two criteria are equally necessary: a thesis should not be so "interesting" or far-fetched as to be insupportable, nor should it be supportable but obvious or trivial. Just as an argument that states only the obvious is a waste of time, so are arguments that are merely frivolous or facetious.

Drafting the Argument

As you begin drafting an argument to support your thesis, you'll need to consider the various strategies you can employ to persuade a reader that your thesis is valid. As we've noted, an argument cannot be merely a series of claims, nor can it be just a collection of facts, statistics, or quotations. An argument must combine claims and support; more exactly, it must support its claims with evidence and reasoning. In academic writing, this support is expected to be particularly strong. So let's review some of the main ways of supporting claims in order to obtain a clearer sense of those that are most appropriate to academic writing.

The Modes of Persuasion:
Ethos, Pathos, and *Logos*

The philosopher Aristotle identified three "modes" or methods by which writers (or speakers) can persuade readers (or an audience): *ethos* (credibility), *pathos* (emotion), and *logos* (logic or reasoning). That is, a writer might persuade readers by convincing them that he or she is a credible source — sincere, fair, caring, amiable, and so on. Or a writer might persuade by appealing to readers' emotions, by bringing them to tears, arousing their anger, or stirring their pride. Finally, a writer can persuade readers by appealing to reason, by explaining how the evidence forces them to reach a particular verdict, for example, or by showing that certain conclusions necessarily follow from principles on which they all agree.

In academic writing, *logos* is the most important of the three modes of persuasion. Yes, an academic essay should show that you are credible (matters like correct spelling, formatting, and grammar suggest that you are a careful writer), but readers are unlikely to be persuaded by *ethos* alone. And yes, appealing to readers' emotions might help to bring home a point or convince them that your argument really does matter (a poignant anecdote to clinch your argument in the last couple of paragraphs can be effective), but an academic essay will rarely persuade by *pathos* alone. Instead, academic arguments persuade primarily by means of *logos*, because the purpose of academic writing is not to win over the reader by any means, but to seek and offer truth. (The only test for *ethos* and *pathos* is whether they have the desired effect. But *logos*, as Aristotle recognized, obeys its own set of rules — which gave birth to the science of logic and ultimately to the scientific method.) By comparison, *ethos* and *pathos* are merely ornamental — not unwelcome, but not the stuff that forms the substance of the argument. It's worth taking a moment, then, to consider how reasoning and logic — *logos* — function in academic writing.

Types of Reasoning

As we noted earlier, an argument is different from a proof. The purpose of academic writing is rarely to *prove* something, but rather to make an argument that is as convincing as possible, given the available evidence. A good academic essay need not make an argument that is unassailably "right," but the reader should feel, by the conclusion, that there's a good chance the argument is right, that its claims are insightful and supported by strong evidence and careful reasoning.

Sound reasoning is essential to academic writing. In developing your argument, you will need to guard against errors of reasoning known as "logical fallacies." In addition, you must explain your reasoning adequately, so that the steps that lead from one claim to another will be clear to the reader. To create a persuasive argument, make sure that your evidence is valid and supports your claims and that your claims support your thesis.

The science of formal logic, concerned with the precise conditions that produce absolutely valid conclusions from premises, need not concern us in detail. (In fact, real-world arguments rarely meet the strict standards of formal logic.) But it may be helpful to distinguish between two kinds of reasoning—inductive and deductive—and to distinguish between two types of deductive reasoning—the syllogism and the enthymeme.

Deduction

Deduction is the term used for deriving a conclusion from other statements, known as **premises**. Thus, a proof can be formed by building a chain of statements, in which each statement rigorously follows from prior statements.

Syllogism   The basic tool of deductive reasoning is the syllogism. Aristotle introduced the syllogism in his *Prior Analytics* as a means of testing the validity of deductive reasoning. He defined the **syllogism** as "discourse in which, certain things being stated, something other than what is stated follows of necessity from their being so."[1] The words "of necessity" are the key here: The deduced statement does not follow because Aristotle wanted it to, or because the ancient Greeks believed in syllogisms, or because the writer finds some advantage in it. The deduced statement *must* be true if the other statements are true.

In simple terms, a syllogism contains two related premises and a conclusion. For example:

> All humans are mortal. **(MAJOR PREMISE)**
> All Greeks are humans. **(MINOR PREMISE)**
> Therefore, all Greeks are mortal. **(CONCLUSION)**

---

[1] Aristotle, "Prior Analytics," trans. A. J. Jenkinson, in Jonathan Barnes, ed., *The Complete Works of Aristotle: The Revised Oxford Translation*, Bollingen Series 71, Vol. 1 (Princeton, NJ: Princeton University Press, 1984), 39.

The subject ("Greeks") and predicate ("mortal") in the conclusion occur in the premises, and both premises also contain a third term ("humans") known as the "middle term," which does *not* occur in the conclusion. The syllogism functions like a machine for producing truths. If you have two related truths, the syllogism makes it possible to deduce a third, new truth. The next two examples are perhaps a bit more practical.

> All drinks containing caffeine affect Michela's sleep.
> Cola contains caffeine.
> Therefore, cola will affect Michela's sleep.

> All shirts with polka dots are on sale.
> All of the shirts on this rack have polka dots.
> Therefore, all of the shirts on this rack are on sale.

In real life, no one argues by means of strict syllogisms, but they show how the validity of an argument can be subjected to strict and precise analysis.

Moreover, in reality we rarely find ourselves working with universally true premises, so it is necessary to argue what is probably true, based on probable premises, rather than what's necessarily true. The point is that you should carefully examine the logic of your deductive reasoning to make sure that your conclusions follow from the premises. Your conclusions don't need to be absolutely, necessarily valid proofs, but they do need to have a high degree of probability.

Enthymeme In formal logic, one conclusion follows strictly from another, and in the process of deducing conclusions from premises, no steps may be omitted. In real-life arguments, however, we can and do omit steps, expecting readers to supply them. An **enthymeme** is an informal syllogism, in which one of the premises is missing. In practice, we're much more likely to say "Caffeinated drinks affect Michela's sleep, so cola will affect her sleep too" or "Cola contains caffeine, so it will affect Michela's sleep" than to spell out the entire syllogism. And this works perfectly well, as long as the reader will understand the missing step. So omit only those steps that you can expect the reader to understand.

Induction

Induction is the method of reasoning from a part to a whole or from particulars to a generalization. When a scientist gathers data from laboratory experiments and draws a conclusion based on that data, he or she is reasoning inductively — reasoning from particulars to a generalization. Of course, some generalizations have greater validity than others; usually, it all depends on the size of the sample on which the generalization is based. Take this statement, for example: "American cars are more reliable than European cars." Although this is a broad generalization, a study of the overall reliability of millions of American and European cars might show that it is valid (or invalid). A smaller study would only be able to *suggest* that it might be valid or invalid.

Types of Evidence

Evidence includes textual evidence, anecdotes from personal experience, statistics, expert authority, graphs and other visuals, facts, and comparisons or other analogies. Each type has its hazards as well as its strengths (see Table 5.1), and each may be more or less appropriate depending on the assignment and the context.

Table 5.1 Types of Evidence

Type of evidence	Example	Strengths	Hazards
Textual evidence (including quotations, paraphrases, and summaries)	In the end, however, Gopnik celebrates the hectic New York way of life: "Busyness is our art form, our civic ritual, our way of being us" (p. 392).	Expected if the assignment asks you to analyze or "close read" a text. Introduces evidence directly into your essay, showing the reader exactly how you drew your conclusions.	If used excessively, direct quotations can obscure the argument you are making. They must be fully integrated into the argument with analysis and commentary, as they rarely speak for themselves.
Stories or anecdotes (including personal anecdotes)	See Carr, in "Is Google Making Us Stupid?": "Over the past few years I've had an uncomfortable sense that someone, or something, has been tinkering with my brain" (p. 347).	Usually engaging, and can be moving, dramatic, powerful.	They often appeal to the emotions (*pathos*) rather than reason (*logos*). May be logically weak, as they describe particular instances rather than general truths.

Table 5.1 Types of Evidence *(continued)*

Type of evidence	Example	Strengths	Hazards
Statistics	See Foroohar: "The Pew Charitable Trusts' Economic Mobility Project has found that if you were born in 1970 in the bottom one-fifth of the socioeconomic spectrum in the U.S., you had only about a 17% chance of making it into the upper two-fifths" (p. 363).	An economical way to summarize a wealth of evidence.	Often abused. They often look compelling but on examination fail to tell the whole story (see Darrell Huff, *How to Lie with Statistics*).
Expert authority	Law professor Michelle Alexander contends that, in many ways, African Americans are doing "no better" today than when Martin Luther King Jr. was assassinated (p. 345).	Reliable sources, especially leading scholars in a particular field writing in peer-reviewed journals, provide strong evidence.	Is the source reliable? No one is beyond question. Some sources, especially Web sites, may seem more authoritative than they really are.
Visuals (including graphics that display statistical data)	See Jane McGonigal's use of a bar graph, "Game Time," in her article "Be a Gamer, Save the World" (p. 397).	Economical yet often rich.	Use only if they truly strengthen the argument, and never for decorative purposes.
Facts	See Foroohar, "Whatever Happened to Upward Mobility?": "Behavioral economics tells us that our sense of well-being is tied not to the past but to how we are doing compared with our peers. Relative mobility matters" (p. 364).	Can be difficult to dispute. At best, they are unambiguous, intelligible, clear.	Facts are often less simple and indisputable than they appear. Cite the source of any fact that is not general knowledge.
Analogies (including comparisons, metaphors, and similes)	Since fraternities have been able to give up hazing traditions, it is likely that the football team will be able to do likewise.	An analogy uses facts or conditions that the reader acknowledges to draw immediate assent to a new idea.	Must be a very close fit, or it will be confusing and ineffectual.

As noted earlier, evidence must be both valid (quotations need to be accurate, facts need to be correct, and so on) and relevant to the claim it supports. Sometimes weaker evidence can be combined with other types of evidence to produce reasonably strong support for a claim.

In college writing, the best kind of evidence is often determined by the nature of the assignment. For an assignment that asks for a close reading of one or more texts, the strongest evidence is typically the words on the page. For a research assignment that asks for a study of a local subculture, the strongest evidence might be your direct observations or the testimony of interviewees. Usually, your assignment will either clearly state or strongly hint at the kind of evidence that you are expected to use. If you are unsure, ask your instructor.

An Argument Matrix

Your notes and informal writing have supplied you with a good deal of raw material to work with. But it *is* raw. You could simply work through all this material and mark or copy out the ideas you plan to use. But the process of working out arguments to support your thesis — including identifying claims and the evidence to support those claims, and working out possible counterarguments — can be made more efficient by using a simple device called an **argument matrix**: a document with three columns, headed "Claims," "Evidence," and "Discussion."

The value of an argument matrix is that you can start in any of the three columns, but at some point you will need to enter notes in all three columns to complete the supporting argument. It reminds you to provide evidence, wherever possible, for your claims and to explain that evidence with discussion (evidence doesn't speak for itself). For example, in the "Evidence" column, you might list a quotation that you feel supports your argument well. Next, in the "Discussion" column, you might add some sentences that explain why this quotation supports your argument. Finally, after this work has clarified how the quotation works in relation to your argument, you can formulate a claim in the "Claims" column. Or you might begin with a claim that you believe to be true and then locate the evidence (a quotation or a fact) that supports the claim.

This method also helps to prevent inadvertent plagiarism, since quotations (other people's words) are clearly distinguished from discussion (your words). Be sure to identify quotations in the "Evidence" column with page numbers. Although your "Evidence" column might include many useful quotations, you don't need to

---

> **→ Guidelines**   ## Making a Three-Column Document
>
> To make a three-column document in Microsoft Word, follow these steps.
>
> - Open a new document and choose "Table" under the "Insert" menu. A dialog box will pop up. (On a Mac, choose "Insert" under the "Table" menu.)
> - In the "Number of columns" text box, type "3."
> - In the "Number of rows" text box, type "2." Click "Okay" and a table will appear in the document.
> - In the top row, type "Claims" in the left-hand column, type "Evidence" in the middle column, and type "Discussion" in the right-hand column. If you wish, select each of these words and click on the icon for centered text and the icon for boldface. Your first entry will begin in the second row.
> - You can add rows as needed: under the "Table" menu, choose "Insert" and then choose "Rows Below" on the submenu that appears.

include them all, word-for-word, in your final essay. You can write paraphrases and summaries or simply insert page numbers. (See Chapter 10's "Integrate Sources Effectively," p. 327.)

Gather material from your notes as well as from the text. Reread the text and your notes with your argument in mind, building support for your thesis.

The following example of an argument matrix is taken from an essay in progress on Nicholas Carr's "Is Google Making Us Stupid?" (p. 347).

Working thesis: that reading has changed further since e-book readers and tablets like the iPad and the Kindle were introduced.

CLAIMS	EVIDENCE	DISCUSSION
Carr was unable to foresee devices that make reading long texts easy and pleasant.	Carr's article appeared in 2008. The Kindle was introduced just a year earlier and hadn't yet had much impact, as it sold out quickly and was unavailable for several months after that. The iPad wasn't introduced until 2010.	The only e-readers Carr would have known about were pretty primitive by today's standards and couldn't offer a reading experience that compared to the reading of books. *(continued)*

CLAIMS	EVIDENCE	DISCUSSION
Technology has become our means for obtaining and reading books.	12.8 million e-readers were purchased in 2010, and as of October 2014, Apple has reportedly sold 170 million iPads (though it's impossible to know how many are used as e-readers).	It's very difficult to find reliable numbers for how many people read whole books on e-readers and tablets.
The Internet may be "remapping the neural circuitry" once again, in ways that Carr would appreciate—thus helping us to be immersed in texts, rather than the opposite.	Carr explains that our brains— "our neural circuitry"—are changed by our activities: we can gain a skill by practicing it, or lose it by not practicing it. Carr writes as if computers can only really be used for surfing of some kind. But we don't just surf on our computers: we read.	I think this brain-changing must work both ways: just as our brains adapt to surfing if computers encourage it, they can adapt to reading again if devices encourage that instead. (Maybe discuss the amazing skills of some gamers? See McGonigal.)
The medium, whether paper or screen, does affect our reading experience, but not necessarily for the worse.	E-readers and tablets are lightweight, can be held at any angle, and can be carried anywhere. They usually have an integrated dictionary, making it easy to look up words. Print size can be adjusted. E-readers like the Kindle often have anti-glare screens that resemble paper. You can easily search for a word or phrase.	Carr writes that, "thanks to the ubiquity of text on the Internet," we may be reading more, but "it's a different kind of reading, and behind it lies a different kind of thinking—perhaps even a new sense of the self" (p. 349). I'm not sure this is so true any more.

CLAIMS	EVIDENCE	DISCUSSION
Technology keeps changing, and recent developments might alleviate some of Carr's concerns.	As Carr himself acknowledges, humans are changed forever by each new technology, whether it's the invention of writing, the printing press, the Internet, or e-readers (p. 355).	There's always going to be loss as well as gain. But reading long texts seems to be making a comeback.

Anticipating and Incorporating Counterarguments

The "Claims" column is also the place to list counterarguments and your rebuttals. A counterargument is an argument that opposes your own argument. Why bring counterarguments into your essay? For two reasons: First, an intelligent reader may well be thinking already of objections to your argument, and you can put these opposing ideas to rest by preemptively responding to them. Second, by addressing counterarguments, you show that you have thoroughly considered every aspect of your argument and are hiding nothing. Anticipating and refuting counterarguments makes your own argument stronger.

Counterarguments are often addressed near the end of an essay, after the main argument has been presented, but they may be included almost anywhere. They may be introduced with phrases such as "although some might argue . . ." or "some readers might object to this argument, saying . . ." No argument should ignore potential counterarguments. At the very least, take some time during this phase of the writing process to play the role of a skeptical reader and imagine how such a reader might challenge the argument you are making. Experienced academic writers learn to play this role constantly as they work, continually seeking out the weaknesses and limitations of their own arguments and figuring out reasonable responses as they put together their claims and support.

You may think of a counterargument that you simply cannot rebut. This is no disaster: it might indicate that your thesis needs to be rethought or qualified — and at this early stage in the process, it certainly can be. If you've drafted a working

⊙ Try This   Developing Arguments

This activity provides an opportunity to practice developing arguments.

Step 1. Choose one of the propositions from the list below and work out an argument for it, based on your own experience, beliefs, and general knowledge. (If time allows, you may choose to conduct research in the library or on the Internet, but research is not required.) As you develop arguments, write out your claims in full sentences, and spell out the support for each claim as fully as you can. Use a three-column argument matrix (p. 124).

Step 2. Trade your work with a classmate. Examine your classmate's argument carefully. Look for places where, in your estimation, your classmate has presented the arguments fully and persuasively, as well as places where the argument needs more development.

Step 3. Look over your classmate's comments on your own work. How might you strengthen your argument by explicating the ideas more fully? With your classmate's help, develop and strengthen your original argument.

Step 4. Work out counterarguments and then address them. Identify two or three unanswered questions or problems that remain.

- Video games do [or do not] have real educational value.
- Americans are [or are not] becoming too materialistic.
- Smoking tobacco should [or should not] be illegal.
- Taxpayer dollars, through government grants, should [or should not] be used to support the arts.
- Physical education classes, three times a week, should [or should not] be a required element in the curriculum throughout grade school, middle school, and high school.
- The United States should [or should not] dismantle all its nuclear weapons, unilaterally.
- Gay men and women should [or should not] have the right to legal marriage in all fifty states.
- Owners of SUVs should [or should not] have to pay a special "gas guzzler" tax.

thesis with the assumption that you'll revise it anyway, you will be less reluctant to shift direction. Often, however, an irrefutable counterargument is not so strong that it requires a total revision of the thesis; it just means that one or more unanswered questions remain. In such a case, don't suppress the question: acknowledge it, and show how it might suggest a direction for further research.

In your argument matrix, identify counterclaims clearly as such in the left-hand column. Your discussion notes for each counterclaim should be a refutation of the claim.

Drafting Paragraphs

Now that you have some claims, evidence, and discussion, you are ready to begin drafting paragraphs. Think of each major paragraph in the body of your essay as making a little argument of its own, beginning with a claim and developing the evidence and discussion that support the claim. (The introductory paragraph works a little differently, as it normally serves to present the purpose of your essay and your thesis statement.) The final shape, number, and arrangement of these paragraphs will change as your work progresses, but it's helpful to put together at least three or four paragraphs as soon as you can so that you have a skeletal structure to build on.

Drafting Introductory Paragraphs

In an argument essay, the introductory paragraph (or paragraphs) serves chiefly to introduce the reader to the essay's purpose. In general, the purpose of an argument essay should be clear by the second or third paragraph. Few readers have the patience to read much further without a sense of where the essay is going.

The introductory paragraph needs to do more than just present the thesis. As we noted, a good thesis offers the solution to a problem, the answer to a question, or a stand on an issue. Moreover, the writer must demonstrate that the problem is real and, if it's not obvious, that it matters because it produces some sort of error or cost. This is the argument's motive. Explaining the motive could require several paragraphs, so your solution — your thesis statement — might not appear until the second, third, or even fourth paragraph. However, in an argument essay, it is usually wise to present the thesis promptly once the motive is clear; delaying it may lead the reader to wonder whether you have anything to contribute.

Consider the following example of how an argument's motive might be presented. The bare thesis statement in this case is "the federal government must develop a more complex method of calculating wealth, one that accounts for local differences in the cost of living." In itself, this doesn't mean much. But an introductory phrase (shown underlined) can be added that positions it as the solution to a problem.

> In order to obtain an accurate count of the number of Americans who live in poverty, the federal government must develop a more complex method of calculating wealth, one that accounts for local differences in the cost of living.

The problem is that government researchers lack an accurate count of the number of Americans who live in poverty. Adding the introductory phrase is an improvement over the bare thesis, of course, because the phrase explains *why* the government should develop better methods of calculating wealth. But it still doesn't explain why solving this particular problem is important. An additional sentence (shown underlined) following the thesis can help.

> In order to obtain an accurate count of the number of Americans who live in poverty, the federal government must develop a more complex method of calculating wealth, one that accounts for local differences in the cost of living. Only when more precise estimates of the number of Americans in need of federal help become available will it become possible to spend taxpayers' money wisely and effectively.

This more complete account of the problem shows that it also entails a *cost* and that the solution confers a benefit. In this case, providing this information can be done simply by indicating that without an accurate count of the number of Americans living in poverty, it's impossible to spend taxpayers' money wisely and effectively. For some arguments, though, you'll need to write more than one or two sentences: if the problem, its costs, and the solution's benefits are not obvious, and if they require a paragraph or more of explanation, be prepared to supply it.

In certain situations, you might need to go even further and relate the narrower problem explicitly to the broader work of the discipline as a whole. Again, the example is underlined.

> In order to obtain an accurate count of the number of Americans who live in poverty, the federal government must develop a more complex method of

→ **Try This**   **Examining the Problem and Solution**

Examine Emily Esfahani Smith's "Life on the Island" (p. 399) carefully, looking for statements that discuss the problem she is addressing. Is it a practical problem or a knowledge problem? What does she suggest, explicitly or implicitly, about the cost or costs of the problem? What solution does she propose, and what is its value or benefit?

calculating wealth, one that accounts for local differences in the cost of living. Only when more precise estimates of the number of Americans in need of federal help become available will it become possible to spend taxpayers' money wisely and effectively. Economists have suggested several alternatives to the method currently in use, but so far none have been considered politically acceptable.

Whether such additional detail is needed depends on the audience and the assignment. In an essay for an economics course, for example, such a statement might not be necessary because any professional economist could be expected to know this; thus you can leave some aspects of the motive unstated and implied. If you are confident that the reader shares your concern with the problem under discussion, you might not need to provide an explicit link between the problem and the aims of the discipline as a whole.

Argument essays sometimes begin with a story or description of a representative case that paints a vivid picture of the problem. A paragraph or two of this kind of narrative can be especially effective because readers will almost always read to the end of a story, simply to find out how it ends.

Drafting Body Paragraphs

When writing a first draft, we tend to leave the claim until late in the paragraph, perhaps even the last sentence, because we develop clarity about what we want to say only gradually, through the process of writing it out. We will begin with some detail that stands out for us, make connections to other details, figure out how it all adds up, and finally state what it means for the main argument as a way of wrapping up. Then we move on to a new paragraph.

Such a process is quite normal in the early writerly stages. But a paragraph organized in this way makes heavy demands on readers, because it reveals the actual *point* so very late. Readers must hold a mass of perplexing details in their heads for several sentences — until finally at the end of the paragraph the point becomes clear. Some readers may get annoyed; some may lose patience and stop reading altogether.

As you draft the body paragraphs of your essay, bear in mind that the first sentence sets the direction. If the reader gets a clear sense of a paragraph's theme from the first sentence, and if the rest of the paragraph keeps to the theme, even as it develops and elaborates it, then your reader will feel that the paragraph has **unity**.

Readers need to find a **topic sentence** — a sentence that declares the paragraph's main concern, theme, or point — at the beginning of the paragraph so that they understand its purpose from the outset and do not have to puzzle through information that lacks any clear purpose. In fact, this need to find the paragraph's main point is so powerful that the first sentence tends to function as the paragraph's topic sentence *whether it is meant to or not.* So, since your reader will assume that your first sentence signals the topic of the whole paragraph, your task is to make sure that it does so as clearly and precisely as possible.

However, an argument essay is not composed of a series of topics. As we've seen, an argument is made up of claims and support for those claims. So in an argument essay, the purpose of most paragraphs will be to present a claim and to support it. The claim really governs the paragraph, as everything else in the paragraph should support it. At least initially, placing your claim in the first sentence is a safe strategy: your point will be clear from the outset.

You can then develop the support for this claim in the rest of the paragraph. Present it fully, laying out the evidence and explaining in detail how the evidence supports the claim. As writers, we tend to assume that readers will understand how a piece of evidence supports a claim — for us, it's perfectly obvious — but to any reader who is new to your ideas or has a different point of view, the relation may not be obvious at all. Spell it out. Evidence — whether it's data, a quotation, or an observation — rarely speaks for itself; it almost always needs to be explained. The "Discussion" column in your argument matrix should give you some words and phrases to begin developing this explanation.

If the point you want to make is complicated and the paragraph must be long, you can strengthen the paragraph's unity by incorporating words or phrases into later sentences that link back to the main topic or theme, thereby showing how these sentences relate to it. Repeating the exact same word frequently will create a sense of tedium, but words and phrases that are related but not identical, that work as variations on a theme, can forge connections and develop your point at the same time.

Here is a paragraph from Nicholas Carr's "Is Google Making Us Stupid?" (p. 347). The first word, "Reading," lets the reader know the paragraph's main theme. Earlier in the essay, Carr discusses the effect of the Internet on brain function, and in the paragraph just before this one he introduces the idea that the Internet may be eroding our ability to read. Here he explains how different ways of reading require different neural circuits. We will examine this paragraph more closely later in this chapter (p. 143), but for now, notice how variations on the theme of reading help tie the paragraph together.

> Reading, explains Wolf, is not an instinctive skill for human beings. It's not etched into our genes the way speech is. We have to teach our minds how to translate the symbolic characters we see into the language we understand. And the media or other technologies we use in learning and practicing the craft of reading play an important part in shaping the neural circuits inside our brains. Experiments demonstrate that readers of ideograms, such as the Chinese, develop a mental circuitry for reading that is very different from the circuitry found in those of us whose written language employs an alphabet. The variations extend across many regions of the brain, including those that govern such essential cognitive functions as memory and the interpretation of visual and auditory stimuli. We can expect as well that the circuits woven by our use of the Net will be different from those woven by our reading of books and other printed works. (p. 350)

Drafting Concluding Paragraphs

At this stage, a concluding paragraph is not really necessary; you can leave it for the revision stage, when your argument is already solid enough that you can step back and reflect on it. At this point, it's enough to say that a conclusion should not repeat points that you have already made clear. Rather than closing off the essay, the conclusion should really open it up, giving the reader a sense of its importance and its broader implications or suggesting directions for further research or questions that remain unanswered. The conclusion should give the reader something to think about, a send-off rather than a wrap-up.

Revising: A Recursive Process

Perhaps owing to the pressure of deadlines, some student writers revise their writing only slightly before submitting it. But failing to revise — or failing to allow enough time to revise — is to miss the opportunity for thinking and learning that writing assignments offer, and almost certainly it means submitting work that misrepresents your real abilities.

Revising is not the same as editing or proofreading. The word "revise" — from the Latin *revisere*, "to look at again" — means to *see* your work *again*. When you revise, you don't just clean up your writing or correct it; you step back from it, identify its strengths and weaknesses, and then do whatever's necessary to improve it — cut, add, rewrite, rearrange, rethink, even start again.

In a sense, writing *is* revision. You began your work with notes in the margins of a text as you read and reread; you developed some of these impressions into phrases and sentences in a notebook; you further developed some of these ideas in your informal, writerly explorations. Finally, as an argument emerged, you began to focus on a thesis, and you developed some paragraphs for a first draft of your essay. At every stage, you *revised* — reconsidered, selected, expanded, developed — some sort of writing that already existed. (You could even call your first reading of a text a kind of revision — a "re-seeing" of the author's point of view by bringing your own point of view to bear on it.) Selecting, rethinking, and rewriting have been essential to the process.

Susan Sontag, one of America's most highly regarded essayists, remarked:

> I don't write easily or rapidly. My first draft usually has only a few elements worth keeping. I have to find out what those are and build from them and throw out what doesn't work, or what is simply not alive. So there is a process of rewriting, of accumulation.[2]

Although her published essays seem spontaneous and confident, Sontag suggests that a great part of her work involves discerning what's worth keeping and what must be cut. We naturally become attached to passages that took a lot of time and effort, and it takes backbone to cut such passages. But cut we must. A careful reader (perhaps a fellow student, a tutor, or a professor) can help identify what should be kept and what needs to go. (Most writers rely on such readers at some stage

---

[2] Charles Ruas, *Conversations with American Writers* (New York: Knopf, 1985), 186.

in the writing process.) But an awareness of what to keep and what to cut also comes from a growing sense of the whole argument that emerges during the revision process.

Rethinking, rewriting, cutting, and rearranging are essential elements in the writing process. They're the way that a writer moves from a messy, informal draft that was never meant to be read by someone else to a clear, persuasive, eloquent, and pleasing final product. Thus, even when we feel ready to move to the next stage in the writing process, we frequently find ourselves circling back to an earlier stage. Perhaps we need to reread a passage and take more notes in order to improve a paragraph that analyzes the text. Or we need to do some more informal writing so that we can figure out more clearly how a certain part of our argument works (it hadn't seemed so important at first, but now it's obviously crucial). And we'll have to revise our thesis statement to reflect this change, and maybe write two more paragraphs to explain it, and so on. So we need to modify our workflow diagram: writers don't move steadily from one phase of the writing process to the next, without ever looking back — they keep circling back through the phases until they get it right. The process looks more like Figure 5.2 below — though even this may be an oversimplification, as any phase can lead back to any other phase at any point.

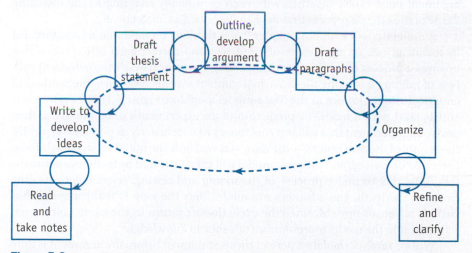

Figure 5.2 **Workflow Revision**

Revising Your Thesis Statement

The process of developing an argument is recursive because an argument evolves as its elements become clearer — as claims and support become articulated in full sentences, as the relation between claims and support and between the various claims themselves begins to emerge distinctly on the page. And as the argument emerges, it becomes possible to shape the thesis statement into a more perfect expression of the argument's central idea. Perfecting the thesis statement, in turn, makes it possible to refine the argument with greater clarity and confidence. A strong argument emerges only by cycling through the process several times. In essence, you must constantly move between the argument in progress and the evidence in order to check, refine, and strengthen your argument.

Inexperienced writers, especially when under the pressure of a deadline, sometimes write out a thesis statement in a first draft and never bother to go back and revise or sharpen it. The result is usually disappointing: either the actual argument doesn't fit the thesis statement very well, in which case the reader can only be confused about the essay's purpose, or the argument gets molded to fit the thesis, no matter what the facts actually show, in which case the reader can only be left feeling unconvinced. But ideas evolve as the writing happens, and both the thesis and the argument must evolve together, with each continually adapting to the changing shape of the other, a process that may be described as "dialectical."

A **dialectic**, as we said in Chapter 2, is a thinking method that moves forward by means of two or more elements that test and correct each other. Often this involves a process of exposing and correcting errors or flaws. This dialectical process of refining a working thesis as an argument evolves resembles the method of empirical science known as the "data-model loop" (see Figure 5.3). Laboratory scientists start with a model or prediction of an experiment's outcome. Next, they devise an experiment that will test this theory as conclusively as possible. Typically, the results of the experiment — the data — reveal how the initial model needs to be corrected or revised, and this new model will then be tested by further experimentation. By this recursive process of theorizing and testing, science gets steadily closer to the truth, and advances are made. Thus the loop is really a spiral that steadily advances upward, since the cycle doesn't return to the same point; each refinement in the model represents an advance in knowledge.

Writers rarely formulate a perfect thesis statement before the argument is fully formed because they seldom have a crystal-clear sense of the entire argument when they first sit down to write. Clarity emerges through the activity of writing and

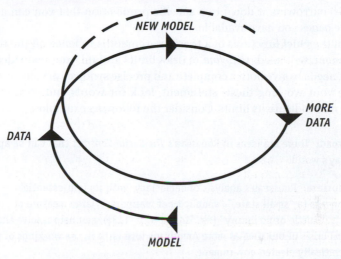

Figure 5.3 The Data-Model Loop

rewriting. A working thesis and an evolving argument have a dialectical relation: as the argument emerges more clearly, it requires corrections in the working thesis, but a clearer and more precise thesis also makes a stronger argument possible. As you develop your argument, expect to revise your thesis several times as your ideas become clearer through the writing process.

Limiting Your Thesis

Earlier in this chapter (p. 118), we identified two criteria for a good thesis: it is fresh, insightful, and interesting; and it can be supported with evidence and strong reasoning. The second of these criteria means that the **scope** of the thesis must be appropriate for the assignment. That is, if the thesis is making a claim that's too broad to argue within the assignment's page limit, you don't have much hope of persuading your reader. For professional researchers, it makes sense to limit the scope of the problem they are working on; the more limited the scope, the better the chances of solving the problem and making a genuine contribution. Likewise, you should narrow your thesis to make it more manageable. Student essays are usually between five and twenty pages. If your thesis is too broad or too ambitious, you won't be able to support it in such a confined space. So it usually helps to limit your thesis, narrowing it down to a specific proposition that you can adequately treat in the pages you have available.

One of the chief functions of a thesis statement is to fence off the territory of your argument, so it needs to *define*, or draw limits around, your main idea. A thesis statement needs to give both a complete and precise synopsis of your argument. As you revise your working thesis statement, look for words and phrases that will sharpen it and indicate its limits. Consider the following examples:

Too broad: There are ideas in Rousseau's *The Social Contract* that can be applied to today's world.

Appropriate: Rousseau's analysis of democracy, with its four essential components (a "small state," "simplicity of manners," "large measure of equality," "little or no luxury" [bk. III, ch. 4, p. 113]), can help resolve the political crisis of our time as more Americans lose faith in the workings of a democratically elected government.

(Student writer Ben Dauksewicz)

Too broad: President Franklin Pierce signed the Kansas-Nebraska Act because he thought it was the best thing for the country.

Appropriate: Although a supporter of states' rights and the Missouri Compromise, President Franklin Pierce signed the Kansas-Nebraska Act into law because he believed that the advantages of a transcontinental railroad were worth the political price: the potential benefits to the country outweighed the anger that the repeal of the Compromise would surely provoke.

(Student writer Zach Peikon)

Too broad: The minimum wage should be increased.

Appropriate: The minimum wage should be raised to a level at which workers can cope with the rising cost of living in each state as determined by the Consumer Price Index (CPI), which "is a measure of the overall cost of the goods and services bought by a typical consumer." Each of the fifty states should be required by a federal mandate to have their own minimum wage based on the average cost of living in each respective state.

(Student writer Tao Lin Pao)

Hedging

Some argument essays are polemic (from the Greek word *polemos*, meaning "war"): their purpose is to defeat a real or imagined opponent, so they state their claims as strongly as possible. But defeating an opponent is rarely the purpose of academic writing; rather, the goal is to get as close to the truth as possible. As a result, academic writers are typically cautious, and they often qualify their claims with words or phrases such as "probably," "perhaps," "possibly," "may," "might," "in most cases," or "could be considered." These are called *hedge words*. Their purpose is not to weaken the argument or to make it wishy-washy. Rather, such words enable writers to convey their degree of certainty. If you present an idea as a possibility rather than a certainty, readers will take you no less seriously; indeed, when you refuse to overstate your claims, you are more likely to be received as a careful and responsible thinker.

But "hedging" is not merely a matter of using qualifiers. It is also a matter of providing an accurate assessment of the strength of the evidence, not only in the thesis statement but throughout the essay. In the following passage, the animal scientist Temple Grandin argues that certain dog breeds are more aggressive than others. Notice how she carefully hedges her claim — not just with hedge words and phrases, but with a frank account of the evidence that makes it impossible to offer more than an educated guess about this matter.

> The genetics of aggression is an especially thorny issue with dogs. Most people don't want to believe that there are some breeds, like pit bulls and Rottweilers, that are more aggressive by nature. (Pit bulls aren't an established AKC [American Kennel Club] breed.) Usually these folks have known or owned individual Rotties or pits who were sweet and good-natured, so they conclude that when a Rottweiler or a pit bull shows aggression the problem is the owner not the dog. But the statistics don't support this interpretation, although it's true that statistics on dog bites aren't hard and fast.
>
> There are lots of problems with dog bite reports. For one thing, there are a few different kinds of dogs that are called pit bulls, including some purebreds like the American Staffordshire terrier and some mixed-breed dogs. Another problem: large dogs do more damage when they bite people, so they're probably overrepresented in the statistics. Also, lots of purebred owners fail to register their dogs with the AKC, so it's impossible to know exactly how many purebred Rottweilers there are in the country and compare that figure to the number of reported dog bites committed by Rottweilers.

Because dog population data is imprecise, no one can nail down *exactly* what each breed's "aggression quotient" is compared to other breeds. Still, you can get an overall picture of which breeds are most dangerous by looking at medical reports of dog bites. *On average*, Rottweilers and pit bulls are so much more aggressive than other breeds that it's extremely unlikely bad owners alone could account for the higher rate of biting. And if you're looking only at anecdotal evidence, there are plenty of cases of nice, competent owners with vicious Rottweilers or pit bulls. Aggression isn't always the owner's fault. Writing about pit bulls, Nick Dodman says, "Originally bred for aggression and tenacity, pit bulls, if provoked, will bite hard and hang on, making them as potentially dangerous as a handgun without a safety lock.... [T]hey can become quite civilized, developing into loyal and entertaining companions. But the *potential* for trouble is always lurking somewhere, as a result of their genes and breeding."[3]

Grandin is speculating here, but speculation is perfectly valid as long as it is presented *as* speculation, and not as near certainty. The purpose of the hedging in this passage is to establish a just relation between the nature of the evidence and the strength of the claim. This hedging is an important part of what it means to be a responsible writer: to overstate or understate, whether deliberately or carelessly, is to engage in a kind of deception, and in academic writing especially, such deception is to be scrupulously avoided.

Revising Paragraphs

When we discussed drafting body paragraphs, we said that the first sentence sets the paragraph's direction and that normally body paragraphs should open with a claim, followed by the supporting evidence and reasoning. But not *every* paragraph has to be structured in exactly the same way; in fact, some variety helps prevent monotony and lets you accommodate exceptional situations (for example, paragraphs that tell a story or raise a question rather than make an argument).

Now that you have drafted a few paragraphs, we can complicate things a bit and distinguish three separate functions that the opening of a paragraph should fulfill: transition, topic, and claim. Recognizing these three functions makes it possible to try different ways of structuring paragraphs while still keeping the argument clear and strong.

---

[3] Temple Grandin and Catherine Johnson, *Animals in Translation: Using the Mysteries of Autism to Decode Animal Behavior* (New York: Harcourt/Harvest, 2006), 148–49.

Transition

A transition guides the reader from the previous topic to the topic of the new paragraph. Transitions can be a word ("moreover," "however," "furthermore," "nevertheless"), a phrase ("in contrast," "in addition," "for example"), or a whole sentence ("Now that we have considered the historical record, let's look at the situation in America today"). Of course, transitions can be used between sentences and clauses as well, but they are often especially helpful when the reader moves from one unit of the argument to a new one — which typically involves moving from one paragraph to another. Transitions give the reader a sense of the relation between this new paragraph and the previous one, whether it be one of contrast, addition, or something else. Avoid using transition words and phrases mechanically or thoughtlessly. A transition is not *always* necessary, but it is often helpful. Think like a reader and use your best judgment. As a rule, make your transitions no longer than necessary; you want to keep the argument moving.

Topic

As we suggested earlier, a topic and a claim are not the same thing. The topic is the general subject of a paragraph, while the claim is the *point* you want to make, the paragraph's real purpose. The first sentence of the paragraph *must* give readers a clear sense of the *topic*; this opening sentence is the chief means by which a paragraph coheres. But as long as the topic is clear, the claim can be moved elsewhere in the paragraph.

Claim

While placing the claim in the first sentence generally works well, it is not absolutely necessary. As long as the paragraph's first sentence clearly states the topic, the claim *can* appear later in the paragraph. It can appear in the second sentence or at the end of the paragraph — both prominent positions. Occasionally, the claim might appear elsewhere. Moreover, the claim can be split between two sentences. For example, it might be stated in general terms at the beginning of the paragraph (to make the main point clear) and in more precise terms later on. Or it can be stated in part early in the paragraph and in part later on.

The main thing to avoid is burying the claim in other material, where it might be overlooked.

In a longer essay, variations in paragraph structure help prevent monotony and predictability. But if there's any possibility of confusion, remember that the point of the paragraph is usually clearest if the claim appears early. To sum up:

- The topic *must* occur in the first sentence.
- The claim may occur in the first, the second, or even the last sentence.
- The claim may be split between two sentences.

It is useful to recall these structural principles as you *revise* a thesis-driven essay because when you draft ideas, there is a natural tendency to begin a paragraph with evidence and end it with a claim. This occurs because we gain clarity as we write: usually we need to work through the evidence before we can be sure what our claim *is* — that is, what claim is truly justified by the evidence and what words best express our claim. Therefore, to work well as readerly arguments, writerly drafts often need to be reorganized: the thesis has to be moved from the last paragraph to the first, perhaps, and claims need to be repositioned at the beginning of paragraphs instead of the end.

Strengthening Paragraph Cohesion

The first requirement of revision is to shift perspective and think like a reader. There are two ways of looking at a paragraph: a bird's-eye view and a globe-trotter's view. As writers we can take the bird's-eye view, looking, as if from above, at the whole paragraph spread out like a map — the topic sentence at the top, supporting material beneath, perhaps a closing sentence at the bottom. But readers do not experience paragraphs this way. They're more like hikers moving through a landscape, or sailors navigating a sea dotted with islands. They encounter one sentence at a time and must work to make sense of each in relation to previous sentences and paragraphs. They don't know what lurks over the horizon, and the horizon changes constantly as they move through the text. A bird's-eye view can be helpful when we position the main elements of a paragraph — topic, claim, support — but we need to imagine the globe-trotter's view to make the paragraph fully clear and coherent.

As we discussed earlier in "Drafting Body Paragraphs" (p. 131), revising a paragraph often means locating the claim and moving it to the beginning of the paragraph. But shaping a paragraph into a coherent unit within your argument may require a little more work. To start with, a draft paragraph that is trying to make more than one claim and address more than one topic may need to be split into two or even three paragraphs. But even after you've revised a paragraph so that it focuses on a single important claim and has unity, you may still be able to strengthen its **cohesion**, the way it *feels like* it holds together for the reader.

Let's look again at that paragraph about reading from Nicholas Carr's "Is Google Making Us Stupid?" (p. 347). We observed earlier that the focus of the paragraph is "reading," and Carr uses variations of that term and related terms to keep this focus in the foreground throughout ("translate the symbolic characters," "the craft of reading," "readers of ideograms," "reading of books," and so on). But there's another theme at work in the paragraph, which we might call "brain functioning." In the copy below, terms related to this theme are underlined.

> Reading, explains Wolf, is not an instinctive skill for human beings. It's not etched into our genes the way speech is. We have to teach our minds how to translate the symbolic characters we see into the language we understand. And the media or other technologies we use in learning and practicing the craft of reading play an important part in shaping the neural circuits inside our brains. Experiments demonstrate that readers of ideograms, such as the Chinese, develop a mental circuitry for reading that is very different from the circuitry found in those of us whose written language employs an alphabet. The variations extend across many regions of the brain, including those that govern such essential cognitive functions as memory and the interpretation of visual and auditory stimuli. We can expect as well that the circuits woven by our use of the Net will be different from those woven by our reading of books and other printed works. (p. 350)

While brain functioning is a theme here, along with reading, it is not a *new* theme in the way that reading is. Carr has discussed reading before in the essay, but never in such a detailed, focused way. Brain functioning, however, has been a theme from the outset, so we could call it a "given" theme rather than a new one, since the reader is already familiar with it. Most paragraphs work this way: there's a given theme, one that has already appeared, and a new theme, one that gives a particular paragraph its special purpose. The writer needs to show the reader how the new relates to the given, and it helps if this connection is made early in the paragraph. Here, Carr makes the connection in the third sentence, but the first two sentences are short, so the reader can manage. And each sentence that follows contains terms that make a clear connection between the new and the given. This repetition of the given theme also helps the reader understand Carr's point about the complicated and varied ways in which the brain processes writing. The repetition of terms relating to the new theme and of terms related to the given theme helps to give the paragraph cohesion and a clear sense of purpose.

Varying Paragraph Length

Paragraphs are sometimes described as the building blocks of the essay. The word "block" suggests unity and cohesion, qualities that paragraphs do need to have. But building blocks are usually alike in shape and size, and the analogy suggests a sameness that could lead to a plodding, repetitive structure. The architectural metaphor we introduced in the opening of this chapter, that of rooms in a well-planned home, might be more useful. Each room is distinct — kitchen, living room, dining room, bedrooms — and each serves a particular purpose. And ideally each room has been designed and furnished to be both functional and pleasing.

If you were to tour such a home, you'd find transitions between rooms — doors and hallways that connect them — and each room would fulfill a particular function. Paragraphs work rather like rooms: each should have its own purpose, but each should contribute to the whole. While paragraphs should cohere, they can be almost any length (though probably not much more than a page); they need not be uniform. A paragraph break marks a pause and gives readers a sense of where one unit of the argument ends and another begins. Since readers usually see the length of a paragraph (perhaps unconsciously, out of the corner of their eyes) before they read any actual words, they know whether to brace themselves for a long trek or whether to relax a little. You can experiment with paragraph breaks, creating shorter or longer paragraphs to suit your argument's needs.

In modern academic writing, paragraphs are usually less than a page in length. It's rare, however, to find many short paragraphs (of, say, less than four lines) in a row. A typical paragraph would be roughly ten to twenty lines in length. But there will be variety. Short paragraphs are sometimes needed; for example, a brief transitional paragraph might sum up all that's been established so far and hint at where the argument will go next.

And sometimes short paragraphs can simply underscore a point.

Concluding Paragraphs

In the body of the essay, you've been taking your reader through a forest of details. But by the conclusion, it may have become difficult, as the saying goes, to see the forest for the trees. Here, you may need to speak to the reader about the forest, the big picture: why all this matters and what it means. As we said earlier, a concluding paragraph should never be redundant and should never merely restate an argument that should already have been made clear. Instead, it should offer *summation*, not summary—a more distant perspective, not repetition. A good conclusion answers the question "So what?" or "What now?" or "Where do we go from here?" or "What else must we consider in connection with this problem?"

So while the concluding paragraph brings the essay to a close, the closure need not be airtight. The most effective closings resonate, leaving the reader with something to think about. The concluding paragraph is often the place to point out questions that remain unanswered or to suggest directions for further research. (You might choose to end the essay with a question.) In this sense, the conclusion is less an ending than a send-off: you are passing the baton to the reader now, to go out and act or reflect or investigate further, as the case may be.

If the rest of the essay has done its job and made a strong case for your thesis, then you might choose to close with a gentle tug at the reader's heartstrings, especially if you feel that action or assent is urgently needed. Earlier in this chapter, we discussed Aristotle's concepts of *logos, ethos,* and *pathos* and noted that in an academic essay *pathos*—an appeal to the emotions—typically takes a backseat to *logos*—an appeal to reason. But the concluding paragraph can be the right place for a little *pathos*. For example, if your opening paragraph describes a problem and its costs, your concluding paragraph might return to the subject of these costs, reminding the reader of the reasons that it is important to address the problem as soon as possible.

✅ Checklist for Developing an Argument

Keep the following in mind as you develop your argument.

- ☐ The argument
  - The argument needs to have a motive. It should respond to a need, such as a problem, a question, or an issue.

- The argument must make a claim. It needs to offer a solution, suggest an answer, or take a stand.
- The argument has to support its claim(s) with evidence and reasoning that are both valid and relevant. The type of evidence should be appropriate for the particular assignment.

☐ The thesis statement
- The thesis statement functions as the "master claim" of the essay.
- It should be fresh, insightful, and interesting.
- It can be supported with evidence and reasoning.
- It may be revised as your argument develops. You can limit and "hedge" the thesis statement as necessary.

☐ Paragraphs
- The introductory paragraph(s) should present the essay's motive and thesis.
- Each body paragraph should usually begin with a claim; support for the claim should fill out the rest of the paragraph. However, if the first sentence makes the topic of the paragraph clear, you can position the claim elsewhere in the paragraph. But avoid burying the claim in a place where it might be overlooked.
- Where necessary, begin paragraphs with transition words, phrases, or sentences. Think like a reader!
- Address counterarguments in one or more paragraphs.
- Vary the length of paragraphs.
- The concluding paragraph should offer a "send-off."

chapter 6

Organizing the Essay

Thinking Like a Reader

If you have drafted and perhaps revised an introductory paragraph, some body paragraphs, and a concluding paragraph, you already have the beginnings of an organizational plan for your essay. But at this point it is a good idea to spend some time refining the organization to give your ideas the most effective arrangement possible. (See the workflow charts on pp. 114 and 135.)

> " It's part of my feeling that what a writer does is to try to make sense of life. I think that's what writing is.... It's seeking that thread of order and logic in the disorder, and the incredible waste and marvelous profligate character of life. What all artists are trying to do is to make sense of life. "
>
> **NADINE GORDIMER**

Organization is most apparent to a reader when it is lacking; good organization is transparent. The reader of a well-organized essay simply proceeds steadily through the argument, admiring how one thought flows smoothly and logically into another and how every question seems to be answered as soon as it arises. The sequence of ideas seems natural, inevitable, even obvious. On occasion, writers achieve this sense of easy flow without effort: the order in which the ideas spilled out onto the page turns out to be the right and best order. But most of the time, writers must give careful thought to the best way to arrange ideas and organize paragraphs. They must work hard to make the organization seem natural and inevitable.

No two essays are organized exactly alike, and no simple formula exists for organizing an essay, because if the writer has anything new to say, the essay will be unique. Organization should be organic in the sense that it should suit the particular subject matter, serve the writer's purpose, and meet the needs of the occasion. (The word "organize," from the Greek word *organon*, meaning "a tool of thought," suggests not just an orderly structure but one that suits its purpose.) So organizing an essay requires some craftsmanship; arguments cannot simply be squeezed into a one-size-fits-all mold, such as the five-paragraph essay format you may have learned in high school or middle school. This format may function well as training wheels — for learning basic principles of argument and paragraph structure — but it lacks the necessary flexibility for the more complicated arguments that college instructors expect. Professional scholars and writers do not employ the five-paragraph format because their ideas can almost never be distilled into just three body paragraphs. Every argument must take its own particular shape, filling as many paragraphs as it requires. The number depends on the nature of the argument.

Organizing your essay is not just a question of arranging ideas; it's also a matter of revealing that arrangement to your reader. So let's first consider some key principles of organization. Following that, we'll consider some strategies for organizing essays, especially longer and more complex ones.

Organizing an Argument Essay

A well-crafted essay follows certain basic principles of organization. These are *principles* rather than rules because variations are certainly permissible (and sometimes advisable, as we shall see later). But even when straying from them, be sure to keep these principles in mind.

Keep Your Own Argument in the Foreground

The first principle of essay organization is to keep the argument in the foreground; that is, make the argument clear at the outset and keep it prominent throughout the essay. Here are some techniques (again, these are not rigid rules).

Place a Well-Crafted Thesis Statement Near the Beginning of the Essay — Usually toward the End of the Introduction. This is where readers expect to find the thesis statement, because the purpose of an introductory paragraph (or paragraphs) is usually to explain the essay's purpose and set the stage for the argument that follows. You may state your thesis again, in different words and perhaps in greater detail, at the end of the essay; however, postponing it entirely could be disastrous if it forces your reader to struggle through the entire essay without grasping your purpose.

Place the Topic and the Claim at the Beginning of the Paragraph. (See Chapter 5, pp. 131–32, for a discussion of the placement of topics and claims.) The first one or two sentences tend to govern the paragraph as a whole because readers expect sentences to indicate the paragraph's topic and to contain the claim. If the paragraph ends up being about something unrelated to the first couple of sentences, readers may become confused. Since complex arguments often require complex supporting evidence — data, reasoning, quotations, claims that support other claims, and so on — readers can easily lose sight of the main point while working through all the details. Placing the claim at the beginning of the paragraph (in the first or second sentence) establishes its importance and shows that the matter that follows is its support.

Create Links between Claims and the Thesis. Use key words and phrases that link back to your thesis statement to show how new arguments connect to the essay's main purpose. Do this thoughtfully and creatively, however, to avoid a tiresome repetition of the same words and phrases throughout. To give yourself a variety of terms and phrases to choose from, take a few minutes to list five or six different ways of expressing your main point. These need not be full sentences; you need just a small storehouse of words and phrases for you to draw from as you revise.

For example, a student writer of an essay arguing that human rights should not be extended to the great apes listed the following connected terms and phrases:

- rights, privileges, entitlements, protections
- recognize, enshrine, preserve, respect
- human being, person, animal, nonhuman animal, primate, ape, great ape
- difference, distinction, contrast

In the end, the writer did not use all these words, but having them on hand made it easier to forge varied and appropriate links between claim sentences and the main argument.

Separate Out Claims and Develop Each Argument Fully

An expository essay (one that explains an idea or makes an argument) must lay out a line of thinking in a systematic and reasonably complete way, making it possible for the reader to weigh the ideas fairly. It *exposes* the whole argument to the reader's view. A common weakness in such essays is a failure to explicate the argument thoroughly, to spell out the component parts and support each one adequately. (The problem, of course, is that the writer is already so familiar with the argument that he or she forgets to explain crucial elements in it.) A good argument essay does not merely state the thesis and the main claims; it also provides evidence for the claims, reasons out the argument, and considers its implications. It addresses as many sides of the issue as possible.

Avoid clumping arguments together or passing over key elements so swiftly that one argument hides behind another. When we first begin to organize an argument in our minds, we need to cluster ideas, chiefly to give us a sense of how the pieces fit together into a whole. But after getting a sense of the argument's main parts, we usually need to shift focus to how each of these component parts will become a fully developed **stage** or "chunk" of the essay — a paragraph or a group of paragraphs on closely related topics (sometimes called a **stadium**; the plural is "stadia"). In other words, after ideas have been brought together into clusters, they need to be separated out into individual paragraphs, and each idea needs to be *fully* developed and articulated.

A good argument answers all the relevant questions that a reader may have and doesn't leave the reader thinking, "Well, if claims x and y are true, then I suppose the argument would be valid. But I'm not sure that claims x and y *are* true." Or, to give a more concrete example: "If it's true that frequent testing helps students remember material better, and if remembering material is the point of a good education, then I suppose the author is correct: teachers should give more tests. But I'm not sure that those assumptions are true." It's the writer's job to produce the strongest possible reasons for believing that claims x, y, and all the others are true. This often means analyzing each argument or component of an argument for implied but unstated claims, or for stated but unsupported claims, and working out support for them. For each of the claims we make, we must ask ourselves, "Why do I believe this to be true?

⊖ Try This   Developing a Claim

Look through the notes, informal writing, argument matrix, and other material that you produced for earlier chapters. Identify one interesting claim of your own, and copy it out at the top of a blank page or word processing document.

Now look through your notes for support for the claim—perhaps a quotation from the text, or evidence of another kind, or your own ideas. List this support under the claim.

Next, generate as much additional support for the claim as you can. You might find other quotations that support it, other evidence, other reasons. Don't be afraid to go a little overboard as you brainstorm; you can always cut out the weaker supports once you have plenty of material. Ultimately, however, the *number* of supports doesn't matter so much as the fact that you have thoroughly considered all the possibilities.

Now develop your material into an argument paragraph. Begin the paragraph with your claim, and explain the support for the claim in the body of the paragraph. Don't simply list the evidence, however; explain as fully as you can how and why each piece of evidence relates to and supports the main claim.

You may find that your paragraph becomes too long and needs to be split into two or even three paragraphs. That's fine. Figure out the best places for a break, and incorporate transitional words or phrases to make it clear that the new paragraphs are still focusing on the claim of the first paragraph.

What reasons do I have for making this claim?" Often the reason is another claim, which will need to be supported in a whole new paragraph.

Now, some claims are so well established already, so unlikely to be at all controversial, that elaborate support and explanation are unnecessary. Other claims may be more controversial, but, having been persuasively argued by another writer, they can be covered by a citation or a footnote without being exhaustively reargued. But every claim that is essential to the argument needs to be treated fully, in one or more paragraphs.

For example, the sample essay "Human Rights for Apes: A Well-Intentioned Mistake" (p. 167) could conceivably be reduced to this: "Human rights should not be extended to apes and the distinction between apes and humans should be preserved, both in law and in ethics, because although apes may be in many ways similar to humans, they lack the cultures and belief systems that make the concept of 'rights' necessary." Such an argument would have the merit of being shorter, but what reason would the reader have for believing the writer's claims? The claims that are being made in this one-sentence version need to be teased out and treated separately, and each must be developed into a sound argument by providing evidence that supports it.

Address the Counterarguments

As we said in Chapter 5 (p. 127), a counterargument is an argument for the *opposing* side or point of view. You should address counterarguments because they will occur to many readers anyway, and so it is prudent to deal with them. The usual readers of student essays are instructors, who are trained to think critically and are in the habit of scrutinizing arguments for their strengths and weaknesses. Often, in fact, they are already deeply familiar with the debate or conversation that you have entered. You are more likely to persuade your readers if you can refute all of the strongest counterarguments or, if not refute them, can at least show that you have considered them and then explain why you believe your own position is stronger.

Some essays devote more space to addressing counterarguments than to presenting the positive side of the argument. This is appropriate when the proposal itself is quite simple and straightforward but when many objections have been voiced against it. For example, an argument in favor of government-funded day care might focus chiefly on the supposed obstacles to it, as there may be general agreement that, if feasible, free day care would be a good thing.

⇒ **Try This** Addressing Counterarguments

If you completed an argument paragraph or paragraphs for the previous "Try This" activity, trade your work with a classmate. Read your classmate's argument carefully and list as many questions and counterarguments as you can, even if you find the argument convincing. (Keep in mind that the ultimate purpose of this exercise is to help make the argument stronger, so you are not really attacking the argument.) Explain your counterarguments as fully as possible. Then exchange papers with your classmate. Using your classmate's counterarguments, as well as any others that occur to you, write one or two paragraphs that address and refute two or three of the strongest counterarguments. (You might begin these paragraphs with a phrase such as "Some might argue that . . .")

Establish Common Ground with the Reader

In presenting your argument, you don't want to alienate your reader by seeming too aggressive. You are not trying to score points against an adversary; you're trying to win over readers to your way of thinking. Remind your readers of the points on which they probably already agree with you. In this way, you get your readers to consent before you introduce more controversial ideas later on. (For more on this kind of rhetoric, see "Rogerian Rhetoric," p. 210.)

In the sample essay "Human Rights for Apes: A Well-Intentioned Mistake" (p. 167), the writer disagrees with those who argue that human rights should be extended to apes but concedes that apes should be considered as having certain rights — animal rights. He makes this concession in the second paragraph, immediately following the thesis statement, in order to put to rest any supposition that he may want to deny any kind of right to apes. In this way, he narrows the scope of his own argument at the outset to the specific question of whether human rights should be extended to apes. And he shows that he is approaching the problem in a fair-minded and reasonable way.

Drafting an Organizational Plan

Clustering and Diagramming

Although at this point you should already have a good sense of your main ideas, you've probably amassed a profusion of notes and informal writing that might seem a little overwhelming. How do you bring order and shape to all these ideas and present them in a way that's clear, economical, and persuasive?

Often, the difficulty is that you've spent so much time arriving at your position that the validity of your argument now seems almost self-evident. You can lose sight of the long road that led to this point. You got here by taking a meandering route through data, questions, arguments, and counterarguments, but your reader has not taken this journey. To the reader, your argument is not at all obvious; in fact, the reader might hold a view of the matter that shares nothing with your own. How, then, can you conceive of your argument as a series of logical steps, a direct path from problem to solution? How will you know where to start and end and how to show the steps that lead to your main argument?

The most practical way to break an argument into steps is to group ideas into clusters. You can then arrange these clusters in a diagram and thereby visualize your whole argument's shape and get a sense of the big picture. As you work, you should be able to see how related ideas can be gathered into groups. The important thing is to begin to see relations among ideas — ways of bringing elements together or separating them.

Diagramming your ideas makes it possible to develop a clear and strong organizational scheme, to keep your main argument in focus throughout your draft, and to concentrate on one element of your argument at a time as you write. It also helps you identify what to keep and what to cut.

If you produced a radial diagram as a reading strategy (see Chapter 3, "Constructing a Radial Map of the Text," pp. 81–83), you are already familiar with this technique. You can create a cluster diagram with pencil and paper or using writing software, mind-mapping software, or a drawing app on your computer. Each medium has its pros and cons, though the computer usually gives a tidier final product. (Nothing is simpler than clustering ideas and drawing diagrams with a pencil, but moving clusters around and making revisions on paper means erasing and rewriting, which quickly gets messy.) If you're working on a long essay involving a complex argument, consider using a pencil and paper initially and moving to the computer later. (See below for guidelines for creating cluster diagrams on a computer.)

There are no rules for this kind of work; in fact, playing around with your ideas and experimenting with different arrangements is really the point. A good way to get started is to write out your thesis statement in the center of the page. Arrange

---

→ **Guidelines** **Creating Cluster Diagrams on a Computer**

Most writing apps, such as Microsoft Word, Apple's Pages, and Google Docs, make it possible to create a cluster diagram. The procedure varies slightly from one app to another, but it typically works like this:

- Insert a text box into a new document, and drag the cursor to create a rectangle.

- Type a line or two of text inside the text box.

- Drag the handles to resize the text box. Double-click to change the fill color.

- Use drawing tools to join boxes with lines or arrows.

An easier way to create cluster diagrams on a computer is to use a drawing app or mind-mapping software. Popular mind-mapping programs include XMind (free and open source), Coggle (a free Web app), FreeMind (free), SimpleMind (free), Mindix (free), MindNode, Scapple, and MindMeister (Web app).

main topics at some distance from the center so that you have plenty of room for other notes. Use a brief phrase to note each main point below each topic heading. (Some topic headings may end up with very few notes, and that's fine. It doesn't necessarily mean the topic is weak or unimportant.)

At first, simply focus on clustering, gathering up the main points that each topic or component of your argument requires. Your cluster diagram might look something like Figure 6.1. Once you've got most of the main components on the

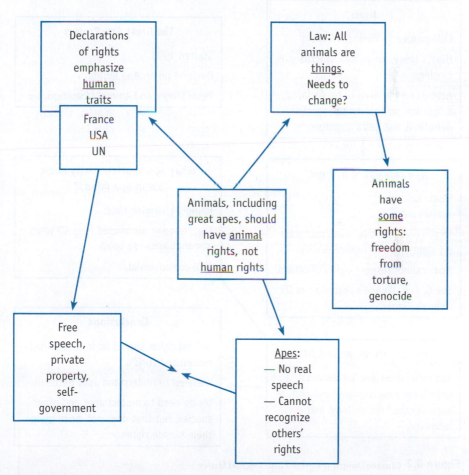

Figure 6.1 Radial Cluster Diagram

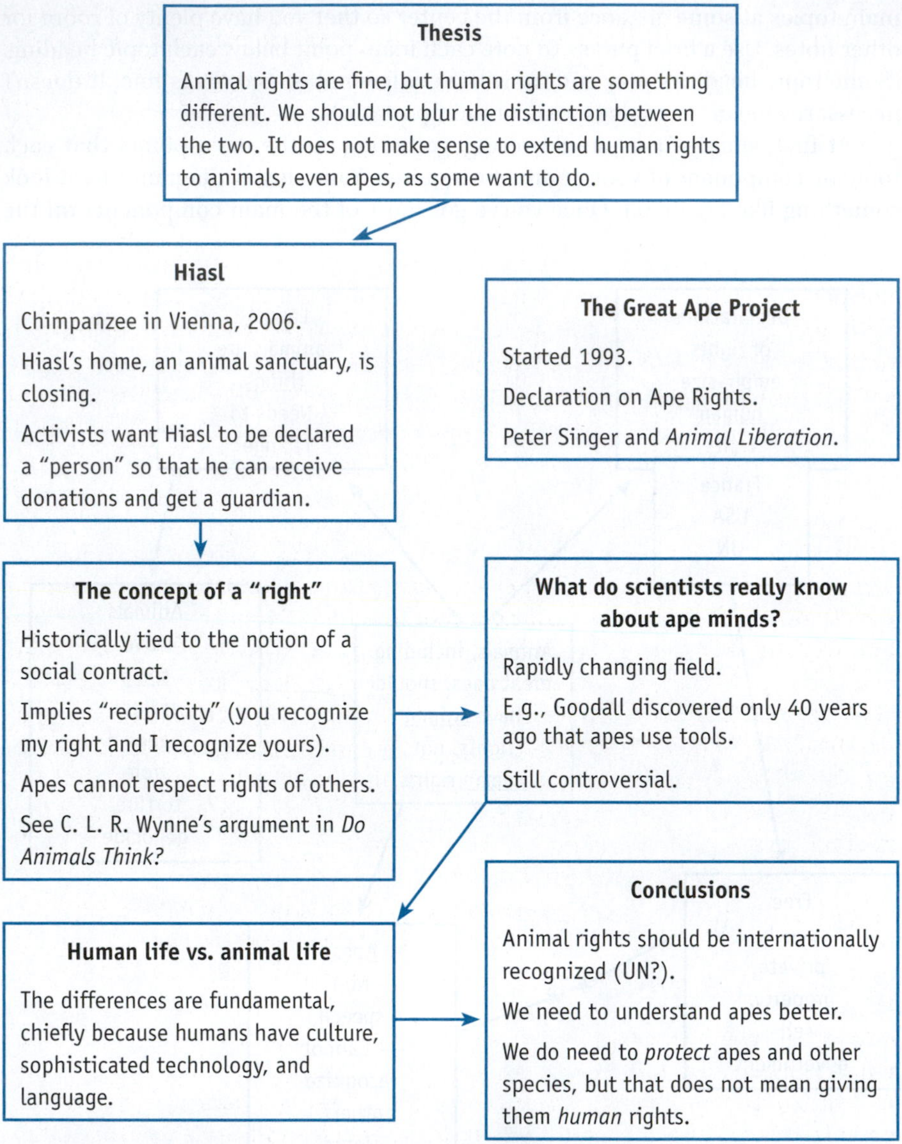

Thesis

Animal rights are fine, but human rights are something different. We should not blur the distinction between the two. It does not make sense to extend human rights to animals, even apes, as some want to do.

Hiasl

Chimpanzee in Vienna, 2006.

Hiasl's home, an animal sanctuary, is closing.

Activists want Hiasl to be declared a "person" so that he can receive donations and get a guardian.

The Great Ape Project

Started 1993.

Declaration on Ape Rights.

Peter Singer and *Animal Liberation*.

The concept of a "right"

Historically tied to the notion of a social contract.

Implies "reciprocity" (you recognize my right and I recognize yours).

Apes cannot respect rights of others.

See C. L. R. Wynne's argument in *Do Animals Think?*

What do scientists really know about ape minds?

Rapidly changing field.

E.g., Goodall discovered only 40 years ago that apes use tools.

Still controversial.

Human life vs. animal life

The differences are fundamental, chiefly because humans have culture, sophisticated technology, and language.

Conclusions

Animal rights should be internationally recognized (UN?).

We need to understand apes better.

We do need to *protect* apes and other species, but that does not mean giving them *human* rights.

Figure 6.2 Cluster Diagram Revised into Logical Order

page, you can begin arranging the clusters. At this point, you can move the thesis statement to the top of the page and organize the argument in a logical order below it, as in Figure 6.2 (see p. 156).

Revising Organization: Constructing a Sentence Outline

Now that you have diagrammed the components of your argument, you are in a position to develop an outline. We have deliberately left a discussion of outlining until after you have developed an argument, even if only a rudimentary one. An outline is a revision tool, one that helps you arrange or rearrange ideas that already exist. If you use an outline too soon, it easily becomes a straitjacket: it inhibits your thinking and shuts out good ideas that haven't yet occurred to you. You need to have material for your argument before you can begin to arrange that material.

You can begin organizing your argument with a very simple outline — little more than your thesis, your motive, one or two claims, and perhaps a note about the evidence that supports these claims. At first, forget about how ideas are arranged in your notes and informal writing; it's time to think fresh and figure out the clearest and simplest way to lay out your ideas. For this purpose, it helps to put into words the **nucleus** or essence of your argument in the form of two or three propositions that explain its basic reasoning (for example, "I think [my thesis] is valid because . . ."). This will help you begin your outline. The important thing is to use *full sentences* and not just words or brief phrases that merely identify topics. An argument is composed not of a string of topics but of ideas that have a logical relationship to one another. Only full sentences can represent your ideas and their relationships.

Ideally, each sentence in your outline will represent a paragraph in your final draft. But it may take a bit of trial and error before you get to that point. Your sentence outline will clarify your sense of the overall shape of the argument and what each paragraph in the essay needs to do. Even after the outline seems complete, however, you may well need to revise it as your essay evolves. Paragraphs can develop in such a way that they cease to correspond exactly to the outline, or a paragraph can grow to the point where it needs to be split in two, or a paragraph may turn out to work better in a different place in the essay than you expected. The organization of an essay changes as it develops, which is just as it should be — that's part of the adventure of the writing process. And because your outline and your essay draft complement each other and take on a reciprocal relationship, each will change to reflect changes in the other. The outline will help guide you, but eventually, after the essay has begun to take its final form, your gauge for making decisions about organization will shift away from the outline and toward your imagined reader — "the reader over your shoulder."

Work Out the Nucleus of Your Argument

To begin, you need to have a reasonably clear sense of your argument's general shape — not yet paragraph by paragraph, but in larger chunks or stages. You can clarify your sense of the main stages by writing out a two- or three-sentence summary of the argument you want to make in support of your thesis. (This summary is not the same thing as the thesis statement itself: rather than being the main point your essay will make, the summary lists the *reasons* that your point is valid.) This nucleus will help you see the logical structure of your argument more clearly. Every argument will differ, of course, but to speak in the most general terms, the nucleus will probably take a form something like this: "If you understand this, then you'll see this next thing. And if you understand that, then surely you'll agree that my thesis is valid." Or "Here's a true story. Here's the lesson I take from the story. If this lesson is valid, it suggests that x [a commonly held belief] may not always be true after all." Or "Because x seems to be true, it follows that y is probably true too. And there's good evidence for z as well. If both y and z are true, then, as you see, my thesis is probably valid. Now, some may say y and z are false, but their arguments are flawed because a, b, and c."

A summary statement includes several stages, and if we separate them out, we have the beginnings of an outline. Each stage might require several paragraphs in the finished essay. (The number of paragraphs assigned to each stage here is just for the purpose of illustration; the actual number would depend on the nature of the particular argument.) Figure 6.3 shows one possible arrangement and paragraph count for the body of an essay.

The model in Figure 6.3 tells us that the body of this essay might require seven paragraphs. (With an introductory paragraph and a concluding paragraph, the complete essay might have nine paragraphs.) But as your writing moves along, you may realize that your summary statement has too few or too many paragraphs. No problem: the outline is not meant to imprison you; its purpose is to help you think like a reader and transform writerly drafting into a readerly finished product.

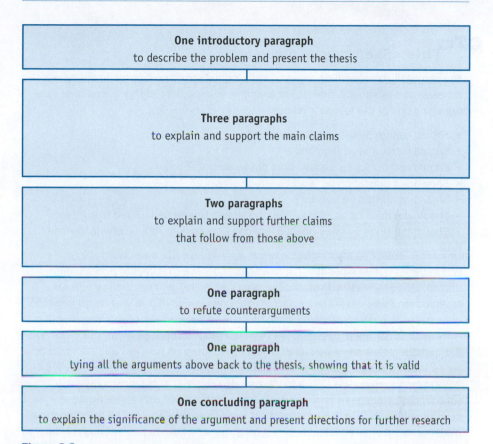

One introductory paragraph
to describe the problem and present the thesis

Three paragraphs
to explain and support the main claims

Two paragraphs
to explain and support further claims
that follow from those above

One paragraph
to refute counterarguments

One paragraph
tying all the arguments above back to the thesis, showing that it is valid

One concluding paragraph
to explain the significance of the argument and present directions for further research

Figure 6.3 Model of a Summary Statement

If you can write out the logic of your argument in two or three sentences, you can usually see its general shape and get a rough sense of how it will need to be organized. You can see what the stages of the argument are and begin to work out what points must be made in order to establish each stage. These points are the claims that make up the skeleton of your argument. Typically, each claim that needs to be argued will require a separate paragraph. Some claims, however, need very little argument, either because they are common knowledge or because a reliable

⊖ **Try This**   **Sketching an Argument**

You can easily try sketching an argument's logical structure by experimenting with an issue that is already familiar. For example, you may already have a point of view regarding one of the following issues:

- Should capital punishment be banned?
- Should marijuana be legalized?
- Should soft drinks be banned from public schools?
- Should sex education be taught in grade schools?
- Should cigarettes be banned?
- Should the drinking age throughout the United States be lowered to eighteen?
- Should the United States adopt a four-day workweek to reduce unemployment?

Or you can select another issue on which you have a clear opinion.

First write out your position (for example, "I believe that capital punishment should not be banned"). Then add the word "because" and list the two or three main reasons why you believe in this stand. Consider what a reader would need to understand in order to be persuaded. This will be the nucleus of your argument.

Now consider the arguments that might be made in opposition to your views and the questions that might be raised. Write some notes on how you would answer or refute these questions and counterarguments.

Now create an outline similar to the model in Figure 6.3, but incorporate your content: your thesis and your main arguments, as well as your response to counterarguments. The outline should not contain all the details or all the supporting evidence, but it should illustrate the logical structure of the argument you envision.

authority has already demonstrated their validity; in such cases, all you need to do is to cite the source. Claims that need little or no argument can usually be folded into other paragraphs.

Get Started with a Basic Sentence Outline

At this point, you are ready to construct a simple outline composed of complete sentences. You should have a clear sense of your motive (the problem or question you are working on), your thesis, and two or three of the main reasons that your thesis is valid.

You can construct this outline on paper, especially if you begin by leaving lots of space between each of the lines. But it's easier to do it on a computer, where you can move lines of text around without having to erase or cross out. Here's how to create a basic sentence outline, along with a few software tips.

- Begin by stating the *problem* that your argument addresses in one or two sentences at the top of the outline. (The wording need not be perfect; just get the idea down.)

- Underneath the problem, write out your working thesis statement. If you're working on a computer, give both the problem and the thesis statement a "heading 1" format.

- Refer to your nucleus to identify the main stages or sections of your argument. Write these out as complete sentences. Indent them one-half inch from the thesis and motive statements. (Or format them as "heading 2.")

- Try to identify two or three of the claims that each stage requires. If you're not there yet, work with the claims that you believe are important for your argument. Indent them one-half inch from the statements of stages. (Or format them as "heading 3.")

- Where possible, briefly explain the evidence or reasoning that supports each of these claims. In each case, use one or two complete sentences. Indent these sentences one-half inch from the statements of claims. (Or format them as "heading 4.")

Be sure to use complete sentences throughout, not words or short phrases that merely represent topics or stand for complex ideas. The purpose of this outline is to represent and clarify the logical structure of your argument — the relationships between ideas — not simply to list a series of subjects to discuss. A mere series of topics — one thing after another, with no logical or meaningful development — is really no organization at all.

Here is an example of the initial basic sentence outline Marc Dumas created for the paper that he eventually titled "Human Rights for Apes: A Well-Intentioned Mistake" (p. 167).

Sample Basic Sentence Outline

Problem: The problem is the controversy over the rights of great apes. Scientists and others in the Great Ape Project argue that the great apes are biologically, intellectually, and socially so much like humans that they should have human rights—and that they need them.

Working Thesis: Chimps and other great apes should not be given the same rights as humans.

    I. The concept of "human rights" is linked to *human* qualities and to *human* society.

        A. For example, free speech and private property are rights that apes cannot exercise.

        B. See Declaration of the Rights of Man and of the Citizen (France) and American Bill of Rights (USA).

        C. See Universal Declaration of Human Rights (UN).

    II. Apes cannot recognize human rights—or even ape rights—so recognizing rights is a one-way street.

        A. Apes can't sit on juries or recognize others' rights or even understand what it means to have a "right" for themselves.

        B. See Clive Wynne, page 226: rights must be "reciprocal."

    III. If we lumped together ape rights and human rights, we would have to limit human rights severely.

    IV. So we should be *protecting* apes rather than creating controversies based on things we can't know about their minds and their feelings.

        A. We don't know much about what apes want, because we cannot really communicate with them.

        B. Maybe the Great Ape Project is a publicity stunt?

Revise the Outline

At this point, you can begin arranging, or rearranging, paragraphs in your draft, or you can continue to flesh out the outline, adding further claims and support for the claims.

Continue working through your diagram, notes, and informal writing to gather up your material, distinguishing claims from supporting evidence and arranging the material within stages in your outline. Move toward an outline that lays out the argument claim by claim.

While you are doing this, you may find that your list of claims changes as you find material that doesn't quite belong with any of the claims you've already listed. This is normal — and part of the recursive or looping nature of the writing process. Each new step tends to require revisions to earlier work, but with each revision the

> **⦿ Guidelines**   ## Constructing an Outline
>
> Many word processors include outlining tools, and you can find dedicated outlining apps such as Microsoft OneNote and OmniOutliner. But it's easy to create an outline in any word processor simply by starting each line with a numeral or letter and using indents to show different ranks. (See the sample outlines on pp. 161–62 and 164–65.) If you want your word processor to renumber the sentences automatically when you change a sentence's position, try formatting your sentences as a numbered list. (The formatting option is often called something like "Bullets and Numbering" or "Bullets & Lists.")

work becomes stronger. The important thing at this stage, as you group supporting material under claims, is to keep claims in the foreground as headings.

Look for Relationships That Suggest an Organizational Plan

Many arguments can be organized in only one way, because certain ideas cannot be introduced until others have been well established. In such cases, the organization of ideas is at least partly dictated by logic and must move from a premise to a conclusion — that is, from an idea that has to be established first (a premise) to an idea that follows from it (a conclusion).

For example, imagine an argument that same-sex couples in America should have the right to marry. First, the writer might argue that there is strong evidence that homosexuality is not typically a choice but is biologically determined or in some other way "hardwired." If this is true, then America includes citizens who are by nature homosexual, citizens who pay taxes and fulfill the other obligations of citizenship. Now (the argument might run) if same-sex marriage does no harm to others, then homosexuals should enjoy the same right to marry as heterosexuals, since to deny this right would be an arbitrary injustice against a subset of the state's own citizens. Arguments like this proceed according to a logical order: if x is true, then y is true, and if y is true, then z must follow.

But you may find that not every element in the argument falls into place according to a strict and necessary logic. Here are some alternative arrangements.

- *Weaker-to-stronger order*. Sometimes, an effective strategy is to proceed from weaker arguments to stronger ones, so that readers feel increasingly persuaded as they read (rather than increasingly doubtful). The weaker-to-stronger arrangement works when you can support a thesis with several distinct arguments, each of which is independent of the others, so that you can sequence them in order of strength.

- *Chronological or narrative order.* When you are discussing events, historical or fictional, it often works best to discuss them in the order of occurrence.

- *Arrangement by theme or type.* Arguments may be grouped by type. For example, arguments that rely on surveys or statistical evidence might be grouped together, and arguments that rely on deductive reasoning might be grouped together. Similarly, arguments that have in common a theme or scholarly discipline may be grouped together. For example, in an essay arguing that the electoral college should be abolished, it might make sense to keep all the arguments from history together and then move on to arguments based on political philosophy.

Organizing a Long Essay

In a long essay (more than about eight pages) involving a complicated argument, you may identify stages within stages, and each substage might involve several points. To keep it all under control, you might want to divide the essay into sections. You might even write a separate nucleus and a separate outline for each section. Each section can be numbered or given a subtitle, or both. You may choose not to keep the section breaks in the final essay, but working with sections of a manageable length at this stage will make it easier to organize them.

Marc Dumas worked on his basic outline, enlarging it and adding further claims and support for them. Here is his revised outline.

Revised Sample Sentence Outline

Thesis: The distinction between the rights of animals and those of humans ought to be preserved, both in ethics and in law.

    I. But legislative bodies should recognize certain *animal* rights.

        A. Under Austrian law Hiasl is considered a "thing."

        B. No third category exists for animals.

C. But it does not follow that he should be made legally a human. Instead, the law should recognize a distinct category for animals.

II. The concept of "human rights" is linked to distinctly human qualities and to uniquely human society.

III. Declaration of the Rights of Man and of the Citizen (France, 1789) emphasizes right to *free speech* and *private property*.

    A. So does American Bill of Rights (USA, 1791).

    B. Universal Declaration of Human Rights (1948)?

    C. These rights are not relevant to apes.

IV. Only an understanding of differences between cultures and histories makes it possible or necessary to recognize "universal" human rights.

    A. Apes lack this understanding.

V. Recognizing ape rights can go in only one direction—apes cannot recognize human rights, or even ape rights.

    A. See Clive Wynne, page 226 quotation: rights must be reciprocal.

    B. Apes can't sit on juries or recognize others' rights or even understand what it means to have a "right" for themselves.

    C. Extending rights to apes might mean we would have to dilute or restrict human rights.

VI. We should be protecting apes rather than creating controversies based on things we can't know about their minds and their feelings.

    A. We don't know much about what apes want because we cannot really communicate with them.

    B. Acquisition of language is still controversial. See Donald Griffin, *Animal Minds*.

VII. **Counterargument:** Great Ape Project says apes' inability to defend their own rights is not a real problem: children and disabled humans need guardians too (p. 5).

    A. But apes don't have human family members to speak for them.

    B. And children and some disabled do not have the same rights (e.g., voting) as others.

VIII. **Closing paragraph:** We need a Universal Declaration of Animal Rights.

Organizing an Argument Essay: A Basic Model

The following student essay by Marc Dumas, "Human Rights for Apes: A Well-Intentioned Mistake," is based on the outline above. It offers a basic model of essay organization. As you might expect, it begins with a one-paragraph introduction that includes a thesis statement. Seven body paragraphs follow, each presenting a distinct argument in support of the thesis. The second paragraph establishes common ground by conceding a point, and the sixth paragraph rebuts a counterargument. The essay ends with a concluding paragraph that suggests some directions for further research and reaffirms the writer's position. As we will see, this structure may be too simple to serve all purposes, but it does provide a starting point for further discussion and exemplifies several principles of good organization. (This essay is in MLA format. See the Appendix for details about formatting conventions.)

Dumas 1

Marc Dumas

Professor Taylor

Composition 101

9 November 2015

Human Rights for Apes:

A Well-Intentioned Mistake

Uses recent news item to show problem vividly and poses a question.

Recently, animal rights advocates in Vienna, Austria, went to court to ask a judge to declare that a chimpanzee named Hiasl (pronounced "heezle") is a "person" ("How to Protect"). To some, their case might sound frivolous, but for at least two decades a group of influential scientists and philosophers has been waging an international campaign to extend human rights to the great apes (chimpanzees, orangutans, and gorillas). The great apes certainly do face dire threats, and recent genetic research has shown just how closely related they are to human beings. But does it therefore follow that *human* rights ought to be extended to a species of nonhuman animal or that this step can be taken without fundamentally changing the very meaning of human rights? I would argue that, while it makes good sense to recognize that higher animals should have "rights" of some kind, we should preserve a clear distinction, in law and in ethics, between the rights of animals and those of humans.

Thesis statement declares writer's response to the question.

First sentence states claim, concedes that some animal rights should be recognized. Reference to Hiasl establishes link to previous paragraph. Rest of paragraph provides support (facts, reasoning, expert opinion).

The case of Hiasl does demonstrate the need for legislative bodies to recognize certain *animal* rights. The chimpanzee's caretakers went to court because the animal sanctuary where he lived for twenty-five years was bankrupt, and Hiasl would soon be homeless. Caring for a chimpanzee is expensive (food, medical bills, and housing cost about US$6,800 a month), and Hiasl's supporters argue that the

Dumas 2

chimp's best hope is to be allowed to receive donations from the public and to be awarded a legal guardian ("How to Protect"). The problem is that Austrian law permits only "persons" to receive personal donations or be adopted. In law, a chimp is merely a "thing"; no third category exists for animals. Hiasl's supporters argue that seeking the status of "person" for Hiasl is their only option ("How to Protect"). However, if Austrian law were not so restrictive, this recourse would not be necessary. It does not follow that Hiasl and every other great ape should be placed in the legal category of human persons. As Rutgers University law professor Gary Francione argues, it would make better sense to recognize animal rights, in particular the right *not* to be treated as a thing, as a distinct category (24).

New claim introduces new argument. Reference to differences between apes and humans establishes link to previous argument. Claim supported by reasoning.

True, animal behaviorists have shown that apes have rich and complex social and emotional lives. Nevertheless, fundamental differences between apes and humans make it inappropriate to grant both species the same rights. Humans live out their lives within cultures and societies characterized by particular belief systems. The differences among these belief systems are what makes a concept of universal "human rights"—a kind of minimum entitlement for every human being—necessary. Similarly, it is only an understanding of a world beyond immediate experience, and a sense of history—both of which are unique to humans—that make it possible to recognize and respect the rights of others.

New claim introduces new argument. Reference to human rights establishes link to previous argument. Claim supported by historical fact, reasoning, expert opinion.

Historically, the notion of human rights has been closely linked to distinctly human qualities and to uniquely human society. It was first worked out during the eighteenth century in Europe. Chief among the rights mentioned by the Declaration of the Rights of Man (1789), issued during the French

Dumas 3

Revolution, and the U.S. Bill of Rights (1791) are the rights to free speech and property—neither of which is relevant to apes. More recently, the Universal Declaration of Human Rights, adopted by the United Nations in 1948, was never intended for nonhuman animals, and Article 1 specifically notes that human beings are "endowed with reason and conscience"— qualities that, as Charles Habib Malik, one of the drafters of the Declaration, commented, "distinguish them from animals" (qtd. in Morsink 298).

New claim introduces new argument. Reference to intellectual capacity of apes establishes link to previous argument. Claim supported by expert opinion (in citations).

In order to apply human rights to animals, we would have to pick and choose the few that are relevant to them. This is what the Great Ape Project has done, identifying specifically the right to life, freedom from slavery, and freedom from torture (4). But even these selected rights can apply in only one direction: we could never expect apes to recognize the rights of humans or even of other apes. Animal behaviorist Clive D. L. Wynne argues that rights, to be meaningful, must be reciprocal:

> As my right to swing my arm stops at my neighbor's nose, so rights in general imply responsibilities. And responsibilities demand comprehension: a defendant must be able to understand what they have been charged with. To express one's rights and accept one's responsibilities one needs a comprehension of others' motivations. . . . (226)

No expert has claimed that any of the great apes except *homo sapiens* is capable of such comprehension.

Background introduces new claim (third sentence) and counterargument (fourth sentence). Rest of paragraph rebuts it (facts, reasoning, expert opinion) to support claim.

We do not really know what any animal, including apes, wants and needs. In the decades since Jane Goodall studied the chimpanzees of Tanzania, our understanding of apes has been improving rapidly, yet primatologists still

Dumas 4

disagree about whether apes are capable of reason, whether
they have a true sense of self, and to what degree their
emotional and social lives resemble humans'. The root of
the problem is that we cannot communicate with apes to
understand their way of understanding the world, except in
the most limited ways. Apes can be trained to use words as
symbols for things; perhaps some apes have even learned
to use a simple form of grammar by combining three or four
signs in American Sign Language—but this too remains
controversial. As Donald Griffin notes, many scientists who
have been studying the evidence carefully for years remain
unconvinced that apes are using language at all: "Terrace
and others have concluded that signing apes are not using
anything that deserves to be called a language, because
of the almost total lack of rule-governed combinations of
signs" (223). And of course, only apes trained in captivity
acquire signing skills. No ape uses language as humans do, to
communicate with others of their species about any number of
topics. Only a handful of apes have ever learned to use even a
hundred signs (Griffin 232).

*New claim,
supported by
reasoning.
Reference to legal
rights establishes
link to thesis.*

Our aim should be to protect apes, not to assume more
than we really know about their needs and desires or to
blur the profound differences between apes and humans.
So by extending human rights to apes, we risk diluting
and weakening the meaning of those rights. No animal can
participate in the rule of law, or participate in the protection
of the rights of others, or even understand what it means
to have a legal right themselves. Does this mean, then, that
those who cannot or will not respect the rights of others can
expect to have their own rights respected?

Dumas 5

Introduces another counterargument. Reference to legal person status establishes link to previous paragraph and thesis. Rest of paragraph rebuts counterargument (facts, expert opinion, reasoning).

The argument that a chimpanzee ought to be given the same basic rights as humans and deserves to be considered a legal "person" has been developed in detail by the Great Ape Project, the brainchild of philosophers Paola Cavalieri and Peter Singer. The project is supported by a number of respected biologists, psychologists, and ethologists. According to the organization's "Declaration on the Great Apes," the fact that apes cannot defend their own interests is not a serious problem. The Great Ape Project argues that "human guardians should safeguard [apes'] interests and rights, in the same way as the interests of the young or intellectually disabled members of our own species are safeguarded" (5). But the young and intellectually disabled have parents or other family members who can speak for them and typically make decisions about their interests. And in fact, we *do* limit the rights of the young and the intellectually disabled, as appropriate to their particular capacities. Small children have very few rights as individuals, as do nonverbal mentally handicapped adults (Singer 55).

Conclusion restates thesis, adds detail, identifies directions for further research.

Hiasl was denied a legal guardian and ended up at the Vienna Animal Protection Center (Stafford). Whatever Hiasl's ultimate fate, however, his case illustrates the problem that societies face when human rights are enshrined in law but no provisions are made for animal rights. This is the case in the United States today. We need to do more to protect ape habitats and defend them from attack, but I believe that the United Nations should compose a Universal Declaration of Animal Rights. Such a declaration might encourage all countries to spare not only the great apes from suffering and indignity but all species of animals.

Dumas 6

Works Cited

Francione, Gary L. "One Right for All." *New Scientist* 8 Oct. 2005:
    24. Print.

Great Ape Project. "A Declaration on Great Apes." *The Great Ape
    Project: Equality beyond Humanity*. Ed. Paola Cavalieri and
    Peter Singer. New York: Griffin-St. Martin's, 1993. 4-8. Print.

Griffin, Donald. *Animal Minds*. Chicago: U of Chicago P, 1992. Print.

"How to Protect Ape's Rights? Make Him a Person." *MSNBC.com*.
    MSNBC Digital Network, 5 Apr. 2007. Web. 17 Oct. 2015.

Morsink, Johannes. *The Universal Declaration of Human
    Rights: Origins, Drafting, and Intent*. Philadelphia: U of
    Pennsylvania P, 1999. Print.

Singer, Peter. *Animal Liberation*. 3rd ed. New York: Ecco-Harper,
    2002. Print.

Stafford, Ned. "Chimp Denied a Legal Guardian." *Nature.com*.
    Nature Publishing Group, 26 Apr. 2007. Web. 15 Oct. 2015.

United Nations. Gen. Assembly. Universal Declaration of Human
    Rights. *UN.org*. United Nations, 2011. Web. 15 Oct. 2015.

Wynne, Clive D. L. *Do Animals Think?* Princeton: Princeton UP,
    2004. Print.

Organizing an Argument Essay: A Second Example

As we noted earlier, there are many ways to organize an argument essay, and no single method can work for every argument. To follow one model every time you wrote an essay would quickly become limiting. In order to understand better the general principles that underlie the organization of argument essays, even sophisticated ones, we can see how they work in a second student paper. This paper, by Wendy Sung, includes paragraphs with greater structural variety than those we saw in the paper by Marc Dumas. (This essay is in MLA format.)

Sung 1

Wendy Sung

Professor Scott

Composition 101

2 April 2015

A Campaign for the Dignity

of the Great Apes

Introduction is two
paragraphs.

René Descartes (1596-1650), often called the father of modern philosophy, believed that animals are "natural automata"—thoughtless and soulless machines (285). In many ways, modern science held to this view even after Charles Darwin showed that *homo sapiens* evolved from primates and after the close similarity of ape and human brain structures and DNA became known. More recently, scientists have learned, both through observation and through direct communication in sign language, that the great apes (chimpanzees, bonobos, gorillas, and orangutans) have rich emotional and even intellectual lives and that they not only sense pain but can suffer in more profound ways as well, experiencing complex emotions such as grief, loneliness, and disappointment. In 1993, two philosophers, Paola Cavalieri and Peter Singer, inaugurated the Great Ape Project, a campaign to secure for great apes fundamental rights that have traditionally belonged only to humans. These rights include the right to life, the protection of individual liberty, and the prohibition of torture, rights that reflect the basic sameness of human and ape needs (Great Ape Project 4).

All the great apes are endangered. Although exact numbers are hard to estimate, great ape populations have declined rapidly in the last two decades, because of hunting,

Sung 2

loss of habitat, and diseases such as SIV[1] and Ebola; most experts predict that the great apes will be extinct in fifty to a hundred years (Bowman; "Species Fact Sheet" 1). Yet despite this risk, and all that we now know about their impressive mental and emotional capacities, apes continue to be used in traumatizing laboratory experiments and to be hunted for meat. America's Animal Welfare Act provides little protection for apes used in research, and none for apes in their natural habitats overseas. Nonprofit organizations such as the World Wildlife Fund, the Jane Goodall Institute, and Save the Chimps are doing what they can with limited funds and powers. But laws are needed that recognize the dignity of the great apes, guarantee their fundamental rights, and prohibit their use in experimental research. Legislation can also provide the means to preserve ape habitats and to help end the hunting of apes for meat, and perhaps can turn the tide in the battle to save apes from extinction.

Thesis: laws are needed to protect apes.

Fifty years ago, chimpanzees in Africa numbered in the millions. Today only about 200,000 remain ("Chimp Facts"). Their habitats are disappearing as the expanding human population turns forest into farmland, and chimpanzees (and their close relatives, bonobos) continue to be hunted both for meat and so that infants can be taken for the live animal trade (Goodall 207). Much of the slaughter would be unnecessary were it not for local economic factors: hunters are driven to killing apes because other sources of income

[1] Simian immunodeficiency virus: Although strains of this virus do not usually cause AIDS in the natural host, they may do so when they cross to another species.

Sung 3

Table 1 Population, Status, and Habitat of Great Apes

Species	Chimpanzees	Bonobos	Gorillas	Orangutans
Estimated population	172,700 to 299,700	5,000 to 60,000	Western gorilla: 100,000 Eastern gorilla: 700	Borneo: 55,000 Sumatra: 7,500
International Union for Conservation of Nature (IUCN) status	Endangered	Endangered	Endangered	Endangered to critically endangered
Location	Central and western Africa	Central Africa	Central Africa	Borneo and Sumatra (Asia)

Sources: Data from "Species Fact Sheet: African Great Apes"; Photos (left to right): imageBROKER/Alamy; robert HENNO/Alamy; Arco Images GmbH/Alamy; blinckwinkel/Alamy.

have disappeared. Social scientist Kerry Bowman's interviews with bushmeat hunters reveal that most of them would accept other employment if it were made available. "All stated they are looking for economic alternatives," he reports.

Of the roughly 2,400 chimpanzees in the United States, the vast majority—about 1,700—are being used for biomedical testing. Only about 500 live in sanctuaries. About 700 are held captive in zoos or used by the entertainment

Statement of fact leading to claim.

Sung 4

industry ("Chimp Facts"). Although the Animal Welfare Act was intended to protect captive animals from abuse, researchers are exempt from its regulations. Animals used in laboratory experiments often suffer horribly after being infected with diseases or poisoned with toxins ("Animal Testing"). This situation persists because we assume that human suffering is more real than ape suffering, and science still treats apes as objects to be used rather than intelligent fellow creatures.

Paragraph begins with a claim.

The cosmetic industry has found alternatives to the use of animals for research, and medical research can do the same. Most—perhaps all—lab research involving apes is unnecessary or even counterproductive, since therapies that work in one species often do not work in another (Singer 89). According to People for the Ethical Treatment of Animals (PETA), 92% of drugs that pass animal tests fail when tested on human beings ("Animal Testing"). The genetic differences between apes and humans mean that clinical trials involving chimpanzees are often of little value. As Peter Singer shows in *Animal Liberation,* experiments that cause animals to suffer are frequently performed but rarely produce new knowledge. Most aim only to confirm the results of earlier research or to repeat an experiment with some minor variation (52-60).

Counterargument is addressed.

Some argue that animals do not have enough understanding of their circumstances to *suffer* in the sense that humans do. But apes almost certainly can suffer. They recall what has been done to them in the past, and they can fear what may happen in the future (Byrne 115). Over the last three decades, scientists have come to understand a good deal about the minds of apes, in particular by communicating

Sung 5

with apes that have learned to use human sign languages such as American Sign Language, or ASL. Apes can be taught to communicate not only with humans but also with each other; they have even attempted to teach one another signs in some instances. While many of their signs focus on immediate needs, apes also converse about social interactions, emotions, private thoughts, and memories (Fouts and Fouts 32). While chimpanzees and bonobos are known to be the most intelligent of the great apes and the ones most closely related to human beings, other great apes are nearer humans in intellectual capacity than we used to think. Psychologist Francine Patterson has tested the IQ of the gorilla Koko repeatedly, using five different tests over the space of five years, and found that his IQ score averaged 80.3 (Patterson and Gordon 61), roughly equivalent to that of a typical four-year-old human. Not only do apes demonstrate self-awareness and have long memories, but they can also anticipate future events. As Richard Byrne writes: "In almost every case, the evidence—though not always conclusive—has pointed to one group of primates, the great apes, as having some ability to imagine future possible states of affairs" (122).

Claim is implied: if humans of low intelligence cannot be killed, neither should apes.

Most people would consider it immoral to deny basic rights to human beings with low intelligence or limited language skills. Modern societies do not consider it acceptable to murder them or use them in medical experiments or use them in any way as the means to an end, no matter how great the rewards of that end might be. Neither intelligence nor the ability to speak is considered necessary for being included in the "human race" and enjoying human rights. If any faculty is considered necessary, it is the ability to feel and to suffer. Only

Sung 6

when a person becomes "brain dead"—permanently incapable of thought or feeling—do we take away life support. But researchers no longer doubt that chimpanzees and other apes are clearly able to think, feel, and experience a range and depth of emotion not very different from that of *homo sapiens*.

This paragraph has an exploratory structure. It includes questions at the start and near the end.

Granted, human beings are different from other animal beings—we build cities, create works of art, send vehicles to Mars, and worry about our fashion sense—but does it make sense any longer to draw one rigid line dividing the human animal from all others? We humans are biologically even closer to chimpanzees than chimpanzees are to orangutans. We share with chimpanzees more than 98% of our DNA. We also share a common ancestor who lived about six million years ago. Richard Dawkins has shown how relatively short a time this is, in evolutionary terms: if parents and children were to hold hands and form a chain representing all the generations between us today and this common ancestor, the chain would stretch less than 300 miles (84). Humans can accept blood transfusions and even organ transplants from chimpanzees (Teleki 298). How can we treat them and other great apes as "just animals"—with the same moral status as the chicken we eat for dinner? I suspect that more of us would understand our special kinship with apes if we could observe them in the wild. Biologist Geza Teleki writes movingly about such an experience in the forests of Gombe, Tanzania:

> As I sat alone on the crest of a grassy ridge watching a spectacular yet common sunset over the silvery waters of Lake Tanganyika in wonderful solitude and silence, I suddenly noticed two adult male chimpanzees climbing toward me on opposite slopes. They saw one another only as they topped the crest, just yards from

Sung 7

my seat beneath a tree, whereupon both suddenly stood upright and swiftly advanced as bipeds through waist-high grass to stand close together, face to face, each extending his right hand to clasp and vigorously shake the other's while softly panting, heads bobbing. Moments later they sat down nearby and we three watched the sunset enfold the park. When dusk fell my two companions went off to build platform nests high in the trees of the valley. Nevermore, I realized as I hastened homeward to my own bed (a lower platform) at the field station before darkness fell, would I regard chimpanzees as "mere animals." (297)

Paragraph begins with a claim.

It is not necessary to make extravagant claims for the intelligence or language skills of great apes in order to believe in their rights. Controversy continues to surround the question of whether apes can really acquire "language" skills in the full sense, as they appear to be unable to form grammatical sentences, but only able to use signs individually or in combinations of two or three. Thus Columbia University ethologist Herbert Terrace and other researchers argue that signing apes "are not using anything that deserves to be called a language" because their signing is ungrammatical and repetitious (Griffin 242). But Donald Griffin counters that, while Terrace's findings have caused many "to dismiss the whole effort to teach language-like communication to apes as unimpressive and insignificant, this dismissal is based on the absence or near absence of combinatorial productivity [that is, grammatical phrases], and it does not seriously detract from the significance of signing as evidence of what apes are thinking" (223).

Conclusion.   Some scientists remain skeptical of the notion that apes and other animals might have emotional lives that resemble our own. But, as primatologist Frans de Waal argues, biologists and animal behaviorists have been so thoroughly trained to avoid anthropomorphizing animals that they may put up excessive resistance to the suggestion that apes are in some ways like us. And consequently, when faced with arguments that apes think and feel much as humans do, they may demand a level of proof that is unattainable in practice. After a critical review of various claims for animal consciousness, animal psychologist Clive D. L. Wynne concludes: "Animals don't need legal rights to be accepted as valuable and worthy of our protection. They are valuable to us because of who we are, not who they are. Things don't have to be like us to be important to us. They don't have to be able to feel pain to deserve our concern" (242). But we are not just failing to value and protect the animals that are most like us; we are actively destroying them, to the point of extinction. Wynne, I believe, is wrong: animals do sometimes need legal rights. When it was recently announced that an animal sanctuary in Vienna, Austria, would be closing, animal rights advocates went to court to ask that one of its residents, a chimpanzee named Hiasl, be granted the legal status of a "person" so that he could be awarded a guardian and become the recipient of donations that would cover the cost of food and shelter ("How to Protect"). Now that we have failed so thoroughly to do what Wynne suggests and to value the great apes "because of who we are," perhaps it is time for stronger measures.

Sung 9

Works Cited

"Animal Testing Is Bad Science: Point/Counterpoint." *PETA*.
    People for the Ethical Treatment of Animals, n.d. Web. 8
    Feb. 2015.

Bowman, Kerry. "The Demise of the Great Apes in Africa."
    Canadian Ape Alliance. The Canadian Ape Alliance, 20
    Apr. 2010. Web. 27 Jan. 2015.

Byrne, Richard W. "Primate Cognition: Evidence for the Ethical
    Treatment of Primates." *Attitudes to Animals: Views
    in Animal Welfare.* Ed. Francine L. Dolins. Cambridge:
    Cambridge UP, 1999. 114-25. Print.

Cavalieri, Paola, and Peter Singer, eds. *The Great Ape Project:
    Equality beyond Humanity.* New York: Griffin-St. Martin's,
    1993. Print.

"Chimp Facts." *Save the Chimps: Speaking Out for Them.* Save
    the Chimps, Inc., n.d. Web. 8 Feb. 2015.

Dawkins, Richard. "Gaps in the Mind." Cavalieri and Singer
    80-87.

Descartes, René. "Animals Are Machines." *Environmental
    Ethics: Divergence and Convergence.* Ed. Susan J.
    Armstrong and Richard G. Botzler. New York: McGraw,
    1993. 281-85. Print.

de Waal, Frans. "Are We in Anthropodenial?" *Discover* July
    1997: 50-53. Print.

Fouts, Roger S., and Deborah H. Fouts. "Chimpanzees' Use of
    Sign Language." Cavalieri and Singer 28-41.

Goodall, Jane. *Reason for Hope: A Spiritual Journey.* New York:
    Warner, 1999. Print.

Great Ape Project. "A Declaration on Great Apes." Cavalieri and
    Singer 4-8.

Sung 10

Griffin, Donald R. *Animal Minds: Beyond Cognition to Consciousness*. Chicago: U of Chicago P, 2001. Print.

"How to Protect Ape's Rights? Make Him a Person." *MSNBC .com*. MSNBC Digital Network, 5 Apr. 2007. Web. 7 Mar. 2015.

Patterson, Francine, and Wendy Gordon. "The Case for the Personhood of Gorillas." Cavalieri and Singer 58-78.

Singer, Peter. *Animal Liberation*. 3rd ed. New York: Ecco-Harper, 2002. Print.

"Species Fact Sheet: African Great Apes." *WWF (panda.org)*. World Wildlife Fund, May 2007. Web. 15 Feb. 2015.

Teleki, Geza. "They Are Us." Cavalieri and Singer 296-302.

Wynne, Clive D. L. *Do Animals Think?* Princeton: Princeton UP, 2004. Print.

Wendy Sung's essay takes a different position from that of Marc Dumas's essay. But it also takes a different approach. Rather than seeing rights for apes as a knowledge problem, Wendy sees the issue chiefly as a practical problem, one that requires action on the part of the reader. She argues that the rights of the great apes should be legally protected.

Wendy's essay also differs from Marc's in structure. Her introduction is more elaborate: it comprises two paragraphs rather than the typical one paragraph; a thesis statement does not appear until the end of the second paragraph. The first paragraph consists of background information that sets up the issue at stake, so a second paragraph is needed in order to present Wendy's position on that issue.

From that point forward, her position remains clear throughout the essay, so clear that there is little danger of it becoming buried. Consequently, she can take some further liberties with paragraph structure; she doesn't need to begin every single paragraph with a claim. Of course, some paragraphs do begin with a claim, such as paragraphs 5 and 9. But others, such as paragraph 4, begin with a statement of fact and lead up to a claim that appears later in the paragraph. In paragraph 7, the claim is never stated outright, yet it is sufficiently clear: if we would never condone the killing of human beings with low intelligence and limited verbal skills and would not condone their use in medical experiments, then we shouldn't do such things to apes, either.

Wendy includes a visual element in the form of a table, to present data in a format that the reader can easily grasp and to avoid tediously listing numbers and facts in a paragraph of background information.

Toward the end of the essay, she includes a paragraph (para. 8) with an exploratory structure: it begins and ends with questions. These are partly rhetorical questions — questions with a clearly implied answer. But the purpose of the paragraph is not simply to argue; it is also to speculate and pose the real question, "Why do we hold onto a rigid distinction between our species and others?" Wendy's concluding paragraph is a little more open-ended than Marc's: she introduces views held by two leading scholars that complicate her argument a little and broaden the perspective, though they do not change the argument fundamentally. The effect of these departures from standard paragraph structure is a degree of variety and unpredictability that is missing from a more basic essay structure.

Clarification Strategies

No matter what kind of essay you are writing, you can employ strategies to clarify your ideas and their organization for the reader. The best time to use these strategies is when your essay is fairly close to its final form, when you have already organized your ideas around a structure and can read a complete draft as if through the eyes of a reader. At this stage, you can ask an actual reader to help identify places where clarification is needed.

Metadiscourse and Programmatic Statements

As we said in Chapter 2, the term "metadiscourse" means writing that refers to the text in which it appears. For example, if I were to write, "You are reading Chapter 6 of *Writing in Response*; this chapter concerns ways to organize a college essay," my words would be making reference to this text itself, rather than to something outside the text. In other words, they would be *discourse about this discourse*. Writers often use metadiscourse to explain their intent or purpose, or to bring the reader back to the main argument, or to remind the reader of their purpose after a long detour. For example:

"I am arguing that . . ."

"We have now reviewed the various types of . . . ; next, we must look at how these types . . ."

"This essay has argued that . . ."

"Looking back over this exploration, I see that . . ."

In a complicated argument, metadiscourse is a useful strategy for clarification. But many essays — perhaps most — require no metadiscourse at all: the argument unfolds without the need for announcements and explanations of purpose and intent. Bear in mind that excessive metadiscourse can be tedious for a reader and can feel like a pointless delay if it's not necessary. Reserve it for moments when clarity truly demands it.

Here is a fairly elaborate example from a book by historian Hayden White, in which he pauses at the end of a lengthy theoretical discussion in order to provide the reader with a road map for the rest of the chapter. In this context, most readers probably find the metadiscourse helpful and welcome.

> All this is highly abstract, of course, and in order to be made convincing requires both theoretical amplification and exemplification. In what follows, therefore, I will try to characterize the historical discourse in somewhat more formal terms and then analyze a passage of "proper" historical prose in order to explicate the relationship that obtains between its manifest and latent (figurative) meanings. After that, I will return to the problem of the relation between "proper" historiography and its historicist counterpart, on the one side, and to some general remarks on the possible types or modes of historical representation suggested by figurative analysis, on the other.[1]

Transitional Expressions

While whole sentences of metadiscourse can clarify the overall direction and purpose of an essay, brief transitional expressions provide a way to express the relationship between ideas. Some examples include "however," "but," "nevertheless,"

---

[1] Hayden White, *Tropics of Discourse* (Baltimore, MD: Johns Hopkins University Press, 1978), 106.

"moreover," "at the same time," "still," and "on the one hand . . . on the other hand." You may use words like these even in your readerly drafts, but you might omit them when the relationship between two ideas seems obvious to you. To the reader, however, such words greatly help to clarify your thinking.

Definitions

Definitions are of two kinds: stipulative definitions and dictionary definitions. A stipulative definition is a special definition for a particular purpose, a meaning that a writer stipulates in the essay. Thus, in an essay on science fiction, a writer might explain, "For the purpose of this essay, the word 'fancy' refers to a particular kind of creative imagination, the faculty of imagining beings and places that do not exist in reality." Writers often need to invest ordinary terms with a special meaning, and these may well need definition since the reader cannot simply go to a dictionary to find the meaning. If the writer does not explain the term, it will remain unclear.

In high school, you sometimes might have included a dictionary definition of a key word in your essay as a clarification strategy, but in a college paper you should assume that readers will use the dictionary themselves, if necessary, to find the general meaning of terms. Include a dictionary definition only if a word has a technical or specialized sense that would not be familiar to an educated reader.

Composing Titles

The title is an important element in any college essay. The title is a clarification strategy because an effective title gives the reader a sense of the scope of the essay, its purpose and argument. Craft a title that points to what is unique about your essay. Titles in the humanities tend to be structured differently from those in the natural sciences. In the humanities, writers often give their essays a two-part title separated by a colon. The first part of the title is more imaginative, and the second part is more

---

> **Try This** **Working with Transitional Expressions**
>
> Working with a classmate, choose two different passages from one of the essays included in this book. Rewrite one of the passages, omitting all the transitional expressions. Your classmate will rewrite the other passage. Exchange your notebooks and write out the passage once more, this time putting transitional expressions back into the passage by considering where they are most needed and which expressions would work best. Compare your rewritten passage to the original. Which is clearer? (You may have made some improvements!)

descriptive. In the natural sciences, titles tend to be strictly descriptive. Consider the following examples, taken from a variety of professional journals:

Ethos and Error: How Businesspeople React to Errors

The Monster in the Rainbow: Keats and the Science of Life

Deep Play: Notes on the Balinese Cockfight

Incorporating Nonverbal Behaviors into Affect Control Theory

Sustained Photobiological Hydrogen Gas Production upon Reversible Inactivation of Oxygen Evolution in the Green Alga *Chlamydomonas reinhardtii*

The second-to-last title, for a sociology article, resembles the last title, for a plant physiology article, in that it is strictly descriptive. But the first, second, and third titles — for articles in composition, English, and anthropology — each have two parts, a more poetic and intriguing first half and a more descriptive second half. This reflects the fact that these disciplines do not insist on detachment, impersonality, and objectivity to the same extent as do the natural sciences. But all these titles strive to signal the essential purpose of the article and help to clarify this purpose for the reader.

✅ Checklist for Organizing an Argument Essay

Be sure to include the following kinds of paragraphs in your argument essay.

☐ Introductory paragraph(s) (usually one, but no more than two)
  - Describe a problem of some kind (a knowledge problem or a practical problem).
  - Offer a solution in a thesis statement, usually in the first paragraph, usually of one or two sentences.

☐ Body paragraphs (usually at least three)
  - Begin with a claim, followed by support for the claim.
  - Develop a new component of the argument. (Complex components may need more than one paragraph.)
  - Address counterarguments, typically toward the end of the essay.

☐ Concluding paragraph(s) (usually one, but no more than two)
  - Bring closure to the essay.
  - Mention questions that remain unanswered and/or directions for further research or thinking.
  - Offer a send-off, not merely a reiteration of the main argument (which should already be clear).

Organizing an Expository Essay

The term "expository" is often used for argument essays, but in a strict sense it refers to writing that explains an idea or a topic in order to *inform* rather than persuade the reader. Much of the advice in this book concerning the reading and writing process (see Chapters 1–4), paragraph structure (see "Revising Paragraphs," p. 140), style (see Chapter 8), and research methods (see Chapters 9 and 10) applies to expository writing as much as to argument writing. Expository writing is often necessary within an argument essay — or you may be given an assignment that asks you to explain or describe something rather than make an argument. For example, you might get an assignment that asks you to explain one of the following:

- how a process functions or how something is accomplished through a series of steps
- how something works or how one thing caused or causes another
- how something happened or how a sequence of events led to an outcome
- how two or more positions or things compare

The aim of expository writing is to define an idea, a thing, or a process and then set it forth in a clear, detailed, and thorough way.

Introduction

The introduction to an expository essay should define the topic clearly. Explaining why the topic is interesting or significant is often useful. This kind of assignment does not usually ask you to make an argument of your own, so a thesis statement is usually not needed. (You may be expected, however, to summarize other writers' arguments within the body of the essay.)

Body Paragraphs

Break your subject into its component parts or aspects and arrange them logically — for example, in their order of importance, in the order they happen or happened, in order of cause and effect, or according to some other logical arrangement. Devote a separate paragraph to each component part.

In each paragraph, incorporate specific details that help the reader understand the process or sequence or operation you are explaining. Explain similarities and contrasts as precisely as possible. Include helpful examples where appropriate. Keep your quotations short: readers usually find an explanation more clear if they do not have to switch from one context to another and back again, as long quotations would require them to do.

When revising, make sure your paragraphs are coherent and unified. Each paragraph should have a topic sentence that governs the paragraph as a whole. Repeating key concepts (using variations on a key word) will help keep the topic in the foreground (see pp. 132–33). Use transitional words and phrases between sentences and paragraphs to show how ideas are connected.

Conclusion

If your exposition has been clear (and it should be), there will be no need to repeat all your main points in the conclusion. Instead, use the concluding paragraph as a place to reflect on the significance of the subject you have explained. What is the subject's importance? Why does it matter? The best concluding paragraphs work more like a send-off than a wrap-up, so you might give your reader something to think about by raising some questions or suggesting a plan of action: What remains to be done? What is not yet understood or known? What problems or mysteries remain unsolved?

Organizing an Exploratory Essay

Normally a thesis is the solution to a problem — either a practical problem or a knowledge problem. But many problems, while interesting and important, are too difficult or complex to be neatly solved, even with a good deal of research. The exploratory essay lets writers explore a difficult problem without necessarily having to offer a complete solution. Such an essay *seeks* a solution, but it may or may not arrive at one — or it may arrive at a partial or provisional or tentative solution. Its chief purpose is to shed light on the problem by thinking it through carefully and to arrive at a deeper understanding of the issues.

Many essays are exploratory in form and purpose — from the essays of Michel de Montaigne, the sixteenth-century French writer generally considered to be the inventor of the essay form, to those we now find in magazines and blogs. Exploratory essays are not the norm in academic writing, where writers typically present the results of scholarly research and make a case for their solution to a problem. However, in some disciplines, especially in the humanities, exploratory essays are becoming more common. As a college student, you may be required to write an exploratory essay in a composition course or perhaps a philosophy or women's studies course, or you may encounter an assignment that, in your view, lends itself to an exploratory approach (but be sure to ask your instructor whether such an approach will be acceptable).

In some respects, an exploratory essay looks like the informal writing that you do when seeking a thesis for an argument essay (see Chapter 4, p. 96): exploratory essays adopt a more informal style and trace a more circuitous path around a problem than thesis-driven essays typically do. However, though they may appear to be more freely organized, successful exploratory essays are nevertheless highly polished and carefully structured — thus they are more readerly than informal writing usually is. They often tell a story, with less focus on claim and evidence, and may have a narrative structure rather than a logical one. They may emphasize suggestion and implication over argumentation. They may move from topic to topic by association rather than through strict logic.

The essay "Bumping into Mr. Ravioli" by Adam Gopnik (p. 385) is a good example of an exploratory essay. The first three paragraphs explain a problem, one that may strike us as amusing and perhaps trivial but that turns out to entail some serious questions about our contemporary way of life. Gopnik takes the reader through his various attempts to understand and respond to this problem — through the stages of a kind of research project, in fact, as he first consults his sister, a child psychologist, then draws on his own knowledge of literary and cultural history, and then studies his daughter's fiction more closely. At each stage, he comes to understand the problem better, reframing it as necessary. Finally, the essay takes a surprising turn, and although Gopnik may not have "solved" his problem exactly, he has come to see it in a different light and is no longer so anxious about it. Exploratory essays frequently offer the reader food for thought rather than a solution.

While the form of the exploratory essay is freer than that of the argument essay, several general principles can guide us. First, instead of being centered on a thesis that governs or drives the argument throughout, an exploratory essay is driven by a central question or problem. So whereas we can describe the argument essay as thesis-driven, we can describe the exploratory essay as question-driven. The sense of the question or problem may evolve as the essay proceeds, but the essay does not meander aimlessly. The search for insight keeps it moving forward. One reason that

→ **Try This** **Analyzing an Episode in an Exploratory Essay**

Adam Gopnik's essay "Bumping into Mr. Ravioli" (p. 385) is composed of four sections or episodes, separated by white space. Read through the entire essay. Then choose one section to reread carefully. How does the section you have chosen move the story forward? What new information or perspective does it introduce? How does it change or complicate the "intellectual quest" or search for understanding? Take detailed notes and write them up in a short essay.

college instructors assign this kind of essay is that sustaining such a quest over several pages requires students to think deeply about the problem at hand.

Exploratory essays are often structured like stories. A story always has a beginning, a middle, and an end, and it often contains several **episodes** that make up the plot. We're all familiar with the notion of episodes from television dramas in which weekly installments, each with its own little plot, together make up a story with a long, complicated plot. An exploratory essay may adopt an *episodic* structure: a series of fairly distinct segments makes up the essay as a whole. (Geoff Dyer's "Blues for Vincent" [p. 358] and Adam Gopnik's "Bumping into Mr. Ravioli" [p. 385], for example, are each composed of several episodes separated by small breaks in the text.) An episode in an exploratory essay does not necessarily have a story, however: an episode could be made up entirely of reflection or description or analysis or argumentation or another type of writing — or of some combination of types. But it should have a certain unity as a segment.

A good way to begin transforming informal exploratory writing into a formal exploratory essay is to identify several episodes — key stages, moments, or incidents in your exploration — and arrange them so that the exploration develops steadily, without all the repetition and circling and dead ends that tend to clog up informal writing. These episodes will make up the middle of the story.

The beginning of the essay will typically define the problem or question that launches the whole exploration. Unlike a thesis-driven essay, however, the exploratory essay does not offer an answer or a solution until the very end (and often not even then). If a solution presents itself prematurely, it must be rigorously questioned: this is what makes the essay "question-driven" rather than "thesis-driven." The essay insists on digging deeper, exploring further, examining more closely. The end of the essay will typically offer some epiphany, clarification, or moment of understanding that brings the essay to a satisfying conclusion even if it does not fully answer the question or solve the problem.

So the exploratory essay presents the story of a quest, an intellectual quest. Like any quest-story, it takes the reader along on an adventure, one that may contain surprising twists and turns and may lead to a quite unexpected destination. But even if the problem remains unsolved, the journey should feel worthwhile, and the reader should be left with a sense of having learned something.

Some exploratory essays tell multiple stories, either in a series or as interwoven strands. Each story or fragment may be offered as a stand-alone segment, with the relationships between the segments suggested only by a similarity in theme or through some other kind of echo. Geoff Dyer's "Blues for Vincent" is a short essay of this type, consisting of four brief sections that at first seem to have little connection to each other. But after rereading the essay, we notice ways in which they may be related after all. Dyer trusts his readers to make sense of his fragments and to find meaning in his disjointed material.

Comparing the Argument Essay and the Exploratory Essay

Table 6.1 (see below) provides a quick overview comparing the two essay forms.

One way to see the difference between the organization of an exploratory (or question-driven) essay and an argument (or thesis-driven) essay is to look at two

Table 6.1 Comparison of Argument and Exploratory Essays

	Argument Essay	Exploratory Essay
Purpose	To persuade the reader that an idea is valid	To explore and deepen the reader's understanding of a problem
Impetus	Thesis-driven	Question-driven
Structure	Logical structure	Mostly narrative structure
Modes of discourse	Keeps primarily to argument mode	Often combines several modes of discourse

sample essays on similar topics, one in argument form and the other in exploratory form. In a course on "The Frontier and American Identity," the instructor assigned a three- to five-page midterm essay on this topic: "Why did President Franklin Pierce sign the Kansas-Nebraska bill (1854) into law?" One student, Kelly Rivera, conducted extensive research in her college library and was ultimately able to draw some conclusions. Even though the historical situation was complicated, she decided that the question posed could be answered, and she felt strongly about the position she had adopted. So she wrote an argument essay in thesis-driven form.[2]

Sample Essay in Argument Form

This essay in argument form presents a thesis at the end of two introductory paragraphs. Body paragraphs present claims that support the thesis. The writer integrates sources to provide support for her claims.

---

[2] Although this paper and the one by Greg Fernandez (p. 202) were written for a dual-credit English and history course and so use MLA documentation, papers for history classes often employ the documentation system outlined in the *Chicago Manual of Style* (see the Appendix for more information). Be sure to check with your instructor about the format you should use.

Kelly Rivera

Professor Lyman

RHET/HIS 201: The Frontier and American Identity

31 October 2015

A Fatal Compromise: President Franklin Pierce

and the Kansas-Nebraska Bill of 1854

Why did Franklin Pierce sign the Kansas-Nebraska bill of 1854 into law? This bill established two new territories in land that had been acquired as part of the Louisiana Purchase and later set aside as Indian Territory. In order to establish these new territories, Congress had to address the delicate question of whether slavery would be allowed in them; it was this aspect of the bill that made it a turning point in American history. Southerners were determined to see that slavery would be permitted, but many in the North feared the political power of the southern slave states and were equally determined that slavery would be prohibited. Earlier agreements on the slavery question left an ambiguous precedent. The Missouri Compromise of 1820 had restricted slavery to territories that fell below 36°30' latitude. But the Compromise of 1850 that established the territories of New Mexico and Utah left the decision in the hands of local residents rather than Congress: in other words, these new territories would decide the slavery question for themselves. The Kansas-Nebraska bill applied this principle of "popular sovereignty" to Kansas and Nebraska and explicitly repealed the Missouri Compromise, which was incompatible with this principle. It was the repeal of this compromise that provoked anger in the North and ultimately led to the creation of the Republican Party and a political standoff that would drag the country into civil war.

Introduction begins with historical context.

Rivera 2

President Franklin Pierce, elected in 1852, had always
supported the principle that the federal government should
avoid interfering in matters that concerned individual states, so
he was a strong supporter of the Compromise of 1850 and the
principle of popular sovereignty. But he was reluctant, at least
initially, to repeal the Missouri Compromise, anger northerners,
and reopen the slavery question once more. Though a
northerner, he agreed with many of his fellow Democrats,
especially those from the South, that slavery was a question
of "states' rights." And he believed, or hoped, that the whole
question had been settled once and for all by the agreements
of 1820 and 1850. However, he became convinced that only a
bill that explicitly repealed the Missouri Compromise had any
chance of passing in the House of Representatives. And he felt
that the advantages of opening the new territories to a railroad
through the center of the continental United States were
worth the political price: the potential benefits to the country
overshadowed the anger the bill would surely provoke. For these
reasons, Pierce signed the bill.

End of introduction presents thesis.

Pierce, like many northerners, was never morally opposed
to slavery. He believed that slavery was a states' rights
issue, and his cabinet included several southern Democrats
who believed deeply that slavery, the South's "peculiar
institution," was morally defensible and protected by the
Constitution. In the words of one biographer, Pierce saw the
United States as "the creation of sovereign states with each
state retaining the right to allow slavery within its border"
(Gara, *Presidency* 79). However, he was opposed to repealing
the Missouri Compromise of 1820; he knew that this would
reawaken a bitter controversy. But he probably overestimated

Claim: Pierce was not morally opposed to slavery but saw it as a states' rights issue.

Rivera 3

the strength of the Democratic Party in the North and underestimated the depth of the anger that the repeal would arouse (Wolff 128).

For many northerners, slavery was more objectionable for the threat that it posed to the balance of power than for the way it abused human beings. The Constitution declared that slaves were to be counted as three-fifths of a white person; they could not vote, of course, but this method of calculating population meant that southern slave states held a larger number of seats in Congress relative to the actual voting population than free states. Most northerners opposed "slave power" rather than slavery itself, so they were more concerned about preventing the spread of slavery than about abolishing it altogether. Few northerners were strict abolitionists; even the Free Soil Party was more concerned with containing the power of the slave states than it was with the conditions or rights of the slaves themselves (Gara, "Slavery" 5-6). Those who did oppose slavery in principle generally saw it as the business of the southern states to abolish it. If northern states were to interfere with southern affairs, after all, what was to stop the South from interfering in northern affairs? As Larry Gara explains, southerners "feared that free territory to the west would make their own slave property insecure. They insisted, through [Senator] Atchison, that legislation creating a new western territory include a provision repealing the 1820 compromise. That was the spark that set a major Free Soil fire in the North. It was clear evidence to the northerners of the influence of the slave power" (*Presidency* 89).

The chief reason for organizing Kansas and Nebraska into territories had less to do with new settlements than with

Claim: fear of "slave power" was greater than opposition to slavery.

Rivera 4

a transcontinental railroad. The Kansas-Nebraska Act came about as a result of a "railroad mania" that was sweeping the country from 1847 to 1857 (Hodder 4). Since the acquisition of California, following the war with Mexico, a transcontinental railroad was considered essential. Pierce, like most of his countrymen, believed strongly in the need for a railroad that would stretch across the country and help unite the nation. He foresaw the "emergence of the United States as a potential two-ocean power requiring transcontinental railroad and telegraph lines to link its various sections" (Gara, *Presidency* 74). A route across the South, from New Orleans to San Diego, had been made possible by the Gadsden Purchase, but such a route would be unacceptable to northerners, who would gain no advantage from it. Uniting the country meant finding a central route, and this meant abolishing what Patricia Nelson Limerick calls the "lingering fiction" of a permanent Indian Territory. Stephen A. Douglas expressed the problem succinctly:

> The idea of arresting our progress in that direction . . . has become so ludicrous that we are amazed, that wise and patriotic statesmen ever cherished the thought. . . . How are we to develop, cherish and protect our immense interests and possessions on the Pacific, with a vast wilderness fifteen hundred miles in breadth, filled with hostile savages, and cutting off all direct communication. The Indian barrier must be removed. (qtd. in Limerick 92-93)

For most white Americans, Indian interests were now of little concern. And in fact, even some Indians, the Wyandot tribe, supported the organization of Nebraska into a territory so that they could receive federal protection (Gara, *Presidency* 89).

Claim: Pierce felt a railroad would unite the nation.

Claim: a central route was key.

Rivera 5

The "key to the whole matter," argues Roy F. Nichols, is "the process of becoming" (197). Nichols argues that we can only understand why the Kansas-Nebraska Act came into being when we stop looking for its cause in the will, ambition, or hope of particular individuals, such as Senator Stephen A. Douglas or Representative Alexander H. Stephens, and instead look at the way that the bill in its final form came into being: it was the product of a long process of bartering and deal-making with congressmen from all over the country who held a wide variety of interests and convictions. The Whig Party was disintegrating, and the Democratic Party was undergoing a transformation. The "real history" of the bill, says Nichols, "is the analysis of how a bill ostensibly to organize a territory had been made an instrument of the fundamental political reorganization that that disintegration of the old parties had made inevitable" (211). This struggle within the parties determined the bill's final form, so that in the end it bore little resemblance to the first bill that Douglas had introduced in 1853. The struggle to win support had resulted in a bill that no single individual really authored. It does not follow that Pierce's support was inevitable, but this does suggest that Pierce too was swept up in a tide of change that he could not control.

Pierce became persuaded that repealing the Missouri Compromise was inescapable during a meeting with Douglas, Jefferson Davis, and other leading senators (Gara, *Presidency* 90). Missouri senator David R. Atchison, president of the Senate (and in effect vice president since the death of Vice President William King shortly after the inauguration), was particularly insistent that the Missouri Compromise must be repealed. Missouri's slave owners worried that if land

Claim: repeal had become necessary.

Rivera 6

to the west of their state was free, their own slaves would run away (Gara, *Presidency* 89). Therefore, even though many southerners did not demand the repeal of the 1820 compromise, the insistence of a powerful few made it seem unavoidable. Without the repeal, no territories, and without the territories, no central railroad. Once Pierce became convinced of this, he worked hard to get support for the bill in the House. Historian Gerald Wolff writes that although Pierce is often described as "an inept and weak President," he proved to be "on the whole, both competent and effective" in winning support for the Nebraska bill among northern Democrats in the House (80).

The election that brought Pierce to the White House had been a triumph for the Democratic Party; in fact, it represented the death of the Whig Party. Pierce could not have foreseen that the Kansas-Nebraska Act would galvanize its opponents, uniting them in opposition to the expansion of slavery, and

Claim: consequences were unforeseeable.

lead to the establishment of the Republican Party. Nor could he have foreseen the bloodshed in Kansas and the Civil War.

Perhaps a president of stronger and more determined character would have been able to resist Senator Douglas and the others who insisted on the repeal of the Missouri Compromise. It is tempting perhaps, but ultimately unfair, to pass judgment with the benefit of hindsight. President Pierce was in a difficult position, and perhaps no one could have prevented the return of a conflict between North and South that had been intensifying throughout the first half of the

Conclusion: we can't judge fairly from the present.

century. And perhaps, if the Kansas-Nebraska Act did hasten the country toward the complete abolition of slavery at last, it was not an entirely bad thing.

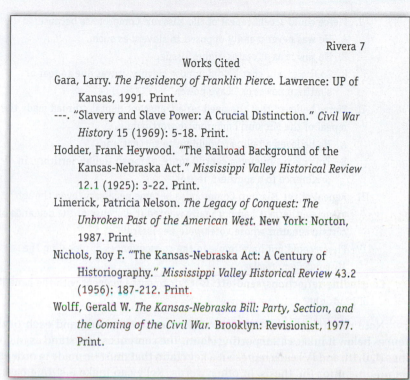

Rivera 7

Works Cited

Gara, Larry. *The Presidency of Franklin Pierce.* Lawrence: UP of
    Kansas, 1991. Print.

---. "Slavery and Slave Power: A Crucial Distinction." *Civil War
    History* 15 (1969): 5-18. Print.

Hodder, Frank Heywood. "The Railroad Background of the
    Kansas-Nebraska Act." *Mississippi Valley Historical Review*
    12.1 (1925): 3-22. Print.

Limerick, Patricia Nelson. *The Legacy of Conquest: The
    Unbroken Past of the American West.* New York: Norton,
    1987. Print.

Nichols, Roy F. "The Kansas-Nebraska Act: A Century of
    Historiography." *Mississippi Valley Historical Review* 43.2
    (1956): 187-212. Print.

Wolff, Gerald W. *The Kansas-Nebraska Bill: Party, Section, and
    the Coming of the Civil War.* Brooklyn: Revisionist, 1977.
    Print.

Analysis

The essay's argument is governed by a clear thesis: "Though reluctant at first to repeal the Missouri Compromise, Pierce signed the Kansas-Nebraska bill because he believed the bill was worth the price." As you would expect, the purpose of the essay is to demonstrate by means of evidence and reasoning that this thesis is valid. So the thesis statement is the essay's main claim, and the other claims play a supporting role. The organization becomes clearer when we look at the essay in outline form, as a sequence of claims that support the thesis. Each claim represents the focus of a different paragraph.

Introduction: historical context of the question.

Thesis: Despite his reluctance, Pierce signed the Kansas-Nebraska bill because he believed the bill was worth the political cost of repealing the Missouri Compromise.

    I. Pierce could accept repeal of the Missouri Compromise because:

        A. He was never morally opposed to slavery as such.

        B. He saw it as a "states' rights" issue.

        C. To the extent that he did oppose slavery, it was due to fear of southern power or "slave power."

    II. Pierce believed that the need for a transcontinental railroad made the repeal of the Missouri Compromise worthwhile.

        A. He believed a railroad would unite the nation.

        B. This meant finding a central route, through Indian Territory, in preference to a southern route.

    III. Repeal of the Missouri Compromise became necessary, even though many southerners had not really wanted it, because of the demands of certain senators whose votes were necessary.

    IV. Pierce could not have foreseen the consequences of repealing the Missouri Compromise.

Concluding reflections/send-off: Is it fair to pass judgment with the benefit of hindsight?

Note that the thesis statement makes a master claim, and each of the sentences below it makes a supporting claim. The sentences that stand as major headings (I, II, III, and IV) each represent a key claim that must be made in order to make an argument for the thesis. In other words, Kelly can make a strong case for her thesis by making a case for each of these claims, or subtheses. Each claim is a kind of miniature thesis, and the sentences that stand as minor headings (A, B, C) also make claims that support the claims that stand above them in the hierarchy.

An essay structured in this way makes it easy for the reader to follow the argument because the structure guides the reader along point by point or claim by claim. The main thesis appears at the end of the introduction, just where the reader expects to find it, and the components of the argument, the claims, have been placed in prominent positions, at the beginning of paragraphs. Thus the argument is firmly in the foreground, and the supporting evidence does what it should do: supporting the claims, not burying them.

→ **Try**This   **Writing an Exploratory Essay**

Write an exploratory essay on the subject of rights for great apes, using the two sample essays (p. 167 and p. 173) as starting points. If you wish, develop your ideas by conducting research in the library or on the Internet, using the bibliographies that follow each of the sample essays as a starting point.

Sample Essay in Exploratory Form

Let's now look at an exploratory (or question-driven) essay on the same topic as Kelly Rivera's argument (or thesis-driven) essay. Greg Fernandez did similar research but ultimately felt that the topic left more questions in his mind than answers. He could see that certain kinds of answers might suffice from certain points of view, but for him the question of why President Pierce signed the Kansas-Nebraska bill opened up perspectives that only led to further questions. After discussing his ideas with his professor, Greg asked if he could write an essay that explored his questions rather than one that made an argument for a definite thesis. Greg's professor encouraged him to give it a try.

Fernandez 1

Greg Fernandez

Professor Delgado

RHET/HIS 201: The Frontier and American Identity

31 October 2015

Exploring the "Whys" of History:

Franklin Pierce and the Kansas-Nebraska Bill of 1854

Why did President Franklin Pierce sign the Kansas-Nebraska bill into law in 1854 and thereby repeal the Missouri Compromise of 1820 and reopen the slavery question? At the start of my research, I found myself focusing almost obsessively on the word "why." It puzzled me because it seemed to point directly toward the question of Pierce's motivation, and motivation can be considered from any number of perspectives. A person might approach it from the point of view of biography: How did the events in Pierce's life story lead him to this crucial decision? Or from the point of view of culture: How did the culture of his time make it possible to allow slavery to expand? Or from the point of view of politics: How did political forces make it necessary for Pierce to sign a bill he may have personally disliked? Or from the point of view of psychology: How did his own inner conflicts make him follow Congress rather than lead it?

And these were, I suspected, just a few of the possibilities.

At this point, it seemed that to provide anything like a sufficient answer to the question "Why?" would be impossible—not only because I faced the usual limitations of time and space but also because it would be impossible to "get inside the head" of a man who lived a century and a half ago. As far as I could tell

Introduction: this is the question that drives the essay.

Fernandez 2

from the biographies, Pierce never left a complete explanation
of why he signed the bill, and even if he had, it would be
difficult to know how much of it to believe (Gara, *Presidency*
119). But after further reading and research, I began to feel
that my initial doubts might be a kind of trap and that, in a
way, I was already answering my question. That is, it may well
be impossible to give any *complete* answer, but the fact that I
had already been able to carve up the question into different
approaches suggested that I might be able to find *some* kind
of answer. As I read historians' accounts of the journey of the
bill from its beginning as one man's idea to its destination as
the law of the land, I realized that historians do know enough
about the events of that time to make it possible to draw some
conclusions and make some educated guesses.[1] I decided to
start with the approach that seemed most practical and feasible:
the political perspective. So I looked at the question in this
way: President Pierce and the Democrats hoped and believed
that the slavery question had been settled by the Compromises
of 1820 and 1850, so how did *political* forces influence Pierce
to sign this bill that repealed the Missouri Compromise of 1820
and reopened the whole question?

In Larry Gara's biography of Franklin Pierce and in
Gerald Wolff's *The Kansas-Nebraska Bill: Party, Section,
and the Coming of the Civil War,* I found some clues. Many,
perhaps most, southerners were not especially eager to see

*A way forward:
answer doesn't have
to be complete;
multiple approaches
are possible.*

[1] For a striking example of a historian's educated
guesswork, about Stephen Douglas's motivation for promoting
the bill with such energy, see Limerick 111.

Fernandez 3

the Missouri Compromise repealed. After all, it did seem to prevent further interference by northerners in the southern

Political approach.

way of life. But some southern politicians, and in particular some from Missouri, were worried that the new territory to their west, Missouri's next-door neighbor, would pose a danger to their own "property" (i.e., their slaves) if it was free. Their only hope for the creation of a slave state on the western border of Missouri was to get the Missouri Compromise repealed; thereafter they might see to it that the referendum in Kansas went in favor of slavery (Gara, *Presidency* 89-90; Wolff 160). Senator Atchison of Missouri was particularly powerful: he was the president of the Senate and, since the death of William King in 1852, vice president of the United States. Without his support, and the support of his cronies (the so-called "F Street Mess"), the bill was dead, and there would be no new territories and no railroad across the country (Nichols 204; Hodder 11-14). So Pierce saw that the repeal of the Missouri Compromise was necessary, and he gave his support to the bill. From that point on, it was inevitable that he would sign it into law once it passed through Congress.

This gave me one kind of answer: a political answer—a partial answer looking at the question from one point of

Transition to other approaches.

view. What about the other points of view—the personal, the cultural, the psychological, and so on? These angles might call for more speculation, but even here it seems possible to say something.

The cultural or moral aspect of the question had already become fairly clear: How could Pierce allow himself to sign the bill, repeal the Missouri Compromise, and open the new

Fernandez 4

territories to slavery? Pierce was not opposed to slavery in principle, it appears, and though he was a New England lawyer and not a southern slave owner, he appointed a number of southern slave owners and defenders of slavery to his cabinet (Gara, *Presidency* 44-47). Racism in the mid-1800s was not confined to the South; it seems to have been a widespread attitude. Most whites seemed to have thought that whites were superior, a point of view supported, they believed, by scripture and by nature. Racist views were deeply ingrained in the American mind and openly expressed by leading politicians of the North as well as the South. For example, in 1839 Lewis Cass wrote in the *North American Review,* "There can be no doubt . . . that the Creator intended the earth should be reclaimed from a state of nature and cultivated" (qtd. in Gara, *Presidency* 75). Senator Thomas Hart Benton asserted that whites had the best claim to the land because they "used it according to the intentions of the CREATOR" (qtd. in Gara, *Presidency* 75). There was even talk of transforming Indians into Christian farmers who would gradually become part of white society, but this suggestion met resistance (Limerick 40). Caleb Cushing, a Massachusetts politician, would not admit as his equals "either the red man, of America, or the yellow man of Asia, nor the black man of Africa" (qtd. in Gara, *Presidency* 75), and Stephen A. Douglas referred to the trans-Mississippi West as "filled with hostile savages" (qtd. in Limerick 93).

It is difficult for a student today to comprehend these attitudes, to understand how intelligent, religious, and apparently moral men and women could be so indifferent to the rights of individuals of a different race or culture.

Cultural approach: racism.

Fernandez 5

Cultural approach: religion.

Perhaps one clue can be found in the religious language used by politicians quoted here: perhaps they genuinely believed that God had made Europeans superior to other races, and men superior to women. Perhaps they believed that the Bible, the Word of God, declared this. They thought of the United States as white and Protestant (Gara, "Slavery" 16). Yet not *all* Americans believed this. Christians like Gerrit Smith believed that slavery was evil and must be abolished, and the former slave Frederick Douglass was revealing the dark truth about slavery; northerners could not really plead ignorance (Rawley 165-66). Did the majority truly believe in white superiority, or did they just persuade themselves of what they wanted to believe, what was convenient to believe?

Why could not Pierce, who, if not a great statesman, was not an evil man, see the evil that slavery represented? Why couldn't most Americans? The Constitution stated that all men were created equal, but evidently Americans did not take this literally or did not apply it to African American slaves. And still today, we cannot say that we have achieved full equality among the citizens of this country: women, blacks, gays, and lesbians remain in certain respects unequal.

Personal approach.

It may be more difficult to draw firm conclusions about the way Pierce's personal life and character influenced his decision, yet I found myself more fascinated with this aspect of the question than with any other. After all, Pierce's personal qualities must have entered into the equation somehow, though it might be hard to say exactly how. I was struck by historians' low estimation of Pierce's abilities and achievements. The reader cannot help pitying him a little: he was a kind of accidental president who never sought the office. His party nominated him because he seemed to provide a way out of a stalemate, and he won the election only by being less objectionable than the Whig candidate, Winfield Scott. He was relatively young, just forty-seven at the start of his presidency, and a heavy drinker, perhaps even an alcoholic. And from the beginning, his presidency was beset by tragedy. After having lost three children in infancy, Pierce and his wife lost their only surviving child shortly before the inauguration. In front of their eyes, he was crushed in a train accident ("Franklin Pierce"). Not long after, Pierce lost his vice president, William King, and a close friend and ally, Charles Atherton (Gara, *Presidency* 76). Perhaps this left the new vice president, Senator Atchison of Missouri, in a position of even greater influence over Pierce.

At the end of my research and after all my reflections and speculations, I felt satisfied that I had learned something about why Pierce signed the Kansas-Nebraska bill. But I also arrived at a further conclusion. In history, answers are always going to be fragmentary and partial—just educated guesses, really. Our knowledge of history is full of holes, like a moth-eaten quilt, and it will always remain so. That, I suppose, is why historians are always debating one another and always coming up with new angles from which to look at old issues. Why did President Pierce sign the Kansas-Nebraska bill? Perhaps we can never know fully *why* historical events occur: the causes are too many, and the record is too thin. But we can discover plausible possibilities. The record teaches us, at least, how one ordinary, flawed human being shaped the country's destiny, without the benefit of foresight.

His conclusion is somewhat tentative.

Fernandez 7

Works Cited

"Franklin Pierce." *Encyclopaedia Britannica Online.*
Encyclopaedia Britannica, 2011. Web. 28 Oct. 2015.

Gara, Larry. *The Presidency of Franklin Pierce.* Lawrence: UP of
Kansas, 1991. Print.

---. "Slavery and Slave Power: A Crucial Distinction." *Civil War
History* 15 (1969): 5-18. Print.

Hodder, Frank Heywood. "The Railroad Background of the
Kansas-Nebraska Act." *Mississippi Valley Historical Review*
12.1 (1925): 3-22. Print.

Limerick, Patricia Nelson. *The Legacy of Conquest: The
Unbroken Past of the American West.* New York: Norton,
1987. Print.

Nichols, Roy F. "The Kansas-Nebraska Act: A Century of
Historiography." *Mississippi Valley Historical Review* 43.2
(1956): 187-212. Print.

Rawley, James A. *Race and Politics: "Bleeding Kansas" and the
Coming of the Civil War.* Philadelphia: Lippincott, 1969.
Print.

Wolff, Gerald W. *The Kansas-Nebraska Bill: Party, Section, and
the Coming of the Civil War.* Brooklyn: Revisionist, 1977.
Print.

Analysis

This essay is governed by its opening question: "Why did President Franklin Pierce sign the Kansas-Nebraska bill into law in 1854 and thereby repeal the Missouri Compromise of 1820 and reopen the slavery question?" The paper explores this question, coming at it from several different angles. While there is no clear thesis, or master claim, that drives the paper and supplies a method of organization, the possible answers to this question (which make up the body paragraphs) serve that purpose. The paper's organization will become clear as we examine its structure. The introduction proposes the question. It is followed by "a way forward," laying out the terms of the writer's intention; Greg writes that his answers may be incomplete but that there is merit in the exploration. This is followed by an explanation of several approaches — political, cultural, and personal — that offer insights into the question. The final paragraph offers a tentative conclusion. Here is the essay in out-line form.

I.   Definition of the problem: the difficulty of answering the question "why," especially because it seems to ask about motivation and we can't get inside his head.

II.   A way forward:
A.   My answer doesn't have to be complete to be worthwhile.
B.   I can choose from among the different angles as a way to get started.

III.   First approach: the political angle.

IV.   Further lines of investigation:
A.   The cultural approach (attitudes toward race and religion).
B.   The personal approach: his tragedies—death of his son and vice president.

V.   Tentative conclusion or upshot: History doesn't offer certain answers—it's a quilt full of holes.

⊕ Try This   Writing the Story of Your Quest

Begin with a problem from a textbook or a writing assignment. Write first to work toward a better understanding of the problem or question. Then figure out ways to find answers: What work does it entail—rereading? research? interviews? a museum visit? archival work? Keep a careful moment-to-moment journal of your work. At some point, you should come to a conclusion of some kind—perhaps not an answer, but at least a point of view, or a theory, or even just a deeper understanding of the question. Then write this up as a quest narrative: identify the key moments in the quest, the missteps as well as the steps forward, and shape your freewriting into a readerly essay.

As we mentioned above, an exploratory essay is structured as a narrative, or story. Any question-driven, exploratory essay will contain three elements — a beginning, a middle, and an end. And since the story is your story, it will typically talk about you. Therefore, you will need to use the word "I" to tell your story, as Greg does.

Now, the story may contain several stories, as well as passages that reflect on the meaning or significance of those stories. For example, in order to define the central problem or question of the essay, you may need to tell the story of how you came to recognize its importance or urgency. Notice how Greg discusses his obsession and puzzlement in his introduction. A vivid account of the context or occasion of the problem is often essential to the reader's understanding of why the question matters and is interesting. And your account of the things you did in order to solve the problem or answer the question may include stories: for example, you might have gone to the library and read a book about some episode in history or someone's life, and such a story might become part of your larger narrative. Or you might have conducted an interview with someone, and this interview becomes a story (itself perhaps containing the interviewee's stories) within your narrative. The skills of storytelling are thus essential to the exploratory essay. The best exploratory essays tell good stories, ones that hold readers' interest and keep them reading even though they do not know what the story's outcome will be. As you revise, bear in mind that the exploratory essay is not the quest itself, but rather a crafted narrative of the quest. You will need to select, shape, and organize your story so that it effectively takes readers down the path of ideas that you have traced.

Rogerian Rhetoric

Rogerian rhetoric is a special kind of exploratory argumentation based on the idea that genuine problem solving involves listening as much as speaking. That is, while traditional rhetoric emphasizes the strategies by which a speaker can persuade his or her listeners, Rogerian rhetoric emphasizes the ways that two individuals with different views or perspectives can arrive at an understanding. How does this work for an individual writer? Essentially, it means constructing a kind of dialogue with an opposing position and taking that other position seriously.

Rogerian rhetoric has its origins in the work of Carl Rogers, a twentieth-century psychologist who applied the lessons he had learned as a therapist to conflicts between social groups and even nations. Even deeply entrenched conflicts could be resolved, he believed, when opponents honestly seek common ground, when each adversary tries to see the situation through the other's eyes. This takes imagination and humility but can be remarkably illuminating. (It could be seen as an extension of the "principle of charity" that we discussed in Chapter 1 — see p. 43.) Rogerian rhetoric takes an exploratory approach to argument in that it encourages a willingness to change or even reverse one's position as the writing proceeds.

The first step is to present an opposing or differing viewpoint *as it would be presented by someone who genuinely holds that view.* So, for example, if you were writing about gun control and started with the belief that all automatic weapons should be banned, your first duty would be to explain the position of someone who believes that all automatic weapons should be legal. And you would need to imagine that person's point of view so fully that you could explain it exactly as he or she would. You would try to understand the values and emotions that lie behind the argument as well as the argument itself. And you would try to avoid imposing your own ideas or way of thinking on the argument too hastily. You would try to put yourself in the other person's shoes and figure out where his or her argument is coming from.

The next step is to begin a kind of dialogue with the opposing position, to sort out the roots of your disagreement and find common ground. Rogerian rhetoric emphasizes caution when evaluating another's views and promotes reluctance to reject ideas or perspectives that may have some value. A mere summary of the opposing argument is not enough: you will need to work out where the argument's strengths lie and why someone might find it persuasive or reasonable. You may find

⊙ **Try**This ## Understand an Opposing Position and Seek Common Ground

Interview a classmate about a controversial issue, one on which the classmate has a different point of view than yours. Write an explanation of *your classmate's* views. Make it as complete and fair an account as possible. Explain the positive values and beliefs that underlie your classmate's position.

Next, explain your own position. Try to identify the values and beliefs that underlie your point of view.

Finally, seek out some common ground. Are any of your fundamental values shared? Or can you find any points on which you and your classmate agree?

that your own position changes (perhaps only a little, or perhaps a lot!). You may find that your argument becomes more complicated or more nuanced. You may need to qualify your argument. All these outcomes are probably desirable and may actually make your argument stronger.

The ultimate purpose of making an argument is not merely to "win" against an opponent (what does that really achieve?) but to come closer to the truth, or at the very least to deepen the reader's understanding. By genuinely considering points of view that differ from our own, we will likely come much closer to actual problem solving than if we merely shut our ears and round up all the reasons that we're right.

✅ Checklist for Organizing an Exploratory Essay

If you are writing an exploratory essay, keep the following narrative structure in mind.

☐ Beginning
   - Begin with a truly difficult problem or question.
   - Explain the problem in the opening paragraphs.

☐ Middle
   - Describe the journey of your quest for insight into the problem.
   - Dig deeper.
   - Explain shifts in direction (for example, if the nature of the problem changes).
   - Highlight moments of insight or turning points.

☐ End
   - Leave the reader with something to think about, such as an insight, a deeper appreciation of the question or problem, or a partial solution.

part 3

Attending
to Style

chapter 7

Crafting Sentences

Sentence Grammar

In this chapter and the next, we shift our attention from the "big picture" or global level of composition to the level of the sentence. We're now in the last phase of the writing process, refining and clarifying (see the workflow chart on p. 114). You already have a great many sentences in your draft, of course, so the focus here is on polishing and correcting these sentences to make them serve their purpose as effectively as possible. Reading poorly constructed sentences is irritating and tedious, but reading well-made sentences, in which the words express thoughts clearly and the sentence structure reflects the movement of thought (its ebb and flow, its rise and fall), can be a real pleasure.

> " To get the right word in the right place is a rare achievement. To condense the diffused light of a page of thought into the luminous flash of a single sentence, is worthy to rank as a prize composition just by itself. . . . Anybody can have ideas — the difficulty is to express them without squandering a quire of paper on an idea that ought to be reduced to one glittering paragraph. "
>
> **MARK TWAIN**

While this chapter focuses on grammar and Chapter 8 focuses on style, the two subjects are closely related. To achieve a pleasing and eloquent style, writers must be able to construct a range of sentence types with confidence, varying the length and complexity of their sentences to suit the need of the moment. This means knowing how to use different forms of punctuation correctly. Some ideas require short sentences. Others need to be woven together in longer sentences that suggest the relationship between ideas and give the reader a clear sense of how one thought depends on another.

Inexperienced writers are sometimes afraid to write a long sentence lest it be a "run-on"; consequently, their sentences tend to be uniformly short, and their style choppy and monotonous. However, a run-on is not a sentence that is excessively long; sentences can be long and still be perfectly readable. In fact, a run-on is an incorrectly punctuated sentence, and even a short sentence can be a run-on. Here's an example:

> We text each other frequently we are always in touch.

This sentence needs some separation between "frequently" and "we" — a semicolon, a period, a conjunction such as "so," or perhaps a dash. Each addition would have a slightly different effect on the sense of the sentence, but any would make the sentence much more readable.

The word "grammar" can refer to the underlying structure of language as it is actually used in speech and writing. In this sense, we are all experts on grammar. But "grammar" can also refer to the rules or conventions of sentence structure and punctuation. At present, we are more concerned with the second sense, because to succeed as a college writer, you need to be familiar with these rules and conventions — even if you choose to break them occasionally. In America, the rules of Standard Written English were developed and standardized in the nineteenth and early twentieth centuries, and although they continue to change with the times, the rules for formal writing change more slowly than the conventions of spoken English do. The way we write will always differ from the way we speak, because writing lacks many of the features of speaking, such as intonation and the presence of a speaker who can be asked to clarify his or her speech. You need to know little about the rules of Standard Written English in order to speak; moreover, concerning yourself with grammar when drafting can be a crippling distraction. But every writer needs to polish and correct a draft so that it expresses ideas as clearly and effectively as possible. Rhetorically, correct grammar is one way to persuade readers that you are serious and careful (appealing through *ethos*; see Chapter 5, p. 119). In the academic context, Standard Written English is expected, and a certain degree of formality is conventional. The same is true in most business contexts. In order to understand grammar as a whole, let's examine the elements of the sentence.

Clauses

Since grade school, you've known how to recognize a sentence: it begins with a capital letter and ends with a period.

But a sentence. Needs more than. Just a capital letter and a period to be complete. The three sentences just before this one are incomplete, of course: they are *sentence fragments*. A grammatical sentence must contain at least a subject and a predicate. A **subject** is the part of the sentence that performs or is associated with an action. It may be a noun, a pronoun, or a noun phrase. A **predicate** is a statement made about the subject. The predicate must include at least a main verb, but often it includes at least one *object* (or complement) as well:

SUBJECT   PREDICATE

This cheese smells.

SUBJECT PREDICATE = VERB + OBJECT

Erin likes bats.

The following sentence contains a longer predicate: a main verb ("is") and a series of predicate adjectives.

SUBJECT   PREDICATE = VERB + PREDICATE ADJECTIVES

The air is full of birds, and sweet with the breath of the pine, the balm-of-Gilead,

and the new hay.   (Ralph Waldo Emerson)

The main verb is the key word in the predicate. Thus a distinction is sometimes made between a **simple predicate**, meaning only the verb (or the verb and auxiliary verb, as in "is typing," where "is" is the auxiliary verb), and a **complete predicate**, meaning the verb plus any complements, objects, and modifiers. (Note that some words that are formed from verbs — called *verbals* — are not *operational* verbs but rather function as adjectives, nouns, or adverbs. For example, in the sentence "Thinking can be hard work," "thinking" is a noun — a verbal formed from the verb "to think" — and "can be" is the verb.)

Sentences may contain more than one main verb; we call the predicate of such a sentence a **compound predicate**:

The judge paused, looked round the courtroom, and proceeded to deliver his sentence.

Many sentences are even more elaborate: they might contain (like the sentence you are reading now) several subject-predicate combinations, not just one. Each group of words that contains both a subject and a predicate is called a **clause**. A complete sentence must contain at least one clause.

Here are some more examples of one-clause sentences.

Andy Warhol became famous for his paintings of Campbell's Soup cans and Coca-Cola bottles.

His 1963 film *Eat* shows Robert Indiana eating a mushroom, or something like a mushroom, for its entire forty-five-minute duration.

In 1966, Warhol produced the Velvet Underground's album *The Velvet Underground and Nico*.

Warhol was sometimes called "the Pope of Pop."

However, many art historians consider other artists, such as Roy Lichtenstein and Jasper Johns, to be no less significant.

Sentences can also contain two, three, or more clauses. Here are some examples.

Many people are under the impression that all black tea is fermented; actually, almost all black tea is oxidized, a process that, unlike fermentation, requires

➔ **Try** **This**   **Identifying Subjects and Predicates**

We can distinguish between the **complete subject**, or "subject phrase," and the **simple subject**, which is usually just one word. For example, in the second one-clause sentence listed above, "His 1963 film *Eat*" is the complete subject. The word "film" is the simple subject. In each of the above sentences, identify the simple subject, the complete subject, the operational verb, and the predicate.

exposure to the air. Pu-erh tea, made from ancient trees in the Yunnan district of China, is an exception: it is fermented and aged for up to ten years. The fermentation process demands that the tea be deprived of oxygen so that the bacteria on the leaves can flourish. The flavor of Pu-erh tea is unusual and does not appeal to all tea-drinkers: it is strong, earthy, and even musty. Though Pu-erh tea is often sold in the form of loose leaves, it is also available in the form of a cake or bar made of compressed leaves. These are often stamped with attractive designs; indeed, many are intended to decorate a table or a wall rather than to be broken up and brewed.

At this point, we can complicate matters slightly. Clauses come in two types: independent (or main) and subordinate (or dependent). An independent clause can stand on its own as a complete sentence, but a subordinate clause cannot.

SUBORDINATE CLAUSE	INDEPENDENT CLAUSE

However, though we continued to be friendly, our relationship was forever changed.

(Glenn Loury)

Here, the word "however" is an introductory word, and the first clause is "though we continued to be friendly." The second clause is "our relationship was forever changed." Note the difference: whereas the second clause could stand alone as a sentence, the first ("though we continued to be friendly") could not. The culprit is the word "though": take it away and suddenly that first clause could stand alone perfectly well. We call "though" a subordinating word: it makes the first clause in this sentence subordinate. So a subordinate clause is one that cannot stand alone as a sentence; it usually begins with a subordinating conjunction (such as "though") or a relative pronoun (such as "who"). Note that a subordinate clause differs from an ordinary phrase. Although a subordinate clause cannot stand on its own as a complete sentence, it is still a clause: it contains a subject and a predicate.

> ➔ **Try This**   **Identifying Clauses**
>
> Identify each separate clause in the paragraph about tea on pages 218–19. For each clause, underline the subject phrase and double-underline the predicate.
>
> Then identify the subordinate clause in the following sentence:
>
> *Grand Theft Auto* is set in Liberty City, which resembles New York City in many ways.

Phrases

Any group of words that makes sense as a unit but lacks a predicate is called a **phrase**. There are five different kinds of phrases — noun, verb, prepositional, absolute, and verbal — categorized according to the part that they play in the sentence. Being able to distinguish phrases from clauses is a useful skill, so it's worth becoming familiar with the different types of phrases. In the chart below, two types of noun phrases and three types of verbal phrases are defined, making for eight phrase types altogether.

Type of Phrase	Definition	Examples[1]
Noun phrase	A noun and its modifiers	*three perfectly happy people*
Noun phrase — appositive	A noun phrase that renames the noun or pronoun that precedes it	I walked up to a tree, *an Osage orange.*
Verb phrase	A main verb and its auxiliaries	as if the leaves of the Osage orange *had been freed*
Prepositional phrase	A preposition, a noun (or a pronoun), and modifiers, if any	*from a spell* *in the form* *of red-winged blackbirds*
Absolute phrase	Usually a noun (or a pronoun) and a participle. It modifies a whole sentence.	Late I lay open-mouthed in bed, *my arms flung wide.*
Verbal phrase — participial	A present or past participle and its modifiers, objects, or complements. It functions as an adjective.	We rock, *cradled in the swaddling band of darkness.*
Verbal phrase — gerund	A gerund (an *-ing* word derived from a verb that functions as a noun) and its modifiers, objects, or complements	The hollow *rushing of wind* raises hair on my neck and face.
Verbal phrase — infinitive	An infinitive (*to* plus the base form of a verb) and its modifiers, objects, or complements. It functions as a noun, an adjective, or an adverb.	The secret of seeing is *to sail on solar wind.*

[1] From Annie Dillard, "Seeing," *Pilgrim at Tinker Creek* (New York: Harper Perennial, 1974, 1998). Longer extracts from Dillard's book appear on pp. 243–44 and 248.

> **→ Guidelines** **Using Grammar Checkers**
>
> Computer grammar checkers are notoriously unreliable. The problem is that a computer does not understand the meaning of a sentence; it can only recognize certain word patterns and make suggestions. Grammar checkers can be helpful if you understand that they offer only basic suggestions and reminders: you must be able to decide for yourself whether these suggestions are appropriate or not.
>
> Nor do grammar checkers distinguish clearly between style advice and grammar advice. Consider the following sentence:
>
> > This sentence contains two independent clauses, but they are separated only by a comma.
>
> The grammar checker suggests changing the second clause to "only a comma separates them"—presumably to avoid the passive voice. That *could* be an improvement. But the original phrasing might be preferable because it puts the word "comma" at the end of the sentence, where it receives some emphasis.

Grammatical Sentence Types

Once you can confidently identify independent and subordinate clauses, you can classify sentences into different grammatical types according to the way these clauses are combined. There are four types of sentences:

- Simple
- Compound
- Complex
- Compound-complex

Sentences that contain just one independent clause and no subordinate clauses — no matter how long and densely packed with modifiers and phrases — are known as **simple sentences**: "This sentence is a simple sentence." Sentences that include one independent clause and at least one subordinate clause are known as

⊙ Try **This** **Identifying Independent Clauses**

Identify the independent clauses in this sentence.

The strategies were as varied as the practitioners; they shared only the theme of special pleading for an a priori doctrine—they knew that God's benevolence was lurking somewhere behind all these tales of apparent horror. (Stephen Jay Gould)

complex sentences. These terms describe the grammatical structure of the sentence, not its length. Complex sentences can be quite short.

SUBORDINATE CLAUSE INDEPENDENT CLAUSE

Where there's life, there's hope.

INDEPENDENT CLAUSE SUBORDINATE CLAUSE

Pepys had more time to make love because he had fewer friends to answer.
(Adam Gopnik, "Bumping into Mr. Ravioli")

Compound sentences contain more than one independent clause, as in this example.

FIRST INDEPENDENT CLAUSE SECOND INDEPENDENT CLAUSE

Astounding and paracosmic tall tales poured out of her: she had been to a chess

THIRD INDEPENDENT CLAUSE

tournament and brought home a trophy; she had gone to a circus and told jokes.
(Adam Gopnik, "Bumping into Mr. Ravioli")

Sentences that contain more than one independent clause and one or more subordinate clauses are called **compound-complex.**

INDEPENDENT CLAUSE DEPENDENT CLAUSE DEPENDENT CLAUSE

We are instructed to believe that we are busier because we have to work harder to

INDEPENDENT CLAUSE DEPENDENT CLAUSE

be more productive, but everybody knows that busyness and productivity have a

dubious, arm's-length relationship. (Adam Gopnik, "Bumping into Mr. Ravioli")

To use punctuation correctly and confidently, you need to be able to identify grammatical sentence types, distinguish between independent and subordinate clauses, and distinguish clauses from other word groups.

There are two ways to join independent clauses.

- With a comma and a coordinating conjunction (*and*, *or*, *nor*, *for*, *yet*, *but*, *so*), as in this example:

  They all invite us for brunch, and we would love to, but we are too . . . busy.
                                      (Adam Gopnik, "Bumping into Mr. Ravioli")

- With a semicolon, as in this example:

  Ronald Firbank is wrung out by his social obligations; Proust is constantly rescheduling rendezvous and apologizing for being overstretched.
                                      (Adam Gopnik, "Bumping into Mr. Ravioli")

In the following example, the first two independent clauses are separated by a comma and a coordinating conjunction, while the second and third independent clauses are separated by a semicolon:

New York is still a subject of television, and we compare *Sex and the City* to sex and the city; they are not yet quite the same.
                                      (Adam Gopnik, "Bumping into Mr. Ravioli)

Here, the first two independent clauses are separated by a comma and a coordinating conjunction. Two more clauses, very short ones, follow the colon; these are separated by only a comma — acceptable here because the clauses are so short and similar.

The crowding of our space has been reinforced by a crowding of our time, and the only way to protect ourselves is to build structures of perpetual deferral: I'll see you next week, let's talk soon.   (Adam Gopnik, "Bumping into Mr. Ravioli")

If you join a subordinate clause to an independent clause, use a comma if the subordinate clause comes first. Usually the comma is unnecessary if the subordinate clause comes after the independent clause. Compare the following two sentences:

When Ellen cooks, Jan cleans the dishes.

Jan cleans the dishes when Ellen cooks.

Properly punctuated, clauses can be linked together to form compound-complex sentences.

Rhetorical Sentence Types

Now that you can recognize the two types of clauses (independent and subordinate) and four sentence structures (simple, complex, compound, and compound-complex), we can move on to consider sentence structures from another angle, the rhetorical rather than the grammatical. Traditional rhetoric divides sentences into three categories, depending on whether the independent clause appears first, last, or both first and last:

- Loose
- Periodic
- Balanced

If the independent clause appears first, the sentence is called **loose**. Here are two examples from Geoff Dyer's "Blues for Vincent":

> I see your face everywhere, wandering through it like rain and the drifting steam of streets.

> The blues is like that, not something you *play* but a way of calling out to the dead, to all the dead slaves of America.

By contrast, a **periodic sentence** places the independent clause, or most of it, at the end of the sentence. This creates a sense of anticipation — but it also asks readers to hold information in their heads as they wait for the subject and main verb to come along and make sense of it all. Here's an example from the same essay:

> Like all who relieve the suffering of others, Theo — in a process that is the exact opposite of a blood transfusion — has taken some of Vincent's pain into himself.

Here's a longer example, by the essayist Richard Rodriguez:

> When armies are victorious, when armies are trodden in the dust, when crops fail, when volcanoes erupt, when seas drink multitudes, it must mean God intends it so.

Lengthy periodic sentences are unusual in modern English writing, though before about 1900 writers frequently used them. Here's an example from the eighteenth-century British statesman Edmund Burke:

> To complain of the age we live in, to murmur at the present possessors of power, to lament the past, to conceive extravagant hopes of the future, are the common dispositions of the greatest part of mankind.

In the third sentence type, the **balanced sentence**, one independent clause follows another; the two (or more) clauses are often parallel in structure. We frequently encounter balanced sentences in political speeches, as their effect is resonant and memorable.

> Ask not what your country can do for you — ask what you can do for your country.
>
> (John F. Kennedy)

> Kings are not born; they are made by universal hallucination.   (George Bernard Shaw)

> Put not your trust in money, but put your money in trust.   (Oliver Wendell Holmes)

We also find them often enough in essays. Here are two examples from Geoff Dyer's "Blues for Vincent":

> Zadkine wanted his sculpture to express the relationship of dependency and trust that existed between Vincent and his brother; in doing so he reveals all the tenderness of which men are capable of offering each other.

> No suffering is so unendurable that it cannot find expression, no pain is so intense that it cannot be lessened — this is the promise at the heart of the blues.

However, as elegant and impressive as balanced and periodic sentences may be, in modern writing and especially in expository or descriptive writing, the loose sentence is the most common and natural-sounding. The word "loose" should not be taken as pejorative: it simply implies that this sentence structure has great flexibility. When the independent clause appears first, we can freely add phrases and clauses to it and produce a sentence of considerable length that remains perfectly clear. Thus the loose sentence is often **cumulative**; that is, it contains modifiers that develop or qualify the main idea in the independent clause.

> And much about my family life was easy then, comfortable, happy in the rhythm of our living together: hearing my father getting ready for work; eating the breakfast my mother had made me; looking up from a novel to hear my brother or one of my sisters playing with friends in the backyard; in winter, coming into the house all lighted up after dark.   (Richard Rodriguez)

> They regarded me silently, Brother Jack with a smile that went no deeper than his lips, his head cocked to one side, studying me with his penetrating eyes; the others blank-faced, looking out of eyes that were meant to reveal nothing and to stir profound uncertainty.   (Ralph Ellison)

> Buffalo Bill comes to the child in us, understood not as that part of ourselves that we have outgrown but as the part that got left behind, of necessity, a long time ago, having been starved, bound, punished, disciplined out of existence.   (Jane Tompkins)

→ **Try** **This**   **Composing Sentences**

1. Compose a single loose cumulative sentence out of the elements listed. Edit them as necessary, and use them in any order, but begin your sentence with an independent clause. Attach phrases and subordinate clauses to the independent clause to include all the remaining elements. (You may find it helpful to look at an image of the Turner painting; you can easily find one on the Web.)

    J. M. W. Turner's 1844 painting *Rain, Steam and Speed — The Great Western Railway* depicts a train.

    The train is crossing a bridge over the River Thames.

    The river flows slowly through the dawn light.

    A tiny rowboat idles in the water.

    The sky is golden, white, and blue.

    The train's black funnel stands out sharply against the sky.

    The train hurtles toward the viewer across the black bridge.

2. Choose a topic of your own, and list five or six attributes or qualities of it. Then combine them into a loose cumulative sentence. Be sure to begin with an independent clause, adding phrases and subordinate clauses as needed to produce an effective sentence.

Punctuation

Once you can recognize independent clauses and distinguish them from dependent clauses and phrases, the rules and conventions of punctuation get a lot simpler. There are actually only a few rules but lots of conventions — conventions you may flout if you do so strategically, for a particular rhetorical purpose. The best way to learn to punctuate is to notice what good writers do and how their practices shade the meaning of their sentences, creating emphasis or inflection or another effect.

Punctuation evolved slowly in the history of writing; different marks were introduced in order to indicate a degree of separation between word groups. End punctuation marks — the period, the question mark, and the exclamation mark — produce the greatest separation between sentences, of course; the semicolon comes a close second, as we have seen, and is normally used to mark off independent clauses that *could* stand on their own as sentences. But we also have several other punctuation marks at our disposal:

- A dash separates a phrase or clause from the rest of the sentence and can be used singly or in pairs. (Don't confuse it with a hyphen — a dash is about twice as long as a hyphen and is used to separate, not to join.)

  > No suffering is so unendurable that it cannot find expression, no pain is so intense that it cannot be lessened — this is the promise at the heart of the blues.   (Geoff Dyer, "Blues for Vincent")

  > I e-mailed this sister for help with the Ravioli issue — how concerned should we be? — and she sent me back an e-mail, along with an attachment, and, after several failed cell-phone connections, we at last spoke on a landline.
  (Adam Gopnik, "Bumping into Mr. Ravioli")

- Parentheses set off a phrase, a dependent clause, or an independent clause from the rest of the sentence and always appear in pairs.

  > While the train and the telegram (and their love children, subways and commuter rails and e-mail) pushed people together, the car and the television pulled people apart — taking them out to the suburbs and sitting them down in front of a solo spectacle.   (Adam Gopnik, "Bumping into Mr. Ravioli")

- Commas set off dependent clauses, phrases, and words where needed.

  > Once I sensed the nature of his predicament, I began to feel more sympathetic toward Charlie Ravioli.
  (Adam Gopnik, "Bumping into Mr. Ravioli")

  > Soon, however, it becomes obvious that while the sky weighs heavily on both figures, one, Vincent, feels gravity as a force so terrible it can drag men beneath the earth.   (Geoff Dyer, "Blues for Vincent")

- A colon creates a sense of anticipation (it is often used before a list introduced by an independent clause).

  > I wake at four in the morning and think of you doing ordinary things: hunting for your glasses that you can never find, taking the tube to work, buying wine at the supermarket.   (Geoff Dyer, "Blues for Vincent")

Punctuation marks give writers choices. They mark a boundary between word groups, a separation of some sort. Some marks create more separation than others — their order, from greatest to least degree of separation:

- End punctuation: period, question mark, exclamation mark
- Semicolon, colon, dash, and parentheses
- Comma

Writing Longer Sentences by Using Coordination and Subordination

As we observed at the beginning of this chapter, writers sometimes hesitate to write longer sentences, fearing that a sentence that contains several clauses might become a "run-on." But a run-on is a sentence that lacks correct punctuation, not a sentence that is excessively long.

Writers need to construct longer sentences for two reasons. First, expressing complicated or nuanced ideas involves expressing the relationship between ideas. Incorporating more than one thought into a single sentence lets you express the close relationship between those thoughts. In the compound-complex sentence that we considered earlier (p. 222), Adam Gopnik expresses a logical relationship by linking an independent clause to two dependent clauses and linking those to another independent clause and a dependent clause. The sentence as a whole is not hard to understand because the thoughts in the first half of the sentence (before "but") are familiar and are logically related, and the opposing thought in the second half is clearly linked to the first half, picking up on the terms "busier" and "productive."

INDEPENDENT CLAUSE   DEPENDENT CLAUSE   DEPENDENT CLAUSE

We are instructed to believe that we are busier because we have to work harder to

INDEPENDENT CLAUSE   DEPENDENT CLAUSE

be more productive, but everybody knows that busyness and productivity have a

dubious, arm's-length relationship.

(Adam Gopnik, "Bumping into Mr. Ravioli")

Second, writing that employs only short sentences will seem choppy and monotonous; a pleasing style varies the length of sentences and imparts a sense of movement and rhythm as it carries the reader along on the swell and ebb of longer and shorter sentences.

Early drafts of an essay tend to rely heavily on simple sentence structures and fairly short sentences. Now, as you revise at the sentence level, you can attend to the rhythm of your writing and to the way ideas are linked or separated. By combining short sentences into longer ones, you can make choppy writing more expressive, elegant, and economical.

Here's a choppy passage from a student's draft.

> Tompkins is plagued by the question of whether to adore or abhor Buffalo Bill. To Tompkins, Buffalo Bill is the antihero. He is the man who roamed the frontier with an itchy trigger finger. Tompkins thinks he also had a knack for spilling blood. Upon further study, he becomes a humanitarian. He tried to save the buffalo from extinction. He becomes a man of culture. He brought civilization to the West. He is also the man who brings a picture of the Wild West back to the civilized East. Bill Cody's final portrait is that of an American hero. He is the "poster boy" of the new era of expansion.

Not only does the prose sound awkward because of the repetition of short, simple sentence structures, but it also feels wordy because of the repetition of empty phrases like "he is." Moreover, the relationship of ideas is less than clear because each clause stands alone, bearing the same relation to the preceding clause as to the following one. However, when the writer, Brendan Barrett, combined closely related sentences into longer ones, the passage improved greatly.

> Tompkins is plagued by the tearing question of whether to adore or abhor Buffalo Bill. To Tompkins, he is primarily the antihero, the man who roamed the frontier with an itchy trigger finger and a knack for spilling blood. Upon further study, he becomes a humanitarian who tries to save the buffalo from extinction; he becomes a man of culture who brings civilization to the West as well as a picture of the Wild West back to the civilized East. Indeed, Bill Cody's final portrait is that of an American hero, the "poster boy" of the new era of expansion.

Brendan took the sentences "He is the man who roamed the frontier with an itchy trigger finger. Tompkins thinks he also had a knack for spilling blood" and turned them into a single **appositive phrase** — that is, a phrase that expands on the term that immediately precedes it (in this case, "antihero"). However, he chose to keep the repetition of "he becomes a" in the next sentence because this repetition helps keep the point clear as the reader enters the more complicated phrases about the Wild West and civilized East that follow. So Brendan joined the second of these sentences to the first with a semicolon, producing a balanced sentence made of parallel clauses. Finally, he turned the last sentence into another appositive phrase, this time expanding on the word "hero."

Combining sentences in this way is called **coordination** and **subordination**. When we combine two sentences and keep them equal to each other (as Brendan has done with the two clauses that begin "he becomes a"), the process is called "coordinating." Coordination is accomplished by joining together clauses, either with a semicolon or with a coordinating conjunction (*and, or, nor, so, yet, but, for*). Some rewording may be necessary.

Turning a sentence into a phrase or a subordinate clause is called "subordinating." Subordination is accomplished in several ways.

Using Subordinating Words Use a subordinating word to turn one of the clauses into a subordinate clause. Subordinating words include subordinating conjunctions (such as *after, because, so that, when, though, in order that*) and relative pronouns (*who, whom, whose, which, that*).

Consider this sentence:

> When propagandists are not demonizing the enemy, they are remaking themselves
> in its image.   (Daniel Harris)

In this example, the clause "propagandists are not demonizing the enemy" has been subordinated to the independent clause ("they are remaking themselves in its image") by placing the subordinating conjunction "when" in front of it.

Here is another example:

> Because there is a generally poetic element in all historical writing, an element
> that appears in prose discourse as rhetoric, great historical works, whether by his-
> torians or historicists, retain their vividness and authority longer after they have
> ceased to count as contributions to "science."   (Hayden White)

In this case, the first clause ("there is a generally poetic element in all historical writing") has been subordinated by placing the subordinating conjunction "because" in front of it.

And here is another example of a sentence that uses subordination:

> One of the grand myths of the American Religion is the restoration of the Primitive
> Church, which probably never existed.   (Harold Bloom)

In this example, the second clause ("which probably never existed") has been subordinated by using the relative pronoun "which" as the subject.

A final example:

> The concept of irony was rediscovered by I. A. Richards, who defines irony . . . as "the bringing in of the opposite, of the complementary impulses," in order to achieve a "balanced poise."
>
> (D. C. Muecke)

Here, the second clause has been subordinated by using the relative pronoun "who" as the subject.

Cutting Words   You can also subordinate by cutting unnecessary words and turning a clause into a phrase, as in the following example.

> Land in Holland being so scarce and expensive, Dutch gardens were miniatures, measured in square feet rather than acres and frequently augmented with mirrors.
>
> (Michael Pollan)

This sentence combines one independent clause and three verbal phrases, of which each could have been an independent clause. In the draft stage, it might have been four separate sentences:

> Land in Holland was scarce and expensive. Therefore, Dutch gardens were miniatures. They were measured in square feet rather than acres. They were frequently augmented with mirrors.

But the repetition of the empty pronoun "they" and the verb "were," the cumbersome "therefore," and the staccato effect of four short sentences in a row all make this version inferior.

Using Appositives   The appositive phrase — a phrase that expands on the term it follows — is an especially useful and effective subordination device. Consider the differences between these versions:

Original   Gioacchino Rossini (1792–1868) is the composer of *The Barber of Seville*, *William Tell*, and other masterpieces of opera. At age thirty-seven, he suddenly stopped composing, though he would live for another forty years.

Revised   Gioacchino Rossini (1792–1868), the composer of *The Barber of Seville*, *William Tell*, and other masterpieces of opera, suddenly stopped composing at age thirty-seven, though he would live for another forty years.

➔ Try This   Combining Sentences

Combine the following pairs of simple sentences into one compound sentence using coordination. You can delete and add words, but don't alter the meaning of the sentence.

1. The *Washington Post*'s Style Invitational is a weekly contest. In Week 278, readers were asked to take any word from the dictionary.
2. The word may be altered by adding, subtracting, or changing one letter. Readers must supply a new definition of the word.
3. For example, one reader made up the word "sarchasm." The reader defined it as "the gulf between the author of sarcastic wit and the person who doesn't get it."
4. Another reader offered the word "inoculatte." It means "to take coffee intravenously when you are running late."

Combine the following pairs of simple sentences into one complex sentence using subordination.

5. The winning entry defined the word "intaxication" as "euphoria at getting a tax refund." It lasts until you realize it was your money to start with.
6. The word "cashtration" refers to the act of buying a house. It renders the subject financially impotent for an indefinite period.

Combine the following sentences into a compound-complex sentence, using both coordination and subordination. Change the order of the sentences if you wish.

7. Some submissions made reference to local landmarks. One of these was awarded "first runner-up." It was sent in by a reader from Arlington, Virginia. He offered the word "giraffiti." He defined it as "vandalism spray-painted very, very high, such as the famous 'Surrender Dorothy' on the Beltway overpass."

Combine the following sentences into a complex sentence, using subordination to subordinate two of the sentences.

8. The word "bozone" was defined as "the substance surrounding stupid people." It stops bright ideas from penetrating. However, the bozone layer unfortunately is showing no signs of erosion.

The appositive in the revised version is "the composer of *The Barber of Seville, William Tell*, and other masterpieces of opera." It simply expands on "Gioacchino Rossini." But the revision is preferable to the original not only because it contains fewer words but also because the first sentence of the original version is dull: it merely explains who Rossini is. Sentences formed around "is" or another form of the verb "to be" are often good candidates for this kind of subordination.

Expanding on Key Words   You can also subordinate by picking up a key word, repeating it, and developing it:

> Rather it is a reconstruction of the field from new fundamentals, a reconstruction that changes some of the field's most elementary theoretical generalizations as well as many of its paradigm methods and applications.   (Thomas Kuhn)

When you combine sentences using coordination and subordination, bear in mind that the aim is to use these techniques judiciously so that the relations between ideas are more clearly and elegantly expressed. Don't simply string clauses together. There's no single correct way to do this. Practice and use your best judgment.

Telling a Story with Active Sentences

When writing seems lively and vivid, precise and varied, verbs typically play a prominent role in many of the sentences. Verbs, especially active verbs, do more than simply link nouns together; they give a sentence energy and movement.

Think of a sentence as a very, very short story. A story comes from the combination of a character (the subject of your sentence) and some sort of action (the verb). Often, the character does something to someone else (the object of the sentence). Consider the following sentence:

> In Sophocles' play *Oedipus Rex*, the murdering of his father and the marrying of his mother are actions taken by King Oedipus of Thebes.

The meaning of the sentence is clear enough, but something's wrong: it seems wordy and convoluted. The sentence fails to tell the story of the play in a forceful, logical way. The operational verb, "are," is a dull one, and the subjects of the verb are "murdering" and "marrying" — nouns formed from the verbs "murder" and "marry" (that is, gerunds).

The problem with the sentence is that murdering and marrying are really the *actions* in the story, not the *actors*. When the actor is the grammatical subject of the sentence and the action is the grammatical verb, the writing becomes clearer. If we rearrange the sentence so that the true actor becomes the subject and the actions become verbs, we get this:

> In Sophocles' play *Oedipus Rex*, King Oedipus of Thebes murders his father and marries his mother.

Let's consider some more examples. Compare the original and revised versions in these three pairs.

Original   The publication of Sigmund Freud's *Die Traumdeutung* occurred in 1899, a translation of which later appeared in English as *The Interpretation of Dreams*.

Revised   In 1899, Sigmund Freud published *Die Traumdeutung*, later translated into English as *The Interpretation of Dreams*.

Original   It was in this book that the introduction by Freud of the theory of the Oedipus Complex took place.

Revised   In this book, Freud introduced the theory of the Oedipus Complex.

Original   The claim of this theory is that the experience of young children is to have a feeling of desire for the parent of the opposite sex and a feeling of hatred for the parent of the same sex.

Revised   This theory claims that young children feel desire for the parent of the opposite sex and hatred for the parent of the same sex.

As we can see, sentences that tell a story are stronger, shorter, and more direct — not only when they concern actual plots (literal people and actions) but also when they concern abstract matters. In the last sentence above, the actor is the word "theory," and the action is "claims." Since theories *do* make claims, we can think of this abstract statement as a kind of story, with an actor and an action.

The more wordy and indirect phrasing that we find in the original sentences is often described as **periphrastic**. Typically, such sentences use a form of the verb "to be" (*is, are, was, were*) as the operational verb, and they frequently use noun forms, adjective forms, or adverb forms of verbs rather than operational verbs.

The way to untangle such sentences is to look for the verbs hiding in the nouns, adjectives, and adverbs. Then revise the sentence so that the actors in the sentence are subjects and objects and the actions are verbs. Table 7.1 (p. 235) shows a small sample of nouns and their verb, adjective, and adverb forms. Though most nouns can be turned into other parts of speech, not all words take all forms.

Table 7.1   **Some Nouns and Their Forms**

Noun Form	Verb Form	Adjective Form	Adverb Form
creation	create	creative	creatively
declaration	declare	declarative	declaratively
discovery	discover	discovered	
finding	find	found	
imagination, imagining	imagine	imaginative	imaginatively
initiation, initiative	initiate	initial	initially
opening	open	open	openly
speech	speak	spoken	
verbalization	verbalize	verbal	verbally
writing	write	written	

⊙ **Try** This   **Working with Word Forms**

Fill in the missing words in the list below.

Noun Form	Verb Form	Adjective Form	Adverb Form
origin, original	originate	_____	_____
_____	emote	emotional	_____
_____	complete	_____	completely
_____	_____	_____	apologetically
_____	reason	rational	_____
compression	_____	_____	
_____	_____	representative	

➔ Try This   Revising Sentences

Revise the following sentences so that the operational verb is no longer a form of the verb "to be." Aim to keep the meaning as close to the sense of the original as possible.

1. Dr. Frank Drake is the inventor of a formula to estimate the number of extraterrestrial civilizations in our galaxy.
2. In 1960, at a meeting of scientists in Green Bank, West Virginia, Drake's formula was an important subject of discussion.
3. A number of variables, including the number of planets that are capable of supporting life and the length of time that a civilization that is in possession of the technology of mass destruction is likely to survive, are components of the formula.

Revise these noun-form or adjective-form sentences to make them active.

4. Primitive life forms such as bacteria may once have had an existence on Earth's neighboring planet, Mars.
5. Life on Earth, biologists now believe, may have had its origin in extreme conditions, around "thermal vents" or "black smokers" on the ocean floor.
6. Similar conditions may be present on other planets and moons that in other respects do not have much resemblance to Earth.
7. This fact, some argue, makes for a great increase in the number of planets that are able to support life.

For the following sentences, revise expletive constructions to eliminate unnecessary words.

8. So far, there are only 150 planets that have been found outside our own solar system, but there are many astronomers who believe that a great many more must exist.
9. There are many planets that have an orbit that is too close to their suns, or too far away, to permit temperatures that would support life.
10. There are some planets, called "extrasolar" planets, that do not orbit a star. There are quite a few climate researchers who believe that some of these, perhaps as many as half a million, may be capable of supporting life.

→ Try This   Examining Sentences

Choose a passage of several paragraphs (about a page) from one of the essays included in this book. Examine how the writer varies the lengths of the sentences, the grammatical sentence types, and the rhetorical sentence types.

Expletive Constructions

Another common type of periphrasis, or indirect construction, is the **expletive**. Expletive constructions use phrases such as "it is ... that," "it was ... that," or "there is ... who," words that can often be omitted without significant loss of meaning. (The word "expletive" derives from the Latin verb *explere*, meaning "to fill out.") Here are a couple of examples.

It was in this book that Sigmund Freud introduced the theory of the Oedipus Complex.

There are some psychologists who dispute Freud's theory of the unconscious.

Still, it is this theory that remains the basis of much modern psychoanalytic practice.

At times, however, expletive constructions are useful. They can throw the emphasis on a particular word in a sentence. Use your ear, and avoid using expletive constructions unnecessarily.

As we shall see in the next chapter, almost every kind of sentence construction has its role to play: passive-verb constructions; active-verb constructions; long sentences and short sentences; loose, periodic, and balanced sentences. The important thing is to keep sentences under control, to be able to construct any type of sentence you need with confidence, analyze sentences for problems, and revise them so that they do what you need them to do.

✅ Checklist for Revising at the Sentence Level

As you revise sentences, keep the following in mind.

☐ Use longer or shorter sentences as needed to express the relationships between ideas.
  - For greater clarity and economy, combine short sentences using subordination and coordination.
  - Express close relationships between ideas by combining simple sentences into compound and compound-complex sentences.
  - Join independent clauses correctly, using a semicolon or a comma and a coordinating conjunction.
  - Use the rhetorical sentence type that best expresses the thought: loose, balanced, or periodic.

☐ Look for the "stories" in your sentences, and ensure that actors are nouns and actions are verbs.

☐ Revise unnecessary expletive constructions.

chapter 8

Writing with Style

Most of us admire those who exhibit that elusive thing we call "style." Certain celebrities (Lady Gaga, George Clooney, Fan Bingbing — perhaps) are renowned for their sense of style; you may have friends whose fine sense of style makes them stand out, and maybe you yourself are so fortunate. Style, like beauty, is one of those things

> " Style is not something applied. It is something that permeates. It is of the nature of that in which it is found, whether the poem, the manner of a god, the bearing of a man. It is not a dress. "
>
> **WALLACE STEVENS**

that we instantly recognize but find difficult to define — in part, perhaps, because uniqueness seems its chief characteristic. But uniqueness isn't the whole story: there are at least a few common qualities that help us pin down what we mean by "style" — a certain harmony of manners, dress, and speech, perhaps; a certain daring, and the poise and confidence to go with it. As the poet Wallace Stevens observes in the epigraph to this chapter, style is something more than a suit of clothes, something more than an outer layer that is just added on at the last moment. Style is not just a surface quality — and this is no less true in writing than it is in anything else. You can say *roughly* the same thing in ugly prose as in stylish prose – but not *exactly* the same thing. And the difference is often crucial.

Any consideration of style in writing is complicated by the fact that the word "style" gets used in two different senses: we find a **normative** sense, which refers to a set of norms or rules that all writers should follow, and a **descriptive** sense, which refers to the characteristic qualities of a particular piece of writing or a writer's whole body of work. Textbooks typically discuss style in the normative sense because they want to offer guidelines and models for writers. Literary criticism, by contrast, frequently uses the word in the descriptive sense, especially when it aims to identify the distinguishing qualities of a great writer — Ernest Hemingway, for example, or Laurence Sterne or Virginia Woolf. This ambiguity in the way that we use the word "style" is more than just a matter of semantic hair-splitting: it affects how we write, and perhaps not always for the better. Writers often feel pulled in two directions at once: on the one hand, they want their writing to express not just their ideas but a personality and a voice; on the other hand, they feel that for their writing to be acceptable or even just intelligible, it must observe a set of impersonal rules — rules of diction, sentence construction, paragraphing, and so on. In other words, writers may feel torn between style as a set of compulsory standards and style as an aspect of self-expression. This sense of being torn in two directions is one of the things that can make the writing process difficult and frustrating.

As with other aspects of revision, it's best to attend to style in the later stages of the writing process, when your ideas are, for the most part, already on the page (or screen). At this point, your style, your voice, will already be evident in your writing to some degree — naturally, and without your having made any conscious effort to develop it. Now you must refine your writing so that it expresses your thinking as clearly and pleasingly as possible. Focusing on style *after* you've already developed your argument helps prevent that feeling of being pulled in two directions.

Some Famous Styles

Here are five representative examples of style.

John Lyly
This young gallant, of more wit than wealth, and yet of more wealth than wisdom, seeing himself inferior to none in pleasant conceits, thought himself superior to all in honest conditions, insomuch that he deemed himself so apt to all things, that he gave himself almost to nothing, but practicing of those things commonly which are incident to these sharp wits, fine phrases, smooth quipping, merry taunting, using jesting without mean, and abusing mirth without measure. As therefore the sweetest rose hath his prickle, the finest velvet his brack, the fairest flower his bran, so the sharpest wit hath his wanton will, and the holiest head his wicked way. And

true it is that some men write and most men believe, that in all perfect shapes, a blemish bringeth rather a liking every way to the eyes, than a loathing any way to the mind.

(From *Euphues: The Anatomy of Wit*, 1578)

Walter Pater

One of the most beautiful passages in the writings of Rousseau is that in the sixth book of the Confessions, where he describes the awakening in him of the literary sense. An undefinable taint of death had always clung about him, and now in early manhood he believed himself smitten by mortal disease. He asked himself how he might make as much as possible of the interval that remained; and he was not biased by anything in his previous life when he decided that it must be by intellectual excitement, which he found just then in the clear, fresh writings of Voltaire. Well! we are all *condamnés*, as Victor Hugo says: we are all under sentence of death but with a sort of indefinite reprieve — *les hommes sont tous condamnés à mort avec des sursis indéfinis*: we have an interval, and then our place knows us no more. Some spend this interval in listlessness, some in high passions, the wisest, at least among "the children of this world," in art and song. For our one chance lies in expanding that interval, in getting as many pulsations as possible into the given time. Great passions may give us this quickened sense of life, ecstasy and sorrow of love, the various forms of enthusiastic activity, disinterested or otherwise, which come naturally to many of us. Only be sure it is passion — that it does yield you this fruit of a quickened, multiplied consciousness. Of this wisdom, the poetic passion, the desire of beauty, the love of art for art's sake, has most; for art comes to you professing frankly to give nothing but the highest quality to your moments as they pass, and simply for those moments' sake.

(From *The Renaissance: Studies in Art and Poetry*, 1888)

Virginia Woolf

Here then was I (call me Mary Beton, Mary Seton, Mary Carmichael or by any name you please — it is not a matter of any importance) sitting on the banks of a river a week or two ago in fine October weather, lost in thought. That collar I have spoken of, women and fiction, the need of coming to some conclusion on a subject that raises all sorts of prejudices and passions, bowed my head to the ground. To the right and left bushes of some sort, golden and crimson, glowed with the colour, even it seemed burnt with the heat, of fire. On the further bank the willows wept in perpetual lamentation, their hair about their shoulders. The river reflected whatever it chose of sky and bridge and burning tree, and when the undergraduate had oared his boat through the reflections they closed again, completely, as if he had never been. There one might have sat the clock round lost in thought. Thought — to call it by a prouder name than it deserved — had let its line down into the stream. It swayed, minute after minute, hither and thither among the reflections and the weeds, letting the water lift it and sink it until — you know the little tug — the sudden conglomeration of an idea at the end of one's line: and then the cautious hauling of it in, and the careful laying of it out? Alas, laid on the grass how small, how insignificant this thought of mine looked; the sort of fish that a good fisherman puts back into the water so that it may grow fatter and be one day worth cooking and eating. I will not trouble you with that thought now, though if you look carefully you may find it for yourselves in the course of what I am going to say.

(From *A Room of One's Own*, 1929)

Martin Luther King Jr.

One of the basic points in your statement is that the action that I and my associates have taken in Birmingham is untimely. Some have asked: "Why didn't you give the new city administration time to act?" . . .

We know through painful experience that freedom is never voluntarily given by the oppressor; it must be demanded by the oppressed. Frankly, I have yet to engage in a direct action campaign that was "well timed" in the view of those who have not suffered unduly from the disease of segregation. For years now I have heard the word "Wait!" It rings in the ear of every Negro with piercing familiarity. This "Wait" has almost always meant "Never." We must come to see, with one of our distinguished jurists, that "justice too long delayed is justice denied."

We have waited for more than 340 years for our constitutional and God given rights. The nations of Asia and Africa are moving with jetlike speed toward gaining political independence, but we still creep at horse and buggy pace toward gaining a cup of coffee at a lunch counter. Perhaps it is easy for those who have never felt the stinging darts of segregation to say, "Wait." But when you have seen vicious mobs lynch your mothers and fathers at will and drown your sisters and brothers at whim; when you have seen hate filled policemen curse, kick and even kill your black brothers and sisters; when you see the vast majority of your twenty million Negro brothers smothering in an airtight cage of poverty in the midst of an affluent society; when you suddenly find your tongue twisted and your speech stammering as you seek to explain to your six year old daughter why she can't go to the public amusement park that has just been advertised on television, and see tears welling up in her eyes when she is told that Funtown is closed to colored children, and see ominous clouds of inferiority beginning to form in her little mental sky, and see her beginning to distort her personality by developing an unconscious bitterness toward white people; when you have to concoct an answer for a five year old son who is asking: "Daddy, why do white people treat colored people so mean?"; when you take a cross-country drive and find it necessary to sleep night after night in the uncomfortable corners of your automobile because no motel will accept you; when you are humiliated day in and day out by nagging signs reading "white" and "colored"; when your first name becomes "nigger," your middle name becomes "boy" (however old you are) and your last name becomes "John," and your wife and mother are never given the respected title "Mrs."; when you are harried by day and haunted by night by the fact that you are a Negro, living constantly at tiptoe stance, never quite knowing what to expect next, and are plagued with inner fears and outer resentments; when you are forever fighting a degenerating sense of "nobodiness" — then you will understand why we find it difficult to wait. There comes a time when the cup of endurance runs over, and men are no longer willing to be plunged into the abyss of despair. I hope, sirs, you can understand our legitimate and unavoidable impatience.

(From "Letter from Birmingham Jail," 1963)

Annie Dillard

Unfortunately, nature is very much a now-you-see-it, now-you-don't affair. A fish flashes, then dissolves in the water before my eyes like so much salt. Deer apparently ascend bodily into heaven; the brightest oriole fades into leaves. These disappearances stun me into stillness and concentration; they say of nature that it conceals with a grand nonchalance, and they say of vision that it is a deliberate gift, the revelation of a dancer who for my eyes only flings away her seven veils. For nature does reveal as well as conceal: now-you-don't-see-it, now-you-do. For a week last September migrating red-winged blackbirds were feeding heavily down by the creek at the back of the house. One day I went out to investigate the racket; I walked up to a tree, an Osage orange, and a hundred birds flew away. They simply materialized out of the tree. I saw a tree, then a whisk of color, then a tree again. I walked closer and another hundred blackbirds took flight. Not a branch, not a twig budged: the birds were apparently weightless as well as invisible. Or, it was as if the leaves of the Osage orange had been freed from a spell in the form of red-winged blackbirds; they flew from the tree, caught my eye in the sky, and vanished. When I looked again at the tree the leaves had reassembled as if nothing had happened. Finally I walked directly to the trunk of the tree and a final hundred, the real die-hards, appeared, spread, and vanished. How could so many hide in the tree without my seeing them? The Osage orange, unruffled, looked just as it had looked from the house, when three hundred red-winged blackbirds cried from its crown. I looked downstream where they flew and they were gone. Searching, I couldn't spot one. I wandered downstream to force them to play their hand, but they'd crossed the creek and scattered. One show to a customer. These appearances catch at my throat; they are the free gifts, the bright coppers at the roots of trees.

(From *Pilgrim at Tinker Creek*, 1974)

Plain Style

Ideas about style in writing, as in fashion, change with the times. A hundred years ago — or two hundred or four hundred — readers brought different expectations to their reading and admired different qualities in writers.

Since the mid-twentieth century, however, a broad consensus has emerged concerning the desirability of clarity and directness in prose. In "Politics and the English Language" (1946), the English novelist and social critic George Orwell argues that pretentious, obscure, or clichéd language poses a real danger to citizens of a democracy because it allows reprehensible or misleading ideas to pass for truth and reason. Not coincidentally, his essay appeared shortly after a world war against fascism.

In America in the 1950s, a textbook by William Strunk Jr. called *The Elements of Style* (first published in 1918 but revised by the *New Yorker* essayist E. B. White) became a best seller — and has remained one for more than half a century. Like Orwell, Strunk and White offer writers a limited set of powerful rules for improving the clarity and freshness of their prose; and like Orwell, Strunk and White assail the laziness that produces obscure and nonsensical writing. "The beginner should approach style warily . . . and he should begin by turning resolutely away from all devices that are popularly believed to indicate style — all mannerisms, tricks, adornments. The approach to style is by way of plainness, simplicity, orderliness, sincerity."[1]

---

[1] William Strunk Jr. and E. B. White, *The Elements of Style*, 3rd ed. (New York: Macmillan, 1979), 69.

Memorable rules such as "Omit needless words" and "Use definite, specific, concrete language" form the foundation of this approach to "plainness." Like Orwell and Strunk and White, most other authorities on style over the last century have similarly championed **plain style**.

For good reason. Ornate writing might seem impressive in its way, but obscure diction and perplexing phrasing come between the reader and the subject matter, making it difficult to see what the writer really wants to say. And as Orwell argues, wordiness, stale metaphors, and excessive abstraction may serve as a cover for false, contradictory, or meaningless ideas. "What is above all needed," he writes, "is to let the meaning choose the word, and not the other way about. In prose, the worst thing one can do with words is to surrender to them."[2] The term "plain style," then, does not mean a dull or flat style; it means a direct, vivid, economical, and readable style, a style that communicates the thought as clearly and precisely as possible.

Any writer who hopes to communicate clearly and effectively would do well to consider the advice of these plain stylists, and we will recapitulate their guidelines in the following sections. But we must bear in mind several caveats or qualifications to this standard (and mostly very good) advice. First, we can draw valuable lessons from some of the older ideas about style, ideas that, though they might at first seem to contradict the principles of plain style, are actually complementary to them. We will discuss these ideas in the section "'Copious' Style: Developing Key Ideas." Second, academic writing has certain stylistic conventions and requirements of its own. We will discuss these in the final section of this chapter. Finally, the principles of plain style are not rules that can be applied mechanically to your writing. They are strategies for making your writing more clear and direct, but every revision will be an experiment; when you tinker with your sentences, you must decide for yourself whether the changes make for real improvement.

Principles of Plain Style

The principles of plain style can be summed up in three precepts: prune excess verbiage, use specific and concrete words, and avoid monotonous sentence patterns.

---

[2] George Orwell, "Politics and the English Language," in *Essays*, ed. John Carey (New York: Knopf [Everyman's Library], 2002), 965.

Ways of Pruning Excess Verbiage

The golden rule of plain style is essentially this: "If it is possible to cut a word out, always cut it out," as Orwell wrote. Or as Strunk and White famously put it: "Omit needless words." In theory, this advice seems easy enough to carry out: just cut any words you can eliminate without changing the meaning of your sentence. But in practice, it takes judgment and experience to recognize which words are really needed and which ones can be dropped without weakening the sense. How much paring is too much?

When speaking, we tend to use many more words than we need—not just those inevitable verbal tics such as "you know?" and "like," but whole phrases and sentences that we subsequently retract or reformulate as we work out our ideas. ("This is terrific coffee. Well, not quite terrific, maybe, but very good. . . . Or at least better than average. Maybe.") Similarly, many of the words in an early draft will prove unnecessary. Some of these you can quickly learn to identify as excess verbiage (see "Phrases That Can Be Eliminated" below); others you might find and revise only by experimenting with alternative phrasing. Read the sentence with the word or phrase, then try reading it without, and see whether the result is greater economy or a real loss of meaning.

1. Seek Out Empty Phrases

In early drafts, almost all writers use empty phrases such as those that follow. But experienced writers learn to look out for them as they revise. ("I'm sorry, but I didn't have time to write you a shorter letter," wrote Blaise Pascal.) Cutting them usually makes the writing more economical, vigorous, and clear.

Phrases That Can Be Eliminated

on the whole

I think that; in my view (in places where it is obvious that the opinion being expressed is your own)

type of; kind of; sort of (when not used literally, as in "Clover is a kind of herbaceous plant")

who is/was (e.g., say "the man in charge" rather than "the man who is in charge")

In other cases, you can substitute a more economical word or phrase for a wordier phrase.

Instead of	Use
come to the conclusion	conclude
the fact that	that
due to the fact that	because
for the reason that	because
each and every	each; every
of a [profound] nature	[profound]
in a [harsh] manner	[harshly]
In [John Updike's story "A & P," he] writes . . .	In ["A & P," John Updike] writes . . .
in terms of	with (e.g., say "I am making progress with my essay" rather than "I am making progress in terms of my essay")

2. In General, Prefer the Active Voice

Compare these sentences:

In 1971, the FBI recovered El Greco's sketch *The Immaculate Conception.*

In 1971, El Greco's sketch *The Immaculate Conception* was recovered by the FBI.

In the first sentence, the verb "recovered" is in the active voice. That is, the subject of the verb ("the FBI") is the *actor* in relation to the verb: the FBI did the recovering. In the second sentence, the verb "was recovered" is in the passive voice. The subject of the verb ("sketch") is the *receiver* of the action, not the actor. Note that the form of **passive verbs** differs from the form of **active verbs**. Passive verbs comprise two (and sometimes three) words—here, the auxiliary verb "was" and the main verb "recovered." So active-verb constructions are always more economical and direct than passive-verb constructions; although both example sentences express the same idea, the second uses two extra words, because the preposition "by" is also needed to identify the actor.

Passive constructions consign specific mention of the actor to a prepositional phrase ("by the FBI") or omit any mention of the actor. Passive constructions that do not mention the actor sometimes express a writer's wish, conscious or unconscious, to hide the actor's identity. "An increase in your interest rate was deemed unavoidable." Deemed unavoidable by whom? By the lender, of course, but the lender appears to be reluctant to reveal that it is acting in this situation. As a rule, active constructions are more forthright and honest: they tell the reader who is doing what to whom. Passive constructions are often indirect and even evasive: they tell the reader only what is being done to someone or something, and not necessarily who or what is responsible.

Although active-verb constructions (such as "Charlie bit the dog") are usually clearer and more direct than passive-verb constructions, we need to consider some exceptions to the rule, situations in which a passive verb is clearer or less awkward than an active verb. Passive-verb constructions allow you to put the thing that is acted upon in the position of the subject: "The dog was bitten by Charlie."

In the following two situations, you might want to use passive verbs:

1. When you want to emphasize the actor by placing it at the end of the sentence. If the identity of the actor is new information, it might make sense to reveal it at the end of the sentence: "Who bit this dog?" "The dog was bitten by Charlie."

2. When the identity of the actor is unimportant and needs no mention. In the sentence "On June 16, 1903, the Ford Motor Company was incorporated," it may not matter who did the incorporating; the writer only wants to tell us the date on which the event occurred.

Consider this passage from Annie Dillard's "Seeing," in which most of the verbs are active.

I chanced on a wonderful book by Marius von Senden, called *Space and Sight*. When Western surgeons discovered how to perform safe cataract operations, they ranged across Europe and America operating on dozens of men and women of all ages who had been blinded by cataracts since birth. Von Senden collected accounts of such cases; the histories are fascinating. Many doctors had tested their patients' sense perceptions and ideas of space both before and after the operations. The vast majority of patients, of both sexes and all ages, had, in von Senden's opinion, no idea of space whatsoever.

There's only one passive verb in the passage above. Can you identify it?

If we simply change as many active-verb constructions into passive-verb constructions as we can, we produce a very awkward paragraph.

> A wonderful book called *Space and Sight* by Marius von Senden was chanced on by me. When a way to perform safe cataract operations was discovered by Western surgeons, Europe and America were ranged across by them so that dozens of men and women of all ages who had been blinded by cataracts since birth could be operated on. Accounts of such cases were collected by von Senden; the histories are fascinating. Their patients' sense perceptions and ideas of space had been tested by many doctors both before and after the operations. In von Senden's opinion, no idea of space whatsoever was had by the vast majority of patients, of both sexes and all ages.

Conversely, we can sometimes make an awkward passage more elegant by changing passive verbs to active ones, or occasionally vice versa. See what you can do with the following paragraph to improve it.

> In 1893, Gandhi and his family moved from Bombay to Natal, South Africa, to practice law for an Indian law firm. Discrimination was suffered by Gandhi, as an Indian in South Africa, and the indignities that were experienced by him there proved to be a turning point in his life. In 1894, the Natal Indian Congress, an organization that was dedicated to working for Indian rights, was founded by Gandhi. Yet at this point in his life, the prevailing racist ideology of South Africa was often reflected in Gandhi's own views. When war was declared by the British against the Zulus, the Indian population of South Africa was encouraged by Gandhi to serve in the British army, and the British regime was urged by Gandhi to accept them. Yet it was during this time that a philosophy of passive resistance was developed by Gandhi, which came to be called "Satyagraha" or "truth-force" by him. In 1915, Gandhi and his family moved back to India.

Sometimes, trying to revise a passive verb creates absurdity.

> Mohandas Gandhi was born in 1869.

Would anyone revise this as "Mohandas Gandhi's mother birthed Mohandas Gandhi in 1869"? In such instances, it is better to use the passive voice.

→ **Try** **This**   **Practicing Concision**

Cut excess verbiage from the following paragraphs.

The Great Cost of Information Overload

A company called Basex, which is a business research firm, recently estimated that "information overload" costs American companies $650 billion a year in lost productivity and innovation. Workers are distracted by a steady barrage of e-mails and instant messages throughout the day. "We send too many things out, and we send them to too many people," says Basex's Jonathan Spira. On the whole, the cost to industry is thought to come not only from the frequent distractions but also from the amount of time it takes a worker to refocus on a task following an interruption of this kind.

Another aspect of information overload is the fact that an almost limitless quantity of information is instantly available to workers through the Internet. In 1997, the aforementioned problem was analyzed by David Shenk in his book that is entitled *Data Smog: Surviving the Information Glut.* "Data smog" was the name invented by Shenk to describe the phenomenon of an "overabundance of low quality information." Looking back on his earlier predictions a decade later, Shenk came to the conclusion that the greater the *quantity* of information we must manage, the harder it is to find information that is *quality*. To offer just one example, while search engines have become tools that are more or less essential, one might say, for finding needed information on the Internet, even a search that has been narrowly defined can result in hundreds of thousands of hits, perhaps even more. Sometimes, one might say, more is less.

In fact, the term "information overload" actually predates the personal computer and the Internet. It was introduced, according to Infogineering.net, by futurologist Alvin Toffler in the 1970s, in the course of predicting that the ever-burgeoning availability of large amounts of information would eventually create problems of a severe kind.

In terms of solutions, Infogineering.net offers workers several useful remedies to the problem. First, workers should spend less time on information that is (or may be) "nice to know" and focus instead on what they "need to know now." Second, they should try as far as possible to focus less on quantity of information and more on quality of information. Third, in e-mail, they should make a point of asking questions in terms that are simple and direct, so that the respondent can respond in answers that are short and precise. Fourth, workers should never try to focus on more than one issue at a time, if possible. Fifth and lastly, workers should never forget to spend part of their day disconnected from e-mail, telephone, and all other kinds of interruptions.

3. As a Rule, Cast Sentences in Positive Form

Generally, it takes fewer words to express an idea in positive form than to express it in negative form.

Negative	Louise did not cease to smoke cigars.
Positive	Louise continued to smoke cigars.

Negative	Throughout the 1960s, the FBI did not stop searching for El Greco's sketch *The Immaculate Conception.*
Positive	Throughout the 1960s, the FBI kept searching for El Greco's sketch *The Immaculate Conception.*

Negative	Arthur does not hate anyone.
Positive	Arthur likes everyone.

Note, however, that the negative form usually carries a slightly different sense: in the first two examples above, the negative statements are a little more emphatic; in the third, the negative statement could mean that Arthur is indifferent to everyone, not that he positively likes everyone.

4. Avoid Unnecessary Qualifiers

A **qualifier** is a word or phrase (usually an adjective or an adverb) that modifies, limits, or attributes a quality to another word or phrase (usually a noun or a verb). In the phrase "a tall tree," the word "tall" is a qualifier. Distinguish between necessary and unnecessary qualifiers, and cut the unnecessary ones.

Some vague qualifiers (such as *rather, very, great, somewhat*) are rarely necessary and should almost always be cut. The sentence will be stronger and more direct without them.

Similarly, colloquial qualifiers (such as *awesome, terribly, literally, really, awfully, definitely*) are often used carelessly and have become almost meaningless. They often can be cut with no loss of meaning.

Check whether the qualifier truly adds something to the sentence, or whether the sentence is stronger, clearer, and more direct without it. In academic style, however, some qualifiers are necessary because they narrow a claim and thereby make it more precise and valid. Without qualifiers, a claim may be too general and thus may be inaccurate. (See p. 263 for more on "hedging" your claims.)

Choosing Specific and Concrete Words

1. Ways of Finding Specific Words

There's a sense in which, as the poet T. S. Eliot put it, "words are general, experiences are particular," and so words can perhaps never express ideas with absolute precision. But although the number of words in the dictionary may be limited, the number of ways they can be combined is not. Thus language can express ideas with a great deal of preciseness, especially when words are used in fresh and striking ways.

When the exact word doesn't come to mind right away, many writers reach for the thesaurus. Now that computer dictionaries typically incorporate a thesaurus, we needn't even reach for it — a couple of mouse clicks will do. A thesaurus can be helpful, but it can also tempt us to choose a word that sounds impressive or fancy but isn't quite right. Before taking a word from the thesaurus, look it up in the dictionary, even if you think you know the word's meaning. The dictionary will give you a more exact sense of its meaning, and sometimes even its history, and will help you choose the best word and use it correctly. In the long run, you may find that the dictionary is more helpful than the thesaurus. Use the thesaurus cautiously; use the dictionary eagerly and confidently.

The seventeenth-century satirist Jonathan Swift defined good style as "proper words in proper places." Your aim should always be to find the exact word, the fitting or "happy" expression — happy in the sense of *fortuitous*, or fortunately happened upon.

The dictionary will help you to avoid a **malapropism** — using a wrong word that sounds similar to the right one. For example, in 2000, presidential candidate George W. Bush said, "We cannot let terrorists and rogue nations hold this nation hostile or hold our allies hostile." He meant "hostage," of course. But good writing requires something more than just avoiding the obviously wrong word. Among the approximately 250,000 words in the English language, there are many that convey similar ideas but carry slightly different shades of meaning. By paying careful attention to how the best writers use language, you will develop sensitivity to these shades and learn not only a word's **denotation** — its dictionary definition — but also its **connotations** — what it suggests or the feelings and ideas it conjures.

> **➔ Try This   Get Happy**
>
> Look up the words "cheerful," "happy," "euphoric," and "jolly." How do the meanings of these words differ? Do they carry different connotations? If so, how might you describe these differences?

2. Choosing Concrete Words

The term **abstract** comes from the Latin word for "drawn away." When a word or concept is distant or remote from lived experience, from things that we can actually see, hear, and touch, we may call it "abstract." The contrasting term is **concrete**, something that is solid and real and exists in material or physical form. Abstractions are necessary and useful, of course. We couldn't possibly limit ourselves to physical objects, especially in academic writing. But words that suggest concrete realities tend to be much more evocative and sensual — and clearer — than abstract words.

Words derived from Latin, such as "operational," "vehicle," and "minimize," often seem more abstract than their near equivalents deriving from Anglo-Saxon: "working," "car," and "lessen." Prefer the shorter, simpler word unless the longer one carries a specific meaning or connotation that you need. Some words are abstract because they refer to concepts that mean different things in different situations and to different people: "democracy," "justice," "progress," "nature," "society," and the like. Such words become devalued over time by overuse or by misuse and should be used with caution.

Abstract words are not bad words — on occasion, they may be exactly the right word in the right place — but most readers object to writing that is *excessively* or *needlessly* abstract, writing that forces them to slog through a thicket of complicated constructions only to arrive at a meaning that could have been expressed more simply.

Compare the following sentences:

> The institution of higher education represents an asylum from the obligation to render pronouncements prematurely.

> College is a refuge from hasty judgment.   (Robert Frost)

Most readers prefer the second sentence.

3. Use Caution with "Fancy" Words, Jargon, and Neologisms

As we noted above, abstract words cannot be avoided entirely, especially in academic writing. But some kinds of words — jargon, neologisms, and pretentious language — should be used with great caution, as they risk obscuring your meaning completely.

Jargon is specialized or technical language that a particular group or profession understands but that the average person does not. Computer engineers, for example, necessarily use a good deal of jargon. In an essay on developments in computer technology, some jargon may be necessary, but it should be kept to a minimum if the reader of the essay is not a computer professional. Use technical terms sparingly, and define each term when you first introduce it.

Neologisms are terms of recent origin that do not yet appear in dictionaries and that readers may not recognize. Some neologisms catch on and eventually become acceptable, familiar words; most fade into obscurity. In the 1990s, the word "digerati" — formed by combining the words "digital" and "literati" — began to be used to refer to people with expertise in information technology; by 2003, the word had entered the *Oxford English Dictionary*, and it is now widely used. By contrast, the word "multidude" (to describe a group of surfers) has never caught on and is now a defunct neologism. The term "mouse potato," meaning someone who idles away too much time at the computer, may yet catch on, but it remains a neologism for now.

4. Using Verbs to Bring Life and Action to Sentences

In Chapter 7, we considered how tangled sentences benefit from being reconstructed so that they tell a story in which the actor is the grammatical subject and the action is a verb. Strong, fresh verbs inject energy into sentences. As action words, they signify not merely abstract relationships but also movement and force. Consciously or unconsciously, the reader sees your ideas in motion when strong verbs show how one concept, thing, or person acts on another; your thought becomes a kind of theater in which characters interact and a plot unfolds.

The verb "be" is probably the least vivid and concrete verb in the language and yet also the most frequently used. Of course, no writer can (or should) avoid forms of "be" entirely, but experienced writers know to avoid them when they can; almost any other verb will serve better than a mere "is" or "was." Many writers find that forms of the verb "be" appear too often in their early drafts. But such sentences often hide another verb that can be revealed to express the idea more vividly.

Look for nominalizations that you can revise into verbs or verb phrases. A **nominalization** is a noun that has been formed from a verb. (The word "noun" comes from the Latin word *nomen*, meaning "name." "Nominalization" comes from the same root.) For example, the noun "defense" is a nominalization of the verb "defend"; "pressure" is a nominalization of the verb "press"; and, as you may have noticed, the word "nominalization" is itself a nominalization of the verb "nominalize."

So a nominalization hides a verb within it: in the previous sentence, each of the clauses features "is" as the verb. But once we recognize that the word "nominalization" is itself a nominalization, we have a way to revise: we might instead write, "The noun 'defense' nominalizes the verb 'defend,'" and so on.

5. Using Metaphors and Figures of Speech

In academic writing, you will not need to concoct elaborate or extended metaphors frequently. But your writing can benefit from an awareness of the metaphors that many English words already contain. Seek out these underlying metaphors in your key terms, and use fitting images and metaphors with care. For example, a writer noticed that she mentioned the "influence" of one thinker upon another: "Walter Benjamin influenced the thinking of John Berger." The word "influence" conceals a metaphor: it comes from a Latin word meaning "flow in." When we speak of how one person influenced another, we are suggesting that something — ideas, probably — flowed from one person into another. So in remarking on how her reading of John Berger changed her understanding of Benjamin, this writer wrote: "The influence flowed against the current of time, however, when I came to read Benjamin's essay in the light of Berger's."

A vivid and fitting metaphor can lodge a memorable image in the reader's mind. (But too many different images can muddy ideas that might otherwise be clear.) In the introduction to his *Complete Poems*, Robert Frost describes the way a poem can take a surprising shape once the writing begins. The poem "has an outcome that though unforeseen was predestined from the very first image of the original mood — and indeed from the very mood." Later in the essay, summing up his thought, Frost writes: "The figure is the same as for love. Like a piece of ice on a hot stove the poem must ride on its own melting."[3]

Avoiding Monotonous Sentence Patterns

1. Use a Variety of Sentence Types

In Chapter 7, we identified four grammatical sentence types — simple, complex, compound, and compound-complex — and three rhetorical sentence types — loose, periodic, and balanced. Sentences differ in other ways too: in function (there are questions, declarations, commands, exclamations), in length, in the number of qualifiers, in the presence or absence of parentheses, and so on. As in other matters of style, your goal should be to vary your sentence patterns not merely for the sake of doing so — as decoration only — but rather to suit your meaning. A pleasing variety of sentence patterns will help to keep your reader interested.

---

[3] Robert Frost, "The Figure a Poem Makes," *The Complete Poems of Robert Frost* (New York: Henry Holt and Company, 1949), vi, viii.

2. Experiment with Word Order

The natural order of words in an English sentence is subject-verb-object. In English, word order conveys meaning: "man bites dog" means something different from "dog bites man," even though the same words appear in both sentences. In the first example, "man" is the subject of the verb "bites," and "dog" is the object of the verb. In the second, "dog" is the subject, and "man" is the object. Because word order expresses meaning in English, readers unconsciously examine sentence patterns to find meaning, and the subject-verb-object pattern is the simplest and clearest way to convey ideas in English.

But we can easily violate this rule, as in the famous line "To the victor go the spoils." Here, the subject of the verb "go" is "the spoils" (the loot or plunder). By reversing the normal word order and writing "To the victor go the spoils," rather than "The spoils go to the victor," the writer throws special emphasis on "spoils." Placing important words at the end of a sentence for emphasis is an effective way to create variety in your sentence patterns.

Some additional examples:

There but for the grace of God go I.

Behind this information lie years of research. (John Berger)

Force, and fraud, are in war the two cardinal virtues. (Thomas Hobbes, *Leviathan*)

As we have seen, word order can be altered by changing an active-verb construction into a passive-verb construction, or vice versa (see p. 247).

A moose wrecked my brand-new Mini.

My brand-new Mini was wrecked by a moose.

The first sentence emphasizes what wrecked the car: a moose. The second emphasizes what was wrecked: the car.

The Roots of English: Simple Words

English dictionaries usually supply information about the roots, or *etymology*, of words as well as their definitions. You will often see abbreviations such as "OE" (meaning Old English) or "Lat." (meaning Latin) in etymological notes. It helps to know a bit about the history of the English language in order to understand how words made their way from one language to another.

English is a Germanic language; the name comes from the Angles, a Germanic people who migrated from northern Germany to England in the fifth century CE. *Old English*, or Anglo-Saxon, was the language of England until the Norman Conquest of 1066 CE. Within a century (about 1150 CE), French, the language of the conquerors, began to blend with Old English to produce *Middle English*. French being descended from Latin, this process introduced into English not only many French words but also many Latin-based words. From about 1500, the language began to stabilize in the form it takes today, largely because of the spread of printed writing; this form is known as *Modern English*. William Shakespeare's English is Modern English; although many spellings and usages have changed — and will continue to change — our grammar and vocabulary are fundamentally the same as his.

Although the English language includes about 250,000 words (not counting strictly technical and scientific terms), many accomplished writers still favor the simple, earthy Anglo-Saxon words (of which there were fewer than 60,000). Typically, these are one- or two-syllable words that native English speakers know from childhood but that resonate with centuries of usage — words like the following:

sorrow (*sorge*)
fear (*fær*)
heart (*heorte*)
thought (*thoht*)
fair (*fæger*)
write (*writan*)

Latinate words with similar meanings are often polysyllabic:

misery (*miseria*)
trepidation (*trepidatio*)
myocardium (*myocardium*)
intellect (*intellectus*)
equitable (*æquitas*)
inscribe (*inscribere*)

Any good dictionary will provide some information about a word's origins. An etymological dictionary, such as the *Oxford English Dictionary*, also provides quotations that illustrate how each word has been used by writers throughout its history. This can give you insight into the connotations that gather around a word, and thus a much more precise sense of its meaning (or meanings) than any definition can provide.[4]

Here are some examples of how English has changed over the years.

Old English

Mæg ic be me selfum soþ-giedd wrecan, siðas secgan, hu ic geswinc-dagum earfoþ-hwile oft þrowode, bitre breost-ceare gebiden habbe, gecunnod on ceole cear-selda fela, atol yða gewealc, þær mec oft begeat nearu niht-wacu æt nacan stefnan, þonne he be clifum cnossaþ.

("The Seafarer," lines 1–8, from the Exeter Book, copied about 940 CE)

A word-for-word translation: "I can about myself a true poem recite, experiences relate, how I laborious-days and hard times often suffered, bitter breast-cares experienced, explored in [my] boat many care-abodes, terrible tossing waves, where anxious night-watch at the boat's prow often occupied me, when by the cliffs it tosses."

Middle English

Whan that Aprill with his shoures soote
The droghte of March hath perced to the roote,
And bathed every veyne in swich licour
Of which vertu engendred is the flour;
When Zephirus eek with his sweete breeth
Inspired hath in every hold and heeth
The tendre croppes, and the yonge sonne
Hath in the Ram his half cours yronne,
And smal foweles maken melodye,
The slepen al the nyght with open ye
(So priketh hem nature in hir corages),
Thanne longen folk to goon on pilgrimages....

(Geoffrey Chaucer, "General Prologue," *The Canterbury Tales*, about 1390)

---

[4] For more information, see Robert McCrum, Robert McNeil, and William Cran, *The Story of English*, 3rd rev. ed. (New York: Penguin, 2002).

➔ **Try This**   Picking the Better Sentence

Compare these sentence pairs. Note the different wording, and choose which of the versions you prefer, A or B. Explain your choices.

A: At the international physics laboratory known as CERN (the European Organization for Nuclear Research), scientists are replicating conditions that existed in the universe when it was only a trillionth of a trillionth of a second old, the instant when matter, energy, space, and even time itself had just come into being.
B: At the international physics laboratory known as CERN (the European Organization for Nuclear Research), scientists are building a model of conditions that were in existence when the universe was only a trillionth of a trillionth of a second old, when matter, energy, space, and even time itself had just been created.

A: Three hundred feet underground, in a tunnel that spans the border between France and Switzerland, subatomic particles race around a 16.2-mile-long accelerator ring called the Large Hadron Collider (LHC).
B: Three hundred feet underground, in a tunnel that lies across the border between France and Switzerland, subatomic particles move in circles through a 16.2-mile-long accelerator ring known as the Large Hadron Collider (LHC).

A: Driven by 9,300 magnets, two particle beams, each containing trillions of protons and ions (hadrons), move through the collider in opposite directions, reaching a speed equal to 99.9999991 percent of the speed of light (almost 300 miles per second).
B: Propelled by 9,300 magnets, two beams of particles, each containing trillions of protons and ions (which are hadrons), hurtle through the collider in opposite directions, reaching a speed equivalent to 99.9999991 percent of the speed of light (almost 300 miles per second).

A: The beams make eleven circuits per second through a vacuum as empty as outer space and then collide with so much force that the energy equals the energy that was released in the first moments following the Big Bang.
B: The beams complete eleven circuits per second through a vacuum as empty as outer space and then crash head-on with such extreme force that it reproduces the energy released a fraction of a second after the Big Bang.

A: The LHC, the world's largest refrigerator, is chilled to a frosty −456.34°F.
B: The LHC, the world's largest refrigerator, is kept to a temperature of −456.34°F.

A: But when particle beams collide, they generate temperatures 100,000 times hotter than the heart of the sun.
B: But when particle collisions occur, there is a production of temperatures that are 100,000 times hotter than the heart of the sun.

Modern English

. . . Come, poor babe.
I have heard, but not believ'd, the spirits o' th' dead
May walk again. If such a thing be, thy mother
Appear'd to me last night, for ne'er was dream
So like a waking. To me comes a creature,
Sometimes her head on one side, some another;
I never saw a vessel of like sorrow,
So fill'd and so becoming. In pure white robes,
Like very sanctity, she did approach
My cabin where I lay; thrice bow'd before me,
And, gasping to begin some speech, her eyes
Became two spouts. . . .

(William Shakespeare, *The Winter's Tale*, act 3, scene 3, about 1610)

"Copious" Style: Developing Key Ideas

In 1512, the great Renaissance scholar Desiderius Erasmus of Rotterdam published *De Copia* (Of Abundance), a handbook for young writers and speakers that offered models for saying the same thing in a variety of ways. In part, these models were meant for orators who often needed to repeat a thought several times in different words, both for emphasis and while they figured out what to say next. But Erasmus also wanted to give writers ways of amplifying or developing an important thought so that the prose would possess richness and fullness. At first glance, Erasmus's advice might seem to contradict the advice of the "plain stylists" and belong to a bygone era when readers had the leisure to linger over ornamental figures of speech that added little to the sense. (John Lyly, a sample of whose writing appears on pp. 240–41, was celebrated for his richly ornamented style.) But in fact, the ideal of *copia*, or abundance, complements the ideals of plain style. The goal of the **copious style** is never mere redundancy or ornament for the sake of ornament, but rather to describe or express a thing *fully*, doing the thought justice by getting it onto the page in all its dimensions. While the principles of plain style put the writer at risk of paring away so much that the result is meager or impoverished, the principles of copious style entail the risk of verbosity and redundancy. The true

→ Try This   Expanding and Contracting

Describe an object in front of you or amplify an abstract thought. For fifteen minutes, focus your attention on the object or idea. Write continuously about it, setting down everything that occurs to you. Let your thoughts flow; do not censor or edit them as they arise, but do try to stay focused on the object or idea you are working with. Without using a thesaurus or a dictionary, use as many different words or phrases to describe it as you can think of.

- Think of associations. (What does the object or idea remind you of?)
- Think of similes (comparisons using "like" or "as"). (What is the object or idea like? What might it be compared to?)
- Consider the object's or idea's opposite. (What is it *not*?)
- Analyze its components. (What are its parts? Its qualities?)
- Imagine you are explaining the object or idea to a child or to someone who is completely unfamiliar with it. (What assumptions do you need to uncover?)

Take a minute to relax, and then come back to the piece you have written. Underline only the words and phrases that seem useful and help to explain the thought. Work these underlined words and phrases into just three or four sentences.

goal is to achieve the right balance of richness and plainness. More precisely, the goal should be to express thoughts fully but to make every word count. Some adjectives and adverbs *do* make an idea more meaningful, vivid, or complete; others are merely excess verbiage, and the prose is stronger without them. The trick is to distinguish between the two. Understanding the difference is perhaps the work of a lifetime, but it is never too soon to begin developing this skill.

Achieving a Balance of Rich and Plain

All of these precepts can and should be broken if doing so makes your meaning more clear. Style is really a spectrum. Plain style embodies certain values (clarity, simplicity, directness), and rich style embodies other values (variety, abundance, completeness). If the danger at one end of the spectrum is verbosity and redundancy, the danger at the other is of "gutting" your writing, paring away all the nuance and subtlety. Once you have a sense of these values and these dangers, the two keys to developing good style are reading and revising. When you are reading, and especially when you are reading a writer you admire, notice how the writing works to express the writer's thought in effective and pleasing ways. And as a writer yourself, allow time in your writing process to work specifically on style. Experiment with different ways of expressing your thought, and see what works best. As with any guidelines concerning style, the principles of rich and plain style must be applied intelligently, not mechanically. You must rely on your own ear. The aim is to achieve the right balance of rich and plain, cutting wordiness and empty phrases but not the valuable content, such that every word contributes to the meaning of the whole. Where you find this balance between rich and plain is where you find your own personal style.

Writing in Academic Style

The principles explained above will serve you well in most writing situations. But many kinds of writing have their own special conventions, and academic writing is one of them. While its peculiarities do not contradict the principles of plain style or copious style, academic writing does frequently display stylistic qualities that suggest some differences of emphasis. Academic writing is typically formal: it avoids colloquialisms and slang (phrases used in speaking but inappropriate in formal writing, such as "chill out, dude" and "that kind of BS is just plain out of bounds"), "chatspeak" (for example, "ROFL" and "OMG"), and contractions (such as "isn't," "can't," or "I'm"). It prefers precise diction, meaning that it often employs technical vocabulary or specialized terms. And it uses qualifiers to indicate the writer's degree of certainty. Academic style reflects scholarly values and habits of mind.

Some Principles of Academic Style

Maintain a Scholarly Tone. Keep a reasonable and critical tone, the tone of a person who is thoughtful and interested, committed to finding out the truth, willing to look at a question from more than one point of view, and able to rise above a merely personal or local perspective.

Aim to Be Clear but Not Simplistic. Aim for clarity, but do not reduce complex, interesting ideas to simple, banal ones. Readers expect academic writing to make reasonable demands on their attention span, patience, and intelligence. Whereas journalists, writing for the general public, must take pains to enable readers to absorb information quickly and easily, academic writers can expect that readers will take more time to dwell on the nuances and complexities of their ideas.

Follow Disciplinary Conventions in Preferring the Active or the Passive Voice. In most college writing, the active voice is generally preferred, as it tends to be clearer and more direct. However, certain disciplines, notably in the natural sciences and some social sciences, conventionally use the passive voice. You might be expected to use the passive voice consistently when writing science papers and reports. If you're unsure, check with your instructor.

Use Qualifiers to "Hedge" Claims. Qualifiers can narrow a claim and thereby make it more precise and valid. Similarly, they can convey the writer's degree of certainty. Academic writers avoid overstating their claims, as they know that new evidence or further argument can always reveal some unforeseen aspect of the question. (For more on hedging, see Chapter 5, p. 139.)

Convey Impartiality. Be cautious when using words that carry emotional or attitudinal connotations. Wherever possible, express a claim as a conclusion that follows from evidence, not as your "opinion." (Opinion is subjective, tied to the personality and experience of the particular individual who holds it; by definition, opinion rests on "grounds insufficient for complete demonstration.") When a claim is only your opinion, you must express it as such, but as we have seen, a strong argument requires something more: claims must follow from strong evidence.

The word "objective" is sometimes taken to mean "factual," as though academic writing deals only with facts or information. But as we have seen, academics typically write in order to make an argument for conclusions they have drawn through research: evidence (including facts) plays an indispensable role, but a supporting role, not a starring one. Academic writing is "objective" in the sense that scholars adopt an attitude of detachment and impartiality. Their ultimate loyalty cannot be to any particular position; it must be to the "truth." (We put the word "truth" in quotation marks, as scholars conventionally do, not because we do not believe in truth but because we can never be entirely sure what it is. Truth is always what remains to be discovered — what, as yet, we only partially know.) Scholars must fix their eyes on the truth; they are not out to win any victories at the truth's expense. Academic style should reflect this attitude.

✅ Checklist for Writing with Style

Understand the principles of plain style.

- ☐ Look for excess verbage.
  - Cut empty phrases.
  - In general, prefer the active voice.
  - As a rule, cast sentences in positive form.
  - Avoid unnecessary qualifiers.
- ☐ Choose clear and direct vocabulary.
  - Use specific, concrete words.
  - Use "fancy" words, jargon, and neologisms with caution.
  - Use verbs to bring life and action to sentences.
- ☐ Avoid monotonous sentence structures.
  - Place important words at the end of the sentence for emphasis.

Understand "copious" style.

- ☐ Strive to express your thought fully while making every word count.
- ☐ Achieve a balance of rich and plain.

Observe conventions of academic style.

- ☐ Maintain a scholarly tone.
- ☐ Aim to be clear but not simplistic.
- ☐ Follow disciplinary conventions in preferring the active or the passive voice.
- ☐ Use qualifiers to hedge claims.
- ☐ Convey impartiality.

part 4

Conducting Research

chapter 9

Getting Started on a Research Project

"Research" can mean many things: carrying out experiments to test a hypothesis, conducting an e-mail survey, interviewing witnesses to an important event, studying old letters in archives, hunting down scholarly articles in the library — or virtually any other means of inves-

" Seeking and blundering are good, for it is only by seeking and blundering we learn. **"**

WOLFGANG VON GOETHE

tigating some question or problem. The novelist Zora Neale Hurston memorably described it as "formalized curiosity."[1] It would be impossible to discuss or even anticipate every type of research that college courses might require, but your instructors almost certainly will ask you to conduct research in your college's library and on the Internet — probably frequently. In many upper-level courses, the research paper is the most common type of writing assignment, and these papers often count for a large portion of the grade. Instructors place considerable weight

---

[1] Zora Neale Hurston, *Dust Tracks on a Road: An Autobiography* (1942; repr., New York: Harper Perennial, 1991), 127.

on such assignments because they give students the opportunity to immerse themselves in a scholarly discussion of a problem in a chosen field of study, to think deeply about it, and to propose ideas of their own. In other words, research papers let students do the work that scholars do. They demonstrate a student's ability to exercise the full range of skills — research, interpretation, analysis, critical thinking, and communication — that are needed to work on almost any problem in the discipline. (These skills are necessary for a great many nonacademic tasks as well.) Research papers allow students to move beyond the more passive and mechanical business of memorizing information and enter into the debates and struggles that represent the leading edge of discovery.

The two most common types of research assignment are the research paper and the research report, which are quite different types of writing. A **research report** usually involves finding reliable information and expert thinking on a topic and presenting your findings in a clear, organized, and objective way. In other words, you present the work of experts. A **research paper** involves not only gathering up information and expert thinking but also developing your own argument, one that is *informed* and *supported* by research but that contributes some new insight or point of view of your own. In this chapter, our focus will be on the research paper, but we will also address most of the information-gathering skills involved in writing research reports.

Whether your campus has one library or a dozen, its collection is likely to be larger and more complicated than your high school's. The library is one of the college's most important resources, and the time you spend becoming familiar with it will be amply rewarded: knowing how to locate material in a large library gives you access to huge reserves of information and ideas. Computers play an essential role in library systems, not only as tools for searching the catalog but also as tools for searching through bibliographic databases and for storing and retrieving complete documents. And the Internet, despite the absence of filters for reliability or quality or value, has nevertheless become an indispensable research tool, providing access to material of all types from sources around the globe. These innovations have made the business of doing research easier and faster — but also more complicated.

Ink and paper, however, are far from being obsolete: the digital revolution is still in progress, and libraries are in a state of transition. The computer world and the print world are increasingly linked together, so to do good research, you must know how to work in, and move between, both worlds. This chapter explains how to use some essential tools to find the material you need.

The Purpose of Research

The purpose of a research paper is to offer an answer to a question or a solution to a problem. Some questions or problems can be solved, or at least addressed with insight, by consulting just one or two sources — and much of our discussion of college writing up to this point has focused on this sort of essay. But other problems require more extensive research. Research can take many forms:

- Fieldwork: Gathering raw data through observation, experiments, surveys, and interviews.
- Library research: Finding books and print articles in scholarly journals, magazines, and newspapers.
- Internet research: Finding Web sites, discussion boards, and electronic editions of books and articles from scholarly journals, newspapers, and magazines.

The materials of a research project can be grouped into primary research and secondary research. Although the meaning of these terms differs somewhat from one discipline to another, in general **secondary research** is at least one degree removed from the object of study. In **primary research**, you directly investigate the object of study yourself and even create the data yourself — perhaps by conducting an experiment or a survey or by studying original materials, such as the letters of a key player in a historical event. In secondary research, you work with the findings or ideas of other researchers or thinkers, perhaps by reading an article or a Web page or by interviewing a scholar. (The same text could function as either primary or secondary evidence depending on what you are writing about. If you were writing a paper on the work of Nicholas Carr, his essay "Is Google Making Us Stupid?" would function as primary evidence, but if you were writing about reading on the Internet, his essay would function as secondary evidence.) Solving a problem might involve one or both kinds of research. Usually, your assignment will make clear what sort of research is appropriate.

Managing the Research Process

Research is always something of an adventure, like detective work. One day, you might come across a source that cracks the case wide open and gives you a whole new understanding of the subject. Suddenly, your project is moving ahead swiftly.

But the next day, you discover there's an important article or book out there that you really can't ignore — but another user has borrowed it, and you won't be able to get your hands on it until after the assignment's due date. Just as suddenly, your project seems to have stalled. What to do?

It may be small consolation to say it, but frustrations and dilemmas like these are all part of the adventure. Wise researchers expect the unexpected and plan for it. If you think about it, unpredictability is in the nature of research, precisely because you don't know in advance where the research will take you; if you did, the research would be unnecessary. So you cannot know in advance what the sources are, which ones are readily available, which ones are essential, and which can safely be ignored. Sometimes the adventure takes less time than you expect, but usually it takes more!

Still, a lot of problems can be prevented by knowing some guidelines for conducting research before you get started. These techniques won't entirely make straight the crooked paths of research, but they will make the journey a little smoother and more enjoyable.

Good research takes both know-how and time management. "Know-how" means possessing the skills to locate the best sources on your topic. Much of this chapter concerns skills of this kind. But time management is equally important: if you allow too little time for hunting down sources or for reading and thinking about them, the writing phase can get so compressed that your best thinking will never make it to the page. So it's important to start a research project early and to gauge, as realistically as possible, just how much time each phase of the project will take and then to schedule these phases around your other commitments. Allow plenty of time for finding sources and developing your argument, as these are the phases in which unforeseeable, time-consuming problems are most likely to occur.

Developing a Research Strategy

Research can be a complex and unpredictable process. But inevitably, it involves a number of different phases:

- developing a research focus
- reading background material
- identifying and locating sources

- reading sources and taking notes
- developing an argument
- outlining
- drafting
- revising, formatting, and polishing

Develop a research strategy that's appropriate for your assignment. What kind of sources will give you the best information and the best understanding of your topic? Where will you find these sources? How much time will it take to gather and digest these materials? You may not be able to answer these questions in detail at the outset, but if you create a strategy and start early, you can more easily make adjustments as the road ahead becomes clearer.

Most academic projects will involve some library or Internet research. Although some assignments may also call for, or benefit from, field research, such as interviews, surveys, or observations, most undergraduate research at least *starts* with texts (whether in print or electronic form).

A typical research project might proceed in this fashion.

- The project begins with the search for a topic area — by reviewing course readings, browsing the Internet, and brainstorming with classmates.

- Once a topic area has been selected, reading in reference sources (encyclopedias, dictionaries, and almanacs) on the Internet or in print reveals the big picture. This includes historical background (key figures, dates, and terms) and also what is currently being discussed — the hot areas of disagreement and interesting issues.

- A list of search terms makes it possible to locate and select an initial cluster of sources. The library's catalog points to relevant books. Electronic databases and Google Scholar list scholarly journal articles on the topic.

- Skimming and reading in this initial group of sources make it possible to narrow the research focus to a specific problem or question, evaluate each source for relevance and reliability, and choose two or three sources to serve as a starting point.

- Careful reading (and rereading, as necessary) provides a sense of the scholarly conversation about the problem or issue. The sources' notes and bibliographies reveal other important books, articles, and Internet sources. Your own notes and questions suggest additional directions for research.

- Further reading and thinking lead to a position on the issues and an argument to support that position. Your understanding of the problem deepens as reading proceeds, notes are compiled, and thoughts and hypotheses are generated.

- Informal writing pulls together thoughts, hypotheses, and notes and helps to identify connections and develop ideas, bringing key themes into focus.

- A working thesis emerges, and you begin to draft an argument with claims and evidence, based on what you have learned from your sources.

- Outlining, revision, and development fill out the draft. The thesis is revised and refined.

- Further revision, through editing and polishing, brings the paper to completion.

This list makes the research process sound complicated — and it often is! However, the process can be boiled down to two phases: (1) *scouting* and (2) *digging deep.* That is, first get the big picture and select a few good, relevant sources. Then use these sources to narrow your focus and build your bibliography as you become more informed.

Too often, inexperienced researchers simply use the first sources that they stumble upon and let these shape the research paper, no matter whether the sources really speak to a specific question or are even pertinent. The result is inevitably a superficial and poorly informed paper.

Two Sample Schedules for Writing a Paper

Here are two sample schedules, one for writing a short paper (roughly five pages, using five to seven sources) to be completed in three weeks, and another for writing a longer paper (roughly ten pages, using ten or more sources) to be completed in seven weeks. Note that about equal time is allotted for research, reading, and writing. But *thinking* — determining the focus and developing ideas — will be happening continuously throughout the process.

Of course, these are only examples, and you will want to adapt these schedules to the particular circumstances of your assignment and your work habits. You might need to complete the activities in a different order (for example, in some cases a working bibliography might be appropriate earlier than week four, and starting a journal to develop ideas might be the very first thing you do). Also, many of the reading and writing activities are recursive: writers move from reading and note-taking to writing and editing and back to reading and note-taking, and so on. Still, the purpose of a schedule is to allot adequate time to every major phase of the research and writing process, so don't allow yourself to get pulled too far off the track.

A Three-Week Schedule

Week One
  a. Brainstorm topics with course readings and classmates.
  b. Do preliminary research in encyclopedias and reference sources. Scan their bibliographies and notes to see what has been published on the topic. Gather search terms and concepts.
  c. Find some sources on the Internet and in the library. Consult a reference librarian. Narrow the topic to a focused research question.

Week Two
  a. Skim sources and select the most useful ones.
  b. Read sources and take notes. Develop a bibliography and locate additional sources.
  c. Keep a journal to develop ideas and formulate an argument. Fill in knowledge gaps with additional research.

Week Three
  a. Write the first draft of the paper.
  b. Revise and edit.

A Seven-Week Schedule

Week One
  a. Brainstorm topics with course readings, classmates, and Google search.
  b. Do "big picture" research online. Make a list of key terms and figures. Note frequently cited sources. Make a list of possible research questions.
  c. Go to the library and do research in reference sources. Consult a reference librarian.
  d. Gather a preliminary group of sources. Skim to select two or three to work with closely.

Week Two

   a. Read selected sources carefully and take notes. Begin developing a working bibliography. Place interlibrary loan requests if needed.

Week Three

   a. Identify additional sources from reading.

   b. Read and take notes. Identify knowledge gaps.

Week Four

   a. Read and take notes.

   b. Brainstorm an argument with informal writing.

Week Five

   a. Read, take notes, and begin drafting.

Week Six

   a. Revise and develop the draft.

   b. Visit the writing center.

Week Seven

   a. Revise, correct, and polish the essay. Double-check notes and bibliography.

Getting Started: Scouting for a Topic

We mentioned "scouting" as one of the two main phases of the research process, the phase that precedes "digging deep." Scouting means searching for an appropriate and interesting topic by using available resources, such as course readings, the Internet, your classmates, and your instructor. What it involves will vary considerably from one assignment to another, but typically it means either

1. choosing an aspect of a course's subject matter that strikes you as interesting and important enough to merit a few weeks of concentrated study, or

2. choosing from among a list of suggested topics included in the assignment.

Reviewing course readings and your notes, brainstorming with classmates, and discussing ideas with your instructor can help you select a topic area. But choosing one also means learning something about potential topic areas, such as historical background and current controversies or questions. Here the Internet is a valuable tool for quickly getting a sense of the big picture. Scouting around on the Internet will be merely preliminary research: the information you find at this point may not be wholly reliable or impartial, and you should not place too much weight on it until your research has progressed further. But perusing the Web will usually help clarify whether a potential topic is appropriate and interesting before you narrow your focus and settle on a specific problem, question, or issue.

Understanding the Big Picture

Using an Encyclopedia

After beginning the scouting process with Internet searches (using Google or another search engine), use an encyclopedia (online or in print) to develop your sense of the big picture. (For a discussion of Wikipedia, see the next section.) To conduct a search, you will need to know key terms associated with your topic and their correct spellings.

As you read the relevant articles, note technical terms, key themes, figures, and dates, as these will help you conduct further research. Most encyclopedias include a brief bibliography with each entry, and some include citation notes. These can guide you to some of the most important books and articles on your topic.

Keep in mind that encyclopedias are an excellent starting point for research, but *not an end point*: they sketch out basic facts, but they take you no further. As you probe more deeply into a subject, you will often be surprised how much more complicated and more interesting the full story is than the mere facts given in an encyclopedia.

A Note on Wikipedia

Wikipedia, founded by Jimmy Wales and Larry Sanger in 2000, differs from other encyclopedias in several important respects. Most notably, it is a free, nonprofit project that allows anyone — not only experts and scholars — to contribute content or edit existing content.[2]

---

[2] This includes you, of course. If you wish to be a contributor, see "Starting an article" at en.wikipedia.org/wiki/Wikipedia:Starting_an_article.

However, Wikipedia does adhere to strict standards and policies. A worldwide community of about 31,000 volunteer editors checks new contributions to make sure these standards are met, and they edit articles as needed. These standards can be summed up as follows.

- Content must adhere to a "neutral point of view."
- Content must be verifiable and must incorporate references to reliable external sources.
- Topics must be "notable" — or covered in at least one reliable and independent source.
- Contributors may not submit articles about their own original research.

Compared to traditional encyclopedias, Wikipedia has some important strengths. Most obvious, perhaps, is its availability as a free resource. Also, its scope is large and growing: the English version of Wikipedia alone includes more than 4.4 million articles. And Wikipedia can be more up-to-date than print encyclopedias that publish new editions or supplements only once a year or less frequently. (Mention of the latest news or developments sometimes gets entered into a relevant Wikipedia article within minutes of being reported.) Finally, Wikipedia allows readers to link directly to external sources in citations and bibliographies, making it a convenient starting point for further research.

Any encyclopedia can contain errors (and Wikipedia does not seem to contain more errors on average than other respected encyclopedias do). Over time, Wikipedia seems to be getting more complete and more reliable. In some areas of natural science, Wikipedia may be the best reference available for the general reader.

But Wikipedia has several clear weaknesses too. It is written by amateurs, and articles — especially newer contributions — may be poorly written. As a work in progress, many of its articles are incomplete. In addition, articles can easily be sabotaged; though obvious cases are quickly corrected, articles on obscure topics may retain errors or distortions for some time. And because Wikipedia is a collaborative project that relies on consensus among its many users, articles on controversial topics may represent a middle-of-the-road compromise rather than the hard truth.

Wikipedia, like any encyclopedia, should be used only as a starting point for research, not an end point. That is, you should not cite Wikipedia or any other encyclopedia in a paper. Instead, go directly to the sources that the encyclopedia references, assess them for yourself, and draw your own conclusions.[3]

---

[3] For more detail, see "Wikipedia: About Wikipedia" at en.wikipedia.org/wiki/Wikipedia:About.

Selecting Sources and Narrowing Your Focus

Once you have chosen your topic, your next step is to pull together an initial collection of sources on your topic — perhaps five to twelve items. Usually these will be scholarly books and articles, but they might also include magazine and newspaper articles or other types of sources. From this group, you will select two or three sources for closer study as a starting point for "digging deep."

Using College Research Libraries

College libraries differ from most public and high school libraries both in size — they are typically much larger — and in function. Their purpose reflects the mission of the institution: a large university research library, for example, will usually carry thousands of scholarly journals, but relatively few popular novels. Increasingly, scholarly journals are being published in digital form, and in many cases, even older journals are being stored electronically rather than in paper form. Thus you can do a good deal of your research at your computer, without actually being in the library. But paper is far from obsolete, and thorough research still almost always requires spending time in the library. In addition, the library provides professional problem solvers in the form of reference librarians.

You may want to begin your research process by finding books on your problem or topic, or you may want to start with journal articles. As a general rule, if your question or problem is a new or very current one, you may find that articles are more up-to-date than books. Otherwise, begin with books, as they are more likely to offer context and a broader frame of reference.

Using Your Library's Electronic Catalog

A few libraries still maintain a catalog made up of index cards, but most have made the transition to an electronic or online catalog, at least for their main holdings. (Special collections or archives may still rely on a card catalog.) Most library catalogs allow users to search by author, title, **keyword**, or subject (see Figure 9.1). A keyword search typically searches through every field in every catalog record (see Figure 9.3, p. 281) for matching terms. Since common words (such as "science," "America," or "war") will usually yield an unmanageable number of hits, keyword searches work best when the terms are fairly specific to a topic or when at least two keywords are combined.

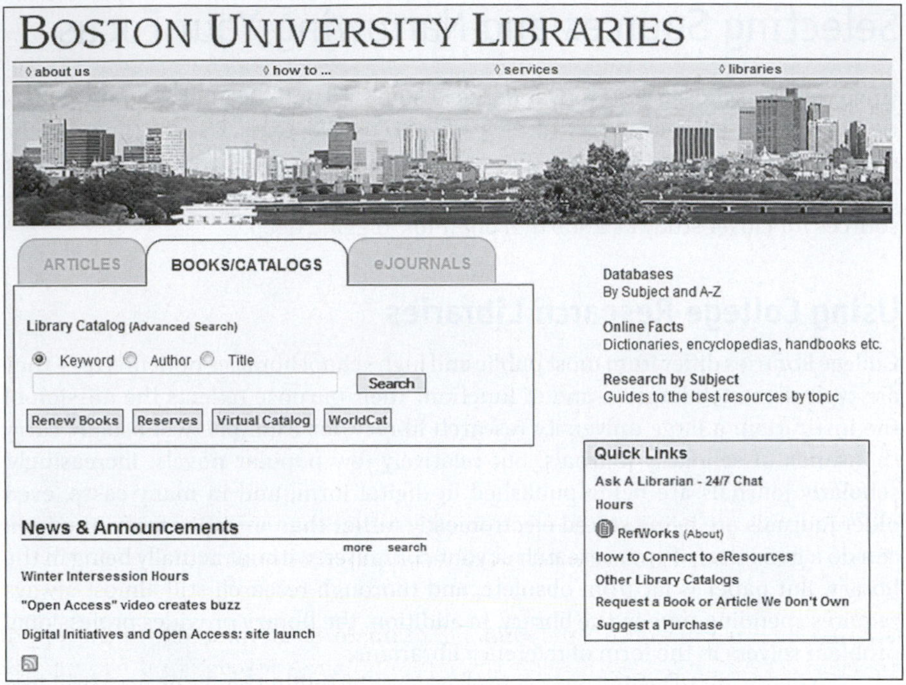

Figure 9.1 Main Search Screen of a College Library's Catalog (Source: Trustees of Boston University)

Some library catalogs let users search by subject. Usually this means "Library of Congress subject headings," a limited and systematic set of subject headings published by the Library of Congress to facilitate cataloging and searching. These subject terms are not always the ones you might expect, but you can explore the Library of Congress subject headings in a set of five large red volumes (many libraries display these volumes prominently in the reference area) or search online at authorities.loc.gov. Alternatively, you can begin with a keyword search, browse the results until you find an item on your topic, and then look at the terms listed under "subject" in the item's record. Many libraries hyperlink subject terms, allowing you to get a complete list of all items on that subject with just one click.

Advanced Searching

Advanced searching allows users to refine a search by including certain criteria and excluding others (see Figure 9.2). The options will differ from one library catalog to

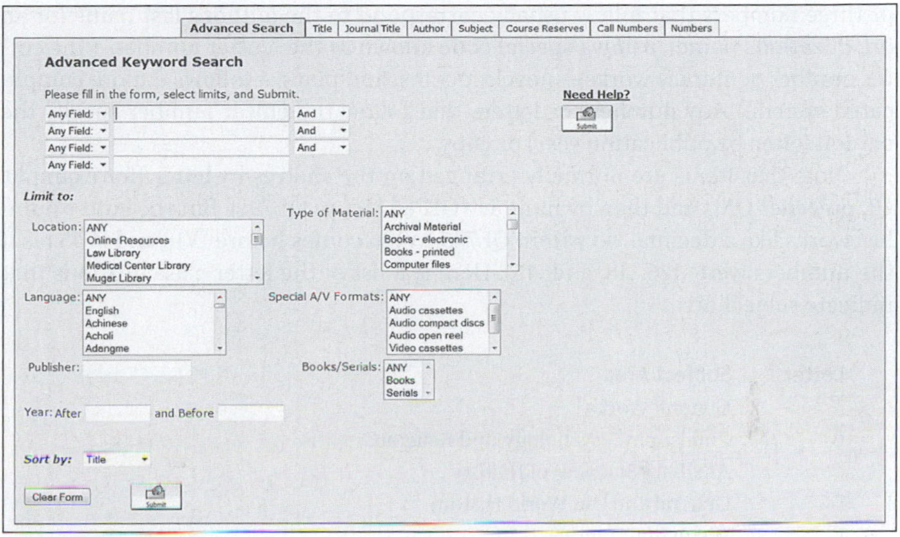

Figure 9.2 "Advanced Search" Screen   (Source: Trustees of Boston University)

another, but the procedure is the same. For example, if you wanted to find a copy of the soundtrack to the 1967 Joseph Strick film of James Joyce's novel *Ulysses*, you could enter "Ulysses" as a title and select "Recordings — music" as "Type of Material." This would eliminate copies of the novel and books about the novel from the search.

Reading a Catalog Record

Catalog records typically contain a good deal of data: in addition to basic information such as the author, title, publisher, and edition of a particular item, they provide a call number and, if your college has more than one library, the location of the item.

The **call number** (for example, QL785 .W126 2001) makes it possible to find the item on the library's shelves (or "stacks"). The Library of Congress classification system, used by most large libraries, begins with one, two, or occasionally three letters that designate subject areas. The first letter corresponds to a broad subject area (see the list on p. 280), and the second and third (if any) letters correspond to a narrower division within that subject area. (Details can be found online at the Library of Congress Classification Outline at loc.gov/catdir/cpso/lcco.) The first set of numbers corresponds to a narrower division of the subject. The letter and the two or three numbers that follow usually correspond to the author's last name (or an organization's name), using a special code known as the "cutter number." (The cutter number of literary works — novels, poems, and plays — follows a more complicated system.) Any numbers or letters that follow the cutter number specify the edition (often by publication year) or copy.

Note that items are normally arranged on the shelves by letter (for example, QL precedes QM) and then by number (QL785 before QL791). But the cutter number works like a decimal, so within QL785, W126 comes before W18 and W45 (as if the numbers were .126, .18, and .45). Here is a list of the letter classifications that indicate subject area.

Letter	Subject Area
A	General Works
B	Philosophy, Psychology, and Religion
C	Auxiliary Sciences of History
D	General and Old World History
E	History of America
F	History of the United States and British, Dutch, French, and Latin American History
G	Geography, Anthropology, and Recreation
H	Social Sciences
J	Political Science
K	Law
L	Education
M	Music
N	Fine Arts
P	Language and Literature
Q	Science
R	Medicine
S	Agriculture
T	Technology
U	Military Science
V	Naval Science
Z	Bibliography, Library Science, and General Information Resources

A catalog record also includes a bibliographic description of the item, including such information as the number of pages in a preface or prefatory material (in small

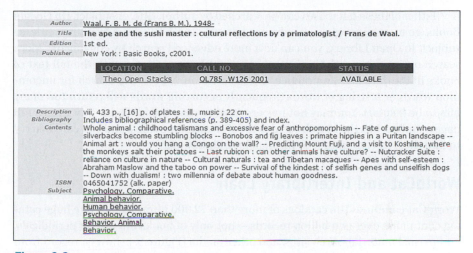

Author	Waal, F. B. M. de (Frans B. M.), 1948-
Title	**The ape and the sushi master : cultural reflections by a primatologist / Frans de Waal.**
Edition	1st ed.
Publisher	New York : Basic Books, c2001.

LOCATION	CALL NO.	STATUS
Theo Open Stacks	QL785 .W126 2001	AVAILABLE

Description	viii, 433 p., [16] p. of plates : ill., music ; 22 cm.
Bibliography	Includes bibliographical references (p. 389-405) and index.
Contents	Whole animal : childhood talismans and excessive fear of anthropomorphism -- Fate of gurus : when silverbacks become stumbling blocks -- Bonobos and fig leaves : primate hippies in a Puritan landscape -- Animal art : would you hang a Congo on the wall? -- Predicting Mount Fuji, and a visit to Koshima, where the monkeys salt their potatoes -- Last rubicon : can other animals have culture? -- Nutcracker Suite : reliance on culture in nature -- Cultural naturals : tea and Tibetan macaques -- Apes with self-esteem : Abraham Maslow and the taboo on power -- Survival of the kindest : of selfish genes and unselfish dogs -- Down with dualism! : two millennia of debate about human goodness.
ISBN	0465041752 (alk. paper)
Subject	Psychology, Comparative.
	Animal behavior.
	Human behavior.
	Psychology, Comparative.
	Behavior, Animal.
	Behavior.

Figure 9.3 **Record in a Library Catalog** (Source: Trustees of Boston University)

roman numerals) and in the text proper (in arabic numerals), the number of pages of plates and illustrations, the number of pages in the bibliography, and the size of the item in centimeters (see Figure 9.3). In many cases, the record also provides a list of the contents, the ISBN (International Standard Book Number), and a list of subject terms. Some libraries also include book reviews in catalog records, where available.

Finding Books Online with Google Books and Open Library

Google Books (books.google.com) is a searchable database of more than 30 million books in over four hundred languages. It grows continuously as more books are scanned into it. Some of the world's largest libraries have partnered with Google on the project, including Oxford University's Bodleian Library, the Harvard University Library, and the New York Public Library. If you have a Google account (free from Google.com), you can view pages of books that are no longer in copyright and those for which the copyright owner has given permission. For most books in print, you can view only a limited number of pages, if any.

Open Library (openlibrary.org) is a nonprofit wiki project to catalog books and to offer the full text of books in the public domain (that is, books out of copyright). It contains the full text of more than a million books.

Either of these databases can be searched by author, title, or subject. (In Google Books, go to www.google.com/advanced_book_search to search by author, title, or subject. In Open Library, you can do a more advanced search by clicking on "More search options" beneath the "Search" button.) You can also search the full text of books in the database. In practice, this is useful only if you can search for uncommon words or a string of words (frequently occurring words will return too many hits to be helpful). You may not be permitted to read the full book — or even a full page — online, but the search can at least give you some titles, and you can then try to find them in your library or through interlibrary loan.

WorldCat and Interlibrary Loan

WorldCat combines the catalogs of more than 72,000 libraries into one huge catalog containing over two billion records — not only of books but also of periodicals, audiovisual materials, Web sites, and other media (Figure 9.4 shows a record from WorldCat). Most large libraries in the United States and elsewhere participate in WorldCat. Many college libraries subscribe to WorldCat and make it freely available to students. A free public version is available at WorldCat.org.

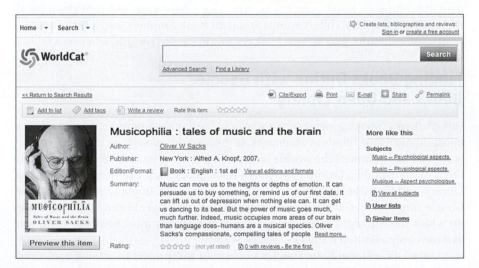

Figure 9.4 **Detailed Record from WorldCat** (Source: Trustees of Boston University)

WorldCat is "location aware," meaning that the detailed record for each item includes a link to a list of libraries worldwide that own a particular item. (If you are accessing WorldCat through your college's network and if your college owns the item, you will see your college's name next to this link.) This list is organized by state, with your own state listed first (if any libraries in your state hold the item), nearby states listed next, and so on. See Figure 9.5 for a sample listing.

This location-listing feature allows you to expand your reach when researching. If your own library does not hold an item you need, you can use WorldCat to find out whether any other libraries in your area (including most public libraries) hold it. If none does, you might able to request an interlibrary loan — by which one library lends a requested item to another library for a short period. Ask at the reference desk whether your library allows such loans.

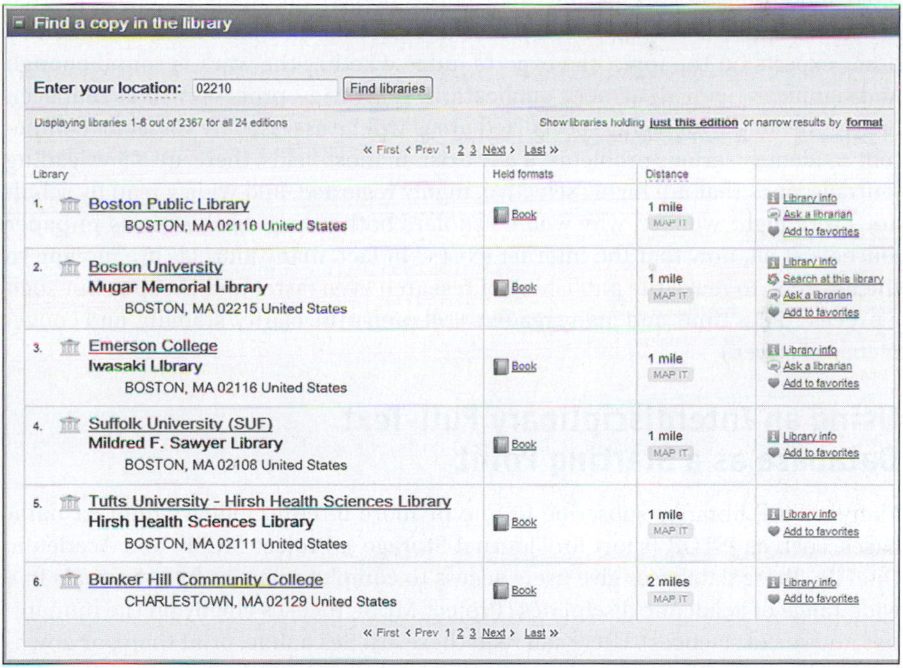

Figure 9.5 **Partial List of Libraries That Own Item, from WorldCat** (Source: Trustees of Boston University)

Finding Scholarly Articles

What Are Scholarly Journals and Articles?

A great deal of scholarly writing is never published in book form; instead, it is published in scholarly journals. Scholarly journals are **periodicals**: like magazines, they appear several times a year (typically three or four times annually; sometimes more or less frequently), but they have a relatively small circulation and a very specific focus. A typical issue might include five to ten articles, four or five book reviews, and several pages of announcements and advertisements. (A year of issues forms a "volume." So, for example, "*PMLA* 131.4" indicates volume 131, issue number 4.)

Journals provide a forum for scholars to share ideas and the results of research with other experts in their field, as articles and reviews can be published and circulated more quickly and cheaply than entire books can. Many scholarly journal articles are **peer-reviewed** or **refereed**, meaning that they have been evaluated by other experts on the topic; the experts judge whether the work is sound enough and significant enough to merit publication. This review process ensures that even articles dealing with highly specialized areas will be assessed by someone competent to identify serious problems, if any exist. In most fields, there are a few leading journals, ones that are highly selective, highly regarded, and widely read by scholars. (You might wonder, why would scholars bother to publish articles in paper journals at all, now that the Internet exists? In fact, many journals are moving to the Internet, to make the publishing of research even faster and cheaper, but such a process takes time, and many readers still prefer the clarity, stability, and convenience of paper.)

Using an Interdisciplinary Full-Text Database as a Starting Point

Many college libraries subscribe to one or more interdisciplinary full-text databases, such as JSTOR (short for "Journal Storage"), Project MUSE, and Academic OneFile. These databases give users access to complete articles from journals in a wide range of academic disciplines (Project MUSE focuses chiefly on the humanities and social sciences). Users can read these articles online, print them, or download them as PDF (portable document format) files. JSTOR offers the full text of more than 2,000 journals, but the actual number of journals available to you will depend on your library's subscription. Project MUSE offers the full text of more than 550 journals, and Academic OneFile that of about 6,000 journals (many of them through JSTOR).

These databases offer a convenient starting point for research because you can quickly try out some search terms, browse a list of hits, and read a few promising articles. Abstracts (or summaries) in the detailed records will help you select the most useful and relevant articles. (Click "item information" in JSTOR or "summary" in Project MUSE; click the title link in Academic OneFile.) Most articles include notes and bibliographies that will point you to other important sources for your research.

However, these databases include only a small subset of all scholarly journals, and the most recent issues of journals (from the past three to five years) are usually not available. So thorough research demands looking further afield.

Using Databases to Find Scholarly Articles

College libraries subscribe to a large number of scholarly journals, including many of the leading journals in the major fields that are taught or researched on campus. Many of these journals are available in electronic format and may be accessible through the library's Web site. But because some journals still publish only in paper and many older issues have yet to be converted into electronic format, researchers must know how to retrieve articles from the shelves of the library as well as from electronic sources.

When a new issue of a journal arrives, librarians record in the catalog only the fact that the issue has been received. They do not enter the title, subject, and author(s) of each separate article. Thus you cannot normally use the library's catalog to search for these articles: if you were to do a subject search in the library's catalog, you would catch most of the books pertaining to that subject, but you would probably miss all the relevant scholarly journal articles. (Likewise, if you were to do a search by author in the library's catalog, you would catch the books by that author but none of his or her scholarly journal articles.) To find materials in scholarly journals, you need to search a different way.

The best way to locate material in scholarly journals is to use a **bibliographic database**. These databases contain all the information about the contents of scholarly journals that the library catalog usually lacks: the titles, authors, and subjects of all the essays that appear in scholarly journals, and often a brief summary (or abstract) of the argument of each article. Bibliographic databases do *not* usually contain the articles themselves, though some library catalogs provide links to some articles. Databases are usually created and maintained by private companies, and libraries pay a subscription fee to give faculty and students access to them. At many colleges, you can access these indexes through the college's Web site if you have a college e-mail address, an ID, and a password.

Because so many scholarly journals exist, indexes typically cover just one broad area of study. For example, *America: History and Life* indexes journals pertaining to North American history, the *MLA* [Modern Language Association] *International Bibliography* indexes journals pertaining to literary studies, and *EconLit* indexes journals in economics. The companies that maintain electronic indexes strive to include information from as many scholarly journals as possible (and many include information about new books in the field as well), so that a search will identify every important article that has been published in recent years on the topic.

You may be able to link from a record in a database to the full text of the article (perhaps in another database). However, in many cases — such as journals or issues of a journal that your library holds in paper only — you will need to enter the library's stacks to retrieve the paper edition. Locating journal articles in print form is typically a three-step process.

Step 1: Conduct a search for articles in a relevant database.

Step 2: Search for journals by title in the library's catalog.

Step 3: Retrieve the volume from the library's stacks.

Let's follow one student, Christina, as she hunts for an article on Davy Crockett's position toward the Indian Removal Act of 1830.

Step 1. Conduct a Search in a Relevant Database

Christina was taking a course in nineteenth-century American history, and one of the essay topics concerned relations between the US government and Native Americans. She decided to work specifically on Davy Crockett's opposition when he served in Congress to the forced removal of Indians from their lands, a fact that had been mentioned only briefly in a lecture but that intrigued her. After finding several books on Crockett's life and politics, she began to look for scholarly articles. Her college library subscribed to several dozen databases, but the *America: History and Life* index seemed the most relevant to her topic.

The index's main search page let her begin with an "all text" search. This allowed her to search every word in every entry in the index — not the full articles, but the abstracts, titles, and descriptor phrases. This approach was thorough, but she

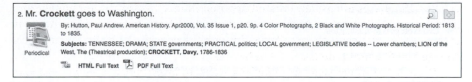

2. Mr. **Crockett** goes to Washington.

By: Hutton, Paul Andrew. American History. Apr2000, Vol. 35 Issue 1, p20. 9p. 4 Color Photographs, 2 Black and White Photographs. Historical Period: 1813 to 1835.

Periodical

Subjects: TENNESSEE; DRAMA; STATE governments; PRACTICAL politics; LOCAL government; LEGISLATIVE bodies -- Lower chambers; LION of the West, The (Theatrical production); **CROCKETT, Davy,** 1786-1836

HTML Full Text   PDF Full Text

Figure 9.6 **Short Entry in a Database**   (Source: Boston Public Library catalog)

quickly learned to avoid terms that were too general. For example, an initial key-word search with the word "Indian" returned more than 16,000 citations — obvi-ously, far too many to browse through.

But a keyword search using the term "Davy Crockett" turned up sixty-two citations — not an impossible number, but still a lot of hits. When she tried "Davy Crockett" as a *subject* search, she got eight hits — far more manageable. And when she combined *two* keyword terms, "Davy Crockett" and "Indian," she got just six hits — a good place to start.

A couple of these hits were identified as book reviews, only a few paragraphs in length and not substantial or informative enough to be useful to her at this stage of her research. Christina passed over these.

One of the hits was an article entitled "Mr. Crockett Goes to Washington" by Paul Andrew Hutton. The citation information indicated that it appeared in the journal *American History* in the year 2000, volume 35, issue number 1, page 21 (see Figure 9.6).

Clicking the "Display Full Entry" button took Christina to a longer version of the entry that included an abstract — a summary of the argument (see Figure 9.7). This revealed that the article discusses Crockett's political career. Since it looked useful for her research, she wanted to find out whether her library carried the jour-nal *American History*, and in particular whether it held volume 35.

So Christina copied down the information from the short entry, being espe-cially careful to copy the citation line accurately, and opened a new browser win-dow to search her library's online catalog.

Step 2. Search for Journals by Title in the Library's Catalog

In the library's catalog she conducted a *title* search for *the title of the journal* — not the title of the article, since the library does not catalog articles by title. Christina entered the words "American History" into the text box on the catalog's main screen and chose "title search" from the menu. The result showed that her library did indeed carry this journal, and it showed a call number for the journal: E171 .A574.

◄ Result List │ Refine Search   ◄ **2 of 11** ►

Mr. **Crockett** goes to Washington.

Authors:	Hutton, Paul Andrew
Source:	American History. Apr2000, Vol. 35 Issue 1, p20. 9p. 4 Color Photographs, 2 Black and White Photographs.
Historical Period:	1813 to 1835
Document Type:	Article
Subject Terms:	DRAMA STATE governments PRACTICAL politics LOCAL government LEGISLATIVE bodies -- Lower chambers
Geographic Terms:	TENNESSEE
Reviews & Products:	LION of the West, The (Theatrical production)
People:	CROCKETT, Davy, 1786-1836
Abstract:	Chronicles the political career of **Davy Crockett** who was a symbol of the "Age of the Common Man" and remembered as an American hero who fought for the rights of the underprivileged. Sold into indentured servitude at the age of 12, with a total of six months' schooling **Crockett** began his political career as a magistrate in central Tennessee, then served as a justice of the peace, and in 1818 was elected colonel of the 57th Militia Regiment. **Crockett's** simple and direct campaign style suited voters and he won the seat to represent Hickman and Lawrence counties in the state assembly. He also served three terms in the House of Representatives. Two of his major issues were defense of squatters' rights and, having participated in the massacre at Tallusahatchee, opposing **Indian** removal. The 1835 House reelection campaign was lost because **Crockett** spent more time promoting his autobiography than working to get the squatters' bill passed. INSET: The Alamo.
Full Text Word Count:	4660
ISSN:	1076-8866
Accession Number:	2809999
Full Text Database:	Academic Search Alumni Edition

Figure 9.7 **Long Entry in a Database** (Source: Boston Public Library catalog)

(Usually, all volumes of a journal have the same call number. Some libraries shelve journals alphabetically by title.)

Step 3. Retrieve the Volume from the Library's Stacks

Entering the library's stacks, Christina found the "E" call numbers on the fourth floor and soon located E171 and the row of bound volumes with the title "American History" stamped on their spines. (Libraries bind issues of journals together by volume and store them on the shelves in a long row. However, the most recent three or four issues are often kept in a separate location reserved for current periodicals.) Pulling down volume 35, she found the article by Paul Andrew Hutton on page 21 of the first issue in the volume. Since her library does not allow journals to be borrowed, she decided to read part of the article in the library—enough to decide whether to photocopy it. In the end, she did make a copy, and she used the article's bibliography to identify two other sources for her paper.

⮕ Try This Writing an Abstract

An *abstract* (from the Latin *abstractus*, meaning "drawn off" or "out of") is a summary that presents the essence of the text's argument as briefly and accurately as possible, usually in just a few sentences, or at most in a few paragraphs. An abstract is strictly objective and impartial; it offers no evaluation or commentary. Writing an abstract can be challenging when the argument is complicated and highly nuanced; the writer must make good decisions about what's *truly* essential to the argument and must choose words carefully to present that essence as clearly and impartially as possible.

Try your hand at writing an abstract.

Option 1. Write an abstract of Michelle Alexander's "Drug War Nightmare: How We Created a Massive Racial Caste System in America" (p. 341).

Option 2. Write an abstract of an article that you find in the library, using *America: History and Life* or another index that provides abstracts. When you have completed your abstract, compare it to the one in the index's "full entry." How does it differ? How would you account for the differences?

Google Scholar

Google Scholar (scholar.google.com) is a specialized search engine that locates scholarly sources. Basic searches are performed in the same way as in regular Google, by typing search terms into a text box.

Google Scholar searches articles and books that have been posted to publicly accessible Web sites; it also searches through some of the subscription-based online indexes and databases of scholarly publications, such as those owned by Elsevier. In addition, it links into library systems so that users can click directly through to the full text of some articles. If you are searching from on-campus via an ".edu" network, you may find that links to items in your library's online holdings appear automatically. If not, you may be able to add your college library in the "Library Links" pane of "Scholar Settings," as illustrated in Figure 9.8. (Click on "Settings" and then "Library Links," and then type in the name of your college.)

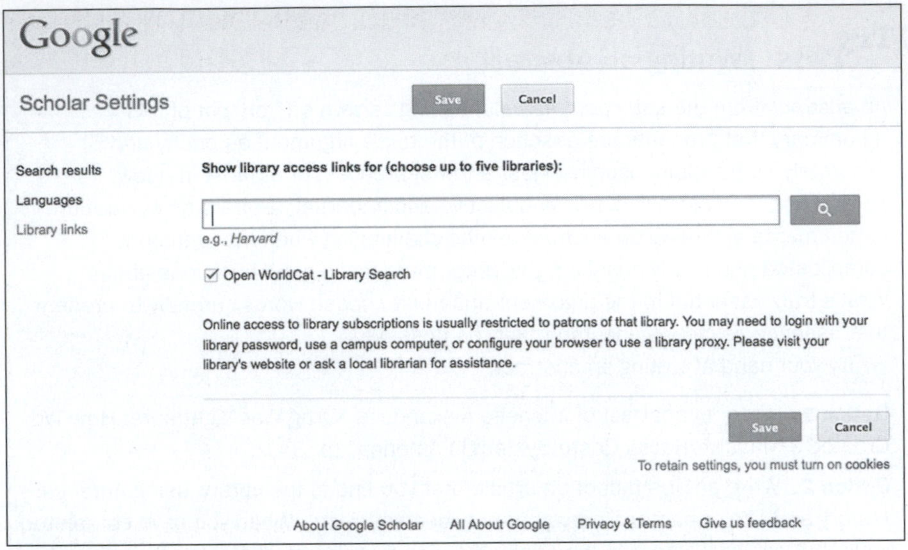

Figure 9.8 Settings Pane in Google Scholar

Google Scholar also searches through the text of the millions of books that have been scanned into the Google Books database. You can access previews of books under copyright as well as entire texts of books without copyright. If only a few pages of a book discuss your topic, Google Scholar attempts to take you directly to those pages so that you can read them right away. Otherwise, the table of contents and preface can give you a sense of the book's focus and help you decide whether you need to hunt it down.

Search results are ranked by their relevance to the search terms (for example, in Figure 9.9, the work that tops the list is the one in which *all* the search terms appear) and by the number of times other writers have cited the work.

One of the powerful tools of Google Scholar is the "Cited by" feature. For example, in the search results shown in Figure 9.9, the article "The city as a growth machine: towards a political economy of place" was cited in 1,774 other works. Clicking on the "Cited by 1774" link will take you directly to a list of these 1,774 items. In turn, each of these items also carries a "Cited by" link.

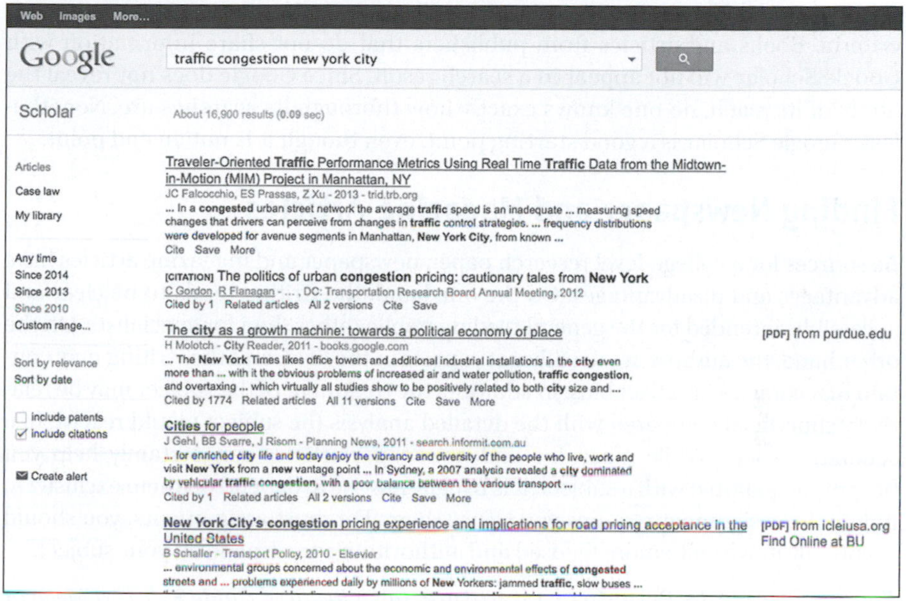

Figure 9.9 Results Page for a Search Using Google Scholar

This daisy chain of citations makes it easier to identify the works that have made a significant contribution to a discussion — the important works that other writers consistently cite. The short list of "key authors" included at the bottom of each results page can also help you identify such works, though it is much less reliable.

Google Scholar searches through the entire text of books and articles, not just keywords and descriptors, so typically it returns exceptionally long lists of results — often in the tens of thousands — many of which will be irrelevant to your search. A good strategy is to read down your list of results until you find one or several items that speak directly to your research question. Once you have identified an article that focuses on the issue you're interested in, you can burrow down into the list of works that cite this article. Not all of those works will be relevant, but likely some will. This technique of working both vertically down a list and horizontally through the "Cited by" pages may help you identify the scholarly conversation about the issue you are researching.

Google Scholar cannot identify *all* the scholarly articles that match your search criteria. Books and articles from publishers that do not share information with Google Scholar will not appear in a search result. Since Google does not reveal the limits of its reach, no one knows exactly how thorough its searches are. Nonetheless, Google Scholar is a good starting point, even though it is not an end point.

Finding Newspaper and Magazine Articles

As sources for a college-level research paper, newspaper and magazine articles have advantages and disadvantages. On the one hand, the writing tends to be clear and accessible, intended for the general reading public rather than for specialists. On the other hand, the authors are usually not experts in the field, and the writing may contain inaccuracies or reflect bias. In addition, the treatment of the subject may be relatively superficial compared with the detailed analysis the subject would receive in a scholarly article. While magazine and newspaper articles can certainly help you become acquainted with a subject, it is usually unwise to depend on them exclusively, unless the assignment requires you to use them. For most assignments, you should eventually move on to more focused and authoritative treatments of your subject.

Readers' Guide to Periodical Literature (also *Readers' Guide Full Text Mega* or *Readers' Guide Full Text Select*) This source indexes articles in about 250 general-interest periodicals (magazines and major newspapers) published in the United States and Canada from 1983 to the present. It also includes the full text of about half the periodicals it indexes, starting from 1994. The *Readers' Guide Retrospective* indexes articles in about 370 general-interest periodicals published in the United States and Canada from 1890 to 1982.

LexisNexis This database is an archive of more than 15,000 newspapers, magazines, and legal sources. Although it was initially designed for business and law professionals, it can be a valuable resource for scholarly research as well. (Your college might subscribe to several LexisNexis databases; if so, the one named LexisNexis Academic is the most useful for finding newspaper and magazine articles. Despite its name, it does not index a large amount of scholarly material.)

Consulting a Reference Librarian

If you run into problems at any point in the research process, consult a reference librarian (usually to be found at a desk in the reference area of the library). Reference librarians are skilled information specialists who can save you time by steering you toward relevant and reliable sources. They can help you not only with the library's own tools and databases but also with Web search engines and other research tools.

If possible, bring a copy of your assignment with you. Be prepared to answer some questions about your research, such as the following:

- What is your topic area or research question?
- In which academic discipline are you writing?
- How much time can you spend on the project?
- How long will the paper be?

If you have a specific question, you may be able to get a quick answer by phoning the reference desk or by using the chat or text-message services that many libraries offer.

Digging Deeper

Now that you have gathered a few sources (for now, five to ten is probably a good number for a paper of about ten pages), you can use them as a starting point for digging deeper. This process involves (1) narrowing your topic to a specific research question or problem (if you have not already done so) and (2) finding additional sources — ideally, *all* the most important sources that speak directly to your question.

First, peruse your sources and select two or three to read carefully. (You might return to the others later, or reject them entirely.) The best ones for your purpose at this point will be those that are most

- relevant to your topic area,
- intelligible,
- current, and
- reliable.

Relevant Depending on your topic, you may not be able to find sources that directly address the topic *exactly*. This is not necessarily fatal — in fact, it can be a good thing if it means that your topic is fresh and original. Sources that may be slightly off your topic may still be highly informative. On the other hand, many scholarly articles and even some books have a very narrow, limited focus. If the scope is too narrow, the source may not be useful at this point. Note the page length. A fairly substantial article (more than five pages) will be most useful at this stage. Choose sources that bear on your topic closely enough to deepen your understanding and inspire questions and ideas.

Intelligible   As we have already noted, scholars often write for other specialists in their field, meaning that some scholarly articles and books are too technical for a nonspecialist to comprehend. A source that's merely challenging to read can be extremely helpful, but one that's *impossible* to understand should be ignored, at least for now. You can probably find other sources that will be more helpful to you. Choose sources that you can learn from.

Current   Recently published books and articles are especially helpful at this stage because you will be using these sources as guides to the conversations around your topic. Most scholarly articles and books will reference or discuss the important works that preceded them, because typically their purpose is to make a contribution to a recognized conversation about a problem in the field. Look for sources with the most up-to-date notes and bibliographies.

Reliable   Evaluating sources can be tricky — we will have more to say about this later (p. 313). For your needs at this point, however, prefer scholarly books and articles — ones that include bibliographies or notes that cite sources. If you're unsure whether a work is scholarly or not, do a Web search for the author's name to find out more about his or her qualifications. If the author is a leading scholar in the field, the work is probably reliable. You can also use Google Scholar to find out how often a book or an article has been cited. Works that have been cited many times are usually more influential.

Now that you have made a schedule for your project, chosen a topic, and found several good sources, you are ready to begin the next phases of your project: narrowing your topic, completing your research, and developing an argument.

✅ Checklist for Planning a Project and Finding Sources

- ☐ Develop a research strategy.
- ☐ Create a project schedule.
- ☐ Choose a topic area.
  - • Review course materials.
  - • Brainstorm with a classmate.
  - • Use an encyclopedia.

☐ Develop your sense of the big picture.
  - Find background information on the Internet.
  - Read relevant article(s) in specialized reference work(s).
  - Develop a list of search terms.

☐ Gather a starter group of sources.
  - Search the library catalog for books.
  - Search databases and Google Scholar for scholarly articles.
  - Search *Readers' Guide* and LexisNexis for magazine and newspaper articles.
  - Search the Internet for additional material.
  - If necessary, consult a reference librarian.

☐ Select two or three sources to read carefully, those that are the most
  - relevant.
  - intelligible.
  - current.
  - reliable.

chapter 10

Working with Sources

Now that you have gathered a handful of useful sources, you can use them as the starting point for research that goes deeply into a narrowly defined question or problem. Some of the sources you've found so far may turn out to be irrelevant in the end, but since they helped you define your research focus, they were certainly worth a look. The next step is to begin gathering

> **"** Meek young men grow up in libraries, believing it their duty to accept the views which Cicero, which Locke, which Bacon, have given, forgetful that Cicero, Locke, and Bacon were only young men in libraries, when they wrote these books. **"**
>
> **RALPH WALDO EMERSON**

materials that address the particular question or problem you have decided to work on, and then to read this material carefully with a view to developing an argument of your own.

Working with Scholarly Articles

As we noted in Chapter 9, scholarly articles can be difficult reading for college students, because they are usually written by specialists for other specialists. The authors usually assume that their readers are already familiar with the subject matter, technical terms, and key concepts of the field. This may not be true in your case — but so much important research is published in scholarly journals that you cannot afford to ignore these articles entirely. And you can use them well if you avoid getting lost in the details and seek instead to understand each article's main purpose. Novice writers sometimes use articles simply as a handy source of facts or quotations that support their position. To treat them this way is a mistake, however: taken out of context, a fact or quotation can fatally misrepresent an author's views, and by neglecting context, the writer fails to learn what the source has to teach.

How can you make sense of scholarly articles and make the best possible use of them? Initially, look for an article's abstract — a valuable tool for making your selections. You may have already read the abstract in the database you used; if not, you can often find it at the beginning of the article or in the journal issue's table of contents. If you cannot find an abstract, read the first two or three paragraphs and the last two paragraphs of the article.

Even if you've already read the abstract, it makes sense to reread it so that you can compare it with the abstracts of the other articles you've gathered. This will help you decide which articles bear most closely on your topic and will be most helpful in your search for a specific question or problem.

Articles in the social sciences and natural sciences often use a "finding system," sometimes called "IMRAD" for **I**ntroduction, **M**ethod, **R**esearch, **A**nd **D**iscussion. For articles of this kind, reading the "Discussion" section *first* often provides a sense of the purpose and significance of the research being presented.

You will need to read the most relevant articles closely; even if you cannot understand every word of an article, you should try to figure out its main idea. In addition to using the reading strategies discussed in Part 1 of this book, you can start by identifying four elements that almost every scholarly article includes or references: a problem, a conversation, an argument, and support. Identifying these elements will help you to recognize and make use of the overall purpose — the *point* — of the article.

The Problem A scholarly article addresses a specific problem, question, or issue — something that is not yet known or is not yet certain. Usually, the article explains this unknown in the first paragraph or two. It occasionally appears later, and very occasionally it goes unmentioned altogether, but only if the problem, question, or issue is so well known that the writer can assume his or her readers will recognize it from other clues. Most of the time, however, it is stated clearly near the beginning of the article.

The Conversation A scholarly conversation takes place largely through articles and books in which scholars present their new research or insights concerning an existing problem. Articles invariably refer to the work of other scholars who have written on the same topic; the most obvious signs are found in citations and bibliographies. But if you look further, you will usually find that authors explicitly *position* their arguments in relation to the work of others, indicating where they stand and where other scholars in the field stand.

The Argument To make a contribution to a scholarly conversation, writers need to make an argument. As we observed in Chapter 3 (p. 75), an argument is a structure that combines a claim and support for the claim. The main claim in a scholarly argument — the thesis statement — is usually found or at least suggested in the first two or three paragraphs of the article. If you can identify the argument and its relation to the problem and see how it makes a contribution to a scholarly conversation, you will have at least a basic grasp of the article's purpose.

The Support Technically, the support is part of the argument. But distinguishing between information that *supports* the argument and words that present or explain the argument will help you understand the article's purpose more fully. For example, many articles in the sciences present the results of an experiment in the form of numerical data, often by means of charts or graphs. Presenting the data and explaining how it was obtained can take up most of the article. But this data is interesting and important only because it supports a claim or thesis, one that resolves some problem or answers some question. If the data is extensive and complicated, one can easily get lost in it and overlook the main point.

Frequently the abstract will at least hint at these four elements. But abstracts are highly condensed, so you'll need to read at least a few paragraphs of the article to see how the four elements reveal the article's purpose.

Though no two articles incorporate these elements in exactly the same way, studying a single article can still give us some idea of how the elements work together in practice. In "Is Google Making Us Stupid?," Nicholas Carr cites the work of Maryanne Wolf, a developmental psychologist at Tufts University. Together with four colleagues, Wolf published an article in *Reading and Writing: An Interdisciplinary Journal* entitled "Links between Early Rhythm Skills, Musical Training, and Phonological Awareness." The entire article occupies thirty pages of the journal, but we can get a good sense of the four elements in just the first couple of pages.

Here are the first two paragraphs.

Introduction

In the development of most academic skills, it is generally assumed that the earlier the better (e.g., Jordan, Grall, Deutsch, & Deutsch, 1985). Reading is among the most important and complex academic skills to be acquired by young learners, and formal reading instruction around the world usually begins in first grade. In recent years, however, many American educators and researchers have looked for ways to use the kindergarten and pre-reading years to better prepare children for the demanding cognitive and linguistic requirements of reading acquisition. Most efforts in pre-school focus on building skills that are directly connected to reading acquisition such as vocabulary, letter, and print knowledge. And, indeed, there exists increasing pressure on many school officials to teach reading precursors early and with more intensity (Elkind, 2010), which could change the dynamics of many early childhood approaches to learning and development. Educators and researchers are exploring whether other developmentally-appropriate, non-academic activities can also bolster a child's reading acquisition skills (e.g., Dana Foundation, 2008).

Claims have been made that musical activity can enhance acquisition of reading skill, even before formal reading instruction begins (e.g., Fisher & McDonald, 2001). However, there have been very few research studies to investigate these claims. In the studies to be reported here, we sought to explore specifically how music and reading acquisition could be connected in pre-readers. Because of overlapping characteristics with regard to timing and segmentation of sound streams, we hypothesized that one way in which music and reading acquisition are connected is through links between rhythm ability and phonological awareness, a central and critical underlying skill for reading acquisition. Working with experimental and control groups of kindergartners, we further investigated whether greater amounts of musical activity with an emphasis on rhythm would be reflected in enhancement of phonological awareness. To lay the groundwork for future investigation of long-term connections between early musical activity and later reading, we also explored whether there are links between kindergarten rhythm ability and second grade phonological skills.[1]

We find evidence of a *conversation* right away, with the phrase "it is generally assumed" and, a few lines down, "In recent years, however, many American educators and researchers have looked for ways. . . ." The second paragraph begins with the phrase "Claims have been made that musical activity can enhance acquisition of reading

---

[1] Catherine Moritz, Sasha Yampolsky, Georgios Papadelis, Jennifer Thomson, and Maryanne Wolf, "Links between Early Rhythm Skills, Musical Training, and Phonological Awareness," *Reading and Writing: An Interdisciplinary Journal* 26, no. 5 (2013): 740.

skill"—another reference to a conversation. The second and third sentences of that paragraph present the particular *problem* that the article addresses: "However, there have been very few research studies to investigate these claims. In the studies to be reported here, we sought to explore specifically how music and reading acquisition could be connected in pre-readers." This is the authors' question: Are music acquisition and reading acquisition connected in pre-readers? The rest of the article attempts to at least partially answer this question by reporting on an experiment that the authors conducted. The data they gathered is *support* for an *argument* that is not fully stated until quite late in the article, in a section headed "Results": "These results support our hypothesis that kindergarten rhythm ability would be significantly related to PA [phonological awareness] in second grade" (758). Postponing the argument is common in science articles, but usually, as here, the author hints at his or her argument strongly in the article's opening paragraphs, giving the reader a sufficiently clear sense of what all the supporting data means.

As you read through the first four or five paragraphs of a scholarly article, mark whatever signs you find of these four elements. (You might mark a *P*, *C*, *A*, or *S* in the margins to keep the elements distinct.) Recognizing them will help you identify and recall the main purpose of the article and will also give you a sense of how scholars present their research findings — how they express their purpose. When it comes time for you to draft your opening paragraphs, try to incorporate these four elements so that your own purpose is completely clear.

Working with Books

Because it takes time to read an entire book, you'll need to use some strategies to select the books that are most useful and to get what you need from them.

- Note the book's date of publication (there may be more than one date if the book has appeared in multiple editions). As a general rule, devote more time to more recent books.

- Read the table of contents. Chapter titles and subtitles may not describe the contents exactly, but they will often give you a good sense of what is covered. (A book might contain only one relevant chapter, but that chapter may be indispensable.)

- To get a sense of the book's overall purpose and focus, read the introduction or preface. It's important to understand the author's position and point of view in the particular chapters you read and use (see p. 320 for more about identifying the writer's position). Often the preface or introduction will also tell you which chapters are most relevant to your topic area and which ones you can skip.

- If the book appears relevant but covers subject matter that lies outside your topic area, use the index to see where your topic is discussed.

Refining Your Research

As you continue your research, you'll want to narrow your search, continue finding relevant material, and keep track of what you find.

Narrow Down Your Topic to a Particular Question or Problem

Perhaps skimming through the sources you've gathered has already helped you identify a specific problem or question for your research. If not, look for one as you read carefully through two or three of your sources. The problem you choose should be appropriate to the assignment you've been given, and it should be sufficiently narrow in scope to be treated within your page or word limit. Moreover, it should be something that interests you, and preferably something you do not already have strong convictions about. (Otherwise, you may be unable to conduct research with an open mind.)

You will probably learn a great deal from reading just two or three sources thoughtfully and attentively, as scholarly works are usually dense with information and ideas. Take notes as you read (include page numbers for any note that refers to a text, so that you can cite the text correctly in your paper). And give yourself time for reflective, informal writing as a way of generating and clarifying ideas (see Chapter 4).

An article or a chapter in a book might spark a new idea that none of your sources directly addresses but that you would like to pursue. If so, it's worth going back to the library catalog and the databases to see what you can find on this new topic, as there's a good chance that a scholar has already discussed it.

If you are not getting much out of the sources that you've found, ask a reference librarian or your instructor for help.

Use Citation Notes and Bibliographies to Point You to Other Sources

As we noted above in "Working with Scholarly Articles," scholarly writers invariably use citations (in-text citations, footnotes, or endnotes) to show readers the source of ideas and information they have used. Most books and articles also include bibliographies. Make a note of any sources that appear to discuss the problem you're working on (see the next section, "Keep a Working Bibliography"). Citations often work like a paper trail: one source points you to others, which point to still more, and so on. If your research is thorough, you'll eventually notice that certain sources get cited repeatedly, and you will develop a good sense of the conversation and perhaps even the field as a whole — who the important contributors are and how the conversation has unfolded over time.

Once you have a more narrowly defined topic, you can conduct a fresh search for sources in databases and the library catalog.

Keep a Working Bibliography

Even as you begin your research, keep a working bibliography to record all your sources. Keep this bibliography scrupulously organized and up-to-date: add works as you learn about them and fill in complete bibliographical information as soon as you can. Delete entries that you have examined and rejected. Include full publication data, and for each entry include a brief note about its usefulness for your project. If your research involves a large number of sources, record the location of your notes (for example, in a folder on your computer or in a notebook) and/or of your printout or photocopy of the item on a separate line. Update this document continually as you work: it will become a crucial component of your research project.

For articles, include the following information:

- Name of the author or authors
- Title of the article
- Title of the periodical
- Year of publication
- Volume number

- Issue number (if the journal is paginated by issue)
- Page range
- Location (name of the database and URL if electronic; library and floor number if print)
- Call number (if print)
- Access date (if electronic)
- Medium (e.g., "Print" or "Web")

For books, include the following information:

- Name of the author or authors
- Title of the book
- Place of publication (city and country)
- Name of the publisher
- Year of publication
- Location (name of the library and floor number)
- Call number
- Medium (e.g., "Print" or "E-book")

For Web sites and other documents found on the Internet, include the following information:

- Brief URL (as much of it as you will need to locate the material again — e.g., loc.gov/rr/program/bib/ourdocs/Louisiana.html)
- Title of the Web page (e.g., "Louisiana Purchase: Primary Documents of American History")
- Author or sponsoring organization (e.g., "Library of Congress")
- Date on which the page was last revised, if available (often found at the bottom of the Web page)
- Access date (the date on which you viewed it)
- Medium (e.g., "Web")

For this working bibliography, you can use a word processing document, a spreadsheet program, a database program, or an online tool such as EasyBib, NoodleTools, Zotero, or RefWorks (see the Appendix, p. 406).

Sample Working Bibliography

Gara, Larry. *The Presidency of Franklin Pierce*. Lawrence, KS: University Press of
Kansas, 1991. Print.
*Only book I've found so far that focuses just on Pierce's presidency. Scholarly
and seems pretty objective. Good bibliography.*
E432. G37 1991
Mugar Library, 4th floor.

Hodder, Frank Heywood. "The Railroad Background of the Kansas-Nebraska Act."
The Mississippi Valley Historical Review 12.1 (1925): 3-22. Web.
Old article, but clearly explains how railroads factored into K-N.
JSTOR: jstor.org/stable/1891782
Accessed: November 16, 2011

Holt, Michael F. *Franklin Pierce*. New York: Times Books-Henry Holt, 2010. Print.
Recent bio of Franklin Pierce. Short. Decent bibliography.
E432. H65 2010
Mugar Library, 4th floor.

Limerick, Patricia Nelson. *The Legacy of Conquest: The Unbroken Past of the
American West*. New York: Norton, 1987. Print.
*Debunks myths about the history of the frontier. Chs. 3, 4 look especially
useful.*
F591. L56 1987
Mugar Library, 4th floor.

Nichols, Roy F. "The Kansas-Nebraska Act: A Century of Historiography." *The
Mississippi Valley Historical Review* 43.2 (1956): 187-212. Web.
Reviews all the historical studies up to 1956.
JSTOR: jstor.org/stable/1902683
Accessed: November 16, 2011

Using Specialized Reference Works

Scholarly articles often treat questions of a very narrow scope, and books may
require a lot of time to read through. So a specialized reference work — an encyclopedia or a dictionary that covers a specific discipline or field of study — can be

useful at this point. Consulting such a reference work is an efficient way to get a clearer sense of the big picture around your research question and to add key sources to your bibliography. Some specialized reference works are available in online versions; others can be found in the reference area of your library. We can list only a few titles here; for a more comprehensive catalog (with more than 16,000 entries), consult Robert Balay's *Guide to Reference Books*, 11th Edition (Chicago: American Library Association, 1996).

Almanacs

American Annual

CIA Factbook

Facts on File Yearbook

World Almanac

Biographical Sources

African American Biographical Database

Biography and Genealogy Master Index

Contemporary Authors

Dictionary of American Biography

Dictionary of National Biography

Who's Who

Specialized Encyclopedias, Databases, and Dictionaries

Contemporary Literary Criticism

Dictionary of Literary Biography

Encyclopedia of Philosophy

Encyclopedia of Sports

The Internet Movie Database

New Grove Dictionary of Music and Musicians

Oxford Dictionary of Art

As you conduct research, you will come across a wide variety of sources. Most of these will belong to a definite type or genre. Each has its own purposes, observes conventions of form and style, and imposes certain expectations on the reader. If you recognize the type of source you are dealing with and understand its conventions, you will be better equipped to use it appropriately in your research.

However, sources do not always make it immediately obvious what type they are, and readers do not always know what to expect from them or why they take a particular form. Table 10.1 below lists the types of sources that students most

Table 10.1 Types of Sources and Their Characteristics

Type of Source	Publisher	Author	Purpose
Scholarly books	University or scholarly press	Expert	Review and add to findings in a scholarly field
Scholarly articles	Scholarly journal	Expert	Publish new findings to scholars in the field
Serious books for general readers	Trade publisher	Usually expert, professional writer, or scholar	General interest
Popular magazines	Usually a for-profit company	Professional journalists and guest writers	General interest
Newspapers	Usually a for-profit company	Chiefly professional journalists	General interest
Sponsored Web sites	For-profit or nonprofit company or organization	Professional and amateur writers and contributors	Varies
Personal Web sites	Individual	Anyone. Author may or may not be identified.	Varies
Discussion forums and listservs	Usually a nonprofit organization or group	Anyone. Authors may use pseudonyms.	Varies from entertainment to serious discussion

frequently encounter in conducting research and identifies some of their pertinent characteristics. It will help you not only identify the type of source you are using but also assess it fairly, weighing one factor against another. A highly selective work, for example, is likely to be more reliable than a nonselective one. But highly selective sources may be difficult to understand. In many situations, a variety of sources will serve your purposes best.

Selectivity	Accessibility	Interactivity
Highly selective and often peer-reviewed	Varies. Specialized language may be difficult for the general reader to comprehend.	None
Highly selective and often peer-reviewed	Varies. Often difficult for general readers to comprehend.	Minimal. Letters from readers are sometimes published, but the process may take months.
Selective, but not usually peer-reviewed	Medium	None
May be selective, depending on the magazine	Easy	Medium. Many publish letters to the editor and reader feedback columns in every issue.
Somewhat selective, depending on the newspaper	Easy	Medium. Most publish letters and comments from readers in every issue.
Fairly selective	Easy	Strong. Many invite comments and e-mails.
Open; not selective	Easy	Varies. Some personal Web sites invite comments or e-mails; some do not.
Open; not selective	Easy	Strong. Posting a question often gets an immediate response.

Other Sources

Field Research

In Chapter 9, we distinguished between primary research and secondary research (p. 269). In primary research, you are typically producing your own findings by directly investigating the object of study — for example, by studying original manuscripts in an archive or by conducting an online opinion poll. In secondary research, you are working with the findings of other researchers. **Field research** — research conducted outside the library or laboratory — is typically primary research, designed to produce original findings. It is not always appropriate in college writing, but some assignments require it (most frequently in the social sciences and natural sciences), and some allow it as an option.

Observations A formal observation involves testing a hypothesis by watching and listening to the behaviors of people or things in a particular setting. Formal observations of human beings are used extensively in psychology, sociology, and anthropology and occasionally in some other disciplines. A typical observation might involve attending a meeting or an event to study how a group of individuals behaves in that setting.

You usually need to do some preliminary research before designing and arranging an observation so that you become familiar with appropriate research questions associated with the particular group or culture. Before conducting the observation, you might want to make notes concerning your own preconceptions and attitudes about the people you will be observing. Testing these preconceptions can help give your observation purpose and focus.

All research involving human subjects, including observations, must be conducted with an understanding of the rights of these subjects. Some institutions require that all research involving human subjects be approved by an Institutional Review Board (IRB) before it proceeds. If your instructor has not already explained your institution's regulations, ask him or her for guidance before making any further arrangements.

If IRB approval is not required, be sure to request permission from the group you plan to observe well in advance of your observation. Use an informed consent form if you will be observing a situation where privacy might be a concern. (For an example, see Figure 10.1.) If you plan to make an audio or video recording, obtain specific permission to do so.

During the observation, use the double-entry method to take detailed notes. On the left-hand side of a page, note only what you see and hear. On the right-hand side, write down your own reactions, questions, and ideas. Note the date, time, place, and conditions of your observation. Fill out your notes at the first opportunity, while your observations are still fresh in your mind.

Finally, minimize the "observer effect." Avoid interacting with individuals in the group and avoid getting involved in the group's activities. As far as possible, minimize your impact on the group's behaviors.

Informed Consent Form

I, [name of participant], give my permission to [your name] to use my written and spoken words in [his/her] research project written for [course] at [your school].

- I understand that I may read and approve the final draft of the material [he/she] uses about me in [his/her] project.
- I understand that I may request that the final draft be kept confidential between [him/her] and the course instructor.

Signature: _____   Date: _____

Address: _____

Telephone Number: _____

E-mail: _____

I prefer to use this pseudonym: _____

Figure 10.1 **Informed Consent Form**

Interviews An interview in person, or by phone, e-mail, or chat, can be an excellent way to learn about your research topic and may provide rich insight in a fairly short period of time. Bear in mind, however, that an interviewee — even an expert — can present only one point of view, and it is unlikely to be definitive. Interviews are typically most useful when they form one kind of source in your research, balanced and complemented by others.

Interviews benefit enormously from preliminary background research. Once you have requested and scheduled an interview, prepare your questions carefully. During the interview, however, listen carefully to answers and be ready to improvise new questions.

Use an informed consent form (see Figure 10.1) if any subject matter may be private or sensitive. Obtain permission if you plan to make an audio or video recording. You can add that stipulation to the consent form if you plan to make a recording.

Surveys Surveys gather data about behaviors or opinions. They are especially useful if your research focuses on a local community, but they may be helpful whenever you need to understand attitudes or opinions on any topic.

The design and implementation of surveys is a science of its own, one we cannot cover in detail here.[2] However, understanding some basic strategies can greatly enhance the credibility and usefulness of your survey or poll.

Surveys work best when their purpose is well defined. Identify the questions you want to ask — and *why* you want to ask these questions: What is the purpose of the survey in your research project as a whole? The more clearly you understand the purpose of your survey, the more effectively you can integrate the results into your writing.

The group you survey is called a "sample" because it represents a small subset of the actual population you hope to learn about. To avoid bias and partiality in your sample, consider the characteristics of the larger group you want to understand, and then build a sample that mirrors these characteristics. The most useful

[2] For a comprehensive discussion, see Arleen Fink, *How to Conduct Surveys: A Step-by-Step Guide*, 4th ed. (Los Angeles: Sage, 2009); Floyd Fowler, *Survey Research Methods*, 4th ed. (Los Angeles: Sage, 2008); or Lawrence Orcher, *Conducting a Survey: Techniques for a Term Project* (Glendale, CA: Pyrczak, 2007).

surveys gather data from a *random* sample that is large enough to be representative of the characteristics of the larger group (containing a similar representation of age groups, income levels, genders, and so on).

There will always be some margin of error because the sample is not identical to the target population; the goal is to reduce that margin as much as possible, though it can never be eliminated. Consequently, it is important to understand the limits of your sample. For example, if you wanted to know whether American college students consider economic growth or protection of the environment a higher priority, you might distribute a short survey to some college friends or classmates. But your sample would need to be much more varied to give you credible information about American college students *as a whole*: to be truly reliable, the sample would need to include a significantly large sampling of students from each region in the country and from different types of institutions as well as different types of students within these institutions.

If you cannot conduct a large survey, and if your sample is limited by geographic area or to certain types of respondents, acknowledge these limitations when you present your results in writing, and recognize the survey's limits as evidence. But bear in mind that the larger and more representative your sample group is, the better.

When you use surveys as a source, keep in mind some practical considerations.

- Find out if someone else has already done a survey similar to yours. It may use a larger sample and offer more reliable and meaningful data than you can gather yourself. For opinion polls, check Gallup polls (gallup.com) and the Polling Report (pollingreport.com).

- Keep the survey as short as you can while still obtaining meaningful data. Shorter surveys usually yield higher completion rates than lengthy ones do.

- Construct questions carefully. Questions should be clear, to the point, and impartial. Guard against phrasing that might lead respondents toward one answer over another.

- Test your questions on friends or classmates to make sure they are clear and produce useful results.

- Multiple-choice and true/false questions lend themselves to gathering numerical data; free-response questionnaires provide more nuanced results but require careful interpretation. A **Likert scale**, which asks respondents to rate their level of agreement with a statement on a scale of 1 to 5, can be a good compromise. (For example, respondents might be asked to enter 1 on the answer sheet for "strongly agree," 2 for "agree," 3 for "neutral," 4 for "disagree," and 5 for "strongly disagree.")

- Include a few questions that ask for relevant information about the participants themselves (for example, sex, age, education level, ethnicity). Analyzing this demographic information will help you to understand the representativeness of your sample and the strengths and limitations of your survey as evidence.

- Use an online tool (e.g., SurveyMonkey, Zoomerang, SurveyGizmo, or Yahoo Groups) to construct a Web-based questionnaire to send to potential respondents. These tools automatically tabulate results from the raw data and create reports.

- In your paper, summarize the key findings. Present the complete results in an appendix.

Dynamic Internet Sources

As you know, the Internet is much more than an archive of documents; it is also a forum for the rapid exchange of information and ideas. If you are researching a current event or any topic of ongoing interest, you might find dynamic Internet tools and sources useful, such as Google alerts, RSS feeds, and listservs.

Google Alerts If you are conducting research on a current event or any topic of ongoing discussion, consider setting up a "Google alert" so that you can receive e-mails about new items on the Web that mention your search terms. Go to google .com/alerts, where you can define your alerts and choose how you would like to receive them (as e-mails or a feed).

RSS Feeds If you need to stay current with a particular site or blog that pertains closely to your research, you may be able to subscribe to updates and the latest news in the form of an RSS feed, which will save you the trouble of visiting the site daily. (RSS stands for Really Simple Syndication or Rich Site Summary.) A Web-based feed reader such as My Yahoo, Feedly, or Digg Reader will let you subscribe to feeds. Many popular browsers and mail programs also incorporate feed readers, or you can use a dedicated app such as Flipboard. Feeds can also be read on mobile devices, using a Web browser or app.

Listservs Listservs are electronic mailing lists focused on a specific area of interest. They exist on a wide range of topics and concerns, and their subscribers are often knowledgeable. You can subscribe to a listserv (even for just a week or two) and pose questions. (Be diplomatic and considerate. It's best to "listen" for a while before jumping into a discussion.) Although a listserv can put you in touch with experts in your research area, you should use information and ideas from this source cautiously: look for corroboration in reliable sources.

To find a listserv on your research topic, send an e-mail to listserv@listserv.net with a blank subject line and a body that reads "list global [topic]," where [topic] is the general topic of your research. For example, "list global Shakespeare" would return all the listservs dedicated to the discussion of Shakespeare.

Evaluating Sources

As you read the sources you've gathered, you will need to assess their reliability. Your argument should lean more heavily on the most credible and trustworthy sources: it cannot succeed if it relies on incorrect information or biased opinion. Yet as a college student, you often have to write papers on unfamiliar subjects, and so you have no choice but to rely heavily on the information and arguments offered in secondary sources. This is a difficult position to be in, but not an impossible one. You need not feel at the mercy of your sources as long as you evaluate them carefully.

Books and Periodicals (Print and Electronic)

Books Scholarly books are often published by an academic press (which usually includes the words "university press" in its name) or a government agency. But trade and mass-market publishers also produce books of a scholarly nature, so the publisher's name is not a sure guide. Scholarly books almost always include a bibliography and references. But so do many books that are not truly scholarly. However, you can take some steps to determine whether the author is an expert and how the book is regarded by other experts.

- Check the preface or introduction for clues about the author's credentials.
- Do a quick Web search for the author's name to find out more about his or her qualifications.
- Find reviews of the book using a database or Google Scholar. Book reviews are usually short and can quickly tell you the book's key findings and its merits and flaws as a work of scholarship.

- Use Google Scholar to check the "Cited by" number (see Figure 9.9, p. 291). This figure tells you how many times a book or an article has been cited in the works that Google Scholar searches. A high number indicates that the book or article is widely cited and probably influential.

Scholarly Articles Scholarly articles are written by experts in the field and in most cases are published only if other experts affirm that the work merits publication. This does not mean, of course, that every word in such works is *true*, but it does mean that scholarly articles occupy a relatively high position on the reliability scale. Scholarly articles satisfy most or all of the following criteria:

- The author or authors are named, often with their credentials or university affiliation.
- The article includes a bibliography or list of references.
- The article is published in a journal devoted specifically to a field of study.
- The language is somewhat technical, suggesting that the intended audience is other experts in the field of study rather than the general public.
- The journal is peer-reviewed or refereed. Sometimes the database will tell you whether the article is peer-reviewed. If not, your library may subscribe to *Ulrich's Periodicals Directory* or Ulrichsweb, a database that contains information about periodicals. After searching for the journal, click on its title in the results list to see the complete record. Look for the line "refereed."
- The article is cited by other scholars. The "cited by" number in the Google Scholar entry for the article indicates how many times it has been cited in the works that Google Scholar searches. Alternatively, your library may subscribe to the ISI Web of Knowledge database, which includes a "times cited" figure for each entry. (Or use Web of Science for articles in the natural sciences.) High numbers indicate that the book or article is widely cited and probably influential.

Magazine and Newspaper Articles Magazine and newspaper articles are typically written not by experts but by professional writers. These writers often must develop some degree of expertise fairly quickly for the purpose of writing the article. The writing must be accepted by the magazine's editors, and the better magazines employ fact-checkers; however, these editors and fact-checkers are not themselves experts, and errors and distortions do occur. Also, because magazines and newspapers strive to interest, inform, and entertain the general reader, their articles are typically more superficial (but also more accessible) than is scholarly writing. So this kind of source (usually known as popular or general-interest periodical literature) tends to be less credible than scholarly writing. However, a substantial article in a reputable magazine may be highly informative and useful if you can confirm the information in at least one other reputable source.

Web Sites, Blogs, and Other Internet Sources

The Internet is a vast and constantly changing agglomerate of information and opinion from all over the globe and from every kind of source — individuals, non-profit organizations, for-profit corporations, advocacy groups, special-interest groups, government agencies, charitable associations, clubs, and so on. You can find an amazing amount of valuable and reliable material on the Internet. But you can also find plenty that is biased, one-sided, ill-informed, incorrect, or just plain crazy. After all, the price of admission to Internet publication is practically zero: anyone with access to a computer can contribute to a public forum or set up a site. Sometimes well-designed sites that look perfectly credible are actually full of distortions and fallacies. So how can you tell whether a site is credible or not? In some cases, you will already be familiar with the site or its sponsor, and you can use it confidently (for example, the Library of Congress Web sites or the *New York Times* Web site), but you don't want to restrict yourself only to these. Since there are no censors or filters for truth and fairness on the Internet, *you* have to be the filter. When in doubt, investigate, using the following process to evaluate Web sites.

1. Cross-Check Information. Responsible writers — on Web sites and elsewhere — tell readers where the information they provide comes from, whether in the text, in a reference note, or with a link. If the writer fails to do so, and if you cannot find corroboration by conducting your own research, discount the information.

The best test of the reliability of information is to check whether it can be found in multiple sources. If you cannot trace the information to a reliable source, don't use it.

2. Determine Whether the Material Is Current. Start by casting a critical eye over the site itself. Good, well-maintained Web sites date their content to tell readers when items were posted. And active Web sites include items posted within the last six months at least, keeping their readers informed about recent developments in their subject area. To determine the currency of material on the Web, ask yourself the following questions:

- When was this material written?
- When was the site last updated?
- Does the site contain more than one or two dead links (nonfunctioning links) to other sites?

3. Test the Site for Signs of Bias. Many Web sites represent a point of view, but some show no interest in being reasonable or fair and may even distort the truth to make it fit a predetermined conclusion. At worst, a Web site may be little more than a vehicle for propaganda and disinformation.

Be wary of writing that seems emotional — a tirade or rant rather than a carefully reasoned argument — and arguments that seem heavily one-sided and neglect or dismiss counterarguments.

Evidence of bias does not necessarily mean that you should ignore the source altogether. Rather, you should use the source with caution, bearing in mind that it may not be telling the whole story and that you will need to look for other sources that present another side and fill in what's missing.

Note that some items within a Web site may be more trustworthy or objective than others. For example, on a newspaper's Web site, you will find news articles along with opinion columns, reviews, and reader comments.

To test a Web site for signs of bias, ask yourself the following questions:

- Does the site reflect only one point of view?
- Is the tone of the writing emotional instead of logical?
- Does the writer cite sources, and do these sources appear to be reputable and trustworthy?

4. Identify and Research the Author or Owner of the Site. You should be able to determine who the author or owner of a Web site is; if not, be suspicious. Often the name of the Web site appears in large type at the top of the page, but the name alone may not tell you much. The details — the sponsoring organization's name, address, and contact information — may appear at the very bottom of the page, perhaps in small type. If you cannot find this information anywhere on the site, you should be quite skeptical. Perhaps this isn't a good source for a college research paper.

The Principal Internet Domain Types

.com, .net, .tv, .fm	Corporate or personal sites (The URL endings ".tv" and ".fm" are actually country codes—for Tuvalu and the Federated States of Micronesia—but these countries license their codes for commercial use.)
.edu	Educational institutions (Personal sites on an educational institution's Web site may also use ".edu.")
.gov	Government agencies
.org	Nonprofit organizations; often sponsors of discussion forums and community blogs (Note, however, that in practice anyone can register a site as a ".org.")

The URLs of Web sites registered in countries other than the United States typically include a country code (such as ".de" for Germany) instead of one of the domain names listed here.

When you are looking for a site's author or sponsor, bear in mind the following:

- The domain name in the URL (the Web site address) — for example, .gov, .edu, .org, or .com — gives you some idea of whether the sponsoring agency is a government agency, an educational institution, a nonprofit organization, or a for-profit company. These domain names are not, however, a sure guide to the type of organization that sponsors the site. (See "The Principal Internet Domain Types," above.)

- Don't confuse the author with the webmaster. A webmaster usually maintains the site but does not necessarily create the content.

➔ Try This   Evaluating a Web Site

Choose a news site, a government site, a personal Web page, and a political discussion forum. Using the guide on the next page, write a brief evaluation of each.

Web Site Evaluation Guide

What is the domain type (e.g., ".com," ".edu," ".gov")?

Is the site current?

- Does material on the site indicate the date it was posted?
- Are the most recent dates within the last two or three months?
- Are all the links active, or do you find dead links?

Does the site show signs of one-sided argument or strong bias?

- Is the site's tone emotional?
- Does the site neglect or dismiss counterarguments or other points of view?

Is the author personal or corporate?

- If corporate, what kind of organization or body is responsible for the site (e.g., nonprofit organization, for-profit corporation, advocacy group, educational institution)?

If corporate, what is the sponsoring organization?

- What is the organization's purpose?
- How is the organization funded?

If corporate, how is the material selected?

- Does the site invite contributions from any user, or does it select material for the site?

If personal, can you determine the author's identity?

- Does the site offer biographical information? (If not, find it using a search engine.)
- What are the author's credentials?

- Some sites require contributions to be anonymous (for example, Wikipedia and certain news sites or sections of news sites). Nevertheless, the identity of the publisher or sponsor of the site should be clear.

Often a link on a Web page will take you to biographical information about the author or background information about the sponsoring organization. Frequently, the author or sponsoring organization will provide an e-mail address or a phone number. If not, use a general-purpose search engine such as Google or Bing to try to find further information about the author or sponsor.

Try to answer the following questions about the author or sponsor of a site:

- What are the author's credentials or qualifications?
- What is the sponsoring organization's purpose? How is it funded?

Reading Critically to Develop a Position

Imagine that you join some friends at a café, and they are deep in conversation about the day's big news story, a court ruling about gay marriage. As you listen, you realize that your friends are having a debate, with two on one side, two on the other, and a fifth who asks questions but seems undecided. As you listen to the arguments, you form a position of your own. One participant mentions facts — new to you — concerning constitutional law, and another mentions some statistics. A third makes an impressive philosophical argument. As you continue to listen, you realize that there are really more than two positions — three or four, perhaps even five. Josh supports civil unions but not marriage for same-sex couples; Judy supports neither and doesn't believe in marriage even for heterosexual couples. Sonja feels that individual states should be free to allow same-sex marriage but that other states should not be required to recognize these marriages, whereas Sue feels that same-sex marriages should be treated no differently from opposite-sex marriages. Steve remains undecided on that question. After you have listened long enough to get a good sense of what's at issue and where everyone stands, you feel ready to contribute your own views, explain your reasoning, and offer something new — based on a poll you remember reading about just this morning.

This situation is similar to the one we face as writers of research papers. Just as a newcomer to a conversation first *listens* to find out where the other participants stand and then, after becoming better informed and deciding on a position, makes a *contribution* to the conversation, so a researcher must first listen to what others have said about the issue, must strive to understand the positions that others have taken, and must try to contribute something new to the conversation. Just as the conversation participant would not merely repeat what everyone else has already said, so a researcher should not merely summarize the views of others, but instead should try to work out a particular stand on the question and then explain the reasons for taking that stand.

When conducting any research, the first step is to find out whether others have investigated this matter before and, if so, what they learned and what conclusions they drew. Usually, you will discover that several other researchers have already explored the matter, that they agree on some points and differ on others, and that a conversation among them has developed, unfolding slowly over time as more research is done and old research is approached from fresh angles. Obviously, there's no point in starting an exploration from scratch as though no one had ever thought about the matter before. In thinking carefully about what others have already said, you may find something fresh and interesting to say of your own.

Because research involves entering a conversation, a necessary element in the research process — just as important as gathering the right sources — is careful, patient *reading* of sources. The reading strategies described in Part 1 of this book, as well as the method described earlier in "Working with Scholarly Articles" (p. 296), can help you make good sense of difficult material. Read sources not only for information but also to understand their main point or purpose — what they contribute to the conversation. Understanding the different positions your sources take will help you to establish your own position and to make a strong argument for it.

Read for the Gist: Identify the Writer's Argument, Purpose, and Position

As you read your sources, look for the writer's argument, purpose, and position. When reading a scholarly article, you can look for signs of the problem, the conversation, the argument, and support, as described in "Working with Scholarly Articles" (p. 296). Other kinds of sources may not contain all four elements — for example, a reference work article might not respond to a problem, and a Web page might not reference a conversation — but many will. Looking for signs of these elements can help you identify the writer's main argument and purpose.

A writer's **position** — his or her stand relative to that of other writers on the subject — is a slightly different aspect of the text from the argument, one that is not always spelled out. The writer may be taking sides in an ongoing debate, or defining a new position never before adopted, or attempting to define a new problem that has not previously been investigated, or raising questions for further study about the conventional wisdom on the subject. The argument is often a narrower, more specific statement than the position.

Scholars often explain the intellectual context of their argument in the first few paragraphs of an article or in the preface or introduction of a book. Here, they will review the conversation — what others have said on the subject — and sketch out the major positions in order to place their own argument in relation to the work of others.

But many writers, and especially scholars who are writing primarily for other scholars in their specialized field of research, save time and space by leaving some aspects of the argument *implied* rather than fully stating it, knowing that their audience will recognize certain well-established ideas and basic assumptions on the basis of a few indications. Of course, this may pose a problem for less expert readers: How can they get access to the rest of the iceberg? One way is to read good reference sources (see "Using Specialized Reference Works," p. 304). Another way is to read a substantial article in a reputable newsmagazine or newspaper or on a trustworthy Web site. Sometimes the full picture emerges as you put the pieces together from various sources; one source tends to illuminate another.

Writers often establish their positions by refuting counterarguments. (Counterarguments are those that oppose the writer's own argument; friendly arguments are those that support it.) When a writer uses a secondary source, it is important to notice whether it is being used as counterargument or as friendly argument. A writer may spend several paragraphs or pages summarizing a work that, in the end, will be questioned or refuted. At times, secondary evidence functions as both argument and counterargument at the same time. For example, a writer (let's call her Smith) might agree with *most* of what another writer (let's call him Jones) has said about an issue but disagree with one part of it. Because Jones has already explained his views in detail in an earlier work, Smith will not bother to repeat in her own work everything she agrees with; she will simply allude to Jones's work briefly and spend most of her time and effort in explaining why she disagrees with the one point that she rejects. This approach might give a careless reader the impression that Smith entirely rejects Jones's views, but that impression would be wrong. A careful reader would see that Smith is greatly indebted to Jones and is paying Jones a kind of compliment by following the same general approach to the issue as Jones, even while she aims to improve on one aspect of it. To understand the position of a writer and use his or her work appropriately, you must recognize these nuances; otherwise, you could end up misrepresenting your source.

Having an understanding of the major voices and positions in a scholarly debate makes it possible to appreciate the basic convictions and beliefs that under-lie a writer's argument. These convictions are not the same thing as *bias*, if we take that word to mean an unfair prejudice. A bias in this sense is irrational and cannot stand up to scrutiny, and a biased argument is a weak one with weak support for its claims. But a position often expresses a deeply held point of view or set of principles that underpins an argument. For example, if the president of the United States were to address the United Nations General Assembly, listeners could expect him to hold the position that a democratic form of government is preferable to a dictatorship. This is not a bias or prejudice; it's a fundamental conviction that he does not need to spell out explicitly because he can assume his listeners know it.

Take Notes

Take notes as you read and reread your sources. The strategies that you learned in Chapters 1 through 3, especially the dialectical notebook, will be useful for note-taking. But in addition, make the following practices your habit.

- No matter what kind of source you're using — a text, an interview, a recording, or anything else — be sure to add full bibliographical data to your working bibliography, and place adequate identifiers in your notes: usually the author's last name, the title, and the number of the page you are working with.

- Always distinguish carefully among the following:

   Direct quotations from the text
   Your paraphrases or summaries of the writer's ideas
   Indirect quotations — words the author quotes from another text
   Your own comments and reflections

- Codes such as the following can prevent confusion:

   For direct quotations: use quotation marks plus the page number.
   For paraphrases: use (PP) at the end, plus the page number.

For indirect quotations: use the original author's name and "qtd. in," plus the quoting author's name and the page number.

For your own comments and reflections: use "(Me)."

Plagiarism is the use of another person's words or ideas without acknowledging the source. It will be discussed in more detail in "Writing an Acceptable Paraphrase" (p. 328). If you make scrupulous note-taking of this kind a habit, you will be unlikely to commit unintentional plagiarism.

- Finally, if you use a computer to take notes, take these precautions:

  Keep all files related to your research in a single folder.

  Back up the folder to an external drive or server at least daily.

Sample Research Notes   The following example shows a student's research notes and corresponding bibliographical information.

Cirincione, Chapter 8, "Nuclear Solutions"

Cirincione realizes that getting rid of nuclear weapons in Middle East will not be easy. But argues that the alternative is a nuclear arms race "with unresolved territorial, religious, and political disputes." (152)

"The latter is a recipe for nuclear war." (152)

Cirincione believes that Israel can be persuaded to shut down its production reactor at Dimona, and Iran can be persuaded to stop processing its own fuel for nuclear power plants — and step by step a nuclear-free Middle East can become a reality. (PP, 152-3)

Maybe a few years ago, but now? (Me)

Cirincione quotes a 2005 Carnegie Endowment report:

"The core bargain of the NPT [Nuclear Proliferation Treaty], and of global non-proliferation politics, can neither be ignored or wished away. It underpins the international security system and shapes the expectations of citizens and leaders around the world." (Carnegie Endowment, "Universal Compliance: A Strategy for Nuclear Security," qtd. in Cirincione, 153-4.)

Cirincione, Joseph. *Bomb Scare: The History and Future of Nuclear Weapons*. New York: Columbia University Press, 2007. Print.

Drafting and Revising

Establish Your Own Position and Develop a Working Thesis

The strategies for writing that we discussed in Chapters 4 through 8 will be useful as you put together your research paper. But keep in mind certain special considerations as you outline, draft, and revise your research paper.

Students sometimes settle on a thesis early in the research process and then treat sources merely as wells of information to draw on to support their argument. True, books, Web pages, and articles are sources of information, but usually they are more than that: they make arguments with a purpose. If you ignore this purpose, you not only misrepresent that writer's ideas but also miss the opportunity of being challenged by men and women of ideas and of thinking more deeply and critically about your chosen research problem. As a researcher, then, it is your responsibility to follow where the sources lead and also to *sift* the arguments carefully and stake out a position of your own.

Understanding the positions of other writers should help you develop a position of your own. But there's no formula for this: you must work out your position by reading carefully and analytically, identifying key positions in the sources, examining the reasoning in your sources, and assessing the strengths and weaknesses of arguments. At some point, discussing what you've learned with classmates or your instructor can also help you figure out your position.

We suggested earlier that it's important to refine a research topic to a specific question or problem. It may, and probably should, evolve as you conduct research, but try not to lose sight of it while immersed in your sources. At regular intervals during the research process (perhaps every couple of days), restate your understanding of the question or problem in your notes. When you are ready — perhaps a little before you feel *quite* ready — draft your current sense of the answer to the question or solution to the problem. Even if it's incomplete, or only one aspect of the answer or solution, your response to this question or problem will often be the source of your thesis statement.

Sometimes the research you've done may seem like a huge muddle, and you might become overwhelmed by the quantity and complexity of the material. At such times, it can be useful to freewrite your way toward some clarity — that is, write casually and informally in order to sort out what the various writers have to say and how their views relate to one another. This sort of writing can help you understand where you stand and why. If you've been taking double-entry notes, review them periodically and build on your comments on the right-hand side of the page. Pose questions, and develop fragmentary thoughts into full sentences. As your own ideas become clear, you will be able to situate your position in relation to others.

Use freewriting and note-taking to seek clarity about two things:

- Your own argument
- The evidence you will be using to support your argument

Once you have a sense of your argument, do the following:

- List your main claims.
- Figure out the main evidence you need to support these claims. This might include strong arguments made by others as well as data.
- Figure out the main counterarguments. You will need to address these too.

At this point, you can sketch out a rough draft in full sentences, based on your notes, to give you a "big picture" sense of your argument. In the first paragraph or two, include a statement of the problem you are addressing as well as your response to it — a thesis statement. Include references to a conversation about this problem — where other writers stand or what other scholars have discovered or theorized about the problem. In the following paragraphs, flesh out your argument: your main claims and the support for those claims.

When you are ready to expand this preliminary draft into a more complete draft, explain your reasoning more fully and consider the role sources will play. Sources can serve a variety of purposes in your argument. They can provide:

- Evidence for a claim you are making
- A counterargument that you will be refuting
- Background information and context to set up your argument

In this rough draft, it is a good idea to omit quotations altogether. You want your reasoning to be clear, both in your own mind and to the reader. And you need to develop the phrases to express your argument fully in your own words. At this stage of writing, leaving out quotations will help you keep the argument in the foreground.

But do include citations (abbreviated if you like) to all the sources you plan to use. You need to be clear about where and how your sources will be used. Don't risk breaking the thread between an idea that comes from another source and the reference to that source. If you don't include these citations in your draft, you risk wasting time later, when you have to hunt down the source of the idea, and you risk committing unintentional plagiarism.

Foreground Your Voice

One of the special challenges faced by writers of research papers is the need to keep their argument in the foreground and not allow other "voices" — quotes or paraphrases from sources — to bury it. Your argument can get buried if the reader cannot easily distinguish the primary voice — your voice — from secondary voices. And your argument can get lost if the reader has difficulty holding on to the thread of your argument and has to keep looking back to the introduction to remember what your paper is supposed to be about. Either, or both, of these failings will result in a loss of focus and purpose. So you have to be like a master of ceremonies, making sure that acts come on- and offstage with appropriate introductions, keeping the audience awake and the show moving briskly, and keeping everything under control.

To maintain control, you need to have clarity about your argument and confidence in it. You are most likely to bury your argument when you're not quite sure what it is, or when you don't quite believe in it. (Even if you don't, write as though you do!)

To keep your argument in the foreground, try these techniques.

- Periodically repeat key ideas in fresh phrases, to ensure that your reader remains aware of your argument.
- Position your principal claims at or near the beginning of paragraphs.
- Relate new ideas to familiar ones. Explain the connection or relationship between new ideas and ones you introduced earlier. Connect your principal claims to your thesis statement.
- Remind your reader of your main argument at critical moments, especially after complex or demanding passages in your argument.

Use Quotations Purposefully

As you refine your argument and your use of sources, continue to work closely with your sources. Typically, as you refine your argument, you'll be alternating between writing and rereading a text that you are writing about.

However, *quote sparingly*. Whenever possible, turn quotations into paraphrases that are more smoothly integrated into your argument. When you quote, you are asking your readers to shift from one context — your argument — to a passage that's been extracted from a different context. You cannot rely on your readers to read quotations as carefully as they read your text, and you should never expect readers to see the same thing in a quotation that you see. Never expect a quotation to "speak for itself" — it almost never does.

Avoid using quotations merely to show that a fact or claim is supported by some source. A paraphrase, a brief reference ("As Sacks shows"), or even just a citation is sufficient to show the reader that your statement has support in some other text.

Use quotations when the wording or style of the original is important to your argument or when no paraphrase could express the text's sense adequately.

Integrate Sources Effectively

Whether you quote or paraphrase a source, integrate the source effectively into your own writing. Avoid the "dropped" quotation: a quotation dropped into the text without attribution and without a clear purpose. The following steps will help you integrate sources into your argument.

- Briefly introduce the source with an introductory phrase.
- Include the writer's name and some indication of why the source is credible (such as the writer's credentials).
- The first time you name the author, use the first and last name; thereafter use only the last name.
- Clarify the connection between the quotation or the paraphrase and your own argument.
- Follow up with commentary or analysis that explains the importance of the source's words or ideas for your argument.

The introductory phrase shows the reader clearly where your reliance on a source *begins*. The citation at the end of a quotation or paraphrase usually shows where the debt to your source ends (see the Appendix, p. 406). Together, the introductory phrase and the citation "frame" the paraphrase or quotation, indicating clearly where your debt to another writer's thought begins and ends. Such framing also keeps *your own* original thought distinct and clear, helping to foreground your argument.

Writing an Acceptable Paraphrase

A **paraphrase** is a rewording of another person's words — whether written or spoken. A paraphrase might be a summary (shorter than the original) or an explication of the text (longer than the original) or just a close reworking of the text (about the same length as the original). As a rule, direct quotations should be used in academic writing only when necessary, so the art of paraphrase is an essential skill, and one that requires particular care and attention. Unless you understand and carefully observe the rules for writing acceptable paraphrases, you can easily commit unintended plagiarism (see the Appendix, p. 406). In general, an **unacceptable paraphrase** is one that either is too close to the wording of the original text or fails to cite its source properly and completely.

A paraphrase must use your own words to convey the ideas or information in the original text. Avoid borrowing distinctive or unusual words or word combinations of more than two words from the original text. Paraphrases can *include* quotations; in fact, quoting brief phrases within a longer paraphrase is a good way to deal with unique expressions that cannot be reworded or omitted. But not only must the words in a paraphrase be your own; so must the sentence structures. So mere "synonym swapping" — replacing the words of the original with close synonyms while keeping the same word order — is unacceptable. A paraphrase in which the grammar and sentence structure of the original remain intact, even though most of the words differ, would be too close to the original and would still be plagiarism.

The best way to write an acceptable paraphrase is to hide the original document by turning off your computer screen or closing the book or journal. Then paraphrase the text in your own words, relying entirely on your memory and doing the best job you can. When you're done, open up the original again, and correct and improve your draft. Finally, edit carefully to make sure your paraphrase is not only acceptable but also accurate and complete.

In practice, however, you will seldom need to produce a strict, straightforward paraphrase; rather, you will want to emphasize some aspect of the original text. After all, you will be using the excerpted text for a new purpose — that is, to support a new argument of your own. Since a paraphrase is usually written for a *purpose*, it will stress certain aspects of the original and downplay others. So a paraphrase should be faithful to the original, but it need not be absolutely *complete* in the sense of representing every word and connotation in the original without exception. Most paraphrasing does involve some summary — as some ideas will be more important to your argument than others. (If you truly need all the detail of the original, then it might be better just to quote the original.) Selective paraphrasing does not imply any distortion or misrepresentation of the ideas in the original; it simply means transplanting ideas from one context into a different context.

Finally, remember that paraphrases *must be cited*, just as quotations must be cited. When conducting your research, be careful to label and identify your notes accurately and completely. Place quotation marks around all direct quotations, even single words, and identify the source of all ideas and information that you write down. If you make scrupulous note-taking of this kind a habit, you will be much less likely to plagiarize unintentionally.

Some students write their rough draft without citations, intending to insert all the citations at a later point. But this is a dangerous strategy, as you will find it difficult to distinguish consistently between your own ideas and those of other writers.

Here are examples of unacceptable and acceptable paraphrases.

Original Text

Humans, Tooby and DeVore suggest, entered the "cognitive niche." Remember the definition of intelligence from Chapter 2: using knowledge of how things work to attain goals in the face of obstacles. By learning which manipulations achieve which goals, humans have mastered the art of the surprise attack. They use novel, goal-oriented courses of action to overcome the Maginot Line defenses of other organisms, which can respond only over evolutionary time. The manipulations can be novel because human knowledge is not just couched in concrete instructions like "how to catch a rabbit." Humans analyze the world using intuitive theories of objects, forces, paths, places, manners, states, substances, hidden biochemical essences, and, for other animals and people, beliefs and desires. (These intuitive theories are the topic of Chapter 5.) People compose new knowledge and plans by mentally playing out combinatorial interactions among these laws in their mind's eye.[3]

Unacceptable Paraphrase

Pinker draws on Tooby and DeVore to argue that human beings came to occupy a "cognitive niche" in the evolutionary tree. Pinker defines intelligence as the ability to use knowledge of the way things work in order to overcome obstacles and reach a goal. Humans became proficient in the art of the surprise attack by figuring out which actions and maneuvers achieve which goals. They use

---

[3] Steven Pinker, *How the Mind Works* (New York: W. W. Norton, 1997), 188.

inventive, goal-oriented strategies to overcome the formidable defenses of other organisms. But these organisms can only respond over evolutionary time. Their strategies can be novel because human knowledge is not just confined to fixed instructions like "how to catch a boar." Human beings analyze their environments by intuiting ideas concerning objects, forces, paths, places, manners, states, substances, biochemistry, and, for other animals and people, beliefs and desires. Humans create new knowledge and plans by working out in their minds how the laws behind these things will interact. (Pinker 188)

This first paraphrase is not acceptable because the wording is too close to the original. Note how this paraphrase repeats such phrases as "art of the surprise attack"; "defenses of other organisms"; "over evolutionary time"; "can be novel because human knowledge is not just"; and "instructions like 'how to catch.'"

Unacceptable Paraphrase

Pinker writes that the human species, as Tooby and DeVore argue, moved into the "cognitive niche." In Chapter 2, he defines intelligence as using understanding of the way things work to achieve objectives in spite of impediments. By figuring out which operations accomplish which objectives, *Homo sapiens* became adept at catching their prey unawares. They employ original, purposeful schemes to defeat the most formidable protections of other creatures, which can react only over many generations. The operations can be original because human understanding is not just formulated in fixed directions like "how to trap a hare." Humans explore their milieu using sensed ideas of things, energies, routes, locations, practices, circumstances, material, unseen biochemical substances, and, for other creatures and humans, convictions and aspirations. Humans innovate understanding and strategies by intellectually working out various combinations among these forces in their imaginations. (Pinker 188)

The problem with this second paraphrase is that its sentence structures too closely mirror those of the original. The writer has simply replaced some of the words in Pinker's sentences with synonyms. For instance, the original "objects, forces, paths, places, manners, states, substances, hidden biochemical essences" becomes "things, energies, routes, locations, practices, circumstances, material, unseen biochemical substances."

Acceptable Paraphrase

Steven Pinker explains Tooby and DeVore's theory of the "cognitive niche," which claims that human beings evolved to occupy a unique position among animals: humans are the only creatures to possess an intelligence that enables them to overcome all manner of difficulties to obtain what they want. Only humans can invent ways to penetrate the defenses of other species and organisms; their victims can develop new defenses only through evolutionary processes that take many generations. And humans can improvise new strategies for new situations: their ideas are not restricted to one fixed set of instructions. Rather, they analyze their environment by grasping its laws and thinking out their strategies in their imaginations. This unique ability accounts for the survival of *Homo sapiens* over the course of evolution. (Pinker 188)

→ Guidelines   **When and How to Paraphrase**

When to Paraphrase

- Whenever you need to incorporate ideas from another source into your own argument, consider paraphrasing those ideas.

- As a general rule, prefer paraphrase (or summary) to quotation, as quotations tend to disrupt the flow of an argument. If you can express the idea in your own words, and if you do not plan to comment on the particular wording of the original, paraphrase.

How to Paraphrase

- Read the original text several times to make sure that you fully grasp the ideas.

- Express the ideas of the original in your own words and sentence structures.

- Never swap synonyms in order to rewrite the original: find new sentence structures as well as new words.

- If key words or phrases in the original cannot be paraphrased, consider incorporating them as brief quotations within the paraphrase.

- Include an introductory phrase to show where the paraphrase begins.

- Cite the paraphrase or summary. (This indicates where the paraphrase ends.)

- Place your own comments on the writer's ideas *after* the citation.

Writing a Summary or an Abstract

In one sense, a summary is just a paraphrase that is substantially shorter than the original, so many of the same rules apply: use your own words and your own sentence structures to convey faithfully and clearly the sense of the original text; if you must use special words or brief phrases from the original, place them in quotation marks.

But writing a summary or an **abstract** presents special challenges because it must be so condensed, containing nothing but the essentials of the argument (or plot, in the case of fiction and drama). Abstracts rarely exceed one or two paragraphs — about 200 words maximum — and a summary in an essay may need to be even shorter.

The challenge in writing a summary is to distinguish the essential from the inessential: to do this, you need to have a clear sense of the argument. The more complicated the argument, the more difficult this is. However, the more familiar you become with the argument, the easier writing a summary becomes. (Think of how easily you could summarize a story you know very well — perhaps *Romeo and Juliet* or *The Wizard of Oz*.) The first two paragraphs and the last two paragraphs of an essay often provide useful clues, but you cannot rely only on these. The first two paragraphs often do define the *problem or question* that the author is addressing, and they may also present the *solution or answer* (that is, the thesis, even if only a partial one). But the complete thesis statement might occur elsewhere in the essay — at the end or even in the middle.

Read through the essay carefully, taking careful notes on the principal *claims* the author makes (you might use one of the strategies suggested in Chapter 2). After you have identified them, work out how they are logically related to one another — how one claim supports or leads to another — and try to write a skeleton outline of the argument using mostly your own words. Now write a draft of your complete summary, beginning with a statement of the problem and the thesis. Then explain only enough of the argument to make good sense of how the author supports his or her thesis. You may need to include a sentence or two to explain something about the method, context, or purpose of the argument as well. Finally, revise and polish the summary, making sure that you use only your own words, except for brief quotations (never more than a phrase).

> **Try This** **Paraphrasing Texts**
>
> Choose a passage of roughly 100 words from three of the essays included in Part 5. Write a paraphrase of each. Check that your paraphrases fulfill all the criteria for an acceptable paraphrase.

Always maintain strict objectivity when writing an abstract, and don't include your subjective reaction or any comments. Even when you write a summary to incorporate into an essay, it is usually wise to avoid confusion by clearly separating the summary from your own comments.

A summary or an abstract includes the following:

- The problem or question that the text addresses
- The solution or answer — the thesis
- The main arguments for that thesis
- If necessary, a brief explanation of the context, method, or purpose
- A citation

An abstract always, and a summary usually, excludes the following:

- Subjective comment, response, or reaction

Using Sentence Templates

Sentence templates are thought structures that can help you keep your own voice in the foreground, use quotations purposefully, and integrate sources effectively.

While sentence templates may seem simple — perhaps even simplistic — they are useful precisely because they are conventional and familiar: they immediately give the reader a clear sense of where you stand in relation to another writer. Once you have tried out templates a few times, you'll begin to internalize the forms and start to use them unconsciously. The exact words used in the following examples are less important than the form of the sentences and the structure of the thought, so you will be able to create your own variations once you get the idea. The templates are powerful tools for incorporating others' views into your work and for making distinctions about parts of arguments.

Presenting What Someone Else Says

In _____, X claims that _____.

X's conclusion is that _____.

On the topic of _____, X contends that _____.

These templates are useful for presenting a brief summary of another writer's views on an issue. Note that the final sample template implies that X has failed to make a convincing argument. (You would then go on to explain why this is the case.)

Incorporating Direct Quotations

In _____, X states, "_____."

X claims that "_____."

After summarizing the topic of _____, X concludes

that "_____."

Using quotations is a powerful way to present another writer's views when the language is especially striking, clear, and succinct. These templates help you employ a key skill in making an academic argument: showing the work that others have done on the issue. After you include a quotation, you then need to introduce your own voice to explain its significance. The following templates suggest ways to do that.

Presenting Another Writer's View and Responding to It

In her essay, X writes _____. This is important because

_____.

In his essay _____, X writes that _____. This

explains why _____. However, we still need to consider

_____.

With this kind of template, you introduce what the author has to say and then take your turn with your own view.

At times you will agree with some of what a writer says but not all of it; in these instances, you must distinguish between the parts you agree with and those you reject. For such a response, you can use the following templates.

Agreeing in Part

Although much of what X writes about _____ is valid, I reject

X's claim that _____.

X is correct to claim that _____. But because of _____,

I disagree with X's contention that _____.

X argues that _____. While _____ and _____

are valid points, _____ is not. Instead, I think that _____.

These sentence templates ask you to identify those parts of the argument that are valid. You will rarely agree with every view expressed by a source. Read the source carefully, and separate out which points are valid and which ones are not. Then respond to the source, explaining why you agree or disagree with certain parts of the source's argument.

At times you'll need to correct a distortion or misstatement of fact. Statistics, for instance, can be manipulated to present a viewpoint in the best light for one side of an argument. You may wish to propose an alternative interpretation or set the statistics in a different context, one more favorable to your own point of view. Of course, be sure that you do not distort statistics. Here are a couple of templates for correcting factual information.

Correcting a Mistake of Fact

While X claims _____, it is actually true that _____.

Although X states _____, a careful examination of

_____ and _____ indicates that _____.

These templates allow you to identify a mistaken claim of fact in an argument and present evidence opposing it.

More often, rather than correcting clear errors of fact, you'll need to refine a writer's argument. You may find that much of the argument makes sense to you but that the writer does not sufficiently anticipate important objections. In those cases, sentence templates such as the following can help you refine the argument to make a stronger conclusion.

Refining an Argument Made by Someone Else

> Although it is true, as X shows, that _____, the actual result is
>
> closer to _____ because _____.
>
> While X claims _____ and _____, he fails to consider
>
> the important point _____. Therefore, a more accurate conclusion is
>
> _____.

Such sentence templates allow you to clarify and amplify an argument.

Sometimes you'll need to distinguish between the views of two different writers and then weigh in with your own assessment of the situation. When two authors write on the same topic, they will frequently share similar views on some points but disagree on others. Similarly, you may find that you agree with some parts of what each writer has to say but disagree with other parts. Your job is to identify the points of contrast between the two authors and then explain how your own position differs from the view of one or both authors. In such cases, you may find the following sentence templates helpful.

Explaining Contrasting Views and Adding Your Own Position

> X says _____. Y says _____. However, I believe
>
> _____ because _____.
>
> On the topic of _____, X claims that _____. By
>
> contrast, Y argues that _____. However, I believe that
>
> _____ is actually correct for these reasons: _____.

Careful writers make sure that their readers understand fine distinctions. The templates above help make those distinctions clear.

Editing and Polishing

When editing a research paper, make sure your voice is in control throughout and that other voices are subordinate to your own.

- Maintain a consistent and credible voice or tone: confident, evenhanded, open-minded.
- Craft strong, well-phrased claim sentences for the opening of paragraphs.
- Introduce paraphrases and quotations fully, and explain their relation to your argument.
- To prevent confusion, add metadiscourse where appropriate — signposts to the reader to clarify the direction of the argument.

In addition, pay close attention to stylistic problems that frequently emerge in complex arguments.

- Look out for convoluted or unclear sentences.
- Look out for vague language or faulty diction.
- Cut repetition and needless verbiage.
- Look out for unsupported claims.
- Check the overall flow of your paper, and keep the proportions between sections roughly equal.

Proofreading

Once you have finished writing, carefully proofread your paper.

- Take advantage of your word processor's spelling and grammar checkers, but don't rely on them (see p. 221).
- Print your paper. Many writers find that it's much easier to detect errors on a printed copy than on-screen.
- Run your finger or a pen along each line as you read slowly, to help you focus on the actual words on the page rather than what you imagine is there. Or place a blank sheet of paper over the page and move it down as you read one line at a time.
- Read your paper aloud.

- Proofread once for each category of error: once for spelling, once for grammar, once for punctuation, once for formatting (especially notes, page numbers, and lists).

Pay attention to the following:

- Make sure all quotations, paraphrases, and information from other sources have been cited (see the Appendix).
- Check the spelling of proper nouns, including authors' names and place names.
- Check the spelling of unusual technical terms.

☑ Checklist for Working with Sources

☐ Narrow your focus to a specific research question.

☐ Keep a working bibliography.

☐ Find additional sources.

☐ Evaluate Web sites with special care.
- Cross-check information, and trace key information to a reliable source.
- Determine if the material is current.
- Test the site for signs of bias.
- Research the author's credentials.

☐ If appropriate, conduct field research (observations, interviews, surveys).

☐ Read sources and take notes.
- Identify the purpose of scholarly sources.
- Look for a problem, a conversation, an argument, and support.
- Include author/title and page number references in your notes.
- Distinguish clearly among direct quotations, paraphrases, and your own comments.

☐ Use informal writing strategies to develop an argument and a working thesis.

☐ Write a preliminary draft.

☐ Revise and develop; get feedback; revise and develop further.

☐ Foreground your voice.

☐ Paraphrase quotations where possible.

☐ Integrate quotations effectively.

☐ Edit and polish.

part 5

Readings

Michelle Alexander

Michelle Alexander (b. 1967) is an associate professor at the Moritz College of Law and the Kirwan Institute for the Study of Race and Ethnicity at Ohio State University. She is also a civil rights advocate and litigator. A graduate of Vanderbilt University and Stanford Law School, she clerked for Justice Harry A. Blackmun on the US Supreme Court and later became director of the Racial Justice Project for the American Civil Liberties Union of Northern California. She won the Soros Justice Fellowship in 2005. In her book *The New Jim Crow: Mass Incarceration in the Age of Colorblindness* (2010), which won the 2011 NAACP Image Award for Outstanding Literary Work—Non-fiction, Alexander argues that the "War on Drugs" and mass incarceration have created a system of segregation in the United States that rivals that of the Jim Crow era (from about 1880 to 1965). The following article, which appeared on the Web sites TomDispatch and AlterNet in 2012, summarizes the main points of that argument.

Drug War Nightmare: How We Created a Massive Racial Caste System in America

1 Ever since Barack Obama lifted his right hand and took his oath of office, pledging to serve the United States as its 44th president, ordinary people and their leaders around the globe have been celebrating our nation's "triumph over race." Obama's election has been touted as the final nail in the coffin of Jim Crow, the bookend placed on the history of racial caste in America.

2 Obama's mere presence in the Oval Office is offered as proof that "the land of the free" has finally made good on its promise of equality. There's an implicit yet undeniable message embedded in his appearance on the world stage: this is what freedom looks like; this is what democracy can do for you. If you are poor, marginalized, or relegated to an inferior caste, there is hope for you. Trust us. Trust our rules, laws, customs, and wars. You, too, can get to the promised land.

3 Perhaps greater lies have been told in the past century, but they can be counted on one hand. Racial caste is alive and well in America.

4 Most people don't like it when I say this. It makes them angry. In the "era of colorblindness" there's a nearly fanatical desire to cling to the myth that we as a nation have "moved beyond" race. Here are a few facts that run counter to that triumphant racial narrative:

- There are more African American adults under correctional control today — in prison or jail, on probation or parole — than were enslaved in 1850, a decade before the Civil War began.

- As of 2004, more African American men were disenfranchised (due to felon disenfranchisement laws) than in 1870, the year the Fifteenth Amendment was ratified, prohibiting laws that explicitly deny the right to vote on the basis of race.

- A black child born today is less likely to be raised by both parents than a black child born during slavery. The recent disintegration of the African American family is due in large part to the mass imprisonment of black fathers.

- If you take into account prisoners, a large majority of African American men in some urban areas have been labeled felons for life. (In the Chicago area, the figure is nearly 80%.) These men are part of a growing undercaste — not class, caste — permanently relegated, by law, to a second-class status. They can be denied the right to vote, automatically excluded from juries, and legally discriminated against in employment, housing, access to education, and public benefits, much as their grandparents and great-grandparents were during the Jim Crow era.

Excuses for the Lockdown

There is, of course, a colorblind explanation for all this: crime rates. Our prison popu- 5
lation has exploded from about 300,000 to more than 2 million in a few short decades, it is said, because of rampant crime. We're told that the reason so many black and brown men find themselves behind bars and ushered into a permanent, second-class status is because they happen to be the bad guys.

"From the outset, the war had relatively little to do with drug crime and much to do with racial politics."

The uncomfortable truth, however, is that crime 6
rates do not explain the sudden and dramatic mass incarceration of African Americans during the past 30 years. Crime rates have fluctuated over the last few decades — they are currently at historical lows — but imprisonment rates have consistently soared. Quintupled, in fact. The main driver has been the War on Drugs. Drug offenses alone accounted for about two-thirds of the increase in the federal inmate population, and more than half of the increase in the state

prison population between 1985 and 2000, the period of our prison system's most dramatic expansion.

The drug war has been brutal — complete with SWAT teams, tanks, bazookas, 7 grenade launchers, and sweeps of entire neighborhoods — but those who live in white communities have little clue to the devastation wrought. This war has been waged almost exclusively in poor communities of color, even though studies consistently show that people of all colors use and sell illegal drugs at remarkably similar rates. In fact, some studies indicate that white youth are significantly more likely to engage in illegal drug dealing than black youth. Any notion that drug use among African Americans is more severe or dangerous is belied by the data. White youth, for example, have about three times the number of drug-related visits to the emergency room as their African American counterparts.

That is not what you would guess, though, when entering our nation's prisons 8 and jails, overflowing as they are with black and brown drug offenders. In some states, African Americans comprise 80%–90% of all drug offenders sent to prison.

This is the point at which I am typically interrupted and reminded that black 9 men have higher rates of violent crime. *That's* why the drug war is waged in poor communities of color and not middle-class suburbs. Drug warriors are trying to get rid of those drug kingpins and violent offenders who make ghetto communities a living hell. It has nothing to do with race; it's all about violent crime.

Again, not so. President Ronald Reagan officially declared the current drug war 10 in 1982, when drug crime was declining, not rising. President Richard Nixon was the first to coin the term "a war on drugs," but it was President Reagan who turned the rhetorical war into a literal one. From the outset, the war had relatively little to do with drug crime and much to do with racial politics. The drug war was part of a grand and highly successful Republican Party strategy of using racially coded political appeals on issues of crime and welfare to attract poor and working class white voters who were resentful of, and threatened by, desegregation, busing, and affirmative action. In the words of H. R. Haldeman, President Richard Nixon's White House Chief of Staff: "[T]he whole problem is really the blacks. The key is to devise a system that recognizes this while not appearing to."

A few years after the drug war was announced, crack cocaine hit the streets of 11 inner-city communities. The Reagan administration seized on this development with glee, hiring staff who were to be responsible for publicizing inner-city crack babies, crack mothers, crack whores, and drug-related violence. The goal was to make inner-city crack abuse and violence a media sensation, bolstering public support for the drug war which, it was hoped, would lead Congress to devote millions of dollars in additional funding to it.

> *"What gets rewarded in this war is sheer numbers of drug arrests."*

The plan worked like a charm. For more than a [12] decade, black drug dealers and users would be regulars in newspaper stories and would saturate the evening TV news. Congress and state legislatures nationwide would devote billions of dollars to the drug war and pass harsh mandatory minimum sentences for drug crimes — sentences longer than murderers receive in many countries.

Democrats began competing with Republicans to prove that they could be even [13] tougher on the dark-skinned pariahs. In President Bill Clinton's boastful words, "I can be nicked a lot, but no one can say I'm soft on crime." The facts bear him out. Clinton's "tough on crime" policies resulted in the largest increase in federal and state prison inmates of any president in American history. But Clinton was not satisfied with exploding prison populations. He and the "New Democrats" championed legislation banning drug felons from public housing (no matter how minor the offense) and denying them basic public benefits, including food stamps, for life. Discrimination in virtually every aspect of political, economic, and social life is now perfectly legal, if you've been labeled a felon.

Facing Facts

But what about all those violent criminals and drug kingpins? Isn't the drug war [14] waged in ghetto communities because that's where the violent offenders can be found? The answer is yes . . . in made-for-TV movies. In real life, the answer is no.

The drug war has never been focused on rooting out drug kingpins or violent [15] offenders. Federal funding flows to those agencies that increase dramatically the volume of drug arrests, not the agencies most successful in bringing down the bosses. What gets rewarded in this war is sheer numbers of drug arrests. To make matters worse, federal drug forfeiture laws allow state and local law enforcement agencies to keep for their own use 80% of the cash, cars, and homes seized from drug suspects, thus granting law enforcement a direct monetary interest in the profitability of the drug market.

The results have been predictable: people of color rounded up en masse for relatively minor, non-violent drug offenses. In 2005, four out of five drug arrests were for [16] possession, only one out of five for sales. Most people in state prison have no history of violence or even of significant selling activity. In fact, during the 1990s — the period of the most dramatic expansion of the drug war — nearly 80% of the increase in drug arrests was for marijuana possession, a drug generally considered less harmful than alcohol or tobacco and at least as prevalent in middle-class white communities as in the inner city.

> *"Millions of people of color are now saddled with criminal records and legally denied the very rights that their parents and grandparents fought for and, in some cases, died for."*

In this way, a new racial undercaste has been created in an astonishingly short period of time — a new Jim Crow system. Millions of people of color are now saddled with criminal records and legally denied the very rights that their parents and grandparents fought for and, in some cases, died for. 17

Affirmative action, though, has put a happy face on this racial reality. Seeing black people graduate from Harvard and Yale and become CEOs or corporate lawyers — not to mention president of the United States — causes us all to marvel at what a long way we've come. 18

Recent data shows, though, that much of black progress is a myth. In many respects, African Americans are doing no better than they were when Martin Luther King Jr. was assassinated and uprisings swept inner cities across America. The black child poverty rate is actually higher now than it was then. Unemployment rates in black communities rival those in Third World countries. And that's with affirmative action! 19

When we pull back the curtain and take a look at what our "colorblind" society creates without affirmative action, we see a familiar social, political, and economic structure: the structure of racial caste. The entrance into this new caste system can be found at the prison gate. 20

This is not Martin Luther King Jr.'s dream. This is not the promised land. The cyclical rebirth of caste in America is a recurring racial nightmare. 21

Questions for Discussion and Writing

1. What is Alexander's critique of the "War on Drugs"? How exactly has the drug war contributed to the creation of a new Jim Crow system?
2. Based on Alexander's analysis, is the "new Jim Crow" an intended effect of the War on Drugs, an unintended effect, or something in-between? How would you characterize the intent behind this effect?

3. Analyze the rhetorical strategies and devices that Alexander employs to persuade her reader. How does she use *ethos*, *pathos*, and *logos* (see p. 119)? How does she employ devices such as rhetorical questions and metaphors? Where does she anticipate counterarguments? How does she arrange her argument? How does she support her claims? Make detailed notes of your observations.

Nicholas Carr

Nicholas Carr (b. 1959) is an American writer whose work focuses chiefly on technology and culture. His writing has appeared in the *Guardian* (London), the *Atlantic*, the *New York Times,* and elsewhere. He holds a BA from Dartmouth College and an MA in English and American literature and language from Harvard University. In addition to numerous essays, he has published four books, most recently *The Glass Cage: Automation and Us* (2014), an exploration of the growing impact of robots and automated tools on our lives. His previous book, *The Shallows: What the Internet Is Doing to Our Brains* (2010), expands on the themes of the essay reprinted here. A finalist for the Pulitzer Prize, *The Shallows* explores the effect of the Internet on the functioning of our minds. Though neither an alarmist nor an uncritical enthusiast of the new technologies, Carr is aware of what they are taking from us as well as what they are giving. In an interview published on the media and education Web site Big Think, he states that "what gets devalued is those . . . more contemplative, more solitary modes of thought that in the past, anyway, were considered central to the experience of life, to the life of the mind certainly, and even to our social lives. . . . What scares me most is that we . . . start to think the way the technology wants us to think."

Is Google Making Us Stupid?

"Dave, stop. Stop, will you? Stop, Dave. Will you stop, Dave?" So the supercomputer HAL pleads with the implacable astronaut Dave Bowman in a famous and weirdly poignant scene toward the end of Stanley Kubrick's *2001: A Space Odyssey*. Bowman, having nearly been sent to a deep-space death by the malfunctioning machine, is calmly, coldly disconnecting the memory circuits that control its artificial brain. "Dave, my mind is going," HAL says, forlornly. "I can feel it. I can feel it." 1

I can feel it, too. Over the past few years I've had an uncomfortable sense that someone, or something, has been tinkering with my brain, remapping the neural circuitry, reprogramming the memory. My mind isn't going — so far as I can tell — but it's changing. I'm not thinking the way I used to think. I can feel it most strongly when I'm reading. Immersing myself in a book or a lengthy article used to be easy. My mind would get caught up in the narrative or the turns of the argument, and I'd spend hours strolling through long stretches of prose. That's rarely the case anymore. Now my concentration often starts to drift after two or three pages. I get fidgety, lose the thread, begin looking for something else to do. I feel as if I'm always dragging my wayward 2 brain back to the text. The deep reading that used to come naturally has become a struggle.

I think I know what's going on. For more than a decade now, I've been spending a   3
lot of time online, searching and surfing and sometimes adding to the great data-bases of the Internet. The Web has been a godsend to me as a writer. Research that once required days in the stacks or periodical rooms of libraries can now be done in minutes. A few Google searches, some quick clicks on hyperlinks, and I've got the tell-tale fact or pithy quote I was after. Even when I'm not working, I'm as likely as not to be foraging in the Web's info-thickets — reading and writing e-mails, scanning head-lines and blog posts, watching videos and listening to podcasts, or just tripping from link to link. (Unlike footnotes, to which they're sometimes likened, hyperlinks don't merely point to related works; they propel you toward them.)

For me, as for others, the Net is becoming a universal medium, the conduit for   4
most of the information that flows through my eyes and ears and into my mind. The advantages of having immediate access to such an incredibly rich store of informa-tion are many, and they've been widely described and duly applauded. "The perfect recall of silicon memory," *Wired*'s Clive Thompson has written, "can be an enormous boon to thinking." But that boon comes at a price. As the media theorist Marshall McLuhan pointed out in the 1960s, media are not just passive channels of informa-tion. They supply the stuff of thought, but they also shape the process of thought. And what the Net seems to be doing is chipping away my capacity for concentration and contemplation. My mind now expects to take in information the way the Net distrib-utes it: in a swiftly moving stream of particles. Once I was a scuba diver in the sea of words. Now I zip along the surface like a guy on a Jet Ski.

I'm not the only one. When I mention my troubles with reading to friends and   5
acquaintances — literary types, most of them — many say they're having similar expe-riences. The more they use the Web, the more they have to fight to stay focused on long pieces of writing. Some of the bloggers I follow have also begun mentioning the phenomenon. Scott Karp, who writes a blog about online media, recently confessed that he has stopped reading books altogether. "I was a lit major in college, and used to be [a] voracious book reader," he wrote. "What happened?" He speculates on the answer: "What if I do all my reading on the web not so much because the way I read has changed, i.e., I'm just seeking convenience, but because the way I THINK has changed?"

Bruce Friedman, who blogs regularly about the use of computers in medicine,   6
also has described how the Internet has altered his mental habits. "I now have almost totally lost the ability to read and absorb a longish article on the web or in print," he wrote earlier this year. A pathologist who has long been on the faculty of the University

> *"And we still await the long-term neurological and psychological experiments that will provide a definitive picture of how Internet use affects cognition."*

of Michigan Medical School, Friedman elaborated on his comment in a telephone conversation with me. His thinking, he said, has taken on a "staccato" quality, reflecting the way he quickly scans short passages of text from many sources online. "I can't read *War and Peace* anymore," he admitted. "I've lost the ability to do that. Even a blog post of more than three or four paragraphs is too much to absorb. I skim it."

Anecdotes alone don't prove much. And we still 7 await the long-term neurological and psychological experiments that will provide a definitive picture of how Internet use affects cognition. But a recently published study of online research habits, conducted by scholars from University College London, suggests that we may well be in the midst of a sea change in the way we read and think. As part of the five-year research program, the scholars examined computer logs documenting the behavior of visitors to two popular research sites, one operated by the British Library and one by a U.K. educational consortium, that provide access to journal articles, e-books, and other sources of written information. They found that people using the sites exhibited "a form of skimming activity," hopping from one source to another and rarely returning to any source they'd already visited. They typically read no more than one or two pages of an article or book before they would "bounce" out to another site. Sometimes they'd save a long article, but there's no evidence that they ever went back and actually read it. The authors of the study report:

> It is clear that users are not reading online in the traditional sense; indeed there are signs that new forms of "reading" are emerging as users "power browse" horizontally through titles, contents pages, and abstracts going for quick wins. It almost seems that they go online to avoid reading in the traditional sense.[1]

Thanks to the ubiquity of text on the Internet, not to mention the popularity of 8 text-messaging on cell phones, we may well be reading more today than we did in the 1970s or 1980s, when television was our medium of choice. But it's a different kind of reading, and behind it lies a different kind of thinking — perhaps even a new sense of

---

[1] University College London, "Information Behaviour of the Researcher of the Future," January 11, 2008, www.ucl.ac.uk/slais/research/ciber/downloads/ggexecutive.pdf.

the self. "We are not only *what* we read," says Maryanne Wolf, a developmental psychologist at Tufts University and the author of *Proust and the Squid: The Story and Science of the Reading Brain.* "We are *how* we read." Wolf worries that the style of reading promoted by the Net, a style that puts "efficiency" and "immediacy" above all else, may be weakening our capacity for the kind of deep reading that emerged when an earlier technology, the printing press, made long and complex works of prose commonplace. When we read online, she says, we tend to become "mere decoders of information." Our ability to interpret text, to make the rich mental connections that form when we read deeply and without distraction, remains largely disengaged.

Reading, explains Wolf, is not an instinctive skill for human beings. It's not etched   9
into our genes the way speech is. We have to teach our minds how to translate the symbolic characters we see into the language we understand. And the media or other technologies we use in learning and practicing the craft of reading play an important part in shaping the neural circuits inside our brains. Experiments demonstrate that readers of ideograms, such as the Chinese, develop a mental circuitry for reading that is very different from the circuitry found in those of us whose written language employs an alphabet. The variations extend across many regions of the brain, including those that govern such essential cognitive functions as memory and the interpretation of visual and auditory stimuli. We can expect as well that the circuits woven by our use of the Net will be different from those woven by our reading of books and other printed works.

Sometime in 1882, Friedrich Nietzsche bought a typewriter — a Malling-Hansen   10
Writing Ball, to be precise. His vision was failing, and keeping his eyes focused on a page had become exhausting and painful, often bringing on crushing headaches. He had been forced to curtail his writing, and he feared that he would soon have to give it up. The typewriter rescued him, at least for a time. Once he had mastered touch-typing, he was able to write with his eyes closed, using only the tips of his fingers. Words could once again flow from his mind to the page.

"We have to teach our minds how to translate the symbolic characters we see into the language we understand. "

But the machine had a subtler effect on his   11
work. One of Nietzsche's friends, a composer, noticed a change in the style of his writing. His already terse prose had become even tighter, more telegraphic. "Perhaps you will through this instrument even take to a new idiom," the friend wrote in a letter, noting that, in his own work, his "'thoughts' in music and language often depend on the quality of pen and paper."

"You are right," Nietzsche replied, "our writing equipment takes part in the form- 12
ing of our thoughts." Under the sway of the machine, writes the German media scholar
Friedrich A. Kittler, Nietzsche's prose "changed from arguments to aphorisms, from
thoughts to puns, from rhetoric to telegram style."

The human brain is almost infinitely malleable. People used to think that our 13
mental meshwork, the dense connections formed among the 100 billion or so neu-
rons inside our skulls, was largely fixed by the time we reached adulthood. But brain
researchers have discovered that that's not the case. James Olds, a professor of neuroscience who directs the Krasnow Institute for Advanced Study at George Mason University, says that even the adult mind "is very plastic." Nerve cells routinely break old
connections and form new ones. "The brain," according to Olds, "has the ability to
reprogram itself on the fly, altering the way it functions."

As we use what the sociologist Daniel Bell has called our "intellectual technolo- 14
gies" — the tools that extend our mental rather than our physical capacities — we
inevitably begin to take on the qualities of those technologies. The mechanical clock,
which came into common use in the 14th century, provides a compelling example. In
Technics and Civilization, the historian and cultural critic Lewis Mumford described
how the clock "disassociated time from human events and helped create the belief in
an independent world of mathematically measurable sequences." The "abstract
framework of divided time" became "the point of reference for both action and
thought."

The clock's methodical ticking helped bring into being the scientific mind and 15
the scientific man. But it also took something away. As the late MIT computer scientist Joseph Weizenbaum observed in his 1976 book, *Computer Power and Human Reason: From Judgment to Calculation*, the conception of the world that emerged from the
widespread use of timekeeping instruments "remains an impoverished version of the
older one, for it rests on a rejection of those direct experiences that formed the basis
for, and indeed constituted, the old reality." In deciding when to eat, to work, to sleep,
to rise, we stopped listening to our senses and started obeying the clock.

The process of adapting to new intellectual technologies is reflected in the 16
changing metaphors we use to explain ourselves to ourselves. When the mechanical
clock arrived, people began thinking of their brains as operating "like clockwork."
Today, in the age of software, we have come to think of them as operating "like computers." But the changes, neuroscience tells us, go much deeper than metaphor.
Thanks to our brain's plasticity, the adaptation occurs also at a biological level.

The Internet promises to have particularly far-reaching effects on cognition. In a 17
paper published in 1936, the British mathematician Alan Turing proved that a digital

> *"People used to think that our mental meshwork . . . was largely fixed by the time we reached adulthood."*

computer, which at the time existed only as a theoretical machine, could be programmed to perform the function of any other information-processing device. And that's what we're seeing today. The Internet, an immeasurably powerful computing system, is subsuming most of our other intellectual technologies. It's becoming our map and our clock, our printing press and our typewriter, our calculator and our telephone, and our radio and TV.

When the Net absorbs a medium, that medium is 18 re-created in the Net's image. It injects the medium's content with hyperlinks, blinking ads, and other digital gewgaws, and it surrounds the content with the content of all the other media it has absorbed. A new e-mail message, for instance, may announce its arrival as we're glancing over the latest headlines at a newspaper's site. The result is to scatter our attention and diffuse our concentration.

The Net's influence doesn't end at the edges of a computer screen, either. As peo- 19 ple's minds become attuned to the crazy quilt of Internet media, traditional media have to adapt to the audience's new expectations. Television programs add text crawls and pop-up ads, and magazines and newspapers shorten their articles, introduce capsule summaries, and crowd their pages with easy-to-browse info-snippets. When, in March of this year, the *New York Times* decided to devote the second and third pages of every edition to article abstracts, its design director, Tom Bodkin, explained that the "shortcuts" would give harried readers a quick "taste" of the day's news, sparing them the "less efficient" method of actually turning the pages and reading the articles. Old media have little choice but to play by the new-media rules.

Never has a communications system played so many roles in our lives — or 20 exerted such broad influence over our thoughts — as the Internet does today. Yet, for all that's been written about the Net, there's been little consideration of how, exactly, it's reprogramming us. The Net's intellectual ethic remains obscure.

About the same time that Nietzsche started using his typewriter, an earnest 21 young man named Frederick Winslow Taylor carried a stopwatch into the Midvale Steel plant in Philadelphia and began a historic series of experiments aimed at improving the efficiency of the plant's machinists. With the approval of Midvale's owners, he recruited a group of factory hands, set them to work on various metalworking machines, and recorded and timed their every movement as well as the operations of the machines. By breaking down every job into a sequence of small, discrete steps and then testing different ways of performing each one, Taylor created a set of precise instructions—an "algorithm," we might say today—for how each worker should work. Midvale's employees grumbled about the strict new regime, claiming that it turned them into little more than automatons, but the factory's productivity soared.

More than a hundred years after the invention of the steam engine, the Industrial   22 Revolution had at last found its philosophy and its philosopher. Taylor's tight industrial choreography—his "system," as he liked to call it—was embraced by manufacturers throughout the country and, in time, around the world. Seeking maximum speed, maximum efficiency, and maximum output, factory owners used time-and-motion studies to organize their work and configure the jobs of their workers. The goal, as Taylor defined it in his celebrated 1911 treatise, *The Principles of Scientific Management*, was to identify and adopt, for every job, the "one best method" of work and thereby to effect "the gradual substitution of science for rule of thumb throughout the mechanic arts." Once his system was applied to all acts of manual labor, Taylor assured his followers, it would bring about a restructuring not only of industry but of society, creating a utopia of perfect efficiency. "In the past the man has been first," he declared; "in the future the system must be first."

"Yet, for all that's been written about the Net, there's been little consideration of how, exactly, it's reprogramming us. "

Taylor's system is still very much with us; it   23 remains the ethic of industrial manufacturing. And now, thanks to the growing power that computer engineers and software coders wield over our intellectual lives, Taylor's ethic is beginning to govern the realm of the mind as well. The Internet is a machine designed for the efficient and automated collection, transmission, and manipulation of information, and its legions of programmers are intent on finding the "one best method"—the perfect algorithm—to carry out every mental movement of what we've come to describe as "knowledge work."

Google's headquarters, in Mountain View, California—the Googleplex—is the   24 Internet's high church, and the religion practiced inside its walls is Taylorism. Google, says its chief executive, Eric Schmidt, is "a company that's founded around the science of measurement," and it is striving to "systematize everything" it does. Drawing on the terabytes of behavioral data it collects through its search engine and other sites, it carries out thousands of experiments a day, according to the *Harvard Business Review*, and it uses the results to refine the algorithms that increasingly control how people find information and extract meaning from it. What Taylor did for the work of the hand, Google is doing for the work of the mind.

The company has declared that its mission is "to organize the world's informa- 25 tion and make it universally accessible and useful." It seeks to develop "the perfect search engine," which it defines as something that "understands exactly what you mean and gives you back exactly what you want." In Google's view, information is a kind of commodity, a utilitarian resource that can be mined and processed with industrial efficiency. The more pieces of information we can "access" and the faster we can extract their gist, the more productive we become as thinkers.

Where does it end? Sergey Brin and Larry Page, the gifted young men who 26 founded Google while pursuing doctoral degrees in computer science at Stanford, speak frequently of their desire to turn their search engine into an artificial intelligence, a HAL-like machine that might be connected directly to our brains. "The ultimate search engine is something as smart as people — or smarter," Page said in a speech a few years back. "For us, working on search is a way to work on artificial intelligence." In a 2004 interview with *Newsweek*, Brin said, "Certainly if you had all the world's information directly attached to your brain, or an artificial brain that was smarter than your brain, you'd be better off." Last year, Page told a convention of scientists that Google is "really trying to build artificial intelligence and to do it on a large scale."

Such an ambition is a natural one, even an admirable one, for a pair of math 27 whizzes with vast quantities of cash at their disposal and a small army of computer scientists in their employ. A fundamentally scientific enterprise, Google is motivated by a desire to use technology, in Eric Schmidt's words, "to solve problems that have never been solved before," and artificial intelligence is the hardest problem out there. Why wouldn't Brin and Page want to be the ones to crack it?

Still, their easy assumption that we'd all "be better off" if our brains were supple- 28 mented, or even replaced, by an artificial intelligence is unsettling. It suggests a belief that intelligence is the output of a mechanical process, a series of discrete steps that can be isolated, measured, and optimized. In Google's world, the world we enter when we go online, there's little place for the fuzziness of contemplation. Ambiguity is not an opening for insight but a bug to be fixed. The human brain is just an outdated computer that needs a faster processor and a bigger hard drive.

The idea that our minds should operate as high-speed data-processing machines 29 is not only built into the workings of the Internet, it is the network's reigning business model as well. The faster we surf across the Web — the more links we click and pages we view — the more opportunities Google and other companies gain to collect information about us and to feed us advertisements. Most of the proprietors of the commercial Internet have a financial stake in collecting the crumbs of data we leave behind as we flit from link to link — the more crumbs, the better. The last thing these companies want is to encourage leisurely reading or slow, concentrated thought. It's in their economic interest to drive us to distraction.

Maybe I'm just a worrywart. Just as there's a tendency to glorify technological progress, there's a countertendency to expect the worst of every new tool or machine. In Plato's *Phaedrus*, Socrates bemoaned the development of writing. He feared that, as people came to rely on the written word as a substitute for the knowledge they used to carry inside their heads, they would, in the words of one of the dialogue's characters, "cease to exercise their memory and become forgetful." And because they would be able to "receive a quantity of information without proper instruction," they would "be thought very knowledgeable when they are for the most part quite ignorant." They would be "filled with the conceit of wisdom instead of real wisdom." Socrates wasn't wrong — the new technology did often have the effects he feared — but he was shortsighted. He couldn't foresee the many ways that writing and reading would serve to spread information, spur fresh ideas, and expand human knowledge (if not wisdom). 30

The arrival of Gutenberg's printing press, in the 15th century, set off another round of teeth gnashing. The Italian humanist Hieronimo Squarciafico worried that the easy availability of books would lead to intellectual laziness, making men "less studious" and weakening their minds. Others argued that cheaply printed books and broadsheets would undermine religious authority, demean the work of scholars and scribes, and spread sedition and debauchery. As New York University professor Clay Shirky notes, "Most of the arguments made against the printing press were correct, even prescient." But, again, the doomsayers were unable to imagine the myriad blessings that the printed word would deliver. 31

So, yes, you should be skeptical of my skepticism. Perhaps those who dismiss critics of the Internet as Luddites or nostalgists will be proved correct, and from our hyperactive, data-stoked minds will spring a golden age of intellectual discovery and universal wisdom. Then again, the Net isn't the alphabet, and although it may replace the printing press, it produces something altogether different. The kind of deep reading that a sequence of printed pages promotes is valuable not just for the knowledge we acquire from the author's words but for the intellectual vibrations those words set off within our own minds. In the quiet spaces opened up by the sustained, undistracted reading of a book, or by any other act of contemplation, for that matter, we make our own associations, draw our own inferences and analogies, foster our own ideas. Deep reading, as Maryanne Wolf argues, is indistinguishable from deep thinking. 32

If we lose those quiet spaces, or fill them up with "content," we will sacrifice 33 something important not only in our selves but in our culture. In a recent essay, the playwright Richard Foreman eloquently described what's at stake:

> I come from a tradition of Western culture, in which the ideal (my ideal) was the complex, dense, and "cathedral-like" structure of the highly educated and articulate personality — a man or woman who carried inside themselves a personally constructed and unique version of the entire heritage of the West. [But now] I see within us all (myself included) the replacement of complex inner density with a new kind of self — evolving under the pressure of information overload and the technology of the "instantly available."[2]

As we are drained of our "inner repertory of dense cultural inheritance," Foreman concluded, we risk turning into "pancake people — spread wide and thin as we connect with that vast network of information accessed by the mere touch of a button."

I'm haunted by that scene in *2001*. What makes it so poignant, and so weird, is 34 the computer's emotional response to the disassembly of its mind: its despair as one circuit after another goes dark, its childlike pleading with the astronaut — "I can feel it. I can feel it. I'm afraid" — and its final reversion to what can only be called a state of innocence. HAL's outpouring of feeling contrasts with the emotionlessness that characterizes the human figures in the film, who go about their business with an almost robotic efficiency. Their thoughts and actions feel scripted, as if they're following the steps of an algorithm. In the world of *2001*, people have become so machinelike that the most human character turns out to be a machine. That's the essence of Kubrick's dark prophecy: as we come to rely on computers to mediate our understanding of the world, it is our own intelligence that flattens into artificial intelligence.

Questions for Discussion and Writing

1. In the few years since Carr published this article, the way we read has changed yet again with the introduction of tablet devices such as the Kindle and the iPad. What difference have these devices made? Do you think their existence has any bearing on the issues that Carr outlines?

---

[2] Richard Foreman, "The Pancake People, or, 'The Gods Are Pounding My Head,'" *Edge*, March 8, 2005, www.edge.org/3rd_culture/foreman05/foreman05_index.html.

2. How are your own reading habits affected by the Internet, mobile devices, and other such distractions? What coping strategies have you developed? How have your reading practices changed (if at all) in the last five years? Write an honest account of your practices as a reader in the Internet age.

3. Presumably, even if we have become less proficient readers and thinkers due to behaviors encouraged by the Internet, we could conceivably reverse the process and recover the ability to read and think. What exactly would a person have to do to make this happen? Devise a strategy that, in your view, would work effectively.

Geoff Dyer

The English writer Geoff Dyer (b. 1958) is best known for his nonfiction. His collection *Otherwise Known as the Human Condition* (2011), in which the following essay appears, won the National Book Critics Circle Award for criticism. His writing gleefully flouts the conventions of genre. *Out of Sheer Rage* (1997), his study of the novelist and poet D. H. Lawrence, for example, largely concerns Dyer's personal (and often hilarious) tribulations in getting the book started. Similarly original and unorthodox are his travel memoirs, *The Missing of the Somme* (1994) and *Yoga for People Who Can't Be Bothered To Do It* (2003). His most recent book, *Another Great Day at Sea* (2014), describes his experience living on the aircraft carrier USS *George H. W. Bush*. Dyer is also the author of four novels, including *The Colour of Memory* (1989) and *Jeff in Venice, Death in Varanasi* (2009). He attended Corpus Christi College in the University of Oxford and currently lives in Venice Beach, California.

Blues for Vincent

It must be four years ago that I first saw Zadkine's sculpture of Vincent and Theo Van Gogh in one of the museums in Amsterdam. Carved in angular-cubist style, the sculpture is of two men sitting, one with his arm around the other's shoulders. I think their heads are touching but I could easily be wrong (works of art that affect you deeply are seldom quite as you remember them). Unusually for a piece so thoroughly committed to the language of cubism, the sculpture works on us very simply, directly addressing the humanity of its subjects where normally the cubist effect distorts and dislocates. Rarely has the hardness of stone been coaxed into such softness.

> *"Rarely has the hardness of stone been coaxed into such softness."*

Zadkine wanted his sculpture to express the relationship of dependency and trust that existed between Vincent and his brother; in doing so he reveals all the tenderness of which men are capable of offering each other.

It is not immediately obvious which of Zadkine's figures is Vincent and which is Theo. Like all who relieve the suffering of others, Theo — in a process that is the exact opposite of a blood transfusion — has taken some of Vincent's pain into himself. Soon, however, it becomes obvious that while the sky weighs heavily on both figures, one, Vincent, feels gravity as a force so terrible it can drag men beneath the earth. From this moment on you are held by the pathos and beauty of what Zadkine depicts: despair that is inconsolable, comfort that is endless. One figure says *I can never feel better*, the other *I will hold you until you are better*.

Last night, a few yards from where I am living, on Third Street, just off Avenue B, I saw 4
a homeless guy the same age as I am (I guessed he was my age because he looked twice that age) grabbing his head and hurling himself at a storefront, falling to the floor screaming, lying still for a few seconds, and then, exhausted but still in the grip of this frenzy, picking himself up and doing it again. An hour later he was unconscious on the sidewalk.

Each morning people are sprawled in the streets, so deeply comatose that even 5
the indifferent kicks of cops fail to rouse them. Throughout the day the destitute and the addicted, the insane and the desperate, sit in pairs in doorways and on steps, heads bowed, hearing each other out or reaching out an arm while the other groans and shivers.

I see your face everywhere, wandering through it like rain and the drifting steam of 6
streets. I wake at four in the morning and think of you doing ordinary things: hunting for your glasses that you can never find, taking the tube to work, buying wine at the supermarket.

Before I unlock the mailbox I can tell if there is a letter from you. I long for your 7
letters and dread the announcements and decisions they might contain, spend whole days waiting for you to call.

I pick up the phone on the second ring, hear an American voice say: 8
"Hi, how ya doin'?"
"Fine."
"What's happenin'?"
"Who is this?"
"I'm just somebody callin' up."
"What about?"
"I'm just a guy hangin' out. So how ya doin'?"
"What?"
"Ah, I'm feelin' kind of low."
"So I don't know you?"
"No."
"I can't talk to you, man."
"No . . . ?" As if he had *eternity* on his hands.

At seven — one in the morning London time — I call you, the familiar English 9
tones becoming bleak after six rings. In case you are just coming through the door I
let it ring another ten times, hoping that when you return you will be able to tell I have
called, furniture and walls preserving a message there was no answering machine to
receive: I miss you, I want you, I love you. Then I just let it ring, the phone pressed to
my head like a pistol.

Halfway through the closing set of a weeklong stint at a club in Greenwich Village, 10
David Murray announces "Ballad for the Black Man."

Murray started off as an energy player but in recent years he's been digging back 11
into the tradition and now sounds like a whole history of the tenor saxophone: in his
playing you can hear Ayler, Coltrane, Rollins, Webster . . .

"The blues is like that, not something you play *but a way of calling out to the dead, to all the dead slaves of America. "*

In the same way, "Ballad for the Black Man" con- 12
tains the cry of all the spirituals and sorrow songs, all
the blues there have ever been. Murray's solo lasts for
ten minutes, climaxing with notes so high they disap-
pear, as if a part of the song were not addressed to
human ears at all. The blues is like that, not something you *play* but a way of calling out to the dead, to
all the dead slaves of America.

The message of the blues is simple: as long as 13
there are people on earth they will have need of this
music. In a way, then, the blues is about its own survival. It's the shelter the black man
has built, not only for himself but for anyone who needs it. Not just a shelter — a
home. No suffering is so unendurable that it cannot find expression, no pain is so
intense that it cannot be lessened — this is the promise at the heart of the blues. It
cannot heal but it can hold us, can lay a hand around a brother's shoulder and say:

You will find a home, if not in her arms, then here, in these blues. 14

Questions for Discussion and Writing

1. On a first reading, this may seem a puzzling essay. The four sections seem
   unrelated, and so different in subject matter and even in tone that they belong
   to different essays altogether. But on a second or third reading, connections
   begin to emerge — though there is still perhaps no single "correct" way to
   make sense of it all. What connections can you find among the sections? How

do you make sense of the essay as a whole? Reread it carefully, and develop an interpretation that explains how these four segments might belong together.

2. Analyze Dyer's description of Ossip Zadkine's sculpture of the Van Gogh brothers in the first section of the essay. (You might look online for an image of the sculpture to assist you in your analysis.) Note the information Dyer gives the reader about the appearance of the sculpture, the language he uses to convey ideas and feelings that the sculpture suggests, and the way he structures the section to move from surfaces to depths. Note how he uses subordination and coordination (see Chapter 7) to make his sentences dense with content. Find a work of art that moves you in a book or online—or (perhaps best of all) simply work from memory—and write a similar description, one that combines detailed information with close interpretation.

3. Write an essay that imitates the form of "Blues for Vincent" but uses different material. That is, write a short essay with four or more distinct sections that differ from each other in subject and tone yet contain "threads" that connect them.

Rana Foroohar

Rana Foroohar (b. 1970; pronounced fo-ROO-har) is an Iranian-born journalist who writes a regular column, "The Curious Capitalist," for *Time* magazine. She is also CNN's global economic analyst, a frequent commentator on shows such as *Face the Nation* and *Real Time with Bill Maher*, and a life member of the Council on Foreign Relations, an independent membership organization and nonpartisan think tank. Foroohar spent thirteen years at *Newsweek* as an editor and a European economic correspondent. But in 2007 she decided to shift her focus from editing to writing. In an interview, she explained, "Being a columnist rather than a manager has allowed me the opportunity to write, build a TV and radio career, work on a book, and speak to influential audiences. . . . It's also given me the flexibility I need to raise my two small children and spend time with my husband, which is harder to do when you are in management and beholden to other people's schedules."

Foroohar wrote the article "What Ever Happened to Upward Mobility?" for the November 2011 issue of *Time*. She sees the recent economic problems of the United States as symptoms of deeper, structural problems related to globalization and technological change and not merely the result of short-term policy decisions by Congress and the Federal Reserve.

What Ever Happened to Upward Mobility?

America's story, our national mythology, is built on the idea of being an opportunity society. From the tales of Horatio Alger to the real lives of Henry Ford and Mark Zuckerberg, we have defined our country as a place where everyone, if he or she works hard enough, can get ahead. As Alexis de Tocqueville argued more than 150 years ago, it's this dream that enables Americans to tolerate much social inequality — this coming from a French aristocrat — in exchange for what we perceive as great dynamism and opportunity in our society. Modern surveys confirm what Tocqueville sensed back then: Americans care much more about being able to move up the socioeconomic ladder than where we stand on it. We may be poor today, but as long as there's a chance that we can be rich tomorrow, things are O.K. 1

But does America still work like that? The suspicion that the answer is no inspires not only the Occupy Wall Street (OWS) protests that have spread across the nation but also a movement as seemingly divergent as the Tea Party. While OWS may focus its anger on rapacious bankers and the Tea Party on spendthrift politicians, both would probably agree that there's a cabal of entitled elites on Wall Street and in 2

> *"The American Dream, like the rest of our economy, has become bifurcated."*

Washington who have somehow loaded the dice and made it impossible for average people to get ahead. The American Dream, like the rest of our economy, has become bifurcated.

Certainly the numbers support the idea that for 3 most people, it's harder to get ahead than it's ever been in the postwar era. Inequality in the U.S., always high compared with that in other developed countries, is rising. The 1% decried by OWS takes home 21% of the country's income and accounts for 35% of its wealth. Wages, which have stagnated in real terms since the 1970s, have been falling for much of the past year, in part because of pervasively high unemployment. For the first time in 20 years, the percentage of the population employed in the U.S. is lower than in the U.K., Germany, and the Netherlands. "We like to think of America as the workingest nation on earth. But that's no longer the case," says Ron Haskins, a co-director, along with Isabel Sawhill, of the Brookings Institution's Center on Children and Families.

Nor are we the world's greatest opportunity society. The Pew Charitable Trusts' 4 Economic Mobility Project has found that if you were born in 1970 in the bottom one-fifth of the socioeconomic spectrum in the U.S., you had only about a 17% chance of making it into the upper two-fifths. That's not good by international standards. A spate of new reports from groups such as Brookings, Pew, and the Organisation for Economic Co-operation and Development show that it's easier to climb the socioeconomic ladder in many parts of Europe than it is in the U.S. It's hard to imagine a bigger hit to the American Dream than that; you'd have an easier time getting a leg up in many parts of sclerotic, debt-ridden, class-riven old Europe than you would in the U.S.A. "The simple truth," says Sawhill, "is that we have a belief system about ourselves that no longer aligns with the facts."

The obvious question is, What happened? The answers, like social mobility itself, 5 are nuanced and complex. You can argue about what kind of mobility really matters. Many conservatives, for example, would be inclined to focus on absolute mobility, which means the extent to which people are better off than their parents were at the same age. That's a measure that focuses mostly on how much economic growth has occurred, and by that measure, the U.S. does fine. Two-thirds of 40-year-old Americans live in households with larger incomes, adjusted for inflation, than their parents had at the same age (though the gains are smaller than they were in the previous generation).

But just as we don't feel grateful to have indoor plumbing or multichannel digital 6 cable television, we don't necessarily feel grateful that we earn more than our parents did. That's because we don't peg ourselves to our parents; we peg ourselves to the

"That's because we don't peg ourselves to our parents; we peg ourselves to the Joneses."

Joneses. Behavioral economics tells us that our sense of well-being is tied not to the past but to how we are doing compared with our peers. Relative mobility matters. By that standard, we aren't doing very well at all. Having the right parents increases your chances of ending up middle to upper middle class by a factor of three or four. It's very different in many other countries, including Canada, Australia, the Nordic nations, and, to a lesser extent, Germany and France. While 42% of American men with fathers in the bottom fifth of the earning curve remain there, only a quarter of Danes and Swedes and only 30% of Britons do.

Yet it's important to understand that when you compare Europe and America, 7 you are comparing very different societies. High-growth Nordic nations with good social safety nets, which have the greatest leads in social mobility over the U.S., are small and homogeneous. On average, only about 7% of their populations are ethnic minorities (who are often poorer and thus less mobile than the overall population), compared with 28% in the U.S. Even bigger nations like Germany don't have to deal with populations as socially and economically diverse as America's.

Still, Europe does more to encourage equality. That's a key point because high 8 inequality — meaning a large gap between the richest and poorest in society — has a strong correlation to lower mobility. As Sawhill puts it, "When the rungs on the ladder are further apart, it's harder to climb up them." Indeed, in order to understand why social mobility in the U.S. is falling, it's important to understand why inequality is rising, now reaching levels not seen since the Gilded Age.

There are many reasons for the huge and growing wealth divide in our country. 9 The rise of the money culture and bank deregulation in the 1980s and '90s certainly contributed to it. As the financial sector grew in relation to the rest of the economy (it's now at historic highs of about 8%), a winner-take-all economy emerged. Wall Street was less about creating new businesses — entrepreneurship has stalled as finance has become a bigger industry — but it did help set a new pay band for top talent. In the 1970s, corporate chiefs earned about 40 times as much as their lowest-paid worker (still closer to the norm in many parts of Europe). Now they earn more than 400 times as much.

The most recent blows to economic equality, of course, have been the real estate 10 and credit crises, which wiped out housing prices and thus erased the largest chunk of middle-class wealth, while stocks, where the rich hold much of their money, have largely recovered. It is telling that in the state-by-state Opportunity Index recently released by Opportunity Nation, a coalition of private and public institutions dedicated to increasing social mobility, many of the lowest-scoring states — including Nevada, Arizona, and Florida — were those hardest hit by the housing crash and are places where credit continues to be most constrained.

But the causes of inequality and any resulting decrease in social mobility are also very much about two megatrends that have been reshaping the global economy since the 1970s: the effects of technology and the rise of the emerging markets. Some 2 billion people have joined the global workforce since the 1970s. According to Goldman Sachs, the majority of them are middle class by global standards and can do many of the jobs that were once done by American workers, at lower labor costs. Goldman estimates that 70 million join that group every year.   11

While there's no clear formula for ascribing the rise in inequality (via wage compression) and subsequent loss of mobility to the rise of China and India, one key study stands out. Nobel laureate Michael Spence's recent examination of major U.S. multinationals for the Council on Foreign Relations found that since the 1980s, companies that operated in the tradable sector — meaning they made things or provided services that could be traded between nations — have created virtually no net new jobs. The study is especially illustrative of the hollowing out of the American manufacturing sector in that period as middle-wage jobs moved abroad. The only major job creation was in more geographically protected categories like retail and health care (another reason wages are shrinking, since many of the fastest-growing jobs in the U.S., like home health care aide and sales clerk, are low-paying).   12

That so many of the jobs we now create are low end underscores a growing debate over technology and its role in increasing or decreasing opportunity. Many of the jobs that have disappeared from the U.S. economy have done so not only because they were outsourced but also because they are now done by computers or robots. Advocates of technology-driven economic growth, like the McKinsey Global Institute, would argue that the creative destruction wrought by such innovations creates more and better jobs in the future; microchip making employs just 0.6% of the U.S. workforce, but chips make all sorts of businesses more efficient so they can develop new products and services. The problem is that those jobs tend to be skewed toward the very top (software engineer) or the bottom (sales clerk). The jobs in the middle have disappeared. According to the New America Foundation, a public-policy think tank, the share of middle-income jobs in the U.S. fell from 52% in 1980 to 42% in 2010.   13

While there's no doubt that so far, technology has been a net plus in terms of the number of jobs in our economy, a growing group of experts believe that link is being   14

"That so many of the jobs we now create are low end underscores a growing debate over technology and its role in increasing or decreasing opportunity."

broken. Two economists at MIT, Erik Brynjolfsson and Andrew McAfee, have just published an influential book titled *Race Against the Machine*, looking at how computers are increasingly able to perform tasks better than humans do, from driving (Google software recently took a self-driving Prius on a 1,000-mile trip) to sophisticated pattern recognition to writing creative essays and composing award-winning music. The result, they say, is that technology may soon be a net job destroyer.

The best hope in fighting the machines is to 15 improve education, the factor that is more closely correlated with upward mobility than any other. Research has shown that as long as educational achievement keeps up with technological gains, more jobs are created. But in the 1970s, that link was broken in the U.S. as educational gains slowed. That's likely an important reason that Europeans have passed the U.S. in various measures of mobility. They've been exposed to the same Malthusian forces of globalization, but they've been better at using public money to buffer them. By funding postsecondary education and keeping public primary and secondary schools as good as if not better than private ones, Europeans have made sure that the best and brightest can rise.

There are many other lessons to be learned from the most mobile nations. Fund- 16 ing universal health care without tying it to jobs can increase labor flexibility and reduce the chance that people will fall into poverty because of medical emergencies — a common occurrence in the U.S., where such medical crises are a big reason a third of the population cycles in and out of poverty every year. Focusing more on less-expensive preventive care (including family planning, since high teen birthrates correlate with lack of mobility) rather than on expensive procedures can increase the general health levels in a society, which is also correlated to mobility.

Europe's higher spending on social safety nets has certainly bolstered the middle 17 and working classes. (Indeed, you could argue that some of America's great social programs, including Social Security and Medicaid, enabled us to become a middle-class nation.) Countries like Germany and Denmark that have invested in youth-employment programs and technical schools where young people can learn a high-paying trade have done well, which is not surprising given that in many studies, including the Opportunity Nation index, there's a high correlation between the number of teenagers who are not in school or not working and lowered mobility.

Of course, the debt crisis in Europe and the protests over austerity cuts in 18
places like Athens and London make it clear that the traditional European welfare
systems are undergoing very profound changes that may reduce mobility throughout the continent. But there is still opportunity in efficiency. Germans, for example,
made a command decision after the financial downturn in 2008 not to let unemployment rise because it would ultimately be more expensive to put people back to
work than to pay to keep them in their jobs. The government subsidized companies
to keep workers (as many as 1.4 million in 2009) on the payroll, even part time. Once
the economy began to pick up, companies were ready to capitalize on it quickly.
Unemployment is now 6% — lower than before the recession — and growth has
stayed relatively high.

The Nordic nations, too, have figured out clever ways to combine strong eco- 19
nomic growth with a decent amount of security. As in Germany, labor and corporate
relations are collaborative rather than contentious. Union reps often sit on company
boards, which makes it easier to curb excessive executive pay and negotiate compromises over working hours. Worker retraining is a high priority. Danish adults spend a
lot of time in on-the-job training. That's one reason they also enjoy high real wages
and relatively low unemployment.

The final lesson that might be learned is in tax policy. The more-mobile Euro- 20
pean nations have fewer corporate loopholes, more redistribution to the poor and
middle class via consumption taxes, and far less complication. France's tax code, for
example, is 12% as long as the U.S.'s. Tax levels are also higher, something that the
enlightened rich in the U.S. are very publicly advocating.

No wonder. A large body of academic research shows that inequality and lack of 21
social mobility hurt not just those at the bottom; they hurt everyone. Unequal societies have lower levels of trust, higher levels of anxiety, and more illness. They have
arguably less stable economies: International Monetary Fund research shows that
countries like the U.S. and the U.K. are more prone to boom-and-bust cycles. And they
are ultimately at risk for social instability.

> *" Unequal societies have lower levels of trust, higher levels of anxiety, and more illness. "*

That's the inflection point that we are at right 22
now. The mythology of the American Dream has made
it difficult to start a serious conversation about how
to create more opportunity in our society, since many
of us still believe that our mobility is the result of our
elbow grease and nothing more. But there is a growing
truth, seen in the numbers and in the protests that are
spreading across our nation, that this isn't so. We can

no longer blame the individual. We have to acknowledge that climbing the ladder often means getting some support and a boost.

Questions for Discussion and Writing

1. Foroohar distinguishes between "absolute mobility" and "relative mobility." What do these terms mean? How does Foroohar support her view that relative mobility matters more than, or at least as much as, absolute mobility?

2. According to Foroohar, America is at an "inflection point," and the "American Dream" of success based solely on an individual's hard work is no longer relevant as it once was. In Foroohar's view, how can government action help increase social mobility? List the measures she suggests. Are these measures practical and realistic? What would need to happen for these ideas to be put into practice?

3. Foroohar is concerned about the demise of the "American dream" and the "myth" that individuals can achieve success through hard work alone. Emily Esfahani Smith in "Life on the Island" (p. 399) expresses concern about the recent emergence of what she calls "hyper-individualism." Consider the two writers' arguments: Do their views contradict each other? Or can both be right?

Malcolm Gladwell

Malcolm Gladwell (b. 1963) is a staff writer for the *New Yorker* magazine and the author of five books, including *The Tipping Point: How Little Things Can Make a Big Difference* (2000) and *David and Goliath: Underdogs, Misfits, and the Art of Battling Giants* (2013). Born in England, Gladwell immigrated with his family to Canada at age six. He earned a degree in history from the University of Toronto in 1984 and subsequently relocated to the United States to pursue a career in journalism. He worked at the *Washington Post* and elsewhere before he began writing for the *New Yorker* in 1996. Gladwell draws on wide-ranging work by academics and journalists to reexamine familiar phenomena, often in the areas of psychology, sociology, and management, and invites us to consider them from fresh angles. In the following essay, which appeared in the *New Yorker* in 2011, Gladwell analyzes the methodology of the well-known and controversial ranking of American colleges by *U.S. News and World Report*. But he also raises questions about the methodology involved in ranking any complex and varied class of objects.

The Order of Things

Last summer, the editors of *Car and Driver* conducted a comparison test of three sports cars, the Lotus Evora, the Chevrolet Corvette Grand Sport, and the Porsche Cayman S. The cars were taken on an extended run through mountain passes in Southern California, and from there to a race track north of Los Angeles, for precise measurements of performance and handling. The results of the road tests were then tabulated according to a twenty-one-variable, two-hundred-and-thirty-five-point rating system, based on four categories: vehicle (driver comfort, styling, fit and finish, etc.); power train (transmission, engine, and fuel economy); chassis (steering, brakes, ride, and handling); and "fun to drive." The magazine concluded, "The range of these three cars' driving personalities is as various as the pajama sizes of Papa Bear, Mama Bear, and Baby Bear, but a clear winner emerged nonetheless." This was the final tally:

1. Porsche Cayman   193
2. Chevrolet Corvette   186
3. Lotus Evora   182

Car and Driver is one of the most influential editorial voices in the automotive world. When it says that it likes one car better than another, consumers and carmakers take notice. Yet when you inspect the magazine's tabulations it is hard to figure out why

Car and Driver was so sure that the Cayman is better than the Corvette and the Evora. The trouble starts with the fact that the ranking methodology *Car and Driver* used was essentially the same one it uses for all the vehicles it tests—from S.U.V.s to economy sedans. It's not set up for sports cars. Exterior styling, for example, counts for four per cent of the total score. Has anyone buying a sports car ever placed so little value on how it looks? Similarly, the categories of "fun to drive" and "chassis"—which cover the subjective experience of driving the car—count for only eighty-five points out of the total of two hundred and thirty-five. That may make sense for S.U.V. buyers. But, for people interested in Porsches and Corvettes and Lotuses, the subjective experience of driving is surely what matters most. In other words, in trying to come up with a ranking that is heterogeneous—a methodology that is broad enough to cover *all* vehicles—*Car and Driver* ended up with a system that is absurdly ill-suited to some vehicles.

Suppose that *Car and Driver* decided to tailor its grading system just to sports   3 cars. Clearly, styling and the driving experience ought to count for much more. So let's make exterior styling worth twenty-five per cent, the driving experience worth fifty per cent, and the balance of the criteria worth twenty-five per cent. The final tally now looks like this:

1. Lotus Evora   205

2. Porsche Cayman   198

3. Chevrolet Corvette   192

There's another thing funny about the *Car and Driver* system. Price counts only   4 for twenty points, less than ten per cent of the total. There's no secret why: *Car and Driver* is edited by auto enthusiasts. To them, the choice of a car is as important as the choice of a home or a spouse, and only a philistine would let a few dollars stand between him and the car he wants. (They leave penny-pinching to their frumpy counterparts at *Consumer Reports*.) But for most of us price matters, especially in a case like this, where the Corvette, as tested, costs $67,565—thirteen thousand dollars less than the Porsche, and eighteen thousand dollars less than the Lotus. Even to a car nut, that's a lot of money. So let's imagine that *Car and Driver* revised its ranking system again, giving a third of the weight to price, a third to the driving experience, and a third split equally between exterior styling and vehicle characteristics. The tally would now be:

1. Chevrolet Corvette   205

2. Lotus Evora   195

3. Porshe Cayman   195

So which is the best car?

Car and Driver's ambition to grade every car in the world according to the same   5
methodology would be fine if it limited itself to a single dimension. A heterogeneous
ranking system works if it focusses just on, say, how much fun a car is to drive, or how
good-looking it is, or how beautifully it handles. The magazine's ambition to create a
comprehensive ranking system — one that considered cars along twenty-one variables, each weighted according to a secret sauce cooked up by the editors — would
also be fine, as long as the cars being compared were truly similar. It's only when one
car is thirteen thousand dollars more than another that juggling twenty-one variables starts to break down, because you're faced with the impossible task of deciding
how much a difference of that degree ought to matter. A ranking can be heterogeneous, in other words, as long as it doesn't try to be too comprehensive. And it can be
comprehensive as long as it doesn't try to measure things that are heterogeneous. But
it's an act of real audacity when a ranking system tries to be comprehensive *and* heterogeneous — which is the first thing to keep in mind in any consideration of *U.S.
News & World Report*'s annual "Best Colleges" guide.

The *U.S. News* rankings are run by Robert Morse, whose six-person team operates out   6
of a small red brick office building in the Georgetown neighborhood of Washington,
D.C. Morse is a middle-aged man with gray hair who looks like the prototypical Beltway wonk: rumpled, self-effacing, mildly preppy, and sensibly shoed. His office is
piled high with the statistical detritus of more than two decades of data collection.
When he took on his current job, in the mid-nineteen-eighties, the college guide was
little more than an item of service journalism tucked away inside *U.S. News* magazine.
Now the weekly print magazine is defunct, but the rankings have taken on a life of
their own. In the month that the 2011 rankings came out, the *U.S. News* Web site
recorded more than ten million visitors. *U.S. News* has added rankings of graduate
programs, law schools, business schools, medical schools, and hospitals — and Morse
has become the dean of a burgeoning international rankings industry.

"In the early years, the thing that's happening now would not have been imagin-   7
able," Morse says. "This idea of using the rankings as a benchmark, college presidents
setting a goal of 'We're going to rise in the *U.S. News* ranking,' as proof of their management, or as proof that they're a better school, that they're a good president. That
wasn't on anybody's radar. It was just for consumers."

Over the years, Morse's methodology has steadily evolved. In its current form, it   8
relies on seven weighted variables:

1. Undergraduate academic reputation, 22.5 per cent
2. Graduation and freshman retention rates, 20 per cent

3. Faculty resources, 20 per cent

4. Student selectivity, 15 per cent

5. Financial resources, 10 per cent

6. Graduation rate performance, 7.5 per cent

7. Alumni giving, 5 per cent

From these variables, *U.S. News* generates a score for each institution on a scale   9
of 1 to 100, where Harvard is a 100 and the University of North Carolina–Greensboro is
a 22. Here is a list of the schools that finished in positions forty-one through fifty in
the 2011 "National University" category:

41. Case Western Reserve, 60

41. Rensselaer Polytechnic Institute, 60

41. University of California–Irvine, 60

41. University of Washington, 60

45. University of Texas–Austin, 59

45. University of Wisconsin–Madison, 59

47. Penn State University–University Park, 58

47. University of Illinois, Urbana-Champaign, 58

47. University of Miami, 58

50. Yeshiva University, 57

> *"A comprehensive, heterogeneous ranking system was a stretch for* Car and Driver — *and all it did was rank inanimate objects operated by a single person."*

This ranking system looks a great deal like the   10
Car and Driver methodology. It is heterogeneous. It
doesn't just compare U.C. Irvine, the University of
Washington, the University of Texas–Austin, the
University of Wisconsin–Madison, Penn State, and
the University of Illinois, Urbana-Champaign — all
public institutions of roughly the same size. It aims
to compare Penn State — a very large, public, land-
grant university with a low tuition and an economically diverse student body, set in a rural valley in
central Pennsylvania and famous for its football
team — with Yeshiva University, a small, expensive,
private Jewish university whose undergraduate program is set on two campuses in Manhattan (one in

midtown, for the women, and one far uptown, for the men) and is definitely *not* famous for its football team.

The system is also comprehensive. It doesn't simply compare schools along one dimension — the test scores of incoming freshmen, say, or academic reputation. An algorithm takes a slate of statistics on each college and transforms them into a single score: it tells us that Penn State is a better school than Yeshiva by one point. It is easy to see why the *U.S. News* rankings are so popular. A single score allows us to judge between entities (like Yeshiva and Penn State) that otherwise would be impossible to compare. At no point, however, do the college guides acknowledge the extraordinary difficulty of the task they have set themselves. A comprehensive, heterogeneous ranking system was a stretch for *Car and Driver* — and all it did was rank inanimate objects operated by a single person. The Penn State campus at University Park is a complex institution with dozens of schools and departments, four thousand faculty members, and forty-five thousand students. How on earth does anyone propose to assign a number to something like that? 11

The first difficulty with rankings is that it can be surprisingly hard to measure the variable you want to rank — even in cases where that variable seems perfectly objective. Consider an extreme example: suicide. Here is a ranking of suicide per hundred thousand people, by country: 12

1. Belarus, 35.1
2. Lithuania, 31.5
3. South Korea, 31.0
4. Kazakhstan, 26.9
5. Russia, 26.5
6. Japan, 24.4
7. Guyana, 22.9
8. Ukraine, 22.6
9. Hungary, 21.8
10. Sri Lanka, 21.6

This list looks straightforward. Yet no self-respecting epidemiologist would look at it and conclude that Belarus has the worst suicide rate in the world, and that Hungary belongs in the top ten. Measuring suicide is just too tricky. It requires someone to make a surmise about the intentions of the deceased at the time of death. In some 13 cases, that's easy. Maybe the victim jumped off the Golden Gate Bridge, or left a note. In most cases, though, there's ambiguity, and different coroners and different cultures vary widely in the way they choose to interpret that ambiguity. In certain places, cause of death is determined by the police, who some believe are more likely to call an ambiguous suicide an accident. In other places, the decision is made by a physician, who may be less likely to do so. In some cultures, suicide is considered so shameful that coroners shy away from that determination, even when it's obvious. A suicide might be called a suicide, a homicide, an accident, or left undetermined. David Phillips, a sociologist at the University of California–San Diego, has argued persuasively that a significant percentage of single-car crashes are probably suicides, and criminologists suggest that a good percentage of civilians killed by police officers are actually cases of "suicide by cop"—instances where someone deliberately provoked deadly force. The reported suicide rate, then, is almost certainly less than the actual suicide rate. But no one knows whether the relationship between those two numbers is the same in every country. And no one knows whether the proxies that we use to estimate the real suicide rate are any good.

> *"A suicide might be called a suicide, a homicide, an accident, or left undetermined."*

"Many, many people who commit suicide by poison have something else wrong with them—let's say the person has cancer—and the death of this person might be listed as primarily associated with cancer, rather than with deliberate poisoning," Phillips says. "Any suicides in that category would be undetectable. Or it is frequently noted that Orthodox Jews have a low recorded suicide rate, as do Catholics. Well, it could be because they have this very solid community and proscriptions against suicide, or because they are unusually embarrassed by suicide and more willing to hide it. The simple answer is nobody knows whether suicide rankings are real." 14

The *U.S. News* rankings suffer from a serious case of the suicide problem. There's no direct way to measure the quality of an institution—how well a college manages to inform, inspire, and challenge its students. So the *U.S. News* algorithm relies instead on proxies for quality—and the proxies for educational quality turn out to be flimsy at best. 15

Take the category of "faculty resources," which counts for twenty per cent of an institution's score. "Research shows that the more satisfied students are about their contact with professors," the College Guide's explanation of the category begins, "the more they will learn and the more likely it is they will graduate." That's true. 16

According to educational researchers, arguably the most important variable in a successful college education is a vague but crucial concept called student "engagement" — that is, the extent to which students immerse themselves in the intellectual and social life of their college — and a major component of engagement is the quality of a student's contacts with faculty. As with suicide, the disagreement isn't about *what* we want to measure. So what proxies does *U.S. News* use to measure this elusive dimension of engagement? The explanation goes on:

> We use six factors from the 2009–10 academic year to assess a school's commitment to instruction. Class size has two components, the proportion of classes with fewer than 20 students (30 percent of the faculty resources score) and the proportion with 50 or more students (10 percent of the score). Faculty salary (35 percent) is the average faculty pay, plus benefits, during the 2008–09 and 2009–10 academic years, adjusted for regional differences in the cost of living. . . . We also weigh the proportion of professors with the highest degree in their fields (15 percent), the student-faculty ratio (5 percent), and the proportion of faculty who are full time (5 percent).

" There's no direct way to measure the quality of an institution — how well a college manages to inform, inspire, and challenge its students. "

This is a puzzling list. Do professors who get paid more money really take their teaching roles more seriously? And why does it matter whether a professor has the highest degree in his or her field? Salaries and degree attainment are known to be predictors of research productivity. But studies show that being oriented toward research has very little to do with being good at teaching. Almost none of the *U.S. News* variables, in fact, seem to be particularly effective proxies for engagement. As the educational researchers Patrick Terenzini and Ernest Pascarella concluded after analyzing twenty-six hundred reports on the effects of college on students:

17

> After taking into account the characteristics, abilities, and backgrounds students bring with them to college, we found that how much students grow or change has only inconsistent and, perhaps in a practical sense, trivial relationships with such traditional measures of institutional "quality" as educational expenditures per student, student/faculty ratios, faculty salaries, percentage of faculty with the highest degree in their field, faculty research productivity, size of the library, [or] admissions selectivity.

The reputation score that serves as the most important variable in the *U.S. News* 18
methodology — accounting for 22.5 per cent of a college's final score — isn't any better. Every year, the magazine sends a survey to the country's university and college
presidents, provosts, and admissions deans (along with a sampling of high-school
guidance counsellors) asking them to grade all the schools in their category on a scale
of one to five. Those at national universities, for example, are asked to rank all two
hundred and sixty-one other national universities — and Morse says that the typical
respondent grades about half of the schools in his or her category. But it's far from
clear how any one individual could have insight into that many institutions. In an
article published recently in the *Annals of Internal Medicine*, Ashwini Sehgal analyzed
U.S. News's "Best Hospitals" rankings, which also rely heavily on reputation ratings
generated by professional peers. Sehgal put together a list of objective criteria of performance — such as a hospital's mortality rates for various surgical procedures,
patient-safety rates, nursing-staffing levels, and key technologies. Then he checked to
see how well those measures of performance matched each hospital's reputation rating. The answer, he discovered, was that they didn't. Having good outcomes doesn't
translate into being admired by other doctors. Why, after all, should a gastroenterolo-
gist at the Ochsner Medical Center, in New Orleans, have any specific insight into the
performance of the gastroenterology department at Mass General, in Boston, or even,
for that matter, have anything more than an anecdotal impression of the gastroenterology department down the road at some hospital in Baton Rouge?

> *"Having good outcomes doesn't translate into being admired by other doctors."*

Some years ago, similarly, a former chief justice of 19
the Michigan supreme court, Thomas Brennan, sent a
questionnaire to a hundred or so of his fellow-lawyers,
asking them to rank a list of ten law schools in order of
quality. "They included a good sample of the big names.
Harvard. Yale. University of Michigan. And some lesser-
known schools. John Marshall. Thomas Cooley," Brennan wrote. "As I recall, they ranked Penn State's law
school right about in the middle of the pack. Maybe
fifth among the ten schools listed. Of course, Penn State doesn't have a law school."

Those lawyers put Penn State in the middle of the pack, even though every fact 20
they thought they knew about Penn State's law school was an illusion, because in
their minds Penn State is a middle-of-the-pack brand. (Penn State does have a law
school today, by the way.) Sound judgments of educational quality have to be based
on specific, hard-to-observe features. But reputational ratings are simply inferences
from broad, readily observable features of an institution's identity, such as its history,
its prominence in the media, or the elegance of its architecture. They are prejudices.

And where do these kinds of reputational prejudices come from? According to   21
Michael Bastedo, an educational sociologist at the University of Michigan who has
published widely on the *U.S. News* methodology, "rankings drive reputation." In other
words, when *U.S. News* asks a university president to perform the impossible task of
assessing the relative merits of dozens of institutions he knows nothing about, he
relies on the only source of detailed information at his disposal that assesses the relative merits of dozens of institutions he knows nothing about: *U.S. News*. A school like
Penn State, then, can do little to improve its position. To go higher than forty-seventh,
it needs a better reputation score, and to get a better reputation score it needs to be
higher than forty-seventh. The *U.S. News* ratings are a self-fulfilling prophecy.

Bastedo, incidentally, says that reputation ratings can sometimes work very well.   22
It makes sense, for example, to ask professors within a field to rate others in their
field: they read one another's work, attend the same conferences, and hire one another's graduate students, so they have real knowledge on which to base an opinion. Reputation scores can work for one-dimensional rankings, created by people with
specialized knowledge. For instance, the *Wall Street Journal* has ranked colleges
according to the opinions of corporate recruiters. Those opinions are more than a
proxy. To the extent that people chose one college over another to enhance their pros-
pects in the corporate job markets, the reputation rankings of corporate recruiters
are of direct relevance. The No. 1 school in the *Wall Street Journal*'s corporate recruiters' ranking, by the way, is Penn State.

For several years, Jeffrey Stake, a professor at the Indiana University law school, has   23
run a Web site called the Ranking Game. It contains a spreadsheet loaded with statistics on every law school in the country, and allows users to pick their own criteria,
assign their own weights, and construct any ranking system they want.

Stake's intention is to demonstrate just how subjective rankings are, to show how   24
determinations of "quality" turn on relatively arbitrary judgments about how much
different variables should be weighted. For example, his site makes it easy to mimic
the *U.S. News* rankings. All you have to do is give equal weight to "academic reputation," "LSAT scores at the 75th percentile," "student-faculty ratio," and "faculty law-
review publishing," and you get a list of élite schools which looks similar to the *U.S.
News* law-school rankings:

1. University of Chicago
2. Yale University
3. Harvard University
4. Stanford University

5. Columbia University

6. Northwestern University

7. Cornell University

8. University of Pennsylvania

9. New York University

10. University of California, Berkeley

There's something missing from that list of variables, of course: it doesn't include 25
price. That is one of the most distinctive features of the *U.S. News* methodology. Both
its college rankings and its law-school rankings reward schools for devoting lots of
financial resources to educating their students, but not for being affordable. Why?
Morse admitted that there was no formal reason for that position. It was just a feeling.
"We're not saying that we're measuring educational outcomes," he explained. "We're
not saying we're social scientists, or we're subjecting our rankings to some peer-
review process. We're just saying we've made this judgment. We're saying we've inter-
viewed a lot of experts, we've developed these academic indicators, and we think
these measures measure quality schools."

> *"U.S. News thinks that schools that spend a lot of money on their students are nicer than those that don't, and that this niceness ought to be factored into the equation of desirability."*

As answers go, that's up there with the parental 26
"Because I said so." But Morse is simply being honest.
If we don't understand what the right proxies for college quality are, let alone how to represent those proxies in a comprehensive, heterogeneous grading
system, then our rankings are inherently arbitrary. All
Morse was saying was that, on the question of price,
he comes down on the *Car and Driver* side of things,
not on the *Consumer Reports* side. *U.S. News* thinks
that schools that spend a lot of money on their students are nicer than those that don't, and that this
niceness ought to be factored into the equation of
desirability. Plenty of Americans agree: the campus of
Vanderbilt University or Williams College is filled with
students whose families are largely indifferent to the
price their school charges but keenly interested in the
flower beds and the spacious suites and the architecturally distinguished lecture
halls those high prices make possible.

Of course, given that the rising cost of college has become a significant social 27
problem in the United States in recent years, you can make a strong case that a school
ought to be rewarded for being affordable. So suppose we go back to Stake's ranking
game, and re-rank law schools based on student-faculty ratio, L.S.A.T. scores at the
seventy-fifth percentile, faculty publishing, and price, all weighted equally. The list
now looks like this:

1. University of Chicago
2. Yale University
3. Harvard University
4. Stanford University
5. Northwestern University
6. Brigham Young University
7. Cornell University
8. University of Colorado
9. University of Pennsylvania
10. Columbia University

The revised ranking tells us that there are schools — like B.Y.U. and Colorado — 28
that provide a good legal education at a decent price, and that, by choosing not to
include tuition as a variable, *U.S. News* has effectively penalized those schools for trying
to provide value for the tuition dollar. But that's a very subtle tweak. Let's say that value
for the dollar is something we really care about. And so what we want is a three-factor
ranking, counting value for the dollar at forty per cent, L.S.A.T. scores at forty per cent of
the total, and faculty publishing at twenty per cent. Look at how the top ten changes:

1. University of Chicago
2. Brigham Young University
3. Harvard University
4. Yale University
5. University of Texas
6. University of Virginia
7. University of Colorado
8. University of Alabama

9. Stanford University

10. University of Pennsylvania

Welcome to the big time, Alabama!

The *U.S. News* rankings turn out to be full of these kinds of implicit ideological choices. 29
One common statistic used to evaluate colleges, for example, is called "graduation
rate performance," which compares a school's actual graduation rate with its predicted graduation rate given the socioeconomic status and the test scores of its
incoming freshman class. It is a measure of the school's efficacy: it quantifies the
impact of a school's culture and teachers and institutional support mechanisms.
Tulane, given the qualifications of the students that it admits, ought to have a graduation rate of eighty-seven per cent; its actual 2009 graduation rate was seventy-three
per cent. That shortfall suggests that something is amiss at Tulane.

Another common statistic for measuring college quality is "student selectivity." 30
This reflects variables such as how many of a college's freshmen were in the top ten
per cent of their high-school class, how high their S.A.T. scores were, and what percentage of applicants a college admits. Selectivity quantifies how accomplished students are when they first arrive on campus.

Each of these statistics matters, but for very different reasons. As a society, we 31
probably care more about efficacy: America's future depends on colleges that make
sure the students they admit leave with an education and a degree. If you are a bright
high-school senior and you're thinking about your own future, though, you may well
care more about selectivity, because that relates to the prestige of your degree.

But no institution can excel at both. The national university that ranks No. 1 in 32
selectivity is Yale. A crucial part of what it considers its educational function is to
assemble the most gifted group of freshmen it can. Because it maximizes selectivity,
though, Yale will never do well on an efficacy scale. Its freshmen are so accomplished
that they have a predicted graduation rate of ninety-six per cent: the highest Yale's
efficacy score could be is plus four. (It's actually plus two.) Of the top fifty national
universities in the "Best Colleges" ranking, the least selective school is Penn State.
Penn State sees its educational function as serving a wide range of students. That
gives it the opportunity to excel at efficacy — and it does so brilliantly. Penn State's
freshmen have an expected graduation rate of seventy-three per cent and an actual
graduation rate of eighty-five per cent, for a score of plus twelve: no other school in
the *U.S. News* top fifty comes close.

There is no *right* answer to how much weight a ranking system should give to these two competing values. It's a matter of which educational model you value more — and here, once again, *U.S. News* makes its position clear. It gives twice as much weight to selectivity as it does to efficacy. It favors the Yale model over the Penn State model, which means that the Yales of the world will always succeed at the *U.S. News* rankings because the *U.S. News* system is designed to reward Yale-ness. By contrast, to the extent that Penn State succeeds at doing a better job of being Penn State — of attracting a diverse group of students and educating them capably — it will only do worse. Rankings are not benign. They enshrine very particular ideologies, and, at a time when American higher education is facing a crisis of accessibility and affordability, we have adopted a de-facto standard of college quality that is uninterested in both of those factors. And why? Because a group of magazine analysts in an office building in Washington, D.C., decided twenty years ago to value selectivity over efficacy, to use proxies that scarcely relate to what they're meant to be proxies for, and to pretend that they can compare a large, diverse, low-cost land-grant university in rural Pennsylvania with a small, expensive, private Jewish university on two campuses in Manhattan. 33

"If you look at the top twenty schools every year, forever, they are all wealthy private universities," Graham Spanier, the president of Penn State, told me. "Do you mean that even the most prestigious public universities in the United States, and you can take your pick of what you think they are — Berkeley, U.C.L.A., University of Michigan, University of Wisconsin, Illinois, Penn State, U.N.C. — do you mean to say that not one of those is in the top tier of institutions? It doesn't really make sense, until you drill down into the rankings, and what do you find? What I find more than anything else is a measure of wealth: institutional wealth, how big is your endowment, what percentage of alumni are donating each year, what are your faculty salaries, how much are you spending per student. Penn State may very well be the most popular university in America — we get a hundred and fifteen thousand applications a year for admission. We serve a lot of people. Nearly a third of them are the first people in their entire family network to come to college. We have seventy-six per cent of our students receiving financial aid. There is no possibility that we could do anything here at this university to get ourselves into the top ten or twenty or thirty — except if some donor gave us billions of dollars." 34

In the fall of 1913, the prominent American geographer Ellsworth Huntington sent a letter to two hundred and thirteen scholars from twenty-seven countries. "May I ask 35 your cooperation in the preparation of a map showing the distribution of the higher elements of civilization throughout the world?" Huntington began, and he continued:

> My purpose is to prepare a map which shall show the distribution of those characteristics which are generally recognized as of the highest value. I mean by this the power of initiative, the capacity for formulating new ideas and for carrying them into effect, the power of self-control, high standards of honesty and morality, the power to lead and to control other races, the capacity for disseminating ideas, and other similar qualities which will readily suggest themselves.

"The reputation of immigrants could be used toward the score of their country of origin, but only those of the first generation."

Each contributor was given a list of a hundred and eighty-five of the world's regions — ranging from the Amur district of Siberia to the Kalahari Desert — with instructions to give each region a score of one to ten. The scores would then be summed and converted to a scale of one to a hundred. The rules were strict. The past could not be considered: Greece could not be given credit for its ancient glories. "If two races inhabit a given region," Huntington specified further, "both must be considered, and the rank of the region must depend upon the average of the two." The reputation of immigrants could be used toward the score of their country of origin, but only those of the first generation. And size and commercial significance should be held constant: the Scots should not suffer relative to, say, the English, just because they were less populous. Huntington's respondents took on the task with the utmost seriousness. "One appreciates what a big world this is and how little one knows about it when he attempts such a task as you have set," a respondent wrote back to Huntington. "It is a most excellent means of taking the conceit out of one." England and Wales and the North Atlantic states of America scored a perfect hundred, with central and northwestern Germany and New England coming in at ninety-nine.

Huntington then requested from the twenty-five of his correspondents who were Americans an in-depth ranking of the constituent regions of the United States. This time, he proposed a six-point scale. Southern Alaska, in this second reckoning, was last, at 1.5, followed by Arizona and New Mexico, at 1.6. The winners: Massachusetts, at 6.0, followed by Connecticut, Rhode Island, and New York, at 5.8. The citadel of

American civilization was New England and New York, Huntington concluded, in his magisterial 1915 work *Civilization and Climate.*

In case you are wondering, Ellsworth Huntington was a professor of geography at   38 Yale, in New Haven, Connecticut. *Civilization and Climate* was published by Yale University Press, and the book's appendix contains a list of Huntington's American correspondents, of which the following bear special mention:

J. Barrell, geologist, New Haven, Conn.
P. Bigelow, traveler and author, Malden, N.Y.
I. Bowman, geographer, New York City
W. M. Brown, geographer, Providence, R.I.
A. C. Coolidge, historian, Cambridge, Mass.
S. W. Cushing, geographer, Salem, Mass.
L. Farrand, anthropologist, New York City
C. W. Furlong, traveler and author, Boston, Mass.
E. W. Griffis, traveler and author, Ithaca, N.Y.
A. G. Keller, anthropologist, New Haven, Conn.
E. F. Merriam, editor, Boston, Mass.
J. R. Smith, economic geographer, Philadelphia, Pa.
Anonymous, New York City

"In spite of several attempts I was unable to obtain any contributor in the states   39 west of Minnesota or south of the Ohio River," Huntington explains, as if it were a side issue. It isn't, of course — not then and not now. Who comes out on top, in any ranking system, is really about who is doing the ranking.

Questions for Discussion and Writing

1. What conclusions should readers draw from the example with which Gladwell opens his essay—*Car and Driver*'s ranking of three sports cars? Gladwell writes, "A ranking can be heterogeneous, in other words, as long as it doesn't try to be too comprehensive. And it can be comprehensive as long as it doesn't try to measure things that are heterogeneous" (p. 371). What does he mean? How does the sports car example help to explain and support this idea?

2. Gladwell argues that the factors measured in *U.S. News & World Report*'s college rankings are "proxies for educational quality." But what, in your view, is "educational quality"? Can you imagine a better way to measure it, or to

compare it from one educational institution to the next? Write an essay that explains your views.

3. Toward the end of the article, Gladwell discusses the ratio between "graduation rate performance" (or "efficacy") and "student selectivity" in the *U.S. News* rankings. In the 2011 rankings, writes Gladwell, *U.S. News* "gives twice as much weight to selectivity as it does to efficacy" (p. 381). But since then, according to the magazine's Web site, *U.S. News & World Report* has made "significant changes" to its methodology. For one thing, that ratio has now changed somewhat, with selectivity accounting for 12.5 percent of an institution's score, while efficacy still accounts for 7.5 percent of the score. However, Gladwell argues that rankings "are not benign. They enshrine very particular ideologies" (p. 381). Read the *U.S. News & World Report*'s explanation of its methodology on its Web site: www.usnews.com/education/best-colleges/articles/2013/09/09/how-us-news-calculated-the-2014-best-colleges-rankings. To what extent does it address Gladwell's concerns? Do the rankings continue to enshrine the same ideologies that Gladwell discerned in 2011, or have they changed significantly? If so, how?

4. Develop and propose a rating system of your own for a category of things that you know about—for example, songs or albums, books, video games, TV shows, or sports teams. You do not need to actually rank all the items within the category, only to develop an acceptable rating system. Identify appropriate "variables" and ways of gathering data, and assign appropriate weights to the variables. Then, drawing on Gladwell, write an essay that makes an argument for your rating system. Explain the system's strengths, but also acknowledge any weaknesses you can detect. (Probably no rating system can be perfect.)

Adam Gopnik

Adam Gopnik (b. 1956) is a staff writer for the *New Yorker* magazine and the author of five books. He has earned a reputation as a master of the familiar essay, the kind of essay that, in the manner of Charles Lamb (1775–1834) or E. B. White (1899–1985), conveys observations about contemporary life in a warm, companionable voice. Much of the charm of these essays comes from the sense of a genuine personality speaking directly to the reader. But Gopnik is a learned as well as an entertaining writer, and though he wears his learning lightly, the remarkable range of historical and cultural reference in his essays is essential to their interest. In a 2001 interview with Robert Birnbaum, he remarked, "I'm an addicted reader. My wife teases me because I read in the shower, when I'm shaving. I read incessantly. I need to be reading a lot. A lot of what I write—I hope it's not too bookish—comes from other books."

Gopnik was born in Philadelphia and grew up in Montreal, Canada, where his parents taught at McGill University. After earning a BA at McGill, Gopnik moved to New York to study art history at the Institute of Fine Arts, New York University. Without completing his doctorate, he began working as a writer and an editor, first at *GQ Magazine* and later at Knopf publishing house. In 1986, he began contributing to the *New Yorker* with the essay "Quattrocento Baseball," which reflected on the connections between professional baseball and Italian Renaissance painting. The magazine soon hired him as a staff writer, and his essays began to appear frequently.

In 1995, the *New Yorker* sent him, with his wife and young son, to Paris, France, to contribute a regular column, "Paris Journal." A number of these essays were eventually published as *Paris to the Moon* (2000). After five years abroad, Gopnik and his family returned to New York (now with a second child, Olivia), where he continued to contribute regularly to the *New Yorker*, often focusing on his experience as a father and on life in New York, now seen through fresh eyes. A number of these pieces were collected as *Through the Children's Gate* (2006). The following essay, "Bumping into Mr. Ravioli," first appeared in the *New Yorker* in September 2002.

Like many of Gopnik's essays, "Bumping into Mr. Ravioli" does not announce a clear argument in its opening paragraphs but rather begins with a puzzle or minor problem of sorts that occasions an informal research project, one that eventually takes in child psychology, social history, the history of technology, the social milieu of New York, and other themes. At the end, the essay takes an unexpected turn; whether this represents a "conclusion" may be up for discussion, but certainly Gopnik has shed new light on the problem of his daughter's too-busy friends.

Bumping into Mr. Ravioli

My daughter, Olivia, who just turned three, has an imaginary friend whose name is   1
Charlie Ravioli. Olivia is growing up in Manhattan, and so Charlie Ravioli has a lot of
local traits: he lives in an apartment "on Madison and Lexington," he dines on grilled
chicken, fruit, and water, and, having reached the age of seven and a half, he feels, or is
thought, "old." But the most peculiarly local thing about Olivia's imaginary playmate
is this: he is always too busy to play with her. She holds her toy cell phone up to her
ear, and we hear her talk into it: "Ravioli? It's Olivia . . . It's Olivia. Come and play? OK.
Call me. Bye." Then she snaps it shut and shakes her head. "I always get his machine,"
she says. Or she will say, "I spoke to Ravioli today." "Did you have fun?" my wife and I
ask. "No. He was busy working. On a television" (leaving it up in the air if he repairs
electronic devices or has his own talk show).

On a good day, she "bumps into" her invisible friend and they go to a coffee shop.   2
"I bumped into Charlie Ravioli," she announces at dinner (after a day when, of course,
she stayed home, played, had a nap, had lunch, paid a visit to the Central Park Zoo,
and then had another nap). "We had coffee, but then he had to run." She sighs, sometimes, at her inability to make their schedules mesh, but she accepts it as inevitable,
just the way life is. "I bumped into Charlie Ravioli today," she says. "He was working."
Then she adds brightly, "But we hopped into a taxi." What happened then? we ask.
"We grabbed lunch," she says.

It seemed obvious that Ravioli was a romantic figure of the big exotic life that   3
went on outside her little limited life of parks and playgrounds — drawn, in particular,
from a nearly perfect, mynah bird–like imitation of the words she hears her mother
use when she talks about *her* day with *her* friends. ("How was your day?" Sighing: "Oh,
you know. I tried to make a date with Meg, but I couldn't find her, so I left a message
on her machine. Then I bumped into Emily after that meeting I had in SoHo, and we
had coffee and then she had to run, but by then Meg had reached me on my cell and
we arranged . . .") I was concerned, though, that Charlie Ravioli might also be the sign
of some "trauma," some loneliness in Olivia's life reflected in imaginary form. "It
seems odd to have an imaginary playmate who's always too busy to play with you,"
Martha, my wife, said to me. "Shouldn't your imaginary playmate be someone you tell
secrets to and, I don't know, sing songs with? It shouldn't be someone who's always
hopping into taxis."

We thought, at first, that her older brother, Luke, might be the original of Charlie   4
Ravioli. (For one thing, he is also seven and a half, though we were fairly sure that this

age was merely Olivia's marker for As Old as Man Can Be.) He *is* too busy to play with her much anymore. He has become a true New York child, with the schedule of a cabinet secretary: chess club on Monday, T-ball on Tuesday, tournament on Saturday, play dates and after-school conferences to fill in the gaps. But Olivia, though she counts days, does not yet really *have* days. She has *a* day, and into this day she has introduced the figure of Charlie Ravioli — in order, it dawned on us, to insist that she does have days, because she is too harried to share them, that she does have an independent social life, by virtue of being too busy to have one.

Yet Charlie Ravioli was becoming so constant and oddly discouraging a companion — "He canceled lunch. Again," Olivia would say — that we thought we ought to look into it. One of my sisters is a developmental psychologist who specializes in close scientific studies of what goes on inside the heads of one- and two- and three-year-olds. Though she grew up in the nervy East, she lives in California now, where she grows basil in her garden and jars her own organic marmalades. I e-mailed this sister for help with the Ravioli issue — how concerned should we be? — and she sent me back an e-mail, along with an attachment, and, after several failed cell-phone connections, we at last spoke on a land line.

It turned out that there is a recent book on this very subject by the psychologist Marjorie Taylor, called *Imaginary Companions and the Children Who Create Them,* and my sister had just written a review of it. She insisted that Charlie Ravioli was nothing to be worried about. Olivia was right on target, in fact. Most under-sevens (sixty-three percent, to be scientific) have an invisible friend, and children create their imaginary playmates not out of trauma but out of a serene sense of the possibilities of fiction — sometimes as figures of pure fantasy, sometimes, as Olivia had done, as observations of grownup manners assembled in tranquility and given a name. I learned about the invisible companions Taylor studied: Baintor, who is invisible because he lives in the light; Station Pheta, who hunts sea anemones on the beach. Charlie Ravioli seemed pavement-bound by comparison.

"An imaginary playmate isn't any kind of trauma marker," my sister said. "It's just the opposite: it's a sign that the child is now confident enough to begin to understand how to organize her experience into stories." The significant thing about imaginary friends, she went on, is that the kids know they're fictional. In an instant message on AOL, she summed it up: "The children with invisible friends often interrupted the interviewer to remind her, with a certain note of concern for her sanity, that these characters were, after all, just pretend."

I also learned that some children, as they get older, turn out to possess what child psychologists call a "paracosm." A paracosm is a society thought up by a child — an invented universe with a distinctive language, geography, and history. (The Brontës invented a couple of paracosms when they were children.) Not all children who have an imaginary friend invent a paracosm, but the two might, I think, be related. Like a lonely ambassador from Alpha Centauri in a fifties sci-fi movie who, misunderstood by paranoid Earth scientists, cannot bring the life-saving news from his planet, perhaps the invisible friend also gets an indifferent or hostile response, and then we never find out about the beautiful paracosm he comes from.

> *" 'Don't worry about it,' my sister said in a late-night phone call. "*

"Don't worry about it," my sister said in a late-night phone call. "Knowing something's made up while thinking that it matters is what all fiction insists on. She's putting a name on a series of manners." 9

"But he seems so real to her," I objected. 10

"Of course he is. I mean, who's more real to you, Becky Sharp or Gandalf or the guy down the hall? Giving a manner a name makes it real." 11

I paused. "I grasp that it's normal for her to have an imaginary friend," I said, "but have you ever heard of an imaginary friend who's too busy to play with you?" 12

She thought about it. "No," she said. "I'm sure that doesn't occur anywhere in the research literature. That sounds *completely* New York." And then she hung up. 13

The real question, I saw, was not "Why this friend?" but "Why this fiction?" Why, as Olivia had seen so clearly, are grownups in New York so busy, and so obsessed with the language of busyness that it dominates their conversation? Why are New Yorkers always bumping into Charlie Ravioli and grabbing lunch, instead of sitting down with him and exchanging intimacies, as friends should, as people do in Paris and Rome? Why is busyness the stuff our children make their invisible friends from, as country children make theirs from light and sand? 14

This seems like an odd question. New Yorkers are busy for obvious reasons: they have husbands and wives and careers and children, they have the Gauguin show to see and their personal trainers and accountants to visit. But the more I think about this, the more I think it is — well, a lot of Ravioli. We are instructed to believe that we are busier because we have to work harder to be more productive, but everybody knows that busyness and productivity have a dubious, arm's-length relationship. Most of our struggle in New York, in fact, is to be less busy in order to do more work. 15

Constant, exhausting, no-time-to-meet-your-friends Charlie Ravioli–style busyness arrived as an affliction in modern life long after the other parts of bourgeois city 16 manners did. Business long predates busyness. In the seventeenth and eighteenth centuries, when bourgeois people were building the institutions of bourgeois life, they seem never to have complained that they were too busy — or, if they did, they left no record of it. Samuel Pepys, who had a navy to refloat and a burned London to rebuild, often uses the word "busy" but never complains of busyness. For him, the word "busy" is a synonym for "happy," not for "stressed." Not once in his diary does Pepys cancel lunch or struggle to fit someone in for coffee at four-thirty. Pepys works, makes love, and goes to bed, but he does not bump and he does not have to run. Ben Franklin, a half century later, boasts of his industriousness, but he, too, never complains about being busy, and always has time to publish a newspaper or come up with a maxim or swim the ocean or invent the lightning rod.

Until sometime in the middle of the nineteenth century, in fact, the normal afflic-   17
tion of the bourgeois was not busyness at all but its apparent opposite: boredom. It has even been argued that the grid of streets and cafés and small engagements in the nineteenth-century city — the whole of social life — was designed self-consciously as an escape from that numbing boredom. (Working people weren't bored, of course, but they were engaged in labor, not work. They were too busy to be busy.) Baudelaire, basically, was so bored that he had to get drunk and run out onto the boulevard in the hope of bumping into somebody.

Turn to the last third of the nineteenth century and the beginning of the twen-   18
tieth, though, and suddenly everybody is busy, and everybody is complaining about it. Pepys, master of His Majesty's Navy, may never have complained of busyness, but Virginia Woolf, mistress of motionless lull, is continually complaining about how she spends her days racing across London from square to square, just like — well, like Charlie Ravioli. Ronald Firbank is wrung out by his social obligations; Proust is constantly rescheduling rendezvous and apologizing for being overstretched. Henry James, with nothing particular to do save live, complains of being too busy all the time. He could not shake the world of obligation, he said, and he wrote a strange and beautiful story, "The Great Good Place," which begins with an exhausting flood of correspondence, telegrams, and manuscripts that drive the protagonist nearly mad.

What changed? That James story helps supply the key. It was trains and tele-   19
grams. The railroads ended isolation, and packed the metropolis with people whose work was defined by a complicated network of social obligations. Pepys's network in 1669 London was, despite his official position, relatively small compared even with that of a minor aesthete like Firbank, two centuries later. Pepys had more time to make love because he had fewer friends to answer.

If the train crowded our streets, the telegram crowded our minds. It introduced 20 something into the world which remains with us today: a whole new class of communications that are defined as incomplete in advance of their delivery. A letter, though it may enjoin a response, is meant to be complete in itself. Neither the Apostle Paul nor Horace Walpole ever ends an epistle with "Give me a call and let's discuss." By contrast, it is in the nature of the telegram to be a skeletal version of another thing — a communication that opens more than it closes. The nineteenth-century telegram came with those busy threatening words "Letter follows."

Every device that has evolved from the telegram shares the same character. 21 E-mails end with a suggestion for a phone call ("Anyway, let's meet and/or talk soon"), faxes with a request for an e-mail, answering-machine messages with a request for a fax. All are devices of perpetually suspended communication. My wife recalls a moment last fall when she got a telephone message from a friend asking her to check her e-mail apropos a phone call she needed to make vis-à-vis a fax they had both received asking for more information about a bed they were thinking of buying from Ireland online and having sent to America by Federal Express — a grand slam of incomplete communication.

In most of the Western world outside New York, the press of trains and of tele- 22 graphic communication was alleviated by those other two great transformers: the car and the television. While the train and the telegram (and their love children, subways and commuter trains and e-mail) pushed people together, the car and the television pulled people apart — taking them out to the suburbs and sitting them down in front of a solo spectacle. New York, though, almost uniquely, got hit by a double dose of the first two technologies, and a very limited dose of the second two. Car life — car obsessions, car-defined habits — is more absent here than almost anywhere else in the country, while television, though obviously present, is less fatally prevalent here. New York is still a subject of television, and we compare *Sex and the City* to sex and the city; they are not yet quite the same. Here two grids of busyness remain dominant: the nineteenth- and early-twentieth-century grid of bump and run, and the late-twentieth- and early-twenty-first-century postmodern grid of virtual call and echo. Busyness is felt so intently here because we are both crowded and overloaded. We exit the apartment into a still dense nineteenth-century grid of street corners and restaurants full of people, and come home to the late-twentieth-century grid of faxes and e-mails and overwhelming incompleteness.

> *"Busyness is felt so intently here because we are both crowded and overloaded."*

We walk across the Park on a Sunday morning and bump into our friend the baker 23
and our old acquaintance from graduate school (what the hell is she doing now?) and
someone we have been avoiding for three weeks. They all invite us for brunch, and we
would love to, but we are too . . . busy. We bump into Charlie Ravioli, and grab a coffee
with him — and come home to find three e-mails and a message on our cell phone from
him, wondering where we are. The crowding of our space has been reinforced by a
crowding of our time, and the only way to protect ourselves is to build structures of perpetual deferral: I'll see you next week, let's talk soon. We build rhetorical baffles around
our lives to keep the crowding out, only to find that we have let nobody we love in.

Like Charlie Ravioli, we hop into taxis and leave messages on answering machines 24
to avoid our acquaintances, and find that we keep missing our friends. I have one intimate who lives just across the Park from me, whom I e-mail often, and whom I am fortunate to see two or three times a year. We are always . . . busy. He has become my Charlie
Ravioli, my invisible friend. I am sure that he misses me — just as Charlie Ravioli, I realized, must tell his other friends that he is sorry he does not see Olivia more often.

Once I sensed the nature of his predicament, I began to feel more sympathetic toward 25
Charlie Ravioli. I got to know him better, too. We learned more about what Ravioli did in
the brief breathing spaces in his busy life when he could sit down with Olivia and dish.
"Ravioli read your book," Olivia announced, for instance, one night at dinner. "He didn't
like it much." We also found out that Ravioli had joined a gym, that he was going to the
beach in the summer, but he was too busy, and that he was working on a "show." ("It isn't
a very good show," she added candidly.) Charlie Ravioli, in other words, was just another
New Yorker: fit, opinionated, and trying to break into show business.

I think we would have learned to live happily with Charlie Ravioli had it not been 26
for the appearance of Laurie. She threw us badly. At dinner, Olivia had been mentioning a new personage almost as often as she mentioned Ravioli. "I talked to Laurie
today," she would begin. "She says Ravioli is busy." Or she would be closeted with her
play phone. "Who are you talking to, darling?" I would ask. "Laurie," she would say.
"We're talking about Ravioli." We surmised that Laurie was, so to speak, the Linda
Tripp[1] of the Ravioli operation — the person you spoke to for consolation when the
big creep was ignoring you.

---

[1] Linda Tripp was a confidante of Monica Lewinsky, the White House intern whose sexual relationship with
President Bill Clinton caused a scandal and led to his impeachment by the House of Representatives in
1998. Tripp illegally recorded her telephone conversations with Lewinsky and, in exchange for immunity
from prosecution, turned the tapes over to Independent Counsel Kenneth Starr. [Editor's note]

But a little while later a more ominous side of Laurie's role began to appear. "Lau- 27
rie, tell Ravioli I'm calling," I heard Olivia say. I pressed her about who, exactly, Laurie
was. Olivia shook her head. "She works for Ravioli," she said.

And then it came to us, with sickening clarity: Laurie was not the patient friend 28
who consoled you for Charlie's absence. Laurie was the bright-toned person who
answered Ravioli's phone and told you that unfortunately Mr. Ravioli was in a meeting.
"Laurie says Ravioli is too busy to play," Olivia announced sadly one morning. Things
seemed to be deteriorating; now Ravioli was too busy even to say he was too busy.

I got back on the phone with my sister. "Have you ever heard of an imaginary 29
friend with an assistant?" I asked.

She paused. "Imaginary friends don't have assistants," she said. "That's not only 30
not in the literature. That's just . . . I mean — in California they don't have assistants."

"You think we should look into it?" 31

"I think you should move," she said flatly. 32

Martha was of the same mind. "An imaginary playmate shouldn't have an assis- 33
tant," she said miserably. "An imaginary playmate shouldn't have an agent. An imaginary playmate shouldn't have a publicist or a personal trainer or a caterer — an
imaginary playmate shouldn't have . . . *people*. An imaginary playmate should just
play. With the child who imagined it." She started leaving on my pillow real-estate
brochures picturing quaint houses in New Jersey and Connecticut, unhaunted by
busy invisible friends and their entourages.

Not long after the appearance of Laurie, though, something remarkable happened. 34
Olivia would begin to tell us tales of her frustrations with Charlie Ravioli, and, after tell-
ing us, again, that he was too busy to play, she would tell us what she had done instead.
Astounding and paracosmic tall tales poured out of her: she had been to a chess tournament and brought home a trophy; she had gone to a circus and told jokes. Searching for
Charlie Ravioli, she had "saved all the animals in the zoo"; heading home in a taxi after a
quick coffee with Ravioli, she took over the steering wheel and "got all the moneys."
From the stalemate of daily life emerged the fantasy of victory. She had dreamed of a
normal life with a few close friends, and had to settle for worldwide fame and the front
page of the tabloids. The existence of an imaginary friend had liberated her into a paracosm, but it was a curiously New York paracosm — it was the unobtainable world outside her window. Charlie Ravioli, prince of busyness, was not an end but a means: a way
out onto the street in her head, a declaration of potential independence.

Busyness is our art form, our civic ritual, our way of being us. Many friends have 35
said to me that they love New York now in a way they never did before, and their love,

I've noticed, takes for its object all the things that used to exasperate them — the curious combination of freedom, self-made fences, and paralyzing preoccupation that the city provides. "How did you spend the day?" Martha and I now ask each other, and then, instead of listing her incidents, she says merely, "Oh, you know . . . just . . . bumping into Charlie Ravioli," meaning, just bouncing from obligation to electronic entreaty, just spotting a friend and snatching a sandwich, just being busy, just living in New York. If everything we've learned in the past year could be summed up in a phrase, it's that we want to go on bumping into Charlie Ravioli for as long as we can.

Olivia still hopes to have him to herself someday. As I work late at night in the "study" (an old hallway, an Aalto screen) I keep near the "nursery" (an ancient pantry, a glass-brick wall), I can hear her shift into pre-sleep, still muttering to herself. She is still trying to reach her closest friend. "Ravioli? Ravioli?" she moans as she turns over into her pillow and clutches her blanket, and then she whispers, almost to herself, "Tell him call me. Tell him call me when he comes home." 36

Questions for Discussion and Writing

1. How would you describe the problem that Gopnik faces at the beginning of the essay? How does his understanding of the problem change as the essay proceeds? Does the essay offer any sort of solution to the problem? If so, what sort of solution is it? How would you describe the results of Gopnik's inquiry?

2. How does this inquiry, this research project, proceed? What are the stages in the exploration, and how do Gopnik's questions push it forward? At what points does Gopnik turn to some new source? Where does he turn, and why? What are the major turning points in the exploration? (Notice the breaks between sections of the essay.) What lesser twists and turns do you notice?

3. We often hear that technology is changing our way of life, but Gopnik approaches the issue from the standpoint of particularly precious and intimate relationships — childhood and the world of imaginary friends. Gopnik wrote this essay in 2002; since then, of course, communication technologies have continued to make rapid strides. How do you experience and understand the ways that communication technologies — including social networking and texting — are affecting your own life and the lives of others? How do you think these new technologies make your life different from the experiences of previous generations? How do these technologies define life for your generation? What do you imagine the future will bring? And what is the value of looking back to the past for insight, as Gopnik does?

Jane McGonigal

Jane McGonigal (b. 1977) is the author of *Reality Is Broken: Why Games Make Us Better and How They Can Change the World* (2011) and director of game research and development at the Institute for the Future, a nonprofit think tank based in Palo Alto, California. Born in Philadelphia and raised in Moorestown, New Jersey, McGonigal earned a BA in English from Fordham University (1999) and a PhD in performance studies from the University of California, Berkeley (2006). She has taught game design and game theory at the University of California, Berkeley, and at the San Francisco Art Institute. She also invented the online game *SuperBetter*, which is designed to help people recover from illness or injury by developing their resilience. McGonigal's work has been influenced by "positive psychology," a movement that focuses on increasing happiness rather than on alleviating illness. In the following article, which appeared in the *Wall Street Journal* in January 2011, McGonigal offers a condensed version of her book's argument that surmounting the challenges presented by video games can help players solve real-world problems as well.

Could games like *Guitar Hero* help cure cancer and end poverty? (Source: Sandy Huffaker/Zumapress.com)

Be a Gamer, Save the World

We often think of immersive computer and video games — like *Farmville*, *Guitar Hero*, and *World of Warcraft* — as "escapist," a kind of passive retreat from reality. Many critics consider such games a mind-numbing waste of time, if not a corrupting influence. But the truth about games is very nearly the opposite. In today's society, they consistently fulfill genuine human needs that the real world fails to satisfy. More than that, they may prove to be a key resource for solving some of our most pressing real-world problems.

Hundreds of millions of people around the globe are already devoting larger and larger chunks of time to this alternate reality. Collectively, we spend three billion hours a week gaming. In the United States, where there are 183 million active gamers, video games took in about $15.5 billion last year. And though a typical gamer plays for just an hour or two a day, there are now more than five million "extreme" gamers in the U.S. who play an average of 45 hours a week. To put this in perspective, the number of hours that gamers world-wide have spent playing *World of Warcraft* alone adds up to 5.93 million years.

> *"But as they devote more of their free time to game worlds, they often feel that the real world is missing something."*

These gamers aren't rejecting reality entirely, of course. They have careers, goals, schoolwork, families, and real lives that they care about. But as they devote more of their free time to game worlds, they often feel that the real world is missing something.

Gamers want to know: Where in the real world is the gamer's sense of being fully alive, focused, and engaged in every moment? The real world just doesn't offer up the same sort of carefully designed pleasures, thrilling challenges, and powerful social bonding that the gamer finds in virtual environments. Reality doesn't motivate us as effectively. Reality isn't engineered to maximize our potential or to make us happy.

Those who continue to dismiss games as merely escapist entertainment will find themselves at a major disadvantage in the years ahead, as more gamers start to harness this power for real good. My research over the past decade at the University of California, Berkeley, and the Institute for the Future has shown that games consistently provide us with the four ingredients that make for a happy and meaningful life: satisfying work, real hope for success, strong social connections, and the chance to become a part of something bigger than ourselves.

We get these benefits from our real lives sometimes, but we get them almost every time we play a good game. These benefits are what positive psychologists call intrinsic rewards — we don't play games to make money, improve our social status, or achieve any external signposts of success. And these intrinsic rewards, studies at the University of Pennsylvania, Harvard, and U.C. Berkeley have shown, provide the foundation for optimal human experience.

In a good game, we feel blissfully productive. We have clear goals and a sense of   7
heroic purpose. More important, we're constantly able to see and feel the impact of our efforts on the virtual world around us. As a result, we have a stronger sense of our own agency — and we are more likely to set ambitious real-life goals. One recent study found, for example, that players of *Guitar Hero* are more likely to pick up a real guitar and learn how to play it.

When we play, we also have a sense of urgent optimism. We believe whole-   8
heartedly that we are up to any challenge, and we become remarkably resilient in the face of failure. Research shows that gamers spend on average 80% of their time failing in game worlds, but instead of giving up, they stick with the difficult challenge and use the feedback of the game to get better. With some effort, we can learn to apply this resilience to the real-world challenges we face.

Games make it easy to build stronger social bonds with our friends and family.   9
Studies show that we like and trust someone better after we play a game with them — even if they beat us. And we're more likely to help someone in real life after we've helped them in an online game. It's no wonder that 40% of all user time on Facebook is spent playing social games. They're a fast and reliable way to strengthen our connection with people we care about.

Today's video games are increasingly created on an epic scale, with compelling   10
stories, sweeping mythologies, and massive multiplayer environments that produce feelings of awe and wonder. Researchers on positive emotion have found that whenever we feel awe or wonder, we become more likely to serve a larger cause and to collaborate selflessly with others.

> **"*Studies show that we like and trust someone better after we play a game with them — even if they beat us.*"**

With so much blissful productivity and urgent   11
optimism, stronger social bonds and extreme cooperation, it's not surprising that so many players feel that they become the best version of themselves in games. That's one of the reasons I believe we can take the benefits of games a step further. We can harness the power of game design to tackle real-world problems. We can empower gamers to use their virtual-world strengths to accomplish real feats. Indeed, when game communities have been matched with challenging

real-world problems, they have already proven themselves capable of producing tangible, potentially world-changing results.

In 2010, more than 57,000 gamers were listed as co-authors for a research   12
paper in the prestigious scientific journal *Nature*. The gamers — with no previous background in biochemistry — had worked in a 3D game environment called *Foldit*, folding virtual proteins in new ways that could help cure cancer or prevent Alzheimer's. The game was developed by scientists at the University of Washington who believed that gamers could outperform supercomputers at this creative task — and the players proved them right, beating the supercomputers at more than half of the game's challenges.

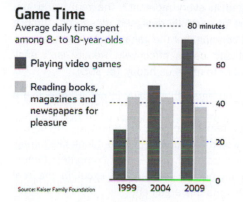

Game Time

Average daily time spent among 8- to 18-year-olds

- Playing video games
- Reading books, magazines and newspapers for pleasure

Source: Kaiser Family Foundation

1999   2004   2009

80 minutes
60
40
20
0

More recently, more than 19,000   13
players of *EVOKE*, an online game that I created for the World Bank Institute, undertook real-world missions to improve food security, increase access to clean energy, and end poverty in more than 130 countries. The game focused on building up players' abilities to design and launch their own social enterprises.

After 10 weeks, they had founded   14
more than 50 new companies — real businesses working today from South Africa and India to Buffalo, N.Y. My favorite is Libraries Across Africa, a new franchise system that empowers local entrepreneurs to set up free community libraries. It also creates complementary business opportunities for selling patrons refreshments, WiFi access, and cellphone time. The first is currently being tested in Gabon.

These examples are just the beginning of what is possible if we take advantage   15
of the power of games to make us better and change the world. Those who understand this power will be the people who invent our future. We can create rewarding, transformative games for ourselves and our families; for our schools, businesses, and neighborhoods; for an entire industry or an entirely new movement.

We can play any games we want. We can create any future we can imagine.   16
Let the games begin.

Questions for Discussion and Writing

1. Should video gaming become part of the American high school curriculum? Write an essay for or against this idea. If you are familiar with particular computer games and the skills they require or develop, draw on that experience in your argument. (How are those skills relevant to skills needed in the "real world"?)

2. McGonigal describes some specialized real-world problem-solving games, but she also suggests that "the real world is missing something":

   > Gamers want to know: Where in the real world is the gamer's sense of being fully alive, focused, and engaged in every moment? The real world just doesn't offer up the same sort of carefully designed pleasures, thrilling challenges, and powerful social bonding that the gamer finds in virtual environments. Reality doesn't motivate us as effectively. Reality isn't engineered to maximize our potential or to make us happy. (p. 395)

   Write a response to this idea. Do you agree that reality is not as effective a motivator as video games?

3. McGonigal makes a forceful and perhaps surprising argument for the educational value of video games. What would the counterargument look like? Imagine the argument for the opposing point of view—that computer games, however enjoyable, do *not* teach us how to succeed or excel in the real world—and write an essay that presents this argument.

Emily Esfahani Smith

Emily Esfahani Smith (b. 1987) is the "Manners & Morals" columnist for the *New Criterion*, a monthly review of "the arts and intellectual life," as well as managing editor of the online journal *Defining Ideas*, published by the Hoover Institution at Stanford University. She is also editor-in-chief of *Acculturated*, an online magazine that explores the meaning and influences of popular culture. Esfahani Smith was born in Zurich, Switzerland, grew up in Montreal, Canada, and attended Dartmouth College and the University of Pennsylvania before establishing a career as a writer and an editor in New York. In the following essay that appeared in the *New Criterion* in October 2013, Esfahani Smith argues that "hyper-individualism" is causing Americans to become not only more isolated from each other but also more anxious and unhappy.

Life on the Island

Emile Durkheim, the father of sociology, died nearly a hundred years ago, but his insights about society and culture seem more relevant now than ever. To understand why, it's worth turning to the French intellectual's groundbreaking empirical study *Suicide* (1897). Durkheim wanted to understand why people killed themselves. Why do some European societies, he wondered, have higher suicide rates than others? It's an interesting question, one that he answered by looking at the relationship between suicide in men and variables like marriage, education levels, and religious orientation. 1

Here in the West, we take individualism and freedom to be foundational to the good life. But Durkheim's research revealed a more complicated picture. He concluded that people kill themselves more when they are alienated from their communities and community institutions. "Men don't thrive as rugged individualists making their mark on the frontier," the University of Virginia sociologist W. Bradford Wilcox pointed out recently: "In fact, men seem to be much more likely to end up killing themselves if they don't have traditional support systems." Places where individualism is the supreme value; places where people are excessively self-sufficient; places that look a lot like twenty-first-century America — individuals don't flourish in these environments, but suicide does. 2

For instance, fewer Catholics, Durkheim found, killed themselves than Protestants, who were, for the most part, better educated than their Catholic peers but less bound by their community. Educated people tend to leave their communities to 3 pursue career advancement — and, thanks to their education, they also are more likely to challenge traditional societal values, something that parents of college-aged students today know all about. Durkheim discovered an exception to this trend among Jewish people. Despite being highly educated, they were also community-oriented, which buffered against suicide. Other factors that strengthened the community, like being a nation at war or having strong marital bonds, were associated with lower suicide rates.

> *"Despite being heavily educated, they were also community-oriented, which buffered against suicide."*

Durkheim's work emphasizes the importance of community life. Without the constraints, traditions, and shared values of the community, society enters into a state of what Durkheim called *anomie*, or normlessness. This freedom, far from leading to happiness, often leads to depression and social decay (as the "twerking" Miley Cyrus perfectly exemplified recently at the Video Music Awards). Durkheim thought that the constraints — if not excessive — imposed on individuals by the community ultimately helped people lead good lives. 4

But we live in a culture where communitarian ideals, like duty and tradition, are withering away. Even conservatives, who should be the natural allies of these virtues, have in large part become the champions of an individualism that seems to value freedom, the market, and material prosperity above all else, leaving little room for the more traditional values that well-known thinkers like Russell Kirk and Richard Weaver cherished. "Man is constantly being assured today that he has more power than ever before in history," wrote Weaver in *Ideas Have Consequences* (1948), "but his daily experience is one of powerlessness. . . . If he is with a business organization, the odds are great that he has sacrificed every other kind of independence in return for that dubious one known as financial." 5

Over the summer, I came across a new study published in *Psychological Science* which brought some of these Durkheimian ideas to mind. The study, by the social scientist Patricia M. Greenfield at the University of California in Los Angeles, examined how American culture changed during the decisive post-Enlightenment years between 1800 and 2000. During this period, the American population — like the world population at large — experienced a major transformation that Weaver, with his agrarian sympathies, followed with distress. People were increasingly leaving behind their rural communities in pursuit of the big city and the opportunities they hoped to find 6 there. "The more closely people are crowded together," Weaver complained of urban life, "the less they know one another."

In 1800, about 95 percent of the American population was rural — that is, people 7 lived in communities with fewer than 2,500 people. Around 1840, people increasingly started moving to urban areas, leaving their rural homes behind — and after 1920, more people were living in urban centers than in rural locales. By 2000, nearly eight out of ten Americans were living in urban areas.

How did this mass migration affect the culture? That's the question Greenfield 8 answered with the help of an interesting new tool called the Google Books Ngram Viewer. This comprehensive database of more than five million digitized books published between 1500 and 2008 lets us see what the culture values and is discussing at any given point. If you enter a word or phrase into the database, it can quickly determine how its frequency has changed over time. In other words, the Google Books Ngram Viewer gives us a quick snapshot of cultural change.

Greenfield was particularly interested in how our culture changed from a more 9 communitarian to a more individualistic ethos over the last two centuries. Here is what she found: as the population became more urbanized, the books of the time mentioned "duty" and "obliged" less and less and mentioned "choose" and "decision" more and more. The crossover occurred right after the 1920s — that was when the books started focusing more on individualistic values than community-oriented ones. Greenfield also unearthed a troubling trend: the use of the words "get" and "acquisition" increased while the frequency of the words "give" and "benevolence" decreased, suggesting a rise in materialism and self-concern, and a fall in being caring and focused on others.

A further consequence of our culture becoming more individualistic over the last 10 two hundred years is that it has also — disturbingly — become more self-absorbed. Greenfield found that over the same period that individualism and urbanization were on the rise, the frequency of words like "authority," "belong," "obedience," and "pray" decreased, while the use of words like "unique," "individual," "self," and "ego" increased. The irony is that as people came together in urban centers, those values that bound people together — those values that put a check on the ego — fell out of fashion.

The reign of ego — this individualism-on-steroids — has another name: narcis- 11 sism. In 1979, during a decade famous for self-obsession, the neo-Marxist-turned-iconoclast historian Christopher Lasch argued, in his bestselling book *The Culture of Narcissism*, that the culture was in the throes of pathological "preoccupation with the self." Thirty years later, our psychologists have found that matters on this score have only gotten worse. In their 2009 book *The Narcissism Epidemic*, the social psychologists Jean Twenge and W. Keith Campbell cite compelling social science research to argue that in many aspects of society, people are focusing on themselves more than they are on others or the world at large.

> *"The reign of ego — this individualism-on-steroids — has another name: narcissism."*

Let's return to the Google Books Ngram Viewer to illustrate the point. When Twenge, Campbell, and their colleague Brittany Gentile analyzed books published between 1960 and 2008, they found that the use of words and phrases like "unique," "personalize," "self," "all about me," "I am special," and "I'm the best" significantly increased 12 over time. Of course, it is not just in our books where this narcissism appears. It is also throughout the popular culture, not least in pop music. When a group of researchers, including Campbell and Twenge, looked at the lyrics of the most popular songs from 1980 to 2007, they found that the songs became much more narcissistic and self-centered over time. In the past three decades, the researchers write, the "use of words related to self-focus and antisocial behavior increased, whereas words related to other-focus, social interactions, and positive emotion decreased."

Consider the song "Roar" by the pop starlet Katy Perry, which, at this writing, sits 13 at the top of the Billboard Hot 100 list. In the song, which is about self-expression, Perry refers to herself three times in the first verse alone:

> I used to bite my tongue and hold my breath
> Scared to rock the boat and make a mess
> So I sat quietly, agreed politely
> I guess that I forgot I had a choice
> I let you push me past the breaking point
> I stood for nothing, so I fell for everything

It would certainly be easy to dismiss narcissists as vain egoists — easy and not 14 incorrect. (Later in the song, Perry sings, "I went from zero, to my own hero.") But the problem with narcissism, as Lasch pointed out in his book, is not just self-obsession. The problem with narcissism lies in the *consequences* of that self-obsession. Narcissists, he writes,

> may have paid more attention to their own needs than to those of others,
> but self-love and self-aggrandizement did not impress me as their most
> important characteristics. These qualities implied a strong, stable sense of

selfhood, whereas narcissists suffered from a feeling of inauthenticity and inner emptiness. They found it difficult to make connection with the world. At its most extreme, their condition approximated that of Kaspar Hauser, the nineteenth-century German foundling raised in solitary confinement, whose "impoverished relations with his cultural environment," according to the psychoanalyst Alexander Mitscherlich, left him with a feeling of being utterly at life's mercy.

This is precisely what we see happening in the culture at large. At a time when we are more connected digitally than ever before, at a time when we live closer together than ever before, rates of social isolation are rising at alarming rates. In 1985, when the General Social Survey asked Americans about the number of confidants they have in their lives, the most common response was three. The survey was given again in 2004 and the most common response was zero. Our connections to others are slowly dissolving, a trend that Harvard's Robert Putnam discussed in his 2000 book *Bowling Alone*. As community goes, so do the values that accompany social connections — values like duty and restraint. 15

Left unchecked by the constraints of the community, individualism has a nasty underside, as Durkheim came to see and as we are now seeing. This past spring, the Centers for Disease Control released an alarming study indicating that the suicide rates of middle-aged Americans aged 35–64 rose 30 percent between 1999 and 2010, with men taking their lives at higher rates than women. More generally across the population, rates of depression have increased tenfold since the 1950s. Young people have been particularly affected. Youth suicide, especially among boys, has risen over the past fifty years in most developed countries. 16

When Richard Eckersley and Keith Dear, two Australian researchers, looked at what is driving youth suicide, they found that, among males, it was associated with several measures of individualism, like personal freedom and control. According to Jean Twenge, levels of anxiety have also been increasing over the past five to six decades, among both adults and children. She has found that this increase in anxiety is linked to a decrease in social connectedness — one more reminder, on top of all the others, that social isolation is not man's natural state. 17

This is an insight that the English poet John Donne grasped long before psychologists and sociologists came to similar conclusions by looking at people and culture as data points. In his oft quoted lines he writes: 18

Any man's death diminishes me, because I am involved in mankind; and therefore never send to know for whom the bell tolls; it tolls for thee.

Though in certain important respects, individuals *are* increasingly living as islands — as isolated beings — Donne reminds us that the individual is not a discrete entity, untethered from those around him and his environment, operating independently in the world at large; he is, rather, part of something bigger, much bigger, than himself.

At the very least, he is part of some social unit. As Aristotle writes in his *Politics*, 19 "man is by nature a social animal":

> an individual who is unsocial naturally and not accidentally is either beneath our notice or more than human. Society is something that precedes the individual. Anyone who either cannot lead the common life or is so self-sufficient as not to need to, and therefore does not partake of society, is either a beast or a god.

Day by day, we are denying this fundamentally social aspect of our nature. We do so at our peril. As we look around the culture at the pathologies that are bubbling to its surface, it is clear that the hyper-individualism — the infatuation with the self — of the last several decades is partly to blame. Though individualism itself is not the problem, the manic individualism of modern life is. For people to thrive, individualism must be in balance with something bigger — it must be rooted in a community or a moral order. Otherwise, it will continue to reveal its dark underbelly in the form of social malaise.

Questions for Discussion and Writing

1. This essay concerns long-term cultural shifts that can be difficult to identify and measure. One of the sources that Esfahani Smith cites used Google's Ngram Viewer as part of its research. This tool is publicly available at books .google.com/ngrams, and you can use it to conduct research of your own on cultural trends over the last two centuries (or over a shorter span). Familiarize yourself with how the Ngram Viewer works by experimenting with it a bit; then choose a topic relating to cultural change and frame a question that can be explored using this tool. Choose search phrases and a "corpus" (the body of work that the Ngram Viewer will search) with care, and explain your choices and the results of your study in a short essay.

2. Cultural change over the course of decades — especially change concerned with subjective matters such as attitude and temperament — can be difficult to measure. Esfahani Smith draws her conclusions, in part, from research that

examines the frequency with which certain terms appear in books and song lyrics. What other methods might be employed to measure a cultural shift (if any) toward "hyper-individualism" and narcissism? In other words, what is another area of life or culture in which such a shift might express itself and become apparent? (Social media? Film?) How might a researcher measure a shift in this particular area?

3. At one point, Esfahani Smith quotes the English cleric John Donne (1572–1631). The quotation is from Meditation XVII of *Devotions upon Emergent Occasions*, which also includes the famous line, "No man is an island, entire of itself; every man is a piece of the continent, a part of the main." In the next paragraph, she quotes the ancient Greek philosopher Aristotle (384–322 BCE) to support her claims about the "fundamentally social aspect of our nature." What does the word "fundamentally" imply here? How does the "social aspect of our nature" reveal itself in a time of hyper-individualism and/or narcissism? Just how fundamental is it, in your view? Drawing on your own experience and observations, write a comment or brief essay on the "social aspect of our nature."

Documentation

Documentation and Scholarship

Documentation — the supplying of information on sources by means of notes and a bibliography — is a hallmark of scholarly writing. Every research paper and most analytical papers must include notes to show the source of all the ideas and infor-

> " [The footnote] lets us peer into the inner workshop of scholars. "
>
> **CHUCK ZERBY**

mation in the paper that are not the writer's own original thoughts or findings.

Scholarly work is fundamentally a collaborative enterprise. Scientists make new discoveries by conducting experiments that have been suggested by the work of other scientists. Historians and literary critics develop new insights by building on, improving upon, or correcting the work of other historians and literary critics. In every discipline, scholars learn from one another and move knowledge forward by sharing their ideas. As Isaac Newton famously put it, not long after the modern scientific method took hold, "If I have seen farther, it is only by standing on the shoulders of giants."[1] This basic truth about scholarly work explains why documentation is so important in academic writing. Indeed, the presence of footnotes and a bibliography, or some similar form of citation, almost defines a work as scholarly.

---

[1] Isaac Newton to Robert Hooke, 5 February 1675/6, in David Brewster, *Memoirs of the Life, Writings, and Discoveries of Sir Isaac Newton*, vol. 1 (Edinburgh: Thomas Constable, 1855), 142.

The Function of Citations in a Scholarly Conversation

Citations have a number of functions, including the following:

- Referencing an authority, as in "Here's my expert source for this claim."
- Referencing an argument, as in "This expert makes this claim here. You can examine the evidence and reasoning behind it for yourself if you wish."
- Referencing related material, as in "If you're interested in a full explanation of this topic, consult this source."
- Acknowledging that another individual or group deserves credit for an idea or for quoted material, as in "Here's where to find the source of this idea or quotation."

Citations—which might take the form of footnotes, endnotes, or in-text citations—serve several purposes in a scholarly work. First, they allow readers to retrace the writer's steps, verify the claims that the writer is making, and weigh the evidence for themselves. Second, citations make it possible for readers to identify the ideas that are really *new* in the work they are reading and to distinguish these new ideas from ones that have already been published elsewhere. Finally, citations tell readers where to look for a more complete discussion of matters that are perhaps not central to the topic at hand. Thus a good scholarly work, by means of its notes, *invites* the reader into the scholarly conversation, because it will show familiarity with (and cite) the most important books and articles that have already been published on the topic.

➔ Try This   Understanding Your School's Code of Academic Conduct

Many colleges and universities maintain a code of academic conduct or academic integrity and impose penalties on students who infringe it, ranging from grade penalties to expulsion. If your college publishes such a code, read it and consider what it implies about your responsibility to cite your sources and document them accurately.

Guidelines — **What to Cite**

You must cite *any* material that you draw from another work—including facts (other than common knowledge), words, ideas, statistics, and hypotheses. This includes material from texts, multimedia sources, lectures, e-mails, interviews, and even ideas that arise in class discussion if they are attributable to a specific person.

Always cite the following:

- Direct quotations
- Paraphrases or summaries of ideas from another work
- References to another work

You should not cite a thought that is your own or is common knowledge that cannot be attributed to any particular source. Common knowledge is information that most people know, the sort of information you would find in a *basic* dictionary, almanac, or encyclopedia—for example, a famous author's date of birth, a country's capital, or a well-known fact such as the name of the current president of the United States.

Do not cite the following:

- Your own ideas
- Common knowledge

→Try This — **Finding Where Citations Are Needed**

All citations have been omitted from the following paper. Place a check mark wherever you believe a citation is needed. Compare your results with those of your classmates and explain your decisions.

Soledad Gonzalez

Professor Takacs

Writing 101

5 March 2015

Do High School Students Share the Right to Free Speech?

In America, the right to free speech is enshrined in the Constitution's First Amendment, which states that "Congress shall make no law . . . abridging the freedom of speech, or of the press. . . ." However, the amendment does not specify whether it applies equally to every American or only to those who have reached the age of majority. An area that remains both unsettled and controversial concerns high school students and their right to question laws and school policies regarding the use of drugs. Should high school students be free to question and even advocate illicit drug use, without restriction? Or do teachers and administrators have the right to limit such speech and to punish students who disregard those limits? Do students have the right to encourage other students to try illegal drugs? In this essay, I will argue that, for better or worse, they do. And high school students' right to free speech should be protected except in rare instances when doing so would create a direct legal conflict for teachers and school administrators.

In 1969, the Supreme Court decided in the case of *Tinker v. Des Moines* that high school students had the right to wear armbands in support of a cease-fire during the Vietnam War. The decision had broad implications. As Justice Abe Fortas wrote for the majority,

> It can hardly be argued that either students or teachers shed their constitutional rights to freedom of speech or expression at the schoolhouse gate. . . . In the absence of a specific showing of constitutionally valid reasons to regulate their

speech, students are entitled to freedom of expression of their views.

Fortas makes it clear that the decision sought to ensure that high school students should enjoy the same right to free speech as adults.

More recently, however, the Supreme Court has imposed certain limits on high school students' speech. In 2007, it ruled in *Morse v. Frederick* that public schools "can punish students for advocating or promoting illegal drug use." This case concerned a high school principal's decision to impose a ten-day suspension on student Joseph Frederick, who had raised a banner reading "Bong Hits 4 Jesus" at a school event. The Court's 5-4 decision was vehemently opposed by the minority, however. Justice John Paul Stevens wrote in his dissenting opinion that the Court's decision "is deaf to the constitutional imperative to permit unfettered debate, even among high-school students, about the wisdom of the war on drugs or of legalizing marijuana for medical use."

Those who argue in favor of limits on students' speech note that school officials can be held liable for failing to maintain an environment that not only is drug-free but also clearly discourages illicit drug use. As Frederick Hess of the American Enterprise Institute claims, "If there are drugs in school, the public is going to come down hard on the schools for not doing enough to prevent drugs in the schools." However, freedom of speech in every circumstance demands that we keep a clear and firm distinction between words and deeds. To use or possess illicit drugs, to offer them to another student—these are deeds that differ fundamentally from words. While some kinds of speech, such as obscenity, hate speech, libel, and sedition, are clearly illegal, the freedom to question laws and engage in political debate is as necessary in high schools as in any public forum.

Gonzalez 3

Some worry that freedom of speech means that the loudest students can cause disruptions and distract students and faculty from their principal task: learning the high school curriculum. But this concerns a different kind of discipline, pertaining to the manner in which something is said, not the content.

Avoiding Plagiarism

A scholarly text does not stand alone but rather exists as a building block in a much larger and more solid structure of knowledge — a structure that continues to expand as insights accumulate and new discoveries are made, but one that would crumble if scholars were to stop linking their own work to others' work. So there are strong practical reasons for carefully documenting sources in scholarly work.

There are also ethical reasons for documenting sources. **Plagiarism** (which comes from the Latin word for "kidnapping") means presenting someone else's words or ideas as your own, without permission or acknowledgment. An act of plagiarism is a triple wrong. It cheats the writer whose work is stolen without credit. It also deceives readers, by misleading them about the true author of the work in front of them. And finally, it robs the plagiarist of an opportunity to think, learn, and create for himself or herself.

Most people prefer to be honest and honorable; the chief reason that some students end up plagiarizing is that, for whatever reason, they panic and think they have no other choice. Most frequently, students plagiarize because they fail to manage their time well or they underestimate the size of the project, and so they find themselves forced to produce a paper at the last minute. Under such circumstances, the temptation to plagiarize — maybe just to get a little too much help from a fellow student, maybe to cut corners when paraphrasing an online source — can be strong. So plan ahead. (See the sample schedules for writing a research paper on pp. 272–74.) The second reason that students sometimes plagiarize is that they feel overwhelmed by the difficulty of an assignment and feel incapable of completing it independently. If this happens, speak to your instructor and explain the problems you're having. The vast majority of instructors are eager to help their students get through such difficulties.

By far the most common sort of plagiarism, however, is unintended plagiarism. A student who does not understand the rules of documentation or the difference between a quotation and a paraphrase or the difference between an acceptable and an unacceptable paraphrase may commit an offense without meaning to do so. *But it is an offense nevertheless*. Every student is responsible for understanding the rules of citation and for knowing how to write an acceptable paraphrase. (See Chapter 10, "Writing an Acceptable Paraphrase," p. 328.)

Documentation in MLA, *Chicago*, and APA Styles

Because they have different needs, academic disciplines have developed distinct formats or styles for document design and citation. The Modern Language Association (MLA) style is widely used in composition and literature courses. The documentation system of *The Chicago Manual of Style* (*Chicago* or *CMS*) is used in many other humanities disciplines as well as in social sciences and in the fine arts. The American Psychological Association (APA) style is used in psychology and other social and behavioral sciences.

MLA format uses in-text citations that typically include just a page number and, if necessary, the author's name; the full citation appears in a Works Cited page at the end of the text. This format does not use footnotes, and endnotes are used only for information, not for citations. *Chicago* style provides the complete reference for a citation in a footnote at the bottom of the page on which the citation occurs or in an endnote at the end of the text. A bibliography or Works Cited page is optional. Like MLA style, APA style includes a list of references. Footnotes are not used for citations.

MLA Style

Main Features

In-text Citations Abbreviated citations occur in parentheses within the text. Complete bibliographical information appears in a list of Works Cited at the end of the paper. In-text citations may take several forms.

A page number is sufficient if the author's name is clearly given in the text.

> As J. Allan Mitchell observes, "Even this comparison underestimates Griselda, who can actually be said to exhibit the proverbial 'patience of Job' that Job lacks" (22).

If the author's identity is not clear from the text, include the author's last name and a page number in parentheses.

> The serfs "could not plead in court against their lord, no one spoke for them in Parliament, [and] they were bound by duties of servitude which they had no way to break except by forcibly obtaining a change of the rules" (Tuchman 373).

If no page number is available (for example, for material from a Web site), use the author's name or the first significant word or two of the title.

> For some weeks afterward, the revolt would break out here and there, but its back had been broken in a matter of days ("Peasants' Revolt").

Works Cited Page A Works Cited page at the end of the paper contains complete bibliographical information for each citation.

The entry for a book includes the name of the author(s), the title in italics, the city of publication, the publisher, the year of publication, and the medium (such as print or Web).

> Miller, Robert P. *Chaucer Sources and Backgrounds*. New York: Oxford UP, 1977. Print.

The entry for an article includes the name of the author(s), the title of the article in quotation marks, the title of the journal in italics, the volume number, the year, the page range, and the medium.

> Ginsberg, Warren. "'And Speketh So Pleyn': *The Clerk's Tale* and Its Teller." *Criticism* 20 (1978): 307-23. Print.

In addition to the information required for print sources, citations for electronic sources include the sponsor of the site (listed before the publication date). Also include the date you accessed the site. (You do not need to include the URL.)

> Aristotle. *Poetics*. Trans. S. H. Butcher. *The Internet Classics Archive*. Web Atomic and Massachusetts Institute of Technology, 13 Sept. 2007. Web. 15 Feb. 2011.

Entries are listed alphabetically by author's last name or, if no author, by the first word in the citation, disregarding "A," "An," and "The." Entries are formatted with a "hanging indent": the first line of each entry is flush with the margin, and each subsequent line is indented half an inch.

Format for a Paper No title page is required; give your name, the name of your instructor, the course name, and the date at top left on the first page. Double-space throughout — including indented block quotations, endnotes, and the Works Cited page.

For more details, see the *MLA Handbook for Writers of Research Papers*, 7th Edition. For examples of MLA papers, see Chapter 6.

Chicago Style

Main Features

Citations Appear in Footnotes or Endnotes Superscript numbers alert the reader that a note at the bottom of the page accompanies the text.

> Women's earnings have been rising faster than men's, but by 2006 women still earned only 77 percent of what men were earning.[1]
>
> 1. Carmen DeNavas-Walt et al., "Income, Poverty, and Health Insurance Coverage in the United States: 2006," U.S. Census Bureau, August 2007, p. 8, http://www.census.gov/prod/2007pubs/p60-233.pdf (accessed November 13, 2007).

Other standard practices for preparing *Chicago*-style notes are as follows:

- Notes can include bibliographic citations or other information.
- Notes may be formatted as either footnotes or endnotes. (The choice is usually up to the author or publisher, but check with your instructor.)
- Number notes sequentially throughout the paper; do not use the same number twice, even if you are referring to a work already cited.
- Footnotes appear at the bottom of the page on which the citation reference appears.

- Endnotes appear in a list on a new page at the end of the paper, under the heading "Notes."

- Provide complete bibliographical information in the notes. Publication data (place, name of publisher, and date) appears in parentheses.

- Each note begins with a number and a period, followed by a space. The first line of each note is indented half an inch, while subsequent lines are flush with the margin.

- Include an access date for Internet sources.

Additionally, the Latin abbreviation "ibid." is used to reference the same source that was cited in the previous note. (See p. 418.)

Bibliography Since the notes contain complete bibliographical data, a separate bibliography is optional. However, a bibliography can be helpful to the reader if the paper cites more than five or six sources. In preparing a *Chicago*-style bibliography, do the following:

- List items alphabetically by author's last name or, if no author, by the first word of the title (ignoring "A," "An," and "The").

- Include complete bibliographical data for each entry. Include an access date for Internet sources.

- Omit parentheses around the place and the name of the publisher. The date appears in parentheses only if following a volume number.

Here are a couple of examples. Note that the first example is for a source with one identified author (David Hosansky), and the author's last name is listed first. The second example is for a source with a governmental entity as the author. This entry would be alphabetized under "U" in the bibliography.

Hosansky, David. "Traffic Congestion: Is the United States Facing Permanent Gridlock?" *Congressional Quarterly Researcher* 9, no. 32 (1999) (accessed January 15, 2012).

U.S. Department of Transportation, Research and Innovative Technology Administration, Bureau of Transportation Statistics. *Transportation Statistics Annual Report 2007*. Washington, DC: printed by author, 2007.

For more details, see chicagomanualofstyle.org and *The Chicago Manual of Style*, 16th Edition.

APA Style

Papers in APA style typically employ the standard structure of scientific papers, in which an abstract (or a summary) is followed by distinct sections entitled "Introduction," "Method," "Results," and "Discussion." The list of references (bibliography) and, if necessary, appendices follow.

Main Features

"Author-Date" In-text Citations Parenthetical references in the main text refer the reader to full bibliographic information in the list of references at the end of the text.

In-text citations may take several forms. Provide the author and date in parentheses (McMahon, 2009) if neither is mentioned in the text.

> One study looked specifically at the effectiveness of music therapy in reducing undesirable behaviors (McMahon, 2009).

If the author is mentioned in the text, provide only the date in parentheses.

> Toth and Aikens (2001) studied the effect of music therapy on patients' moods, as measured by the frequency of responses such as smiling, laughing, and singing along with the music.

No parenthetical reference is needed if both the author and date are mentioned in the text. Full bibliographical information appears in the list of references.

> Mary Ellen Geist's 2008 memoir, *Measure of the Heart: A Father's Alzheimer's, A Daughter's Return*, describes her father's remarkable memory for music even after he had lost virtually all other memories.

Include a page number when quoting text or citing a specific passage in a text. If page numbers are unavailable (for example, on a Web page), cite the paragraph number, using the abbreviation "para." (para. 6).

> Curiously, people with dementia are often able to recognize and enjoy familiar music, and perhaps even play an instrument or sing flawlessly, long after they have lost other brain functions (Sacks, 2008, pp. 379-380).

If the reference list contains several works published in the same year by the same author, distinguish between them in the text by using a letter following the year of publication (2003a, 2003b, and so on).

The List of References A references page at the end of the paper contains complete bibliographical information for each citation. Items in the list of references appear alphabetically, under the heading "References."

For a book, list the author(s), the year of publication (in parentheses), the title (italicized), the city of publication, and the publisher. Entries in the references invert the author's name and use initials for first and middle names. In APA style, only the first words in titles and subtitles of sources are capitalized; other words are not.

> Aldridge, D. (1996). *Music therapy research and practice in medicine: From out of the silence.* London, England: Jessica Kingsley.

For an article, list the author(s), the year of publication (in parentheses), the title of the article, the title of the journal (italicized), the volume number (italicized), and the page range. If a journal is paginated by issue, place the issue number in parentheses.

> Koger, S. M., Chapin, K., & Brotons, M. (1999). Is music therapy an effective intervention for dementia? A meta-analytic review of literature. *Journal of Music Therapy, 36*(1), 2-15.

If the item is a chapter from a book, place the page range in parentheses following the title of the book.

Endnotes Endnotes may be used for informational material that does not fit well into the body of the text, but not for bibliographical citations.

For more details, see apastyle.org and the *Publication Manual of the American Psychological Association*, 6th Edition.

Latin Documentation Terms

You may encounter a variety of Latin abbreviations in the notes of scholarly texts. Here's an explanation of the most common Latin documentation terms, followed by an example of "ibid." used in footnotes.

et al.	An abbreviation of *et alii* (or, if feminine, *et aliae*), Latin for "and others." Used in footnotes and endnotes to shorten a series of authors' names. (For example, "John Adams, Joan Bentley, Susan Critchley, and Linda Smatter" might be abbreviated "John Adams et al.")
op. cit.	An abbreviation of *opere citato*, Latin for "in the work cited." Used in footnotes or endnotes to indicate that the reference is to a work already cited; now obsolete. When "op. cit." is used, a short form of the full citation is given, including only the author's name and the page reference. If more than one work by the author has been cited, a short title is also included.
loc. cit.	An abbreviation of *loco citato*, Latin for "in the place cited." It was used in the same way as "op. cit." and has also become obsolete.
ibid.	An abbreviation of *ibidem*, Latin for "in the same place." Used in footnotes or endnotes to indicate that the reference is to the work cited in the immediately preceding note. A page reference is still necessary if different from the page number in the preceding note.

1. David Hosansky, "Traffic Congestion: Is the United States Facing Permanent Gridlock?" *Congressional Quarterly Researcher* 9, no. 32 (1999): 733.

2. Ibid.

3. Ibid., 740.

Tools to Help with Citation

Web-based or desktop bibliography managers, such as RefWorks, Zotero, EndNote, JabRef, Scholar's Aid, EasyBib, or NoodleTools, can help you build your own database of sources and can automatically generate a bibliography from that database in the style you choose. If your college library subscribes to a Web-based citation manager, you may be able to upload references from your library's catalog, from electronic databases, and from Google Scholar directly into your own online database of sources. In some cases, you can attach the source itself, as a PDF file, to the reference information, and you can add notes about each source.

While these tools are certainly a convenience, you must check their output carefully, as the formatting is not always correct and key information may be missing.

✅ Checklist for Documentation

Keep these guidelines in mind as you document your sources.

- ☐ Always cite:
  - Direct quotations
  - Paraphrases or summaries of someone else's words
  - References to another work
- ☐ Do not cite:
  - Your own ideas
  - Common knowledge
- ☐ Avoid plagiarism.
  - Start your project early and manage your time.
  - In order to write appropriate paraphrases, avoid using the language of the original text, and avoid using the original text's sentence structures.
- ☐ Observe the assignment's formatting style (e.g., MLA, *Chicago*, or APA).
- ☐ If using a bibliography management tool, check the output carefully for formatting errors.

Glossary

abstract (1) *noun:* A summary of an argument. (2) *adjective:* Denoting a thought, an idea, or a quality rather than a concrete thing.

academic discourse The characteristic language use, or conventions of speaking and writing, practiced by members of institutions of higher education.

academic literacy A familiarity with academic discourse that enables a person to understand it and speak it.

active reading A kind of reading that brings all of one's mental faculties to bear, including questioning, analyzing, weighing, drawing inferences, and more.

active verb A verb form in which the subject performs the action: "Stephen King wrote this book." Sentences constructed in this way are in the "active voice." (See PASSIVE VERB.)

annotate To add a note to a text or graphic, usually as a comment or an explanation.

appositive phrase A phrase that expands on the term that immediately precedes it. For example, "Barack Obama, the first African American president, was born in Honolulu." Here, "the first African American president" is an appositive phrase.

argument A logical structure made up of a claim and support for the claim.

argument matrix A device for developing arguments that consists of a document divided into three columns for noting claims, the evidence that supports the claim, and the discussion that links and explains the two.

audit of meaning A reader's active assessment of the sense of a text. The term is a definition of "dialectic," offered by the critic I. A. Richards (*How to Read a Page* [New York: W. W. Norton and Co., 1942], 240) and employed by professor of English Ann E. Berthoff to explain how readers and writers must continually review and revise their understanding of meaning as it emerges. In *Forming/Thinking/Writing*, Second Edition (Portsmouth, NH: Heinemann–Boynton/Cook, 1988), Berthoff writes, "Just as a bookkeeper has to account for income and expenditures in order to balance credits and debits, an audit of meanings would have to balance what one sentence seems to say against what others seem to say; how one way of saying something compares with another; what one word seems to refer to in a certain context with what it seems to refer to in another" (23).

balanced sentence A sentence that uses parallel sentence structures, usually two or more independent clauses joined together. For example, "He liked to like people, therefore people liked him" (Mark Twain, *Joan of Arc*).

bibliographic database An electronic index to journal, magazine, or newspaper articles, usually including citations. It may also include abstracts, full text, and links to full text.

call number A number or combination of numbers and letters used to arrange and locate items on a library's shelves.

citation A note that attributes referenced, paraphrased, or quoted material to its source.

claim An assertion that something is true or valid.

clause A group of words that contains a subject and a predicate.

close reading A careful, detailed analysis or interpretation of a text (or other artifact such as a visual or a piece of music). Such a reading attends to diction, syntax, imagery, structure, voice, and other features.

cohesion The fact of cohering or holding together as a unit; the quality of forming a united whole.

complete predicate A predicate's verb plus its complements, objects, and modifiers.

complete subject The noun or pronoun that performs the action of a clause's main verb together with its modifying words. Also known as the "subject phrase."

complex sentence A sentence that contains one independent clause and at least one subordinate clause.

compound-complex sentence A sentence that contains more than one independent clause and at least one subordinate clause.

compound predicate A predicate that contains more than one main verb.

compound sentence A sentence that contains more than one independent clause.

concept An idea or a general notion, usually one that is widely held and drawn from many instances or examples.

concrete Existing in a material form or as an actual reality, or pertaining to such things (as opposed to ABSTRACT).

conjunction A word used to join words, phrases, or clauses (for example, "and," "if," "or," "yet").

connotation The associations, ideas, or feelings that a word conjures, as distinct from its literal meaning. (See DENOTATION.)

coordination Connecting two or more ideas or clauses of roughly equal weight or emphasis in a sentence, usually with a semicolon or a coordinating conjunction. For example, "She loved Barcelona, but she could not visit often." (See SUBORDINATION.)

copious style A style of writing described by Erasmus in *De Copia* (1512), characterized by its abundant embellishments, amplifications, and descriptive details.

counterargument An argument or a line of reasoning in opposition to another argument or line of reasoning.

critical thinking The process of skillfully applying, analyzing, evaluating, and synthesizing ideas and information in order to solve problems and answer questions.

culture The customs, arts, way of life, and social practices of a people, society, period, or social group.

cumulative loose sentence A loose sentence in which words and phrases that develop or qualify the main idea appear after the independent clause. (See LOOSE SENTENCE.)

current belief An idea or a set of ideas that is widely accepted based on available evidence in a given historical period, though new evidence might negate it.

database In general, a set of data stored in a computer. Often used as shorthand for BIBLIO-GRAPHIC DATABASE.

deduction The inference of particular instances from a general truth, or of one general truth from another. (See INDUCTION.)

denotation The literal dictionary definition of a word. (See CONNOTATION.)

descriptive Serving to portray the characteristic qualities of a thing (or person or place).

dialectic A method of arriving at insights or truths through the back-and-forth of debate, discussion, or an exchange of ideas.

dialectical notebook A type of double-entry notebook, developed by Ann E. Berthoff, that uses a divided page to allow direct observation, transcription, or quotation on one side of the page and reflection or commentary on the other. "The point of this double-entry system is that it encourages you to think about your thinking and to carry out an audit of the meanings you are making" (in Berthoff, *Forming/Thinking/Writing*, 2nd ed. [Portsmouth, NH: Heinemann–Boynton/Cook, 1988], 26). (See AUDIT OF MEANING.)

diction The choice of words and phrases in a text or speech.

documentation The supplying of information on sources by means of notes and a bibliography.

drafting The act of making a preliminary, rough version of a text.

editing The act of correcting and improving a text, or preparing it for submission or publication.

enthymeme An argument in which one premise is unstated.

episode An incident, a scene, or a segment that forms part of a larger story.

epitome A brief summary.

evidence Facts or information that support a claim, showing it to be valid.

exegesis (*plural:* exegeses) An interpretation, an explanation, or a paraphrase.

expletive A phrase that fills out a sentence without adding to the sense, often using the word "there" or "it" and a form of the verb "to be," as in "There are nine muses who are celebrated in Greek mythology."

fact A well-established item of information or knowledge, usually based on actual observation or trusted testimony.

fallacy A failure of reasoning or an error in logic.

field research Studies conducted outside the library or laboratory, producing original data. Common types of field research include observations, interviews, surveys, and opinion polls.

genre A category or type of work, usually defined by similarities in form or purpose.

gerund A word form derived from a verb that functions as a noun — for example, the word "writing" in the sentence "Writing is one of my favorite activities."

grammar The structure of a language; the study of relations between words in a sentence; the rules for using language in accordance with accepted usage.

induction The inference of a general truth from particular instances. (See DEDUCTION.)

informal writing Free, casual, relaxed writing, normally performed to generate and clarify ideas rather than to present ideas to a reader. (See REVISING.)

intellectual property The right of individuals and organizations to own their original ideas or data.

keyword Any significant word in a database or catalog record.

knowledge problem The question that remains unanswered, the mystery that remains unsolved, or the need that remains unfilled.

Likert scale A type of multiple-choice survey or questionnaire in which respondents indicate their level of agreement with a series of statements. Named for the twentieth-century psychologist Rensis Likert.

logic Systematic reasoning conducted according to strict rules of validity.

loose sentence A sentence in which the independent clause appears first, followed by any modifying clauses and phrases.

main argument A work's major claims and the reasons given in support of these claims.

malapropism An incorrect use of a word or phrase that sounds similar to the correct one.

marginalia Notes in the margins of a text.

metadiscourse Words that explain or discuss the text (or speech) of which they are a part.

monograph A written study of a single specialized subject.

nominalization A noun formed from a verb.

normative Relating to a norm or standard.

nucleus (of an argument) The core ideas that make up an argument.

opinion A view, belief, or judgment that rests on grounds insufficient for certainty.

paraphrase A rewording of a text. An acceptable paraphrase does not use the same words or the same grammatical structures as the original.

passive verb A verb form in which the subject is acted upon rather than performing the action. The actor may or may not be stated — for example, "The book was beautifully written" or "The book was beautifully written by Stephen King." Sentences constructed in this way are in the "passive voice." (See ACTIVE VERB.)

peer-reviewed Evaluated for publication by other experts in the same field. (See REFEREED.)

periodical A journal, magazine, or newspaper published at regular intervals.

periodic sentence A sentence in which the independent clause appears at or near the end, preceded by modifying phrases and clauses.

periphrasis (*adjective:* periphrastic) A roundabout, indirect, or wordy expression or style.

phrase Any group of words that makes sense as a unit but lacks a predicate.

plagiarism Taking another person's words or ideas and presenting them as one's own.

plain style A style of writing characterized by economy, clarity, simplicity, and directness.

position A writer's stand or point of view relative to that of other writers on the subject.

predicate A group of words that says something about the subject and includes a main verb.

premise A proposition that supports a conclusion. In logic, a statement from which another follows as a conclusion. Either of the first two statements in a syllogism, from which a conclusion is drawn.

prepositional phrase A group of words beginning with a preposition and ending with a noun, pronoun, gerund, or clause — for example, "at home," "before noon," "by force."

primary research Research in which the researcher gathers or produces the data himself or herself, as distinct from secondary research, in which data and ideas are gathered from other sources.

principle of charity The proposition that readers should give an author's views fair consideration before making criticisms and raising questions.

proof Evidence or argument that establishes the fact, certainty, or truth of a statement.

proposition A statement that asserts or denies something, or a statement offered for consideration.

qualifier A modifier; a word or phrase that limits or attributes a quality to another word or phrase.

qualify To modify, limit, or add reservations (to a statement).

readerly Concerning the reader, or with attention to the reader's needs and enjoyment (as opposed to WRITERLY).

reading with a purpose Reading in order to generate ideas of your own, with the aim of responding, rather than reading simply to understand the writer's ideas or to expand your own knowledge. It is reading as a means to an end, rather than as an end in itself.

reasoning A sequence of logically connected statements.

recursive A process that repeats the same functions but produces advances with each repetition.

refereed Evaluated for publication by other experts in the same field. (See PEER-REVIEWED.)

relevant (support) Connected to, and appropriate for, an argument.

research Systematic investigation aiming to contribute to knowledge; a systematic investigation conducted to gather material for an original essay, article, report, or other document.

research paper A composition that presents the results of a systematic investigation.

research report A composition that summarizes the research conducted by other scholars on a topic or question.

response A verbal or written reply to, or comment on, a statement or an idea.

revising Altering and improving a text; one of the two principal phases of the writing process (the other being INFORMAL WRITING).

rhetoric The art of argument or persuasion.

rhetorical structure The arrangement of the elements of an argument, especially the relationship between claims and their support.

Rogerian rhetoric A special kind of exploratory argumentation based on the idea that genuine problem solving involves listening as much as speaking. While traditional rhetoric emphasizes the strategies by which a speaker can persuade his or her listeners, Rogerian rhetoric emphasizes the ways that two individuals with different views or perspectives can arrive at an understanding.

scholarship Learning or erudition; the attainments and methods of a scholar.

scope The range or extent of an argument, a topic, or a theme. To "broaden the scope" of a topic is to make it more general; to "narrow the scope" is to make it more specific.

secondary research Research in which data and ideas are gathered from other sources, as distinct from primary research, in which the researcher gathers or produces the data himself or herself.

sentence structure The arrangement of words, phrases, or grammatical elements in a sentence.

simple predicate The verb (including auxiliary verbs) of a predicate.

simple sentence A sentence that contains only one independent clause and no subordinate clauses.

simple subject The noun or pronoun (without its modifiers) that performs the action of the clause's main verb.

stadium (*plural:* stadia) Another word for a STAGE in an argument.

stage A major segment of an argument; a group of related arguments that together form part of a larger argument.

strategy A technique or plan of action designed to achieve a significant aim.

subject The part of a sentence that performs an action. It may be a noun, a pronoun, a noun phrase, or a clause that functions as a noun.

subordination Connecting an idea of lesser weight or emphasis in a sentence by turning it into a phrase or dependent clause. For example, "Although she loved Barcelona, she knew she would never visit it again." ("Although she loved Barcelona" is the dependent clause.) (See COORDINATION.)

support In rhetoric, the evidence and reasoning that back up a claim.

syllogism A form of logical argument frequently used in deductive reasoning in which a conclusion is drawn from two premises — for example, "All men are mortal. Aristotle is a man. Therefore, Aristotle is mortal." (See ENTHYMEME.)

thesis The main argument of an essay or a longer text.

thesis statement A statement of the author's main argument; the "master claim" for the argument as a whole. It may be one sentence or several.

tone A quality in writing that expresses or suggests a particular voice, inflection, character, or mood.

topic The subject matter or theme of a text or discourse.

topic sentence A sentence that declares the main concern, theme, or point of a paragraph.

turning point In a text, a place where a significant change of direction occurs, from one topic to another or from one approach or method to another.

unacceptable paraphrase A version of a text that is too close to the wording or the grammatical structure of the original, or one that fails to cite its source properly and completely. (See PARAPHRASE.)

unity In paragraphs, the quality of consistency of purpose, wholeness, and cohesion.

valid (support) Logically sound and to the point; grounded in logic, fact, or truth.

whole subject See COMPLETE SUBJECT.

working thesis statement A provisional thesis statement that will be developed or improved later. (See THESIS STATEMENT.)

writerly Concerning the writer, or with attention to the writer's own needs (as opposed to READERLY).

writing to communicate A kind of writing, or phase in the writing process, that emphasizes sharing ideas with a reader or conveying ideas clearly and effectively.

writing to learn A kind of writing, or phase in the writing process, that emphasizes discovery, invention, and the generation of ideas (as opposed to their communication).

Acknowledgments

Index